PROTESTING JORDAN

Stanford Studies *in* Middle Eastern *and* Islamic Societies *and* Cultures

PROTESTING JORDAN

Geographies of Power and Dissent

Jillian Schwedler

STANFORD UNIVERSITY PRESS

Stanford, California

STANFORD UNIVERSITY PRESS

Stanford, California

©2022 by Jillian Schwedler. All rights reserved.

No part of this book may be reproduced or transmitted in any form or by any means, electronic or mechanical, including photocopying and recording, or in any information storage or retrieval system without the prior written permission of Stanford University Press.

Printed in the United States of America on acid-free, archival-quality paper

Library of Congress Cataloging-in-Publication Data

Names: Schwedler, Jillian, author.

Title: Protesting Jordan : geographies of power and dissent / Jillian Schwedler.

Other titles: Stanford studies in Middle Eastern and Islamic societies and cultures.

Description: Stanford, California : Stanford University Press, 2022. | Series: Stanford studies in Middle Eastern and Islamic societies and cultures | Includes bibliographical references and index.

Identifiers: LCCN 2021041615 (print) | LCCN 2021041616 (ebook) | ISBN 9781503630376 (cloth) | ISBN 9781503631588 (paperback) | ISBN 9781503631595 (ebook)

Subjects: LCSH: Protest movements—Jordan. | Demonstrations—Jordan. | Government, Resistance to—Jordan. | Jordan—Politics and government.

Classification: LCC HN661.A8 S34 2022 (print) | LCC HN661.A8 (ebook) | DDC 322.4095695—dc23

LC record available at https://lccn.loc.gov/2021041615

LC ebook record available at https://lccn.loc.gov/2021041616

Cover design: Kevin Barrett Kane

Cover art: Nidal El-khairy

Typeset by Newgen North America in 10.5/14.4 Brill

For Jake and Nick Ronin

Contents

Acknowledgments   ix

List of Photos, Drawing, and Maps   xiii

1 THE SHIFTING POLITICAL STAKES OF PROTEST   1

2 TRANSFORMING TRANSJORDAN   27

3 BECOMING AMMAN: FROM PERIPHERY TO CENTER   63

4 JORDANIZATION, THE NEOLIBERAL STATE, AND THE
   RETREAT AND RETURN OF PROTEST   97

5 AN ETHNOGRAPHY OF PLACE AND THE POLITICS OF
   ROUTINE PROTESTS   127

6 JORDAN IN THE TIME OF THE ARAB UPRISINGS   150

7 THE TECHNIQUES AND EVOLVING SPATIAL DYNAMICS OF
   PROTEST AND REPRESSION   193

8 PROTEST AND ORDER IN MILITARIZED SPACES   226

9 PROTESTING GLOBAL ASPIRATIONS   250

Notes   287

References   321

Index   355

Acknowledgments

THE ANALYSIS IN *PROTESTING JORDAN* WAS SHAPED BY AN OFF-hand comment made by one of my interlocutors in Amman around 2003. They had asked me to share some English-language analyses of Jordanian politics, and I had brought them several books and articles, including my own work. Sometime later, I asked what they thought, and the response was both devastating and revelatory: "I just don't recognize Jordan." Our work was empirically solid, they said, but much of it focused on elections, political parties, and state institutions—big topics in political science but not where many Jordanians saw and experienced the political. I wanted to see the politics that they saw, and to capture a political landscape that they would recognize even if they disagreed with my analysis. I thought I was good at field research, but now I really started to listen. I asked questions that weren't structured by a prefabricated research question or a "puzzle" that the "literature" had not adequately addressed. Instead of ending interviews with "what am I missing?" I led with that question. One unexpected answer sent me in an entirely new direction: "The places where we protest are disappearing." "Wow," I thought, and I dove into the literatures on space, geography, and urban planning, as well as the work of anthropologists, historians, and political scientists who had already made the "spatial turn." I began to look at Jordan in completely different ways, seeing both protests and the built environment ethnographically and through

Henri Lefebvre's notion of the "right to the city." This book is the result of that intellectual journey as well as several personal ones, and I am indebted to those who sent me down new paths and made me see in new ways.

I began writing this book in 2005, just after my boys were born and as I finished *Faith in Moderation.* My world went haywire for some years, but I continued working slowly on this project. I finished a full draft and then lost most of it in May 2016, when my computer spectacularly crashed just two weeks before a book workshop. Yes, I had been backing up my computer every day with an automatic virtual program. But I had unknowingly configured it to back up only my photos and music, which I did not discover until I looked to retrieve the files. Much tequila was followed by a cleanse and a restorative cross-country camping trip. I started rewriting from near scratch in June 2017 during a Ramadan trip to Tunis. I workshopped the new manuscript in October 2019 and twice during the pandemic. It's a wonder to me that it's finished—a book that seemed to resist coming into existence. And, without question, I could not have done any of it, or even survived those difficult years, without the love and support of colleagues, friends, and family.

The book spans my tenure at three institutions—the University of Maryland, the University of Massachusetts Amherst, and Hunter College and the Graduate Center at the City University of New York. Generous colleagues at each of these schools have encouraged and supported my vision. Over sixteen years, I have presented my work and received feedback dozens of times—too many to mention individually—but I am deeply grateful for the audiences and interlocutors whose questions and suggestions helped me shape what appears on these pages. I need to mention, however, several venues where I have presented parts of the manuscript on multiple occasions: the CUNY Graduate Center's Comparative Politics Workshop, the Graduate Center's Protest and Politics Workshop, Charles Tilly's Contentious Politics Workshop at Columbia University, and the New England Middle East Political Science Workshop. The "On Protest" collective at the University of Maryland led by Sonia Alvarez and Barbara Cruikshank was a critical incubator for developing my ideas outside of the social movement framework. And my work has benefited immeasurably from the feedback that I received at four separate book workshops, sponsored by the Project on Middle East Political Science (POMEPS), the CUNY Graduate Center's Middle East and Middle East-American Center (MEMEAC), and the

Sidi Bou Said School of Critical Protest Studies (twice). Field research was funded by the Project on Middle East Political Science (TRE Grant), the United States Institute of Peace (3SG-073–06s), and the National Science Foundation (0527339).

In Jordan, I'm grateful to the countless activists, researchers, journalists, party leaders, and government officials who generously shared their time and patiently answered my (sometimes tedious) questions. I benefited tremendously from serving as scholar-in-residence at the Arab Archives Institute, the Center for Strategic Studies, and the New Jordan Research Center. Mohammad Asad and Ammar Khammash patiently answered my questions about urban planning and helped me understand Amman's history and built environment. For multiple conversations about protests and Jordan, I am likewise grateful to Laith al-Ajlouni, Lina Ejailat, Hani Hourani, Saeda Kilani, Sufian Obeidat, Naseem Tarawneh, and many others who have asked to remain unnamed. Hisham Bustani and Basel Burgan have become dear friends (and tough critics), and their insights and experiences have deeply shaped my work. Aida Dabbas, who died of cancer in November 2003, was a tireless warrior for justice and a dear friend whose loss is still felt.

At Stanford University Press, I'm lucky to work with the incredible (and patient) Kate Wahl, Susan Karani, and Caroline McKusick as well as the amazing series editors Joel Beinin and Laleh Khalili, both of whom are dear friends. Susan Olin did a phenomenal job copyediting the manuscript. Nidal Elkhairy provided the cover art, and Eliana Abu-Hamdi, Kyle Craig, Tally and Samuel Helfont, Dana M. Moss, Muhammad Zakaria, *7iber*, and the Anti-Gas Deal Campaign provided additional photos. Tariq Adely and another whose name escapes me generously shared an old travel guide to Jordan. In Brooklyn, the patient and kind people at Ozu Sushi, My Little Pizzeria, and Brooklyn Wine Exchange delivered me sustenance during writing binges and the dark days of the pandemic.

Numerous friends, colleagues, and students have given detailed feedback on portions of the manuscript, including Fida Adely, Tariq Adely, Steven Brookes, Barbara Cruikshank, Yazan Doughan, Darah Grant, Sune Haugbølle, Najib Hourani, Amaney Jamal, James Jasper, Mark Levine, Ellen Lust, David Patel, Sayres Rudy, Dean Schafer, Fred Schaffer, Sandy Schramm, Erica Simmons, Nicholas Rush Smith, Dimitris Soudias, Tareq Sydiq, and Frédéric Volpi.

xii ACKNOWLEDGMENTS

I am deeply grateful to friends and colleagues who have generously commented on full drafts of the manuscript, including Ziad Abu-Rish, Laith al-Ajlouni, Betty Anderson, Hisham Bustani, Youssef El Chazli, Kyle Craig, Lilly Frost, Sarah El Khazaz, Adrienne LaBas, Matthew LaCouture, Rima Majed, Zachariah Mampilly, José Ciro Martínez, Jacob Mundy, Agnieszka Paczynska, Sarah Parkinson, Robert Parks, Nicola Pratt, Thoria El-Rayyes, Stacey Philbrick Yadav (and the incredible students in her class), and Sean Yom. Some friends have (insanely) read multiple full drafts: Eliana Abu-Hamdi, Anne Marie Baylouny, Laryssa Chomiak, Janine Clark, John Krinsky, Marc Lynch, Pete Moore, Curt Ryan, Lisa Wedeen, and Susan Woodward. If I have forgotten anyone, please shame me and I'll buy the next round. Along with astute comments from two anonymous reviewers as well as Kate Wahl, the careful comments from these friends and colleagues improved the work and clarified the argument immeasurably. All flaws are unquestionably my own.

My dearest friends along this journey, who have lived with me and this project for years, are Amel Ahmad, Paul Amar, Shiva Balaghi, Sara Kepler Brenz, Hisham Bustani, Janine Clark, Barbara Cruikshank, Patti Eaddy, Gregory Gause, Lisa Hajjar, John Krinsky, Marc Lynch, Laleh Khalili, Shana Marshall, Pete Moore, Sarah Parkinson, Curtis Ryan, Susan Woodward, and Stacey Philbrick Yadav. Most of these friends have kept me company during the pandemic with sometimes weekly Zoom "Quarantinis" or via long message threads, which kept me sane as well as productive. And my especially beloved besties, with whom I speak or communicate daily, are Eliana Abu-Hamdi, Kathleen Cavanaugh, Laryssa Chomiak, Agnieszka Paczynska, and Lisa Wedeen. To all my friends: Your friendship, patience, brilliance, and encouragement have nourished, inspired, and sometimes even saved me, and I love you endlessly. Finally, I am deeply grateful to Joel Sherman, whose encouragement and belief that I could write this book were unwavering, even during turbulent times. This book is dedicated to our gentlemen, Jake and Nick Ronin, who have brought endless joy and light into the world. Keep being your badass selves.

Photos, Drawing, and Maps

PHOTOS AND DRAWING

Figure 1.1. Protesters hold flatbread as placards

Figure 2.1. Workers repairing the Hijaz Railway

Figure 3.1. Amman circa 1920

Figure 3.2. Protest in downtown Amman in 1933

Figure 3.3. Military parade

Figure 3.4. Women's march in Amman

Figure 4.1. Routine protests return to the Grand Husseini Mosque

Figure 4.2. Typical vista of Amman

Figure 5.1. Protesters with mixed flags

Figure 5.2. A view from behind the gendarmerie

Figure 5.3. Women move to confront the gendarmerie

Figure 5.4. Plainclothes *baltajiyya*

Figure 6.1. Police blocking a march in downtown Amman

xiii

xiv PHOTOS, DRAWING, AND MAPS

Figure 7.1. Man holding photos of his son

Figure 7.2. "Cute Darak at the Fourth Circle"

Figure 7.3. Muslim Brotherhood parade guards

Figure 7.4. Anti-gas deal banner

Figure 8.1. Concrete barriers at the Fourth Circle

Figure 8.2. Underpass at the Fourth Circle

Figure 8.3. Political graffiti and redaction

Figure 8.4. Turnstile entrance to Hashemite Plaza

Figure 8.5. Heavy security forces at the Abdali interchange

Figure 8.6. Concrete wall at the Fourth Circle

Figure 9.1. Abdali Boulevard

Figure 9.2. Billboard at Abdali Boulevard

Figure 9.3. Author selfie in Jebal Amman

Figure 9.4. Anti-gas deal protest near the Jordan Gates Towers

Figure 9.5. A banner at the Royal Court reading "Dhiban District: The Unemployed"

MAPS

Map 2.1. The Transjordanian area

Map 3.1. Amman city center

Map 9.1. East Amman and West Amman

PROTESTING JORDAN

Chapter 1

THE SHIFTING POLITICAL
STAKES OF PROTESTS

IN JANUARY 2018, THE JORDANIAN GOVERNMENT ANNOUNCED A 10 percent tax increase on 164 basic goods, including grain, dairy, and produce. The price of bread doubled. Outside of the capital, Amman, protests broke out in the city of Salt and the town of Dhiban. By February they had spread south to the mountain town of Karak, and protests in those places continued through March. Demonstrators in all three locations held up bread and chanted, "Bread, Freedom, Social Justice!"—a slogan used across the region during the Arab uprisings in 2011.[1] Although bread was just one of many goods to see price increases, it long has been associated with a basic and dignified life.[2]

Two months later, on May 21, the government proposed increasing taxes on Jordan's middle class. The Union of Professional Associations announced a general strike on May 30. Both the private and public sectors were called to strike, as was "anyone affected by the government's policies." At least thirty-nine striking unions and professional associations were joined by small and medium capital owners whose businesses were feeling the diminished purchasing power of the lower and lower-middle classes.[3] These "middle-class" protests—which brought tens of thousands to the streets nationwide, including many first-time protesters[4]—quickly evolved to include people whose incomes were too low to be affected by the tax increases.[5] Demonstrators began chanting against corruption, the lifting of subsidies earlier in the year, and the regime's embrace of neoliberal economic reforms. They again wrote slogans on pita bread and carried them as placards. With participation crossing class lines, the protests created the conditions of possibility for new forms of solidarity; the question, however, was whether those solidarities would be thwarted or cultivated.

Jordanians refer to these protests (May 30–June 7, 2018) as *Habbit Huzayran* (June rage) or *Habbit Ramadan* (Ramadan being the month on the Islamic calendar).[6] *Habbi* means to catch on fire—for example, *habbit al-nar* means to burst into flames. In using the term to describe protests, it conveys a sense of exploding in sudden action or bursting forth in rage—an uprising or rising against an intolerable situation.[7] The term also indexes an emotional outburst—anger or rage—that connects the economic to the political through the act of Jordanians flooding the streets, occupying major intersections, and engaging in loud claim-making. The label *habbi* also evokes a connection to earlier anti-austerity protests: the *Habbit Nisan* (April rage) protests of 1989 (concerning petrol subsidies) and the *Habbit Tishreen* protests of 2012 (electricity and fuel subsidies).

At most protests, Jordanians direct their anger toward the prime minister or Parliament, even though the king dictates or at least approves all policies. *Lèse-majesté* is a punishable offense in Jordan under multiple laws, including Article 195 of the Penal Code, which forbids one to raise one's voice—literally one's tongue—against the king.[8] Punishments can include years of hard labor and hefty fines as well as more informal practices such as punishing one's extended family through the denial of employment or university admission. Since at least 2010, however, a small but growing number of Jordanians have dared to cross that "red line"[9] and brazenly criticize the king. The most explicit criticism has come primarily from Jordanians of East Bank descent—those with long-standing affective connections (pre–twentieth century) to lands east of the Jordan River. A significant portion of these Jordanians—who are often seen as the regime's support base—view King Abdullah II as having failed to honor the social contract[10] established in the 1920s between his great-grandfather (and namesake) and the East Bank local authorities of his time.

Criticism from East Bank communities is worrisome for the regime because they are a core constituency for the monarchy. Economic grievances among their numbers have been growing since the 2000s, particularly over the

SHIFTING POLITICAL STAKES OF PROTEST   3

FIGURE 1.1. Protesters hold flatbread as placards during the 2018 *Habbit Huzayran/Ramadan* protests. Source: Muhammad Hamed for Reuters.

privatization of state industries and state efforts to attract foreign investment. Many East Bankers feel that they are disproportionately suffering under the king's economic policies, so they turn to protests to express their outrage over corruption, unemployment, and neoliberalism in general. Activist Ali Brizat, for example, declared in a recorded speech during the winter 2018 protests, "These decisions [cutting subsidies] are beyond reckless. The real recklessness is that of the king and none other than the king." The Brizat family belongs to the powerful Bani Hamida tribal confederation, one of a number of large, extended sets of East Bank families that see themselves as sharing a common descent, social practices, local authority structures, and spatial attachments to specific lands.[11] Brizat was arrested for his comments in February but released a few weeks later.[12] Similarly in June 2018, another opposition figure, Fares al-Fayiz of the powerful Bani Sakhr tribal confederation, was arrested after criticizing the king at a protest. "We want to change the political formula," he said in a speech that was filmed and posted to social media. "We will not accept you as a king, prime minister, defense minister, police chief, and governor. You are everything! You became a demigod, according to this constitution, and we are slaves!"[13]

Fayiz's comments reflect another common complaint: that while Jordan is officially a constitutional monarchy, in practice as well as law the king is all powerful. He articulated in public what many say privately: that the privatization of state industries since the 2000s has unfairly benefited those close to the royal family. Fayiz, however, went so far as to describe Queen Rania as "Satan" and accuse her family members of looting Jordan for their personal wealth. While his arrest for his comments was expected, members of his tribe still responded with outrage. At one news conference, his son threatened that unless his father was released, the Bani Sakhr would block the Amman–Madaba road—built on historically Bani Sakhr land—to disrupt traffic to the airport. Fayiz was released. As we shall see in coming chapters, blocking major transit routes is a long-standing part of Jordan's protest repertoire—the tactics and spatial techniques for public political claim-making that are embodied in a kind of circulating public knowledge.[14] How did the regime's supposed support base become the source of its loudest and harshest critics?

LOCATING PROTESTS IN THE POLITICAL LANDSCAPE

Protesting Jordan argues that protests and other public acts of political dissent provide an ideal entry point for understanding Jordanian politics while also being worthy of greater theorization in their own right. What role do protests play in both challenging and reproducing state power? Why do protests emerge in particular locations and moments and take the form they do? Why are state coercive apparatuses deployed unevenly against protests? What are the political effects of routine protests, given their ritual character, the repetitiveness of their demands, and the fact that they do not translate into political disruptions? And how do regional and global financial and security arrangements shape protests at the local level and vice versa?

To answer these and other questions, I leverage the rich literature on space and geography to make three main interventions that have broader theoretical purchase. The first is that protests are integral to processes of state-making and state-maintaining. How would-be political leaders contend with resistance to and claims about their efforts to establish authority shapes the institutions and practices of governance. As occasions for publicly airing grievances, protests can work to both challenge existing power structures and reproduce them—sometimes simultaneously. Protests are also not exceptional "events" that rupture "normal" institutional politics. Rather, challenges to political authority are routine and ongoing, and protests work to structure the political terrain on which authorities seek to produce and maintain their power.[15] Public expressions of dissent also expose as well as build the affective connections and spatial imaginaries that would-be authorities strive to bring into alignment with their own political ambitions.

A second theoretical intervention explores how and why protest and repression vary across space, and how they shape the built environment and vice versa. The ways in which the built environment is mapped and organized can facilitate some forms of protest but lead to the easy suppression of others. I show, for example, that even within a given city, protest repertoires can take utterly different forms in one place compared to an adjacent neighborhood, and that, for this reason, the state's responses are also distinct. Protests can also expose as well as shape how social, economic, and political powers are organized, distributed, and located spatially and geographically.

A third intervention is that geographies of regional and global entanglement shape protests and vice versa. These include imperial and colonial projects and the spatial imaginaries they seek to bring into being. For example, an imperial project built around the control of trade routes and the extraction of taxes differs in scope and substance from a colonial project aimed at creating a territorial state with a centralized administration. Patterns of regional and global financialization and securitization likewise shape, and are shaped by, patterns of protest and how they are located in material and symbolic space. Neither the subnational nor the transnational scales have analytic primacy, as they together coproduce politics at the national scale. This multiscalar approach helps bring into view spatial variations in repertoires of protest and repression, while showing how Jordan's attachment to regional and global security arrangements has effects on protests and vice versa.

In the remainder of this chapter, I define what I mean by protests and present a multiscalar framework for thinking about protest and repression in terms of spaces and geographies of power and dissent. I outline the theoretical and empirical contributions of the three main interventions, previewing arguments developed in the coming chapters. Then I revisit the 2018 *Habbit*

Huzayran protests, showing how the grievances expressed by protesters bring into view competing narratives about Jordan's past and visions of its future. Increasingly, protests have become routine occasions for the regime's East Bank constituency to publicly air grievances and threaten to withdraw support for king and throne. And as we shall see, Jordanians turn to protests because they often bring results. Finally, I discuss my methodology and preview the chapters to come.

Defining Protests

Protest is the expression of dissent. It can be done loudly or quietly, collectively or individually, and publicly or secretly. Protest is dissent externalized, even if done without hope of affecting change, and the perpetrators need not be part of an organization or movement. Demonstrations, riots, marches, strikes, and sit-ins are all familiar forms of protest. Passivity can likewise be a form of protest, as can boycotting or not showing up.

Much of the social science literature on protests has focused on the forms or tactics of public claim-making. Why do protests take the forms that they do? What factors explain the dynamics and trajectory of protests and whether they are able to achieve their objectives? Erica Chenoweth's work on nonviolent action is exemplary of such outcome-oriented analyses. She asks, for example, whether nonviolent protests are more successful in realizing change than violent protests; and, under what conditions are nonviolent protests able to affect decolonization, revolution, or structural reform?[16] *Protesting Jordan* addresses these questions, but it also looks beyond the success/failure model to explore how protests can have a wide range of observable political effects.

Another dimension of outcome-oriented analyses is that the object of study is often a movement or uprising (or revolution, wave of protests, and so on), and the primary puzzle to be explained is what might be called its "life cycle." As a metaphor, life cycle invokes a temporality that directs our attention to the object of study's origin, trajectory, and fate. Most work on protests in Jordan follows this tendency to focus on specific movements—of teachers, laborers, or political parties—and whether their movements are successful in achieving their goals by mounting protests as occasions for claim-making. When did the movement/uprising start? How did it evolve? How many participated and what forms did the protests take? And again, was it successful? Beyond the case of

Jordan, many early analyses of the Arab uprisings of 2011 sought to explain variations in the trajectories and outcomes of different uprisings. In such studies, each state is treated as an autonomous unit, and the conditions that define which had an "uprising" hinge on judgments about the size of the mobilization and its potential for affecting political change. Here, a book-length analysis by Jason Brownlee, Tarek Masoud, and Andrew Reynolds is illustrative of the limits of such an orientation. They ask why some uprisings led to regime reform while others led to repression, and why uprisings failed to materialize in cases like Saudi Arabia and Algeria.[17] They find that successful uprisings emerged in places without a hereditary executive or significant oil rents—explanatory variables internal to each case. What is missing in their analysis is the extent to which these states are differently situated in regional and global financial and security arrangements, and how other states intervened in often aggressive ways to affect the trajectory and outcome of otherwise domestic uprisings. Each uprising certainly had dynamics unique to it; but focusing primarily or even exclusively on domestic factors overlooks the role of regional and global factors in shaping the trajectories of individual instances.[18]

Protesting Jordan asks a different set of questions than these outcome-oriented and movement-centric approaches, although it does explore the outcomes and broader political effects of protests. The analysis situates individual protests—including those of the uprising period—within long-term patterns and repertoires of protest and repression, with additional attention to spatial variation at the subnational level and connections at regional and global scales. It also adds an additional question: How do protesters, counterprotesters, political authorities, and those observing the protests understand these acts of public claim-making? Bringing these diverse standpoints into focus allows us to see the meaning-making work done through protest and repression as well as how that matters for both contesting and reproducing state power.

How to define "protest" in such a capacious analysis spanning a century and a half? The definition used here is simply "people assembling in public to express some form of claim-making." This broad understanding of protest can accommodate such diverse acts as revolts and rebellions; obstruction of transportation routes; destruction or sabotage of property and infrastructure; traveling to government offices to demand jobs or benefits; and all manner of demonstrations, strikes, marches, riots, and sit-ins. The approach takes up the invitation made by Doug McAdam, Sidney Tarrow, and Charles Tilly in 2000 to think broadly about contentious politics and move away from compartmentalizing different "types" of contentious claim-making (e.g., the distinct literatures on revolutions, social movements, civil wars, etc.).[19] I show how twenty-first-century repertoires of contention—including their geographic and spatial dynamics—are built around the memories and practices of earlier acts of rebellion. The state and its challengers both learn and innovate as well by observing, adopting, and even training in the tactics and techniques of protests and repression elsewhere.

Of course, there are nontrivial distinctions in what Jordanians understand protests to mean—in the nineteenth century as today. Because not all Jordanians understand rebellion and dissent in the same way, I attend carefully to the language used to describe diverse acts of claim-making that I collect under the umbrella "protest." Early Bedouin raids, for example, were and still are described as *ghazawat* (pl.), the same term used to describe conquests in the early Islamic period. Some non-Transjordanian anti-Ottoman writers label anti-Ottoman revolts as *thawra* (also translated as "revolution"), but in Jordan the local word for those early revolts is most often *hayyi* (a local variation on *habbi*, or "rage," discussed above), as in the *Hayyit al-Karak* detailed in the next chapter.[20] By comparison, the more large-scale Great Arab Revolt of 1916–18 (*al-thawra al-'arabiyya al-kubra*) is labeled a revolt or revolution, as are the Palestinian revolts of the 1930s (*al-thawrat al-filistiniyya*). The few uses of *thawra* to describe early revolts in Jordan seem to be efforts to exaggerate their breadth and impact.[21] Few Jordanians describe even massive protests in Jordan as *thawrat* (pl.), and the term is seldom invoked during protests (but see chap. 6). Most activists call the 2011 uprisings in Egypt and Tunisia *thawrat*, but they call their own nationwide protests during that period merely *ihtijajat* (pl., protests)—a noun that did not come into wide usage until the 1950s. Nationwide anti-austerity protests, however, are labeled *habbat* (pl. of *habbi*), public outbursts of rage, and those titles are widely recognized by even those who opposed the protests. *Intifada*, a term closely associated with the Palestinian intifadas of 1987 and 2000, is also sometimes used to describe a nationwide uprising. For different forms of protest, Jordanians also use the vocabulary of *mudthahira* (demonstration), *masira* (march), *zahf* (slow procession or crawl), *'idrab* (strike), *tamarud* (revolt), and *i'tisam* (sit-in).

Finally, because of the way social science has studied protests, many analyses overlook small or routine protests, and scholarship on Jordan largely follows this trend. Nationwide protests receive scholarly and journalistic attention, but thousands of smaller and localized acts of public claim-making often go entirely unnoticed, particularly nontransgressive protests—those that do not seek to overturn existing political institutions or power relations.[22] I will show how examining protests that are not disruptive or seem to have failed to achieve their goals provides a richer understanding not only of politics in Jordan but of the political work of protests more generally.

Protests, State-Making, and State-Maintaining

Protests are integral to processes of state-making and state-maintaining. Numerous scholars have already shown how states came into existence in Europe as elites forged allies with financiers that enabled them to support standing armies and extend their authority over a territory.[23] One method for diffusing challenges to would-be political authorities was to integrate the rebellious into the emerging state—for example, by bestowing aristocratic titles or via other forms of clientelism. Colonial state-making differed from the European model, of course, but co-optation and accommodation proved enduring techniques for deflating dissent, and how those techniques were deployed shaped the structure of emergent territorial states. John Chalcraft makes this argument in his ambitious study about the making of the modern Middle East, showing how contentious mobilization shaped overall patterns of historical change.[24]

Following this sensibility, I show how the making of the Jordanian state beginning in 1921 was not a top-down process, as often portrayed, but a dialectical one. The colonial project of creating a territorial state with a centralized administration was undertaken by an alliance of British forces and the powerful Hashemite family that had for years ruled the Hijaz region in western Arabia. My analysis, however, begins fifty years earlier in order to bring into view the geographies of power and dissent—along with the repertoires for protest and repression—that characterized the Transjordanian area prior to the establishment of British-Hashemite colonial rule.[25] I use the term "Transjordanian area" to refer to the territory on which the colonial state would be established, while also foregrounding how the people residing there recognized various local authorities over particular lands. I pay particular attention to imbricating spatial imaginaries and their affective connections with places and people beyond their local communities and the territorial state that would later emerge (chap. 2).

Transjordanians' articulations of their desires, and their reactive demands to British and Hashemite efforts to establish centralized authority, contributed to form the new state as much as, or perhaps even more than, the colonial authorities that dominated Jordanian society. Bedouin revolts in the 1920s and 1930s created so many problems for the would-be centralized authority that the colonial powers could stop them only by providing the Bedouin with permanent employment and benefits. Settled tribal leaders during the same period—frustrated with both favoritism toward rival tribes and government employment of people hailing from elsewhere in Greater Syria (*Bilad al-Sham*)—frequently revolted and sometimes marched to Amman to express their grievances and make demands on the new regime. Aided by British largess, the Hashemite regime eventually gained the backing of powerful East Bank tribal leaders—the relationship of patronage and favoritism that Jordanians refer to as the social contract. Perhaps most tellingly, the colonial powers created an entirely new geography of political authority in the Transjordanian area by establishing the new capital in small-town Amman. Had they chosen one of the larger towns, budding Hashemite authority would have had to compete with existing local authority structures.

The new capital was instead established in a small town with a railway stop, populated by merchants and refugees with little more than a generation of ties to the area. Powerful tribal authority structures elsewhere in the Transjordanian area were left largely undisturbed, but within only a few decades the political center and periphery were largely inverted. Large flows of Palestinian refugees after the 1948 and 1967 wars also profoundly altered the newly independent nation's demographics, more than doubling the population and turning Amman into the nation's largest city. But because the regime continued to rely on East Bank support to shore up its authority, state-maintaining required that the regime continue to honor the social contract.

Over the decades, the Hashemite regime has faced down repeated challenges to its rule, including by leftists and Arab nationalists, Palestinian militias, violent conflicts on its borders, Islamist extremists, and nationwide protests that periodically bring the country to a standstill. Many analysts half-jokingly describe the Hashemite regime as "forever on the brink"; even thoughtful scholars deploy the phrase while noting its irony.[26] But rather than dismissing the phrase as an unhelpful cliché, I unpack its contradictions to show what kind of political work that perception of Jordan does for reproducing state power. Indeed, the Hashemite regime itself has advanced notions of both stability and looming instability—sometimes to different audiences—as part of a strategy to insure the survival of its rule. It puts forth the image of Jordan as a stable and unified nation, for example, to attract foreign investment and reassure its allies. Maintaining that "stability," however, relies on a massive security apparatus and a militarized built environment, made possible only with considerable economic and military assistance from the United States and, to a lesser extent, the Gulf states. The security state not only seeks to crush political dissent, it also enables Jordan to remain open for business, projecting the regime's stability into the future to assuage the concerns of potential investors as well as regional and global allies. At the same time, however, the regime concomitantly invokes ever-present, looming threats: Islamist extremism, violent conflicts in neighboring states, and fiscal problems exacerbated by multiple influxes of refugees. It uses those "looming threats" to justify efforts to silence political dissent through a wide range of techniques, including expanding security forces as well as the reach of antiterror and cybercrime laws enacted in the name of national security. Jordanians thus live under the tyranny of "crisis" times while enjoying little of the benefits of stable "normal" times. When deployed not by scholars but by the state, the "forever on the brink" trope works as a technique for insuring the maintenance of the Hashemite regime.

All political regimes, of course, strive to project stability as a means of creating it, and challenges to state authority are the rule rather than the exception.[27] Here a politics of time comes to the fore during protests, and the case of Jordan is ideal for such a theoretical exploration. By invoking alternative futures, protests seek to challenge the state and thus destabilize its assertion of stability in ways that might open real space (and not just discursive space) to disrupt the temporality of the regime's stability extending into the future. In this way, we can recognize that the real threat for the Hashemite regime—one it does not want domestic or international audiences to see—is that its authority has been repeatedly called into question in recent decades, most publicly at protests by the regime's supposed East Bank support base. But here it is important to not treat East Bank communities as monolithic and unified. Indeed, while Jordanians of East Bank descent have been the regime's most vocal critics, East Bankers also dominate the state security sector and turnout as loyalist counterprotesters. And even seemingly stalwart loyalists—conservatives who oppose real democratization because they wish to maintain East Bank political power—can pose challenges for the Hashemite regime. Some even embrace a kind of chauvinistic and racist nativism—the idea that only those people with long-standing roots in the Transjordanian area, specifically those residing there prior to World War I, are true Jordanians. In such a formulation, the Hashemite royal family are outsiders, a claim that calls into question its moral authority to rule. King Abdullah II has struggled to contain this and other dissent in East Bank tribal areas, illuminating the extent to which accommodating political dissent works alongside repression in the maintenance of state authority.

The Interaction between Protests, Repression, and Space

The dynamics of protest and how states deploy forces against them vary not only depending on who is protesting, what they are demanding, and how they are doing so, but also on where protests take place. The vast literatures on social movement and contentious politics began to explore questions concerning space in the late 1990s,[28] and a growing number of scholars across a number of disciplines (including geography, urban studies, political science, sociology, history, and anthropology) took up the spatial aspects of contentious politics in earnest by the 2000s. This diverse literature brings multiple kinds of spatialities—including scale, place, network, positionality, and mobility—into analyses of contentious politics.[29] Scholarly attention to the spatial dimensions of protest (as opposed to social movements or revolutions) remains more limited, however, but it has begun to increase in recent years.[30]

The interaction between protests and space has several dimensions. First, the physical space of the built environment can shape protests by creating obstacles to assembly or movement and by limiting what can be seen or heard—thus affecting the disruptive potential of protests (positively or negatively). Space is not merely a container or location for protest, as it can structure the impact of protests, convey meaning, and present both possibilities and obstacles for protests to have political effects. Second, protesters also interact with the built environment, for example, by blocking roads, damaging property, and sabotaging infrastructure. Protests can work as acts of place-making, creating and shaping the memories and symbolism embodied in particular physical spaces and at particular moments. Third, states seek to constrain the potential challenges of protests by altering the built environment, both materially and symbolically. These processes include the militarization of the city; spatial repertoires of repression; and regime efforts to construct a nationalist history through the built environment that bolsters the regime's claims to authority.

The relationship between protest and the built environment is thus dialectic: protests shape the meaning and form of particular spaces and vice versa. Repression of protests has similar dynamics, shaping protest and the built environment but also being shaped by both. In his discussion of four hundred years of protest and rebellion in New York City, Don Mitchell details how the violence of protests—undertaken by those engaged in claim-making as well as those seeking to silence them—can produce meaningful change in the built environment as well as how the city operates socially, economically, and politically.

> Violent upheaval influences investment decisions—how capital circulates in or flees from the urban landscape—and thus where and how New Yorkers can live, work, and play. Urban violence, whether organized or disorganized, shapes laws, leads to new strategies of policing, and influences the development of institutions (like the police department itself).[31]

Because protests are mounted in identifiable physical spaces, new meanings and histories about those places can also invoke and evoke alternative narratives of the past and new imaginaries of the future.

The coming chapters will detail how the interaction of protest and repression with the built environment has played just such a role in state-making, place-making, and state-maintaining. Thinking beyond conventional notions of scale, as Neil Brenner does, allows us to see how urban and national spaces are constitutively multiscalar.[32] Since the 2000s, King Abdullah II has used state policies and resources to more aggressively direct flows of capital across Jordan, reshaping the built environment in some locations (such as Amman,

Aqaba, and tourist and investment zones) while leaving other areas relatively untouched; those decisions (e.g., neoliberal reforms) are the subject of protests, as we have already seen. The state also creates material obstacles to protest in the built environment, aiming to deflate the potential for protests to be disruptive and foreclose place-making that might challenge the official narrative about Jordan's past and future. The coming chapters explore these processes from before the Hashemite state-making period through the neoliberal period beginning in the 1980s, and I introduce a new typology for understanding state strategies for controlling protests in the built environment.

Geographies of Regional and Global Entanglement

Finally, *Protesting Jordan* situates Jordan within regional and global entanglements, asking how they shape the spatial and geographic dimensions of protest and protest repression in the Hashemite Kingdom, and how and why those geographies have changed over time. Configurations of domestic, regional, and global power relations (and the challenges to them) project a set of social, economic, and political geographies that at times clash and at times imbricate but are never fully congruent. These are the geographies of trade, patronage networks, local histories, electoral maps, urban planning, energy sources, affective connections, agricultural production, water availability, tribal authority and rivalries, imperial and colonial ambitions, and pastoral and nomadic practices—not to mention the regional and international geographies of neoliberal austerity, urban megaprojects, free trade zones, foreign trade and investment, military alliances, and networks of policing and securitization.

My approach leverages the notion of geographies of power and dissent to bring into focus flows, practices, affinities, understandings, and histories that are spatially and historically situated but do not always correspond to the territorial borders of the Hashemite Kingdom of Jordan. In the first quarter of the twentieth century, for example—the period surrounding the arrival of the Hashemites in the Transjordanian area—we can identify multiple spatial imaginaries and the political forces seeking to reshape them. While Ottoman imperial and later British colonial powers each aimed to assert their control over the lands and peoples that most interested them, Great Britain eyed a much larger territory and the creation of multiple centralized, territorial states in the region. Local inhabitants, however, had their own affective connections to and understandings of their lands and the people who lived in them; those spatial imaginaries were incongruent with those of the colonial state.

The arrival of Abdullah I in the southern town of Maʿan in late 1920 marked a shift from the imperial Ottoman project to a new territorial colonial project that envisioned an entirely new political geography—that of a sovereign state with fixed borders and centralized administration. Efforts to realize that project clashed with the existing practices and geographical understandings of the various peoples residing in the broader Transjordanian area. In this sense protest and resistance at the time were *about* the terrain of the emerging Hashemite state, and not merely taking place *on* that terrain. Not just glimmers but forerunners of later political contention existed, in rich and undiluted form, in forgotten preindependence episodes, and in liminal spaces overlooked by focusing the analysis exclusively at the national level. The arrival of hundreds of thousands of Palestinians after 1948 and 1967 again restructured Jordan's political geography, connecting Transjordan to Palestinian lands west of the Jordan River. The regime's annexation of the West Bank strained the East Bank social contract and complicated the question of Jordanian identity as well as whom the state serves. And throughout his near fifty-year reign, King Hussein, Abdullah I's grandson, clung to a larger spatial imaginary, a wished-for unified Hashemite entity that would not only include Palestine's West Bank but would also extend over Iraq.

Today, Jordan is deeply involved in a Saudi-led regional security network (particularly the alliance among Sunni states against perceived and real encroachment of Iranian influence), itself part of a larger US-centered global security arrangement. Jordan not only sends its security forces to participate in the policing of protests elsewhere in the region, it also operates multiple training sites for gendarmerie and counterterrorism forces from across the globe, with direct US assistance. These investments in securitization and policing both produce and project the appearance of the kind of political stability necessary to attract foreign investment, embark on the construction of foreign-funded multibillion-dollar megaprojects, and operate zones of economic exception that function as shared sovereign spaces with the United States and Israel. Many Jordanians voice contentious claims against Jordan's role in these regional and global arrangements, and *Protesting Jordan*'s multiscalar approach brings all of these into clear view.

DIVERGENT FUTURES, ALTERNATIVE PASTS

The 2018 *Habbit Huzaryan* protests introduced at the outset of this chapter marked an escalation in the willingness of some Jordanians—particularly those from the regime's East Bank tribal support base—to openly criticize the king during protests. That opening dates to the uprisings that began in 2011 (chap. 6), during which slogans, chants, and speeches began to advance narratives about Jordan that clashed with the official narrative of Hashemite rule. The political stakes of competing narratives are perhaps highest when they call into question who has the right to political authority and whether those in power are ruling justly. As E. P. Thompson showed in his study of the English working class, protests break out not in response to grievances but when a strong sense that some egregious injustice has occurred.[33] Competing political actors, of course, seldom agree on the meaning of historical or even current political happenings. This is not to suggest that all actor evaluations are equally valid, or that some empirical claims are not better supported by historical evidence than others. But protests work as moments of public interpretation, and they advance alternative narratives that index competing projects, visions, and political stakes. How rebellions, uprisings, and demonstrations are publicly remembered and commemorated work to both assert claims on the past and stake claims on the future.

Michel-Rolph Trouillot begins his meditation on power and the stakes of historical narratives with a discussion of the events that unfolded in nineteenth-century Texas—then a Mexican province—where Mexican general Antonio López de Santa Anna roundly defeated the English-speakers occupying the Alamo mission in San Antonio. Tables turned a few weeks later, as Santa Anna fell prisoner to Texan troops under the command of Sam Houston. The political stakes of that history lie not only in who won—which certainly matters most—but how those events are remembered, anchored in narratives that assert moral as well as material claims. As Trouillot writes,

> Houston's men had punctuated their victorious attack on the Mexican army with repeated shouts of "Remember the Alamo!" With that reference to the old mission, they doubly made history. As actors, they captured Santa Anna and neutralized his forces. As narrators, they gave the Alamo story a new meaning. The military loss . . . was no longer the end point of the narrative but a

necessary turn in the plot, the trial of the heroes, which, in turn, made final victory both inevitable and grandiose.[34]

Victors always get to narrate history, of course, and the narrative of ultimate Texan victory following the Alamo defeat is reproduced in textbooks, at annual commemorations, and spatially through the site's enshrinement as a major event in Texan and US history. But just as state power must be constantly reproduced, the historical narratives that authorize them must also fend off competitors. The Alamo story's competitor is that the Inter-Tribal Council of American Indians seeks to have the burial grounds of more than a thousand Native American Catholics adjacent to the Alamo mission recognized as sacred grounds by the state of Texas and the city of Antonio. This "second battle of the Alamo," as Trouillot puts it, questions the very meaning of the siege: was the Alamo a brutal slaughter of brave English-speaking pioneers who decided to fight until death rather than surrender to a corrupt Mexican dictator? Or was it instead an example of brutal and racist expansionism, "the story of a few white predators taking over what was sacred territory and half-willingly providing, with their death, the alibi for a well-planned annexation?"[35]

Control of physical space is obviously central to state-making and state-maintaining, and the US-centric Alamo narrative is dominant in large part because Texas won. But while the United States exerts authority over that territory, thousands of Native Americans literally occupy parts of that land in their graves. The Inter-Tribal Council wants that occupation to be officially recognized, which would force the dominant narrative to accommodate those moral claims. Furthermore, if the graves are recognized as Native American sacred ground, visitors to the site would directly confront the place-making of marking the grounds as sacred and off-limits. Here the challenging narrative struggles to inscribe its alternative temporality and moral and material claims in the built environment, insisting that past events have other meanings. If they are successful, however, they will also invoke a possible alternative future. Will the United States maintain absolute sovereign control over the whole Alamo site, or will it be forced to cede space to Native American control and allow its place-making? Could such a loss be the first in a series of coming US losses, however small and symbolic? Temporally, competing narratives signal potential turns in the plot, bringing forth both incongruent spatial imaginaries and narratives of the past and the present. They also project into

CHAPTER 1

the future moral and material claims, and the stakes of some disagreements are higher than others.

*   *   *

How do competing narratives in Jordan signal potential turns in the plot? What are the challenges to the state's official narrative of the past and the present? In June 2016, Jordan celebrated the centennial of the Great Arab Revolt, when the Hashemites (then based in the Hijaz region of western Arabia) joined British forces to help bring down the Ottoman Empire during World War I. The revolt is celebrated annually on or around June 10, which is also Jordan's Army Day. The 2016 centennial celebration included massive displays of Jordanian military forces, including a brigade on horses. Such pageantry both invokes and romanticizes the time of the revolt, when horses were also the primary means for Bedouin raids. The mounted soldiers and many spectators donned the red-checkered scarf that symbolizes Transjordanian identity. (The black-and-white keffiyeh is also worn in Jordan, but it symbolizes Palestinian identity.) While these celebrations invoke a time when the Hashemites did not exert political authority over Transjordanian lands, they seek to connect Hashemites with a longer history of Arab tribal victory over foreign powers.

That history, and sometimes even Hashemite authority in Jordan, is publicly challenged at protests. Despite the battery of laws criminalizing criticism of the king, many of the regime's most outspoken critics enjoy relative protection because they belong to powerful East Bank families or tribes. Yet criticism does not come only from the wealthy and well-connected; poor and unemployed Jordanians of East Bank descent have also not hesitated to directly blame the king for their dire circumstances. Some protest chants invoke the king indirectly, as in this one from the 2018 *Habbit Huzayran* protests referencing an upscale neighborhood in West Amman, where several royal palaces are located: "You, who live in Dabouq, down with the rule of the [International Monetary] Fund!"[36]

In 2019, weekly protests at a parking lot adjacent to the Jordan Hospital expressed anger at King Abdullah II. At one protest commemorating the thirtieth anniversary of the 1989 *Habbit Nisan* protests (detailed in chap. 4), some two dozen protesters were surrounded by a diverse group observing them:

journalists, bystanders, retired military officers, political figures (including parliamentarian Hind al-Fayiz of the Bani Sakhr), and at least two dozen plain-clothes intelligence officers filming the protesters on their phone cameras. The parking lot was ringed by some hundred uniformed officers from at least three security forces. Yet the protesters were unintimidated, chanting against the king for more than two hours. One chant, for example, criticized Abdullah II's economic failures, albeit without mentioning the king by name: "Twenty years on the throne, nothing green or dry remains!"[37] In the latter part of this chant, "green" invokes fresh food as well as bank notes, and "dry" is a reference to stale bread—effectively, "we are so broke that we don't even have stale bread to eat." To have nothing to eat, no money, and not even bread is to say that one does not have even the basics of a dignified life. Blame for this hardship is placed directly on the king, who has failed to improve their condition after two decades of rule.

Another chant at that protest defiantly informed the king that people would no longer publicly celebrate him: "We stopped saying 'long live you,' why should we die, and you live?"[38] The "you" is again a clear reference to the king, a direct play on the phrasing of the familiar, reverential chant.[39] But because the king neglects his people and indeed appears to be unaware of their suffering, why should Jordanians declare, "Long live his majesty the great!" when they are unemployed and starving?

Another chant directly challenges the regime's historical narrative, the one advanced at celebrations like the anniversary of the Great Arab Revolt. Whereas the official narrative connects the Hashemites to Jordan's Arab and Bedouin tribal heritage, one chant invoked an alternative spatial imaginary: "Our [house/land] was Jordanian before the Great Arab Revolt!"[40] This chant is quite a provocation, as it asserts that the only true Jordanians are those who called the Transjordanian area home prior to World War I. Since the Hashemites arrived only in late 1920, they therefore are not Jordanian.[41] Such provocations have come to characterize a growing segment of the protest landscape, with a steady increase beginning in 2010. From a few individuals willing to call out the regime at that time, larger crowds now openly criticized the king. As the coming chapters will show, however, growing criticisms have not translated into unified calls to remove either Abdullah II or the Hashemite regime from power. Indeed, most Jordanians of East Bank descent see the

20   CHAPTER 1

preservation of Hashemite authority as key to maintaining East Bank tribal privilege. In that sense, some of the criticisms of the king at protests are more conservative than revolutionary.

The analyses presented in the coming chapters explore the political history of Jordan from the standpoint of diverse local peoples asserting claims that have shaped the Hashemite state-making and state-maintaining projects. The title, *Protesting Jordan*, therefore has two meanings. First, it highlights the centuries-old practices of people living in the Transjordanian area of asserting claims against political authorities through collective public expressions of dissent: Jordanians are endlessly protesting. Second, it brings into view growing anger among East Bank tribes toward the Hashemite regime and radical nativist claims about who is Jordanian and whether the Hashemites have a place in Jordan's future: Jordanians are protesting about whom the state serves. *Protesting Jordan* is also a regional and global story, one that cannot be fully comprehended without acknowledging the Hashemite regime's multiple entanglements with global economic processes and regional and global security arrangements.[42] Finally, the substantial original empirical material provides a rich opportunity to also theorize about protests in their own right by exploring their meaning-making and their spatial dimensions at multiple scales.

METHODOLOGY AND OUTLINE OF THE BOOK

Protesting Jordan is an avowedly interdisciplinary and interpretivist work that engages debates in the fields of political science, anthropology, history, geography, and urban planning. It examines the geographies of power and dissent in the Transjordanian area through multiple theoretical approaches, including networks, place-making, spatial imaginaries, and the militarization of space. The analysis is situated at multiple scales,[43] showing how particular spatial arrangements are implicated and coimplicated in challenges to the regime and in regime responses to those challenges.[44]

But the analysis is not a case study in the conventional sense of examining Jordan as an object that objectively exists "out there." I adopt the alternative approach that Joe Soss calls "casing" (a verb). Casing allows the researcher to create "new standpoints for interpretation, new paths for generalization, and new terms for relational, processual, or comparative analysis."[45] I "case" my study of protests in Jordan from the standpoint of the people resisting, engaging, and seeking to shape the evolving power structures in the Transjordanian area as well as state responses to them. Thus, instead of treating Jordan exclusively as a spatially bound, territorial state (although it is that), I move between multiple scales, sometimes zooming in to a single building and at other times zooming out to the regional and global levels. My aim is not merely to dislodge the conventional narrative of top-down state-making in Jordan but also to theorize about protest and space in ways that can advance our understanding of how political authority and challenges to it are mutually constituted in part through acts of public claim-making.

In addition to questions about space, I also examine multiple time frames and temporalities. These include the temporalities of my own analysis as well as those that different Jordanians themselves invoke, contest, and embrace.[46] I consider pacing, eventful moments, "normal" versus "crisis" times, and the affective connections that people invoke as they make claims about the past, present, and future. As shown, some protest chants convey a time frame that anchors "true" Jordanians spatially in the Transjordanian area prior to the Hashemite era. The Hashemite regime, however, anchors Jordan's past less spatially than culturally, weaving Bedouin, Islamic, and Biblical references into a Jordanian heritage that is broad enough to encompass Hashemite familial history.[47] I also reflect on the temporalities of my own analysis at various junctures. More than mere stylistic choice, the chosen analytic temporality in each chapter structures the arc of the analysis and brings certain things into view while obscuring others. Before previewing the multiple temporalities in the coming chapters, however, I pause to note that a scholar's choice of temporality can also do work that is political, often in unintended ways. Many early studies of the Arab uprisings, for example, were quick to proclaim the uprisings to be over by 2012, concluding that all of them had failed save the Tunisian uprising. And yet for years to come, hundreds of thousands across the region continued to protest. In such analyses the life-cycle temporality of the uprisings worked to reinforce the very narratives being advanced by autocratic regimes, namely, that the uprising period was "over" when the larger crowds diminished. Protesters struggled to keep the uprising period alive, and along with it the promise of an alternative future. *Protesting Jordan* seeks to avoid this pitfall, giving voice to multiple narratives and their sometimes clashing temporalities.

22   CHAPTER 1

In my analysis here, long-term temporalities illuminate shifting geographies of power and dissent related to empire, colonialism, state-making, and state-maintaining in the face of considerable dissent. These struggles unfold over the course of decades and sometimes centuries, and I bring into view multiple spatial imaginaries for patterns of trade, urban settlement, foreign intervention, tribal authority, conflicts over resources and territories, and migration for education and employment. I show how the increasing pace of urban growth in the capital—and variations in development across the city—contrast with the relative stagnation of the outlying governorates. Modes of slowing down—such as marches on foot that converge on locations in the capital representing not government power but the monarchy—can at times raise the stakes for challenges that the regime is then unable to ignore.

I also utilize medium-term temporalities to explore particular series of protests, but I directly probe the limits of the life-cycle time frames by drawing multiscalar connections across space and time. My discussion of Jordan's protests during the time of the Arab uprisings, for example, situates those protests within a shift in spatial practices of protest that preceded the uprising period by several years while exploring people's affective connections to other significant periods of protest in Jordan as well as the other uprisings in the region. Finally, I employ short-term temporalities and local scales to examine the microdynamics of protests that unfold in particular spaces over a matter of minutes or hours. I consider how diverse political actors understand the temporalities of change as well as how the histories and futures that they invoke challenge those advanced by the regime.

Beginning with chapter 4, most of the empirical material is original and comes from my field research in Jordan from 1995 to 2020—some two dozen trips totaling approximately five years of residence. Field research methods include elite interviews, ethnographies of protests, and public ethnography of places in the built environment.[48] I attended some three dozen protests, interviewed journalists and members of political parties and professional associations, served as scholar-in-residence at three Jordanian research institutes, interviewed more than a hundred activists, attended organization meetings with activists, and socialized with activists. I pored over personal, newspaper, and government archives in Amman, London, and Washington, DC. I incorporated insight from both Jordanian and foreign-funded public opinion surveys. This mixed methodology is well suited for analyzing as well as theorizing geographies of power and dissent, the spatial practices of protest and repression, interactions between protests and the built environment, and the political stakes of competing narratives about past, present, and future.

Because one goal of this book is to expose state techniques for silencing dissent, the voices of protesters and their activities are largely limited to what they do or say that is already within public view. This decision aims not to silence protesters or erase their agency; on the contrary, the analysis restores the agency of Jordan's diverse population in shaping their political, economic, and social arrangements for more than 150 years. I also focus on what is already in public view at the request of activists in order to protect them from additional harassment and exposure to state repression of the sort examined in chapter 7.

Chapter 2, "Transforming Transjordan," deploys the concept of spatial imaginaries to bring into view various political projects in the Transjordanian area before and during the British-led Hashemite colonial project. I adopt a scale and time frame that is sweepingly historical but zoomed out from the boundaries of modern-day Jordan in order to reveal regional patterns and contests over political authority for a period of many decades. Examining how political and social forces were mutually constituted through rebellions, repression, and accommodation, I show that the Ottoman, British, and Hashemite efforts to impose authority were met not with sporadic rebellions but with sustained resistance and proactive efforts to shape those imperial and colonial projects. I examine the emergence of the territorial state with a central administration, and its new spatial imaginary, from the standpoint of those inhabiting the Transjordanian area. This approach highlights the agency of various actors and the ways that they shaped emergent Hashemite rule. The analysis begins in the nineteenth century to identify the existing repertoires of claim-making and resistance, tracing changes in spatial imaginaries and geographies of power and dissent through the establishment of the independent state of Jordan in 1946.

In chapter 3, "Becoming Amman: From Periphery to Center," I bring the scale of analysis down to the level of the city but maintain a long-term time frame to examine patterns of urban development and political resistance. I examine place-making in the city and trace the transformation of Amman from a seasonally inhabited town in the late nineteenth century to its establishment

24   CHAPTER 1

as the Hashemite capital in 1928, and how that transformation led to a restructuring of the political geography of the Transjordanian area whose profound effects would not be fully realized for two decades. Urban planning documents throughout the period convey the colonial spatial imaginaries of a planned and ordered capital, only portions of which were realized. I examine the massive protests of the 1950s and Amman's rapid transformation through the Black September violence of 1970–71. I show how, as the growing capital became the new state's economic center, a new fiscal geography relegated the existing East Bank towns to the periphery.

Chapter 4, "Jordanization, the Neoliberal State, and the Retreat and Return of Protest," returns to the national scale to examine techniques of Hashemite state-maintaining in the wake of Black September. I explore the massive *Habbit Nisan* protests of 1989 through a spatial lens, showing how those protests marked a major juncture in Jordanian politics and introduced new spatial patterns of protest. Protests in the outlying East Bank governorates, which put some of the greatest pressure on the Hashemite regime, revived portions of the repertoires of early twentieth-century revolts, notably blocking roads and destroying infrastructure. In Amman, by comparison, the rapidly changing built environment reshaped the city's own geography of protests, with new spaces developing highly localized protest routines.

In chapter 5, "An Ethnography of Place and the Politics of Routine Protests," I bring the scale down to the microlevel, examining protests on a street adjacent to the Kalouti Mosque in West Amman. There, protests against the normalization of Jordan's relations with Israel became so routine in the 2000s that they hardly seemed contentious at all. I present an ethnography of place to examine the microdynamics and temporality of those protests over the course of several hours, including how they alter the political atmosphere of the neighborhood. The spatial dynamics of routine protest and policing practices reveal that permitted protests can work to shore up the regime's power even as protesters challenge government policies and maintain existing spaces for protest.

Chapter 6, "Jordan in the Time of the Arab Uprisings," returns to a national level but with the timing and spread of the regional uprisings considered in tandem with protests in Jordan. I examine the gradual escalation of protests beginning with labor protests in 2006 through the violent repression of anti-austerity protesters in fall 2012. The uprising period saw shifts in protest repertoires as well as newly mobilized segments of the East Bank communities, forces that the regime scrambled to divide and weaken. I also examine the rise of the radical nativist movement that indexes Hashemites as outsiders, a serious problem for a regime that relies on support from East Bank communities. The escalating rhetoric of the period set the stage for increased public criticisms of the regime discussed in this introductory chapter.

In chapter 7, "The Techniques and Evolving Spatial Dynamics of Protest and Repression," I examine the resurgence of protest in the mid-2010s, with attention to the most active sectors of protest as well as the evolving spaces and repertoires for protest—including virtual spaces. I explore how proximity to Amman enabled deeper connections between new groups of activists compared with activists residing farther south. I also show how a new tactic for East Bank unemployment protesters—marching on foot to the capital to demand jobs outside the Royal Court—entailed significant spatial and temporal innovations.

Chapter 8, "Protest and Order in Militarized Spaces," returns to the scale of the city to show how securitization, neoliberal development, and the attraction of foreign investment affected changes to the urban built environment. Along with a building boom, Amman enjoys upgraded infrastructure that is militarized to provide the kind of "normal"-time stability—or at least the appearance of it—the regime needs to reproduce its authority as well as secure foreign investment. These diverse public and private projects have altered the possibilities for political protests, some intentionally and others unintentionally, by creating blockages, reducing the visibility of certain established places of protest, and rendering other spaces more exposed and visible for surveillance. Here I contribute an original typology to the small but growing literature on space and protest, one that examines the spatial techniques used by the state to weaken the potential impact of protests by creating material obstacles to protest in the built environment.

Chapter 9, "Protesting Global Aspirations," ties it all together. I connect the evolution of Jordan's geographies of power and dissent to regional and global geographies of neoliberal investment, military alliances, and policing and securitization networks. King Abdullah II has a vision for Jordan, one in which the Hashemites are responsible for leading the kingdom from its noble Bedouin, Islamic, and Biblical past into a modern, fast-paced, and cosmopolitan future. But as was true a century ago, Hashemite authority today is maintained not only with the support of East Bank communities but via tremendous financial and military assistance from external states and institutions—each with its own interests and agenda. While the regime struggles to realize its regional and global aspirations, protests across Jordan reveal large-scale opposition to neoliberalism and particularly its austerity policies. Although protests can work as a kind of negotiation between the regime and its constituents, the exchange is not only transactional. Protests also bring into view moral as well as material claims. And they reveal deep tensions over who is Jordanian and what Jordan is or should be, the stakes of which are the future of Hashemite political authority. This final chapter also examines Jordan's location in regional and global security networks and its multiple training facilities for counterterrorism and riot police.

Let's now see how and where people were protesting in the Transjordanian area some 150 years ago.

Chapter 2

TRANSFORMING TRANSJORDAN

TERRITORIAL STATE-MAKING IS A POLITICAL PROJECT, ONE THAT aims to discipline and control diverse populations in ways that facilitate centralized authority. Seeing such state-making projects from the standpoint of those seeking to preserve and expand their own local and regional authorities brings into view more complex and multiscalar political configurations and practices than the top-down view of state-making reveals. In the face of imperial and colonial projects, diverse local populations advance and defend their own understandings of their political worlds and the social and political attachments those views entail. While state-making—and colonial state-making in particular—is always a story of coercion, dependency, and patronage, this does not mean that local subjects are hapless victims or that they have lost their political voice or capacity to assert agency. The early part of Jordan's modern period shows just how central resistance and rebellion were to the form of the new political configurations that emerged, including the political geography of the centralized territorial state.

Instead of beginning with the Hashemite-British colonial state-making project following World War I, my analysis begins half a century earlier, with the first Ottoman imperial efforts to impose greater authority over portions of the Transjordanian area than they had previously. Late nineteenth-century Transjordan was not a cohesive political or social entity. Characterized by overlapping social, economic, and political networks, the people residing in the area—some for decades, others for centuries—held strong attachments to the area but differed in how they saw themselves connected to others across geographic space. A helpful way of understanding these multiscalar social and political attachments is to think not in terms of political authority—who controlled what territory—but in terms of the spatial imaginaries that diverse people produced and embraced.

The concept of spatial imaginary aims to capture the spatiality of how people understand their social and political worlds—its contours, coverage, and limits.[1] Spatial imaginaries are how people see themselves attached to or differing from other people across space, and thus they are a primary mode of meaning construction, social interaction, and calculating collective action.[2] Spatial imaginaries reflect how people are attached in meaningful ways and how they spatially understand political authority, social connections, and movements. They are both ontological and normative, embodying understandings of how things are as well as how they should be.

Spatial imaginaries are also productive of sociopolitical connections. They reflect a set of sociospatial entwinements, each with distinct authorities, practices, networks, and affinities.[3] They are at the heart of colonial rule[4] and, indeed, of all visions of modernity and later postmodernity.[5] The Ottoman imperial spatial imaginary, for example, was primarily concerned with the urban centers, towns, outposts, and agricultural land located along the north-south pilgrimage and trade route. The people residing in those areas, however, had diverse familial roots and thus affective attachments not only to the Transjordanian area but also to locations in Palestine, Greater Syria (*Bilad al-Sham*), and, to a lesser extent, Iraq and Egypt. Merchants in the towns of Salt, Madaba, and Ajloun, for example, saw themselves as more connected to Damascus and Nablus than to "Transjordanian" towns to the south.[6] Indeed for most northerners, even those living for decades under Ottoman control, affective spatial imaginaries extended well beyond the Transjordanian area into Greater Syria (and still do, as we will see in chap. 6). By comparison, the people of the central and southern highlands, including the towns of Karak, Tafileh, and Shoubak, identified somewhat with Greater Syria but had stronger and more autonomous local identities. These identities and their histories were forged in part around conflicts within and among tribes (alliances were always open to reconfiguration), but also around their shared willingness to rebel against Ottoman practices they believed to be unjust. As we will see, tribes with long-standing animosities sometimes coordinated anti-Ottoman activities, even as other tribes allied with the Ottomans. The larger tribal confederations as well as the families that constituted them also had differing attachments to their lands or, for nomadic tribes, their larger domains of seasonal migration. Many central and southern people had longer attachments to their lands than did some people in the north, many of whom had migrated for economic opportunities more recently. Familial ties to Damascus, for example, were common in the north but weaker or nonexistent in the central highlands. Thus, the spatial imaginary of highland towns and adjacent agricultural land captured their self-sense as proud, independent, and fiercely assertive people.

Further south, some people identified even less with northerners, embracing instead affective attachments as the northernmost part of the Hijaz region of the western Arabian Peninsula. This spatial imaginary explains why the Hashemite emir Abdullah I was readily welcomed in Ma'an upon his arrival in 1920 as well as why some Ma'anis today have greater sympathies (than elsewhere in Jordan) with strains of salafism originating in the Arabian Peninsula. By comparison, the steppe or desert hinterland dominated the spatial imaginaries of nomadic Bedouin tribes that migrated between the outer steppe in the winter and regions closer to the north-south transit corridor during the summer. The Bedouin were not a single or united force, of course, siding at times with townsfolk against Ottoman taxation and authority while maintaining their practices of pillaging and raiding those same towns as well as each other.

Across much of the region, however, the primary basis of affiliation and prestige was the tribe ('ashira).[7] This mode of belonging entailed shared forms of localized political authority but also extended across much of the Arabian Peninsula and Gulf region, weakening somewhat in major urban centers like Damascus and in towns where most residents were migrants. It is important to pause here to discuss what "tribal" means. As mentioned in chapter 1, tribes are extended families that see themselves as sharing a common descent, social practices, local authority structures, and spatial attachments to specific lands or domains. These extended families tend to be clustered into larger tribal confederations, which may or may not be led by a recognized "shaykh

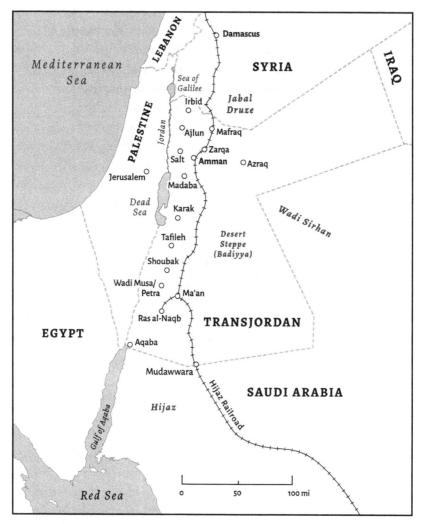

MAP 2.1. The Transjordanian area, with developments from the nineteenth century to the 1950s.

of shaykhs." But tribes are also not primordial or homogeneous in their composition, practices, or self-understanding. Some are powerful, with proud oral histories that extend back centuries. Others have weaker attachments, with members adhering less strictly to the directives of tribal authorities. Like states, tribal attachments and authority structures must be actively maintained, and as such the meanings and practices of "tribes" and "tribal authority" evolve considerably over time, as we shall see. Tribes are often in conflict over land, resources, and leadership. Alliances among tribes also frequently change, and challenges to tribal authority are common and occur even within a family. One's reputation is based in part on how one asserts power and meets challenges, although membership in a prominent family can yield its own rewards.[8]

Key for the moment is to recognize that tribes were powerful during this period across much of the Transjordanian area, but merchant and northern settled areas were less insularly tribal than in the central and southern areas or among Bedouins. And while nomadic, semisettled, and settled Bedouins are all tribal, the settled tribes are not Bedouin. In important ways, therefore, spatial imaginaries and the affective attachments of tribes and the people living in the Transjordanian area should be seen as imbricating rather than exclusive, with various attachments more-or-less salient depending on the situation or its political stakes. Unpacking these complex sets of affinities will prove crucial for understanding the political configurations of the emerging territorial colonial state.

FROM THE OTTOMAN IMPERIAL PROJECT TO THE BRITISH COLONIAL ONE

In the second half of the 1800s, the Ottoman Empire—a political force in the Transjordanian area since the sixteenth century—sought to assert greater control over the transit corridor between Damascus and Mecca through modern forms of statecraft and administrative practices. Between 1851 and 1893, the Ottomans established militarized outposts at most towns. They sought to collect taxes and forge economic relations with local authorities but without aiming to fully displace existing power structures or local authorities. Many local shaykhs received cash stipends in exchange for accepting Ottoman authority.[9] The Ottomans tried unsuccessfully to settle the nomadic Bedouin, but they were able to create new settlements of Circassians (in Amman), Caucasians (in Ajloun and the Balqa), and Turkomen (in Lajjun and al-Humman).[10] These newly settled communities effectively created spaces of "local" Ottoman support unencumbered by the tribal practices and authority structures that characterized the previously settled and nomadic areas. In short, these new communities had no attachment to existing spatial imaginaries in the Transjordanian area. Meanwhile, nomadic Bedouin continued their seasonal migrations, some pushing west into the Jordan River Valley (Ghor) and the lands of Palestine, northeast into what would become Iraq, and east and southeast into the Arabian Peninsula.

Expanding Ottoman communication and trade infrastructures worked to integrate the settled areas of the Transjordanian area. Gradually, a form of "Arabism" emerged among intellectuals in the Greater Syria area, particularly in Damascus. Some of these began to call the whole region *Suriya*, including northern portions of the Transjordanian area, likely influenced by European use of the term. The spatial imaginary of Greater Syria gradually took on meaning as a distinct homeland (*watan*)—one among other Arab homelands as well as among the worldwide community of homelands.[11] Other new spatial imaginaries emerged as ideas about nationalism spread not only in the Arab world but also globally.

Whereas the Ottoman imperialists sought to tax the locals, establish garrisons, and induce Bedouin settlement,[12] the British colonial forces following World War I advanced a colonial spatial imaginary of a territorially defined state with central governing structures. The Hashemites, for their part, had designs on a much larger domain, eyeing Damascus as the potential capital of a larger Hashemite kingdom. But they eventually accepted the British offer to establish Hashemite authority over the Transjordanian area as a start, although Abdullah I and his grandson, King Hussein, held on to expansionist dreams throughout the twentieth century. The British also offered Sharif Hussein's other son, Faysal, rule over Iraq, so the Hashemites essentially got two kingdoms. Meanwhile, the creation of Transjordan as a territorial nation-state worked as a political technology employed in the exercise of power, one that sought to bring into being a new political spatiality.[13] But that new centralized state took years to solidify by means of British money and forces, and it was profoundly shaped by the claim-making and resistance of the diverse peoples inhabiting those lands. In the first instance, the British had to bring Abdullah I's ambitions into alignment with their own plan for ruling over Transjordan.

The remainder of this chapter examines the ways in which people residing in the Transjordanian area responded to, resisted, or engaged the Ottoman imperialist project and later the British and Hashemite colonial one. It shows how the imperial and colonial spatial imaginaries did not eclipse the existing multiscalar ones but rather worked to assert authority through a combination of accommodation and repression. I show how the emergent new state and society were mutually constituted through these acts of rebellion, repression, and accommodation, and how the new political geography of the Hashemite centralized state failed to entirely supplant the affective spatial imaginaries of the peoples living in the broader Transjordanian area. As we will see, those affective spatial attachments continue to shape Jordanian politics into the twenty-first century.

INVADERS, RAIDERS, RESISTANCE

Spatial imaginaries are historically situated, and these different communities developed their own repertoires of resistance, albeit with knowledge of other local struggles. Rebellion in the area far predates the nineteenth century, with significant revolts against the Ottomans, such as by the Bani Tamim tribe in the seventeenth century. Some areas were more resistant to Ottoman efforts to collect taxes and establish local authority than were others. The northernmost regions were often less resistant than those farther south, which were proud of their independence and fierceness in battle. The central region of Balqa, for example, has a long history of resisting Ottoman encroachment.[14] When the Ottomans planned to launch raids on Balqa in 1867 to subdue local authorities, a prominent shaykh from the Adwan tribe in the region coordinated resistance among residents of Salt in alliance with local Bedouin tribes. Adwani tribesmen on horseback fought the Ottoman forces in a four-hour battle a few months later, again pushing back Ottoman efforts to assert authority. In another act of rebellion in 1869, members of the Bani Hamida tribal confederation who were angry with Ottoman authorities destroyed the recently discovered Moabite Stone dating to the ninth century BCE, heating it with a fire and then pouring cold water over it so that it broke into pieces.[15] Subsequent clashes between Ottoman forces and tribe members led to several of the latter's deaths.

Later that year, multiple tribes in the area set aside their animosities to join forces to resist Ottoman authority again, especially the Bani Sakhr and Adwan tribal confederations.[16] Indeed, the latter half of the nineteenth century was characterized by so many changes in the official administrative arrangements over the Transjordanian area that it is hard to miss the extent of Ottoman failure and concomitant success of the local people in resisting.[17]

One region known for rebellion, the highlands of Karak, is exemplary of the resistance to outsiders aiming to weaken local authorities. Located in the mountains immediately east of the Dead Sea, Karak takes its name from its twelfth-century crusader castle, Crac des Moabites.[18] In the nineteenth century, the region flourished with trade, agriculture, and pilgrim traffic under the local leadership of the Majali family, Palestinians who had come to Karak as merchants from Hebron in the late eighteenth century.[19] The region had suffered considerable destruction in 1834 by Muhammad Ali's invading Egyptian army but was rebuilt under Majali authority, further cementing the family's local power.[20]

When the Ottomans sought to deepen their control of the region a few decades later, they employed a combination of administrative redistricting and the use of force.[21] But Muhammad Majali retained de facto authority over Karak, and multiple attempts to collect taxes between 1861 and 1876 proved futile. Indeed, Majali used his own funds to maintain independent forces that could protect both locals and pilgrims against pillaging by others in the region. When Ottoman forces next tried to enter Karak in 1893, European missionaries reported that locals greeted the forces with gunfire and rolled huge stones down on them from the mountaintop town center. The Ottomans attacked Karak for nearly a week, with its administrators only permitted to enter after extensive negotiations and bribes.[22] Ultimately the resistance in Karak allowed it to maintain considerable local authority while refashioning its role in a changing region.[23] Compared to regions farther north, the Ottomans in the nineteenth century were only able to establish limited garrisons and minimal administrative offices in the central and southern highland areas.[24] As Eugene Rogan writes, "certain areas would break out in open rebellion and revolt if the Ottoman measures were too disruptive of local power arrangements, or if the Ottomans were unable to develop a significant constituency in a given area."[25]

When the Ottomans failed to establish military control over certain local communities, they began to create new settlements beholden to their largess.[26] Three related developments altered the political geography of the Transjordanian area. First, from 1867 to 1878, peasants who had left local towns to seek economic opportunity or to escape intercommunal strife created new settlements largely unattached to local power structures. Second, from 1878 to 1906, the Ottomans settled Circassians, Chechen-Circassians, and Turkmen at various sites in the Transjordanian area, including near the Roman ruins of seasonally inhabited Amman. These refugees of Russian wars were key to establishing Ottoman authority in the area since they were grateful for the land and protection but unbeholden to tribal authorities in the area. Third, as a result of the refugee settlements, the Bedouin were losing control of land they had used previously, and the Ottomans responded to their claims bureaucratically, with reference to whether the Bedouin had paid taxes or registered their lands with Ottoman authorities. The Ottomans concluded that lands that the Bedouin had not cultivated were outside of the bounds of legitimate claims. As a result, poor Bedouin began to protect what they viewed as their land by creating mud-hut plantations, often farmed by Palestinian and Egyptian peasants. As Bedouin villages began to appear, the Ottomans granted land titles to individuals who were then required to pay taxes to the Ottoman authorities.[27] The nominal Ottoman successes in administering these new settlements contrasted sharply with their inability to easily overcome the resistance by locals in many of the established towns.

By the end of the nineteenth century, the lands of the Transjordanian area were home to diverse peoples with their own spatial imaginaries, many of whom continued to move within and across the land. Merchants from other regions in Greater Syria, especially from Damascus, continued to settle in Salt, Madaba, and Ajloun for economic opportunities; Circassians, Chechen-Circassians, and Turkmen refugees were settled by the Ottomans; Egyptian and Palestinian peasants migrated to the region for agricultural work; and Bedouin tribes still seasonally traversed the lands of today's Syria, Jordan, Palestine, Iraq, and Saudi Arabia. These are the people who together are described as the Hashemite regime's East Bank tribal support base, a category that unhelpfully obscures differences of interest, identity, and attachment that distinguish them to the present day.

THE REVOLTS OF THE EARLY TWENTIETH CENTURY

Acts of resistance in the early twentieth-century Transjordanian area largely registered anger at Ottoman infrastructural projects and practices of extraction, notably taxation. Infrastructure has always worked as a terrain of power and contestation, as locations through which "sociality, governance and politics, accumulation and dispossession, and institutions and aspirations are formed, reformed, and performed."[28] As a technique of power, infrastructure has both spatial and temporal dimensions. Roads, railways, and electrical lines, for example, extend spatially in ways that connect as well as divide. They reduce travel time and make political control of outlying areas easier.[29] Infrastructure projects also project political power into the future, creating new nodes and spaces for both economic prosperity and exclusion. Yet despite the powerful political effects of infrastructure, political authorities treat such projects as depoliticized technical issues—an outlook that is itself a technique of power.[30] Chapters 8 and 9 will examine additional dynamics between infrastructure and political protest in the contemporary period, but here I consider the infrastructure projects that created faster-paced connections across space while disrupting the practices and spatial imaginaries of some local populations.

In the latter part of the nineteenth century, infrastructure development projects accelerated the movement of peoples within and across Greater Syria, the Transjordanian area, and the Hijaz area of western Arabia. In 1867, ferries shuttled people and goods across the Jordan river, meeting roads that connected to Nablus and Jerusalem. A small fleet of boats connected Jericho to a landing near a road leading up the mountains to Karak.[31] Telegraph lines extended along the Hijaz Highway south from Damascus, reaching Salt by 1900 and southward locations soon thereafter. When they were not tearing down the telegraph lines in protest,[32] locals used them to send petitions to the Ottoman provincial authorities in Damascus and to the sultan in Istanbul.[33] The sabotage and destruction of the new transportation and telecommunication infrastructure became part of the local repertoires of resistance.

The most significant infrastructure project of the early twentieth century was the Hijaz Railway along the existing route from Damascus to Medina. Construction began in 1900 and reached Medina in 1908. While beneficial for Ottoman administrators and those urban merchants based at stops along the

FIGURE 2.1. Workers repairing the Hijaz Railway after a Bedouin raid in 1918.

route, the infrastructure created economic hardship for the Bedouin, who lost significant revenue because merchants, pilgrims, and the Ottoman authorities stopped leasing Bedouin camels to transport goods and people.[34] A trip across the Transjordanian corridor that used to take weeks could now be made in a few days, and the increased speed meant fewer stops along the way. By 1908, the pilgrimage caravans stopped almost entirely.[35] Indeed, the railway proved economically devastating for the Bedouins, even as some found employment guarding it. Other Bedouins sought to raid the trains themselves—usually unsuccessfully—and sabotaged the railway by stealing the wooden sleepers, to which the rails were secured, and using them for firewood.

Changes in modes of extraction and patronage were also met with resistance. Locals objected to higher taxes and the fluctuating stipends paid by Ottoman authorities to local officials. In 1900, for example, the shaykhs of Karak threatened a rebellion when the Ottomans reduced subsidy payments. The Ottomans sent more soldiers instead, quelling talk of a revolt but leaving a simmering discontent as taxes were increased over the next decade.[36]

Two major revolts are exemplary of these decades of rebellion. The first took place in the town of Shoubak in 1905, home of the crusader Montreal Castle, where locals had previously revolted five years earlier. During the 1905 revolt, a major grievance was taxation, but locals also objected to Ottoman officials demanding that local women carry water to them daily from a spring in a nearby valley. A group of townsmen climbed to the citadel and killed some of the Ottoman troops stationed there. Nearby Bedouin—angered by Ottoman efforts to end the practice of Bedouin pillage, a major source of income for their communities—joined the Shoubak rebels and helped occupy the citadel for several days. A hundred Ottoman troops arrived and demanded that the rebels evacuate the citadel and that local leaders provide a written apology to the Ottoman administrators.[37] The rebels met some of the demands but sought to use the rebellion to renegotiate the terms of Ottoman authority. The specific demands are worth examining closely:

1. The Ottoman government must improve the selection of staff and governors who manage the administration in the region and be aware of the customs and traditions of the people of the region.
2. The government must punish the gendarmerie forces and the garrison that abused the women of Shoubak. Those forces must be permanently transferred elsewhere.
3. The government must prevent soldiers from entering Shoubak neighborhoods unless necessary for security purposes.
4. The people of Shoubak—both men and women—are not obliged to bring water from the springs to the garrison, its soldiers, or the homes of strangers, regardless of those individuals' rank.
5. The sons of Shoubak or the people of the nearby Shoubak villages will be selected to fill the role of security and tax collection.
6. The rebels will not be arrested, punished, or held accountable for the raid.

A careful look at their demands reveals some details of the local spatial imaginary—the identification of boundaries to Shoubak neighborhoods and nearby villages—and an insistence that local norms of behavior within that area must be respected by Ottoman officers. The demands also do not reject Ottoman authority but rather articulate what local authorities saw as its moral and material boundaries.

The Ottoman administration resoundingly rejected the demands and violently put down the revolt, killing as many as 150. Three rebel leaders were sent to Damascus to be prosecuted for treason; two of them died there in prison. Even as news of the fate of the Shoubak Revolt (*Hayyit al-Shoubak*) spread, however, it did not temper revolts elsewhere across the region. In 1907, additional Ottoman forces were sent to Ma'an to fend against attacks by the nomadic Bani Sakhr tribal confederation pushing south from the Balqa region.[38] In 1908, tribal leaders again put aside their rivalries and organized a general tribal revolt, uniting disparate local authorities around common grievances; six thousand additional Ottoman troops were sent to put it down, and relative peace was restored only through the payment of increased subsidies to tribal leaders.[39]

A second major revolt during this period is exemplary of repertoires of resistance shaped by both infrastructure and political struggles outside of the Transjordanian area: the 1910 Karak Revolt, remembered today as *Hayyit al-Karak*. Karakis were frustrated by Ottoman taxation,[40] and they had lingering anger over the violent suppression of the threatened revolt earlier in the decade. Karak was located less than ten miles from the Qatrana stop on the Hijaz Railway, and at the time had a population of 2,000 to 3,000.[41] In Istanbul, the Young Turk Revolution (1908–9) sought to realize consistent rule of law across the empire, at the expense of some of the established accommodations with local authorities in numerous locations. In Greater Syria north of the Transjordanian area, massive Ottoman forces took months to put down a Druze revolt, from August through November 1910. The Druze were forced to pay taxes (including arrears) and submit to Ottoman conscription.[42] The Ottomans then turned their sights south to the Transjordanian area, first disarming Ajloun and forcing conscription. Ottoman troops tightened control over towns just to the south of Ajloun, including Salt (then the largest in the Transjordanian area with a population of some 3,300), and continued pushing south into Madaba in the central Transjordanian area, preparing locals for conscription but not immediately taking conscripts.

Sami Pasha, an Ottoman administrator in Damascus, telegraphed authorities in Karak and warned them to prepare for major administrative changes: weapons would be confiscated and banned, taxes increased, and the male population counted in a census—a preparatory step for conscription. Karaki authorities signed a petition refusing to disarm, arguing that the weapons were needed to defend themselves from Bedouin raids. Their petition also complained of higher taxes and lowered subsidies to local authorities, and it demanded that the prominent local shaykh Qadr Majali be given a seat on the local Ottoman administrative council, as had his predecessor, Salih Majali.[43]

The Ottomans ignored the petition and carried out the census over the next two weeks. As Rogan puts it, they acted "as if they had no intention of conscripting, and the Karakis went along with the registration as if they had no intention of rebelling."[44] Karaki leaders, however, had already decided that they would revolt, and Qadr traveled around neighboring areas seeking support by arguing that a revolt might enable them to negotiate a more favorable arrangement with the Ottomans.[45] A charismatic leader adept at mobilizing people, Qadr argued that disarmament and conscription would weaken the town's defenses.[46]

The region-wide rebellion had an additional spatial dimension: Karaki leaders hoped to draw Ottoman troops to multiple rural battles in order to lessen the number of troops in the mountaintop town. If successful, the move might enable townspeople to capture the government buildings quickly. But the plans were overheard by Ottoman soldiers, and at least one rival shaykh, Hussayn Pasha Tarawneh, agitated against the plan. On December 4, one Ottoman census team was attacked and killed, launching a massive revolt early the following day. The rebellion spread south to Tafileh and Ma'an as well as to several stations along the Hijaz Railway. In Karak, locals burned Ottoman administrative records and buildings and killed several administrators. Rebel patrols outside of town attacked the railway and tore up some rails and sleepers. Local Bedouin tribes joined in the rebellion, entering Karak town and attacking stores owned by non-Karakis.[47] In Tafileh, rebels attacked Ottoman troops and nearby railway stations; Bedouin tribes in that area also joined in. Members of the Atiyya tribe killed several railway employees at the Qatrana station and pulled up rails to prevent trains from running.[48] Some Bani Sakhr tribes also joined the rebellion.[49]

Ten days later, Sami Pasha arrived in Karak with a massive Ottoman army and crushed the rebellion. His forces laid siege to Karak and reportedly threw some rebels off the cliffs to their deaths. The wives of several of the organizers were arrested and sent to Ma'an prison in an effort to compel the revolt's organizers to surrender.[50] Rafıfan Majali's pregnant wife, Bandar, gave birth in prison to a son.[51] To insure that their imprisonment not be forgotten, she gave him the unusual name Habis, which in Arabic means "locked up" or "confined." Even as Ottoman forces took control of the town, it remained a frontier area and not "actual Ottoman domains," as was the fate of Ajloun and

Salt to the north.[52] But by January 1913, the Ottomans had fully established rule over the broader Karak region and granted an amnesty to remaining rebels. They agreed to recognize the rights, customs, and authority of the tribes in the surrounding regions, and the Majali family regained some of its authority.[53] Although the revolt itself was crushed, the Karakis established a reputation for resisting the imposition of a centralized government.[54]

Despite Ottoman recognition of some local tribal authority and customs, however, the revolt marked a turning point for Karak with the extension of more direct Ottoman control over the region. Many scholars therefore portray the revolt as a complete failure, for example, the Jordanian historian Tariq Tell:

> The Karak revolt is better seen as the dying spasm of the local order, a doomed attempt of a tribal system to defend itself against an encroaching state. The Ottoman hold on the district was rapidly reestablished, and the Karakis for the most part remained loyal Ottomanists throughout the subsequent years of war and revolt.[55]

Tribal authority was certainly weakening, but, as we shall see, it was evolving more than it was simply dying out.[56] Such conclusions also underappreciate the central role revolts and other acts of dissent would play over the next decades in shaping the colonial state-making project. These revolts are remembered today, and they shaped the repertoires of resistance inherited by future generations. And while these anti-Ottoman rebellions sought to negotiate terms with the imperialists while maintaining local authority structures, the imperial spatial imaginary did little to disrupt Transjordanians' own domains and attachments. They were, however, about to encounter new forces with a different spatial project: the establishment of a colonial territorial state with a centralized administration, one that aimed to assert direct control over the whole of the Transjordanian area and, indeed, beyond.

COMPETING SPATIAL IMAGINARIES AND THE COLONIAL PROJECT

The first years after the fall of the Ottoman Empire marked less a political rupture than a handover of power from one semi-absent authority to another. Land use, trade patterns, and infrastructural development show considerable continuity. In July 1917, the Great Arab Revolt against the Ottoman Empire reached Transjordan in the midst of World War I, led by Sharif Hussein bin Ali of the Hashemites of the Hijaz region of western Arabia. As he and his troops pushed into the Transjordanian area, local tribes differed on whether to join the revolt or side with the Ottomans. Those decisions were largely based on material incentives and specific economic and social conditions, but also on calculations shaped by their level of local autonomy or allegiance to the Ottomans. Some tribes suffering from local food shortages joined the rebellion in order to eat, whereas areas that enjoyed plentiful food and where the Ottomans played a significant role in local trade were less likely to support the revolt.[57]

Sharif Hussein and his troops met resistance in Aqaba but found allies in Tafileh and Wadi Musa. In Ma'an, families within the powerful Huwaytat tribal confederation fought on both sides.[58] In Karak, the now-strong bargain with the Ottomans gave local leaders little appetite for joining the revolt.[59] Some parts of the Bani Sakhr in the central Balqa area, however, also fought on both sides.[60] British troops provided support for the revolt, particularly in the north. But they failed to take control of Amman and only briefly occupied Salt. While Tell argues that northern tribes, notably the Adwan, were insignificant actors in the revolt,[61] Mathew Madain documents how the people of Salt welcomed the British and rebelled against the Ottomans, inflicting "sizeable casualties" on the latter, raiding an Ottoman outpost and attacking settler communities on traditional tribal land.[62] Overall, Transjordanians took sides based on their local interests and calculations, underlining the extent to which the area still lacked a unifying allegiance or collective identity.

At the end of the war and with the collapse of the Ottoman Empire, France and Great Britain secretly planned to divide colonial control of the Arab lands formerly under Ottoman control, first via the secret Sykes-Picot Agreement of 1916. According to that agreement, France would oversee control of Syria and Lebanon, and Great Britain would oversee control of Palestine, Transjordan, and Iraq; the European colonial spatial imaginary of the agreement severed Greater Syria into two. Most of Transjordan's local populations, urban and rural, opposed foreign efforts to assert authority. But while some saw in the advance of the British new opportunities for employment or patronage, others saw only new efforts to displace local authority structures. Janine Astrid Clark argues that Great Britain initially envisioned regional governments with their own administrative apparatuses in the districts of Ajloun, Salt, and Karak. When those administrative units failed to function as the British hoped, it revisited its earlier promises to Sharif Hussein, wagering that leadership from the prominent tribal Hashemite family, which descends from the Prophet Muhammad, could bring Bedouin and tribal leaders in line with British colonial state-making aspirations. One of Hussein's sons, Abdullah, received a monthly stipend and was instructed to keep Transjordan as free as possible from nationalist agitations while maintaining peace with Syria and Palestine.[63]

Sharif Hussein and his sons Abdullah and Faysal, however, envisioned a much different territorial entity: a Hashemite domain that would put all of Greater Syria and Iraq under their control. They believed, not unreasonably, that the British had promised independent Arab rule of those lands in the letters exchanged between Sharif Hussein and Sir Henry McMahon, the British High Commissioner to Egypt. Faysal sought to act on those promises by establishing authority in Damascus, initially with British permission. But when he declared the fully independent Arab Kingdom of Syria in March 1920, Britain failed to recognize it and French forces drove Faysal and his supporters out by late July. Clearly, the Hashemites' aspirational spatial imaginary was incongruent with the colonial division of the lands into French and British domains. But it bears noting as well that the borders drawn in the secret Sykes-Picot Agreement of 1916 and at the later 1920 San Remo Agreement met resistance on the ground and never fully took the forms initially imagined.[64] It was a moment of competing spatial imaginaries, and the states that would emerge had as much to do with local resistance as they did with European aspirations. Although Faysal was driven out of Damascus, the British offered the Hashemites authority over its planned colonial states of Transjordan and Iraq, wanting to install Arab authorities who would be their allies. Although less than the hoped-for larger Hashemite domain, Iraq and Transjordan were a start, although the Transjordanian area was more of a consolation prize compared to Damascus.

Abdullah first arrived in Ma'an by train in November 1920. Ma'an was itself a kind of border town between the southernmost part of Greater Syria and the Hijaz. The town consisted of two parts: Ma'an Shamiyya was a small northern neighborhood, *Shamiyya* being a reference to the spatial imaginary of *Bilad al-Sham* (Greater Syria). That neighborhood was largely inhabited by Syrians who had migrated south. The larger portion of the town was Ma'an Hijaziyya, referencing connection to the Hijaz region of western Arabia. Abdullah camped in tents in the Hijazi neighborhood, as it was part of the traditional Hashemite area of authority; he did not immediately cross into the Shami northern part, which was under British control. (Indeed, Ma'an's strong sense of its own identity during the Hijaz period was retained even after it became formally annexed to the Emirate of Transjordan in 1925; the neighborhood names remain today.) Abdullah appealed to local leaders by asking them to recognize Hashemite tribal authority, posing less of a threat to their practices and local authority than might other possibilities, such as direct European colonial rule. Indeed, winning the support of local tribes would prove essential to establishing Hashemite authority. As Laurie Brand argues, this recruiting from and rewarding the tribes had the effect, over the decades, of reinforcing the salience of tribal affiliation to East Banker identity, even if all tribes did not enjoy the same level of support.[65]

Abdullah and his forces remained in Ma'an for three and a half months, discussing his aspirations with various local authorities.[66] During this period, he was courted by the nomadic Bani Sakhr tribal confederation of the central area, which owned some small towns that cultivated land through Palestinian and Egyptian labor. The Bani Sakhr had a reputation as fierce warriors and were unhappy with British efforts to assert control in Salt and other towns and villages in and near their domain. Other prominent tribal families and paramount shaykhs, however, threw their support behind the British, creating tensions among tribes in areas like the Balqa.[67] The paramount shaykh of the Bani Sakhr saw opportunity in Abdullah's arrival, however, and sought to establish an alliance that would elevate Bedouin interests over some of the more settled and semisettled tribes like the Majali and Adwan. Other nomadic Bedouin tribes, however, strongly opposed Abdullah as an outsider, looking instead to prominent local tribal leaders who might rule over their historic lands.

At this stage, British and Hashemite visions for the future state were incongruent. The British envisioned a centralized state, perhaps annexed to Palestine. Abdullah shared the broader Hashemite vision of building a larger tribal confederation that would fall under Hashemite authority but allow considerable local authority to remain in the hands of the traditional tribes.[68] Both British and Hashemite efforts to establish authority were disputed in many places, and British forces were repeatedly needed to bring local communities into line. Forms of resistance included attacks on the directors of railway stations, sabotage of telegraph railway lines, and kidnapping for ransom. On several occasions, one prominent shaykh led villagers to raid British military bases and Jewish settlements in the Jordan Valley, stopping only when the British Royal Air Force attacked their positions.[69] Local authorities appealed to Abdullah with telegraphed petitions, but he preferred to meet face-to-face as is customary for tribal practices of negotiation and conflict resolution.[70] Given the Ottoman power vacuum, many local authorities sought to expand their own areas of influence. Towns suffered raids from Bedouins even as they resisted centralized Hashemite authority. Spatial imaginaries were in flux, and the whole of Transjordan appeared to be mobilized in a bid for greater local or regional power.[71] A number of tribal notables sent direct appeals to Herbert Samuel, the high commissioner for Palestine, who soon thereafter promised that the British would not demand either conscription or disarmament. The tribal leaders were disappointed with early British rule, however, and quickly concluded that the British were not up to the task. British officers routinely also mistook the warm welcome by tribal leaders as indication that they had reached accommodations with various local centers of power, misunderstanding the customary politeness toward strangers.[72] Thus, while the British worked directly with leaders in the larger towns, Abdullah was tasked with bringing the tribal and Bedouin leaders in line with Hashemite authority. Some leaders saw opportunity and took him up on the offer, gaining cash payments, positions in various new government offices, and preferential tax rates (or no taxes at all). But when bargaining and accommodation failed to produce acceptable results, local communities turned to more assertive forms of resistance.

Mithqal al-Fayiz, the paramount shaykh of the Bani Sakhr, lobbied Abdullah to move north and set up camp in Amman, the trading town populated largely by refugees and merchants from Palestine and Syria. Located in the traditional Bani Sakhr domain, Mithqal and the mayor of Amman (his brother-in-law) saw Abdullah as preferable to the British, who were trying to establish centralized authority that would weaken their local authority. Familiar in tribal ways, Abdullah and the Bani Sakhr forged an alliance that would not only prove important to Hashemite rule but would itself create tensions that would lead to major revolts.[73]

The Kura Revolt

On April 11, 1921, Britain formally named Abdullah emir of the Transjordanian area on which they planned to create a centralized territorial state. The first major rebellion against the emir was the Kura Revolt (*Hayyit al-Kura*), which lasted for nearly a year. That April, Abdullah's representatives sought to establish authority in Ajloun by collecting taxes. Kura is a district adjacent to Irbid, and it was overseen by Kulayb al-Shurayda, a leader who a year earlier had reached some accommodations with French authorities in Damascus. The greater Ajloun area, however, was under the leadership of Ali Khulqi Sharayiri, who was appointed by the emir to the position of minister of security in the fledgling Hashemite government. Sharayiri was also a personal rival of Shurayda. When Abdullah declared that Kura was to be administered as part of the Irbid district, Shurayda stirred up other locals to oppose the integration.

In the Kura district's village of Rahaba, locals encouraged by Shurayda refused to pay taxes to the emir's collectors, complaining that they had recently paid animal taxes to the previous government. Troops accompanying the tax collectors tried to confiscate property in lieu of taxes, with one confrontation resulting in a local's death. Anticipating an escalated confrontation over the death, the emir's Ajloun administrator sent some 150 members of the Reserve Forces, who were met by as many as a thousand armed tribesmen. In short order, Abdullah's forces were defeated with between fifteen and twenty killed.[74] The Royal Air Force then bombed Shurayda's hometown of Tibna, and he and several of his leaders were arrested and sentenced to prison. But under pressure from other tribal leaders, and with strong nudging from British officials, Abdullah agreed to utilize the tribal custom of 'utwa—a truce period during which tribal practice for negotiating conflict would be used. Both sides agreed to pay reparations for those killed in the fighting. The emir traveled to Kura to hold the discussions in person, where Shurayda promised his loyalty in exchange for a general amnesty.[75]

Abdullah's compromise with Shurayda, however, encouraged other areas to revolt to gain better accommodations. Over the next year, revolts broke out in Wadi Musa, Karak, Tafileh, Ajloun, and Balqa.[76] Increasingly frustrated, the emir sought British help to put down the rebellions by force, with the Royal Air

Force at times bombing sites of resistance into submission. In 1923, Shurayda again pushed against the emir's rule, but this time British aerial bombing quickly crushed his rebellion.

The Adwan Revolt

In early 1923, tensions flared between the leaders of two powerful Bedouin tribal confederations—the nomadic Bani Sakhr and the semisettled Adwan, both based in the central Balqa region. As discussed above, the emir had forged a close relationship with the Bani Sakhr's Mithqal al-Fayiz, offering perks in exchange for support in fighting Ibn Saud's Wahhabi raiders (discussed below).[77] The arrangement angered Majid Adwan and his son, Sultan,[78] who began agitating against the emir's rule with members of other tribes in Irbid, Salt, and Karak. Opposition spread among the more educated members of those tribes, expressing frustration at the emir's autocratic style and favoritism of Bedouin over the settled and semisettled tribes.[79] Among their grievances was the staffing of the administration with technocrats from Beirut, Damascus, and Palestine rather than with Transjordanians. In addition to anger over the Bani Sakhr paying lower (or no) taxes, the Adwan thought that they should have access to lucrative employment opportunities.

On September 3, 1923, hundreds of Adwani tribesmen on horseback rode into Amman led by Sultan and his eldest son, Majid. As Yoav Alon describes the scene,

> They surged through the centre of Amman in an impressive and provocative demonstration of power. Shouting and shooting in the air, the demonstrators expressed their discontent with the regime and the way it treated them and the thousands more they represented.[80]

Following the repertoire for claim-making established during the Ottoman period, Sultan arrived with a petition that spelled out their grievances and made what they felt were reasonable demands. The petition addressed the economic needs of the Balqa region and asked for employment opportunities in the new capital. But they also challenged the emir's authority, demanding the establishment of a constitutional monarchy with an elected parliament.[81] The demonstration in Amman perhaps also aimed to show that the Adwan (and not the Bani Sakhr) were the real powerholders of the Balqa region.[82] Sultan spoke with Abdullah and demanded that the emir reform his government and improve its relations with the Adwan.

Many Transjordanians sympathized with the Adwan.[83] A small group of Amman-based Transjordanian intellectuals supported them, pointing out that the emir's administration had been flush with Syrians and other foreigners. Majid even used a slogan, "Jordan for Jordanians"—meaning not for the British, Hijazi Hashemites, or those from cities in Syria and Palestine. It was a first clear articulation of the view that only certain of the people living in the Transjordanian area were true Jordanians and not outsiders. The emerging use of the term *aghrab* (foreigners) suggests that an incipient spatial imaginary for a Transjordanian identity was emerging. This early form of nativism juxtaposed the existing tribal populations with the nonnative interlopers there only with British backing. The specific identity of this emerging anticolonial nationalism may have been in flux, but its "other" (i.e., British colonialism) was absolutely clear.[84] Decades later, some of these early revolts and demonstrations would be reinterpreted as expressing a collective "national" sentiment. But at the time, they reflected diverse communities objecting to the particularities of colonial control and not a unified nationalist identity or movement.

Meanwhile, Abdullah promised and then reneged on meeting with Sultan on Adwan lands outside of Amman, having been cautioned by tribal allies that giving in to the Adwan would diminish his power. The British were also in no mood to appease rebelling tribes, and they were frankly frustrated with Abdullah's failure to bring them in line. Outraged, Sultan decided it was time for a second show of force. This time, however, the Balqa tribes were divided on whether to join the revolt, with some having sworn allegiance to Abdullah after the first demonstration in Amman. But Sultan had been in correspondence with British officers, and he believed that, as with his first march on Amman, the British would not intervene with a second demonstration in the capital. He led three hundred of his tribesmen on horseback and five hundred on foot in another march to Amman. This time he and his forces paused in Sweileh, a town to the northeast of Amman, where they took over the police station, blocked the main road connecting Amman with Jerusalem, and cut the telephone and telegraph lines.[85] The next morning, before Sultan's forces began to move on Abdullah's camp in Amman, Arab Legion troops with the support of British armored vehicles moved on Sultan's forces. With superior weapons, they surrounded the town and crushed them in less than an hour, killing dozens as Sultan fled north to Jebal Druze in Syria.[86]

In many accounts, the crushing of the revolt marked the end of an era and the defeat of traditional tribal authority. Andrew Shryock, for example, concludes that "the power to break the state and smash its minions came to a decisive end in 1923, the year of the ill-fated Adwan revolt."[87] But such assessments underestimate the profound ways in which these revolts deeply shaped the colonial state-making project, forcing the fledgling Hashemite authorities to seek long-term accommodations of the interests and desires of powerful tribes. Like earlier revolts (including under Ottoman rule), the Adwan Revolt was aimed at negotiating terms and affecting its relationship with the colonial authorities that were allied with a rival tribal confederation, the Bani Sakhr. In this sense, the revolt may have been crushed but it also brought results. Most immediately, it shaped the composition of Abdullah's cabinet. Whereas the first cabinet (appointed April 11, 1921) included members of Hijazi, Syrian, and Palestinian origin along with only one Transjordanian, the remaining cabinet positions filled after the revolt largely went to Transjordanians. The emir also abandoned efforts to collect arrears taxes for the years 1918–20, and he increased taxation on the Bani Sakhr, who had been paying far less as a result of their early alliance with Abdullah.[88]

The revolts also shaped the emir's alliances with local tribal leaders and the Adwan. Relations between the emir and the Balqa tribes dramatically improved, and Sultan and Majid became closely allied with the regime.[89] Majid's immediate family today recounts the close relationship between Majid and Abdullah and downplays the Adwani "defeat" in the conflict. Less prominent Adwani members, however, recall the 1923 revolt with pride,[90] although for others it remains a source of embarrassment. Alon reports that during his research, a group of students from the Ajarma tribe even urged him to call the revolt *Thawrat al-Adwan wa al-Ajarma*, because they wanted the participation of their forefathers to be remembered.[91] Their asking for the term *thawra* (revolt or revolution) is also notable, as my interlocutors predominantly described the events as *Hayyit al-Adwan* or *Hayyit al-Balqa* (rage or revolt). The term *thawra,* while it is sometimes used, works to exaggerate the scale of the revolt by suggesting a broader, more revolutionary movement with multiple battles, something akin to the Great Arab Revolt (which is labeled *thawra*). Although not all Jordanians remember the Adwan Revolt, in recent years talk of it has revived, particularly with the publication of Abdullah Assaf's book on the topic in Arabic. As Yazan Doughan notes, Assaf's argument advances the idea that an alternative to Hashemite rule was within reach but was aborted by colonial intervention; Jordan could have had Jordanian leadership from the beginning of the modern state.[92] Assaf also labels the rebellion *thawra*, a term that exaggerates its reach.

Meanwhile, the British grew frustrated with the emir's inability to effectively bring the local Bedouin and tribal authorities in line, presenting him in August 1924 with an ultimatum "to reform his administration and accept British supervision or to give up his throne."[93] Gradually the British state-making project sought to transfer historically tribal functions to the state, a project that unfolded over the next decades.[94] The Adwan Revolt was the last major use of arms in a battle against the new regime, but people continued to rebel. In 1926, for example, residents of Wadi Musa refused to pay the administration's tax collectors, seizing and looting the government's local military outpost. Unable to prevail in the face of British ground and aerial forces, however, Transjordanians began to innovate their repertoire for resistance, based in part on the realities of the emerging centralized state.

FROM ARMED REBELLION TO PUBLIC DEMONSTRATIONS

The British and Hashemite state-building project ran up against local spatial imaginaries that embodied affective and historical connections with people outside of the Transjordanian area. The increasing speed of trade, transit, pilgrimage, and education put Transjordanians in greater contact with other peoples, and news of rebellions outside of the emerging Hashemite state was received quickly and widely debated. The Druze Rebellion in southern Syria in 1925–27 brought a flow of refugees into northern Transjordan, along with some militants who launched attacks into Syria from Transjordanian territory. Talk of large-scale resistance to Abdullah was heard in pockets across the territory, making the emir nervous enough to briefly declare martial law in places like the Azraq oasis east of Amman.[95]

The infrastructure that the British built for trade and transport was constructed with an awareness of potential challenges to the Hashemite regime. Roads were built along the Transjordanian-Syrian "border" during the Druze

Rebellion, for example, so that troops could be transported quickly should the rebellion spread south. Indeed, upgraded transit infrastructure proved essential for a wide variety of security reasons. Settled townspeople sometimes welcomed paved roads as facilitating trade, while at other times they viewed them as threatening. In 1926, for example, the residents of Wadi Musa saw danger rather than economic opportunity in Britain's desire to connect their village to the town of Ma'an. The official justification for the road was to facilitate tourist travel to Petra, but it was also designed to give tax-collectors easy access to a historically independent and rebellious community. Locals organized a revolt to stop construction of the road, but it was quelled, and the road opened in 1930.[96] In this way, infrastructure should be seen not only as service provision but as a technique for bringing the colonial spatial imaginary into existence by rendering outlying locations more connected and thus also more easily dominated.[97]

Protests of the sort recognizable today as street demonstrations began during the 1920s. As the Bani Sakhr were lobbying Abdullah to come to Amman in early 1921, for example, townsfolk in Amman mounted anti-British demonstrations that prompted the British to withdraw troops from the town.[98] Sometimes these forms of protest were aimed at condemning political events happening outside of the Transjordanian area, such as the growing solidarity with Palestinians resisting Zionist settler colonialism.[99] But Transjordan's first large "nationwide" protests came in April 1928, when massive demonstrations erupted in Amman and most towns against the Organic Law, which established Abdullah as head of state with concentrated powers to declare martial law, appoint and dismiss the cabinet, and convene and dissolve the legislative assembly (which in any case held only advisory powers). Even many regime-allied communities were outraged at the audacity of the announcement. The provision that perhaps sparked the most anger was the one establishing the Hashemite regime as a hereditary monarchy. These protests marked a significant shift in the repertoires of resistance, as crowds assembling in town centers replaced the armed revolts of the past. As we will see, however, violence often continued, if not in the same form.

The Organic Law protests brought much of Transjordan to a standstill. Strikes closed the Irbid souk for a week and stopped work in Salt for three days. Townsmen blocked roads to stop transit and commerce. Messages were

CHAPTER 2

telegraphed to the emir from across the fledgling nation, some congratulating him and others condemning him as a traitor. People nationwide did not hesitate to openly criticize the emir, even in the capital. As Betty Anderson writes,

> In Salt, schoolboys threw onions at Abdullah, while in Amman a student demonstration forced Abdullah to give the final oral exams that year himself, passing and failing students according to their political loyalty. A delegation of forty notables from Ajloun presented a petition to the Emir protesting the Agreement.[100]

The leaders of the petition drive included the poet Mustafa Wahbi al-Tell, widely known by the pen name Arar and considered Jordan's greatest poet. Arar had spent his high school years in Damascus, where he participated in student strikes against Ottoman policies, activism for which he was repeatedly exiled. Now in Transjordan, he and others tapped their earlier experiences and knowledge about various modes of claim-making.

What is striking about the Organic Law protests is that while they expressed opposition to the establishment of the Hashemite monarchy, they simultaneously worked to bring the spatial imaginary of a new territorial state into existence by uniting outlying areas and diverse tribal leadership against the centralization of power in the hands of the emir. Indeed, one group of intellectuals, urban merchants, and tribal leaders sought to establish a legal and institutionalized mechanism for sustained resistance to the regime's authority even as they embraced the idea of a Jordanian nation. Prominent among them was Rashid al-Khuza'i of the Furayhat family, the "Prince of Ajloun" whose own historic domain included Dara'a (now in Syria) and Nablus in northern Palestine. Khuza'i struggled against the British colonial state-making project, allying with the Adwan in efforts to resist the division of his Ajloun emirate which his family had ruled for hundreds of years.

Outraged by the provisions of the Organic Law, Khuza'i and others now called for limits on monarchical power. Some 150 gathered in Amman on July 25, 1928, establishing the National Conference, a democratic organization with Husayn al-Tarawneh from Karak elected as the body's president. The group drafted the National Pact, which called for only Transjordanians to be hired into government positions, the establishment of a constitutional monarchy with an elected legislative assembly, and for Great Britain to cease its involvement in domestic Transjordanian affairs. Although the group sought to limit British power and to resist efforts at reorganizing the existing tribal domains into new administrative governorates, as a "national" conference it also worked to advance a new spatial imaginary of Transjordanian residents as a single people, a nation. The government, however, moved forward in early 1929 with preparations to hold elections for a consultative body under the Organic Law framework, despite strong calls for a boycott by opposition voices. Only some 3 percent of the population voted, but the signers of the National Pact won a small opposition bloc of five seats.[101]

In the span of less than a decade, most armed revolts gave way to street demonstrations nationwide, while acts of sabotage and property destruction continued. Demonstrations erupted in towns and villages across the country and now also on university campuses. Unarmed demonstrators increasingly clashed with government forces seeking to break up the gatherings. Talk of Transjordan as a nation began to gradually take hold, particularly in articulating opposition to British colonial authority.

MORAL AND MATERIAL BASES FOR RESISTANCE

The earlier spatial imaginaries were not, however, entirely erased. Tribal leaders and paramount shaykhs sought to maintain authority over their traditional domains, and those who allied with the regime earliest saw more success in doing so. Bedouin raids from the steppe and desert hinterland remained frequent in the 1920s, including among tribes who continued to move between their summer and winter grazing lands. Raids were an established practice for raising revenue and making claims, including via attacks on transport infrastructure. New on the scene, however, were Wahhabi militants backed by the Saudi king, a political rival in Arabia who had defeated the Hashemite for control of the Hijaz early in the twentieth century. Both the continuation of Bedouin raids and the escalation of Saudi-backed attacks threatened Hashemite authority over the emerging state, so the British worked to develop new techniques for deflating resistance to the centralized colonial state.

From 1920, the British created a series of armed units to police the towns and steppe in an effort to stop Bedouin raids and infrastructure sabotage. The first was the Mobile Force, an armed unit based in Zarqa (northeast of Amman) intended to help the Hashemite regime establish its authority among

54   CHAPTER 2

tribes there. Some 80 percent of the thousand-man force was drawn from the Chechen in Amman who had no allegiances to Bani Sakhr authority over the area. The force also included some Bani Sakhr, who were known as fierce warriors and whose paramount shaykh, Mithqal al-Fayiz, had forged an early alliance with Abdullah. The force was renamed the Arab Legion in 1923. The Transjordanian Frontier Forces were created on April 1, 1926, by the British high commissioner for Palestine to secure Transjordan's porous northern and southern borders in the face of the Druze Rebellion and Ibn Saud's raids. Its soldiers were drawn primarily from Palestine, Syria, and Lebanon, as well as some Circassians from Amman.[102] Ibn Saud ordered numerous raids from Arabia into the Transjordanian area by Wahhabi bands called *Ikhwan*.[103] Ibn Saud sought to secure a corridor into Syria through the desert as a rival to Transjordan's north-south artery. The first of these raids was launched in 1922 against two Bani Sakhr villages south of Amman, where the *Ikhwan* massacred the residents. In a two-day battle, the Bani Sakhr and neighboring Hadid tribesmen then defeated the *Ikhwan* raiders without British assistance. But as Abdullah and Ibn Saud fought over control of the steppe and desert hinterlands, the nomadic Bedouin who migrated seasonally posed a problem for both. First, Bedouin raiding practices and pastoral patterns complicated British and Hashemite efforts to centrally administer the land. The newly declared "borders" defined in the agreements mostly drawn up in Paris and London were alien to Bedouin spatial imaginaries, as they were to most people in the area.[104]

Meanwhile, Ibn Saud's *Ikhwan* raids continued. In August 1924, a contingent of 4,500 *Ikhwan* forces marched up from Hijaz and again fought the Bani Sakhr. This time, the British deployed aerial forces that caused 500 *Ikhwan* casualties, compared to 130 locals. *Ikhwan* bands again raided the Bani Sakhr in February 1925. This time, Ibn Saud's forces were able to extract taxes from the Bedouin in Wadi Sirhan, leaving the Hashemite authorities with the question of whether to make them pay double tax or concede Saudi authority there.[105] The Royal Air Force faced a double challenge in trying to both stop the *Ikhwan* raids and prevent angry Bedouin from retaliating; the new border was being disregarded from both sides. Meanwhile, the Saudis obstructed the traditional tribal payment of restitution for what had been lost in the raids, and Bedouin tribes struggled with few remaining resources. Locust infestations around the southern town of Ma'an combined with droughts in the south and east of Amman led to further conflict among the now starving and struggling Bedouin. To survive these hardships, they pushed closer to villages and towns and raided more settled areas.[106]

In 1929, authorities in Jerusalem and Amman concluded that they needed to extend their direct control over the steppe.[107] They created a Tribal Control Board and sought to assign an intelligence officer to engage Bedouin in securing the desert area from raids coming from "inside" Transjordan (local Bedouin) and "outside" (Saudi-sponsored *Ikhwan*). The board had considerable spatial and jurisdictional reach, investigating Bedouin raids, handling all tribal court issues, and controlling where Bedouin could migrate and camp.[108] In November 1930, British officer John Bagot Glubb was assigned to head a project to address the conflicts and violence among the Bedouin tribes and to oversee a new commission to adjudicate disputes among competing tribes across the Saudi-Transjordanian frontier. Bedouin raids in the 1920s and 1930s so disrupted the state-making project that Glubb started distributing cash to Bedouin shaykhs, and by 1932 most raids stopped. Bedouin were also recruited into the Desert Patrol as a form of welfare, but they initially took up arms not out of newfound loyalty to the Hashemite or British authorities but out of economic necessity.[109] Within a generation, their economy had largely collapsed: they lost the ability to raid for profit; they lost most of the lucrative camel market (with the completion of the Hijaz Railway); and they lost access to and control of many pastoral lands as shifting "international" borders severed tribes from their winter grazing lands.[110] The establishment of a territorial state thus had a violent effect on Bedouin practices and livelihood, imposing new borders, encouraging them to settle, and upending the spatial imaginary of their traditional domains of authority.

The rebellious Bedouin won a prominent place in the emerging new regime without having to abandon many of their tribal customs or local authority, but the cost was economic dependence on the state. That transactional relationship brought only some of them security while exacerbating tensions among the tribes. As the steppe became increasingly connected to the regime's administrative and security apparatuses, the term "Bedouin" began to be used not only for nomadic tribes but more broadly to refer to formerly settled tribes like the Bani Hamida, who only in 1935 began to move into the desert for part of the year. Meanwhile, some nomadic Bedouin, like the Bani Sakhr, adopted sedentary lives during portions of the year. These shifting migratory and settlement patterns led to clashes, as newly settled populations (which the government encouraged) violated long-standing tribal spatial imaginaries or were less aware of tribal customs and practices. Bedouin also found employment guarding the Iraq Petroleum Company pipeline, further reducing Bedouin raids on settled land and on each other. Intertribal clashes in winter 1937 were eased with more direct cash subsidies. By that summer, the Desert Patrol began to be used to put down dissent by other tribal groups, as when it was sent to break up a large demonstration by the Zabn section of the Bani Sakhr.[111] In less than a decade, most formerly rebellious areas were falling in line with the Hashemite state-making project, with Bedouin troops in the state's employ now joining the British in crushing rebellions against Hashemite and British colonial rule.

LAND FOR LOYALTY

A final spatial and geographic transformation during this period entailed the use of land reform as a means of appeasing dissent and rewarding those who allied with the new regime. In 1922, British authorities were eager to regain control of vast swaths of land in the area—including land "owned" by the Ottomans—to generate revenue. Locals often disputed such ownership, complaining that the Ottomans had illegally seized lands for years. The British frequently rejected such claims because they wanted to seize ownership of those lands as "state" lands, but individuals and often whole tribes pushed back.[112] Abdullah used land as a bargaining chip to win the loyalty of tribal leaders, even as British authorities tried to stop the sale of "state" land to political allies at low cost.[113] The state enacted a popular land registration policy that increased the value of land and gave legal rights to the owners in exchange for light taxation. Villagers who cultivated the land often benefited, and the policy became central to the creation of a substantial base of support for the new regime.[114]

A system of land registry was initiated in 1927 and more fully taken up in 1929 with the establishment of a new Department of Lands and Surveys located in Amman.[115] The plan was shaped by Sir Ernest M. Dawson, who received a commission to address taxation, land tenure, and land registration. Dawson advised that the British should directly supervise the process rather than leave it to the emir or locals.[116] The land registry also created a class of newly landless people, many of whom made their way to Amman in search of work and housing.[117] Then in 1932, a delegation led by Alec Kirkbride—who had participated in a 1930 meeting in Paris at which European leaders again sought to demarcate the precise boundaries between the mandate states—arrived with a Syrian and Jordanian delegation to establish the national boundaries on the ground.[118] In a trip that took him across Transjordan, Kirkbride discovered that the boundaries—agreed upon by delegates who had never visited the area—resulted in a number of houses being bisected.[119]

The new land settlement and state boundaries together altered patterns of social control and cultivation in some areas, in part through increased individual property ownership and by creating mechanisms whereby the formerly marginalized could challenge elites. Some enterprising cultivators cleared forests so that they could claim the land when the settlement parties arrived. But when the state sought to maintain the forests by registering them to the state, many tribal authorities were indignant at the large-scale appropriation of their traditional domains. Then in 1933, property owners demonstrated outside government offices in Amman after the state adopted a policy of confiscating the property of those who defaulted on land loans. As a result of those demonstrations, the state eased its confiscation policy toward those who had defaulted.[120] Once again, resistance from the local communities played a direct role in shaping government policies as well as the very relationship between the state and the people.

A NEW ERA OF PROTEST

By the 1930s, political demonstrations over a wide range of issues were common in towns large and small, and locations for protest in the built environment gradually developed their own spatial routines. In Salt, for example, Ayn Square emerged as the primary destination for protest,[121] while marches in Karak often ended at the plaza adjacent to the castle. Across the emerging Hashemite state, new forms and tactics of protest gradually reshaped the repertoires of resistance, and repression evolved alongside them. Meanwhile, the colonial spatial imaginary of a territorial state with a centralized bureaucracy gradually took form and substance. But affective connections of older spatial imaginaries remained, while new and imbricating ones emerged. With the rise of Arab nationalism across the region, many Transjordanians felt connections with Arabs in other states, just as pious Muslims see themselves belonging to a global Muslim community, or *Umma*. For both, European colonial power was a target of dissent. All forms of colonialism led people to demonstrate in the streets, but none more so than Zionist settler colonialism that sought not only to assert control but to displace and expel Palestinians from their land.[122] Rashid al-Khuza'i, the aforementioned "Prince of Ajloun," was active in agitating against the British and in support of Arab nationalism. After the British executed three Palestinian activists on June 17, 1930, Khuza'i led a major demonstration in Irbid. During the Palestinian revolts against Zionist settler colonialism in the mid-1930s, he and other tribal leaders supported those revolts, supplying weapons and conferring with Palestinian rebel leaders. Protests and demonstrations were common across Transjordan during this decade, in support of Palestinians but also against British authority in Palestine and Transjordan. Sabotage of infrastructure was widespread, blocking roads, tearing down telegraph lines, and damaging government property. Alon reports that the British feared losing control of the tribes as they rebelled.[123]

In April 1936, the Palestinian Revolt against the British and colonizing Zionist settlers raised fears in Transjordan that the Hashemite regime might face a similar uprising, particularly given the increase in solidarity protests over the past eighteen months. Workers in towns and cities nationwide held anticolonial and anti-Zionist demonstrations and strikes, while the semiclandestine opposition movement, the Trans-Jordanian National Congress, organized the sabotage of oil pipelines, government offices, and communication infrastructure. Solidarity with the protests spread into the steppe, with some prominent Bedouin shaykhs expressing support for Palestinians and with the Transjordanian saboteurs. Widespread demonstrations continued as the summer wore on, with some of the most contentious gatherings emerging in southern towns. In June, a number of prominent tribal leaders convened a congress that encouraged Jordanians to protest in large street demonstrations. By September, a protest in Ma'an turned violent as activists attacked the shops of merchants known to trade with Jews. When the emir did not publicly reject the Peel Commission's recommendations for partitioning Palestine the following summer, more protests broke out, including general strikes that reached from Irbid in the north to Tafileh and Ma'an in the south.[124]

But one old-style revolt emerged in 1937, led by Khuza'i in Ajloun. He formed and led an anticolonial group called the Rebels of Ajloun that clashed with the Arab Legion for control of Ajloun. Although the Ajloun Revolt (*Hayyit Ajloun*) is not widely covered in scholarly writing, one interlocutor from the area conveyed the local narrative that the revolt was put down only by the Royal Air Force's bombing of Khuza'i and his rebels, killing perhaps hundreds in the process. Other interlocutors from Ajloun describe this version as exaggerated. Either way, Khuza'i fled to Saudi Arabia, where he remained for eight years until he was pardoned and returned to his birth town of Kufranja.[125] His followers in Ajloun continued smaller acts of rebellion for the next years. Although his revolt was defeated, his leadership and support for Palestinian rebels is celebrated in poems and oral history by his descendants, and the British bombing of the revolt is remembered as excessive and unjust.

Overall, protesters mixed old repertoires (attacks on property and blocking roads) with new (merchant strikes and peaceful marches) throughout 1938. When the son of a former Amman mayor died fighting in Palestine, his funeral turned into a huge political demonstration in Amman.[126] Routine clashes broke out between the Desert Patrol and Palestinian rebels. As many as 250 Transjordanian Arab nationalists joined the rebels, with whom they identified as sharing the struggle against British and French intervention across the region.[127] With British cash, the emir tried to quiet the unrest by increasing cash payments to a number of shaykhs in exchange for not supporting the rebels, but he found only partial success.

By the late 1930s, then, demonstrations around Arab nationalist issues were common, invoking an affective connection with Arab communities across the region. The 1940s, however, marked a turning point. The new state as well as the organized Transjordanian opposition had by that time advanced a national spatial imaginary, and Abdullah now controlled the apparatuses of a modern state, albeit with limited administrative capacities and heavy reliance on British support. With the major global powers tied up fighting Nazi Germany in World War II, however, Arab nationalist and anticolonial mobilization escalated. Mass demonstrations in neighboring lands refracted in Jordan, particularly as Hashemite rule in Iraq was challenged. France and Great Britain were overextended as they tried to deal with challenges across the region that commanded attention and resources.

60 CHAPTER 2

In Iraq in spring 1941, nationalists led by Prime Minister Rashid Ali al-Gaylani launched a coup against the young King Faysal II in Iraq (Abdullah's great-nephew). British forces hoping to crush the Gaylani Revolt against Hashemite and British authority paid Transjordanian Bedouin to guide them through the desert. Some tribal leaders of the Bani Sakhr, however, expressed sympathies with the Iraq nationalists and called on their kinsmen to boycott the expedition. When those calls were ignored, one dissenting shaykh, Haditha al-Khraysha of the Bani Sakhr, left for Saudi Arabia, where he remained for a short period before returning to make peace with Abdullah. His rival, Mithqal al-Fayiz, decided to storm the Prime Ministry in protest of the neglect of local tribal chiefs, but he was surprised to find himself arrested and forced to apologize to the minister.[128]

The protests in Iraq and their repercussions in Transjordan—along with the numerous Palestinian solidarity demonstrations across Transjordan—underline the extent to which, even by the mid-twentieth century, Transjordanians continued to see themselves connected to other communities in the region and identified with political resistance in neighboring states. Repertoires for resistance had evolved from the raids and armed revolts of the early twentieth century to include the demonstrations, strikes, and marches more typical of centralized, territorial states. Many of these new tactics were introduced by Transjordanians who learned new forms of protest and forms of solidarity during their travels to Damascus and Baghdad, and their studies in places like the American University in Beirut.[129]

Karak again is illustrative, with its significant early support for Arab nationalism as well as strong contingents of the Jordanian Communist Party and the Baath Socialist Party by the 1950s. But even prior to the presence of political parties—as recalled by the former secretary-general of the Communist Party, Yaqoub al-Zayadin—Karak saw many public demonstrations on Transjordanian as well as regional issues. The town hosted the leader of the Great Syrian Revolution, Sultan Pasha Atrash, along with numerous other activist exiles.[130] Their presence added to the political atmosphere in Karak, which locals connect to Karakis' long history of resistance.[131]

Suleiman Nabulsi—a prominent figure in Jordanian national politics in the 1950s—worked in Karak as a teacher in 1946. On the thirtieth anniversary of the Balfour Declaration, he led his students into the street for a demonstration.

He found Karakis eagerly joining his students as they marched, but seemingly without understanding the purpose of the protest. As Peter Gubser recounts, at one point, Nabulsi led his students with the chant,

> "Falyasqut wa'd Balfour!" which, figuratively translated, means: "Down with the Balfour Declaration!" The crowd in the street was ignorant of its meaning and started yelling: "Falyasqut Karkur!" ("Down with Karkour!"). Karkour was a local Armenian shoemaker and he ran out into the crowd, crying, "Balfour, oh people, Balfour!" Others yelled "Falyasqut wahid balkun!" ("Down with a balcony") and "Falyasqut wahid min fawq!" ("Down with one from the top!").[132]

This humorous anecdote suggests that Karak had by the mid-1940s established a repertoire of chanting at protests, as locals understood immediately that the students were protesting and unhesitatingly joined them. They maintained a strong local identity attached to a history of rebellion and protest but also identified with the political plights of people outside of Transjordan.

In 1948, Jordan entered the war to liberate Palestine from Zionist control; waves of Palestinian refugees flowed into Jordan. Abdullah—now king with Jordan's independence on May 25, 1946—seized the opportunity to expand his domain and annexed the West Bank on April 24, 1950. Although the move perhaps brought back the Hashemite dreams of controlling a larger territory than Transjordan, annexation was met with months of nationwide protests expressing solidarity with Palestinians and opposition to the king's decision for annexation, including massive demonstrations in hotbeds of protest like Karak.[133]

CONCLUSION

By bringing into view the diverse spatial imaginaries and geographies of power and dissent, the role of protests in Jordan's state-making comes into sharp focus. Indeed, acts of resistance and rebellion profoundly shaped the emergent state. The interactions between the local people and the British and Hashemite colonizers—interactions that included rebellion, accommodation, negotiation, and modern forms of protest—came to be understood by Jordanians of East Bank descent as a form of social contract. The creation of that contract was crucial to the emergence of the spatial imaginary of the nation and the spatial imaginary of East Bankers as affectively connected. The moral and material

CHAPTER 2

claims embodied in the contract saw East Bankers as privileged in relationship to the state, particularly as large waves of Palestinian refugees dramatically altered Jordan's character and demographics. The perceived violation of that contract a century later would be at the center of East Bank grievances, as we shall see in detail beginning in chapter 6.

Meanwhile, let's continue examining Jordan's changing political landscape. While we see the emergence of a new political and economic center in the capital, the East Bank area became a new kind of periphery. Even into the mid-1950s, for example, as much as 80 percent of East Bank villages remained inaccessible to motor traffic, with the most remote villages accessible only by foot traffic or pack animals[134]—so the temporal pace of the capital became increasingly disconnected from the slow-moving East Bank areas and their lingering inaccessibility. To explore that stark and growing divide, let's bring the scale down from the broader Transjordanian area (and the spatial imaginaries of imperial, colonial, and local authorities) to focus on the capital city of Amman and its emergence as a central place for expressing political dissent. From a rather insignificant outpost in the late nineteenth century to a bustling urban center by the time of independence, Amman's urban development shaped and was shaped by massive demonstrations. Indeed, the decision to establish the capital in Amman was itself shaped by resistance. Then a small town, Amman was populated primarily by Ottoman-settled refugees and merchants who had migrated there recently. Although located within the domain of Bani Sakhr authority, the town was not in any way its seat of power. It proved a more welcoming location for the new regime than the existing towns with their long histories of rebellion. Indeed, earlier considerations about settling in Salt were abandoned precisely due to local resistance. Locating the seat of power of the emergent state in Amman left aspects of the existing tribal authority structures and their spatial imaginaries intact, but it radically altered Jordan's political geography.

Chapter 3

BECOMING AMMAN

From Periphery to Center

CITIES HAVE HISTORICALLY BEEN CENTERS OF PROTEST. Symbolically they are often seats of political and economic power, and spatially they can be ideal for attracting attention and disrupting governance and commerce. Amman in the late nineteenth century was not such a place. Its downtown was characterized by the remnants of the ancient Roman city of Philadelphia—including an amphitheater, nymphaeum, and citadel. Despite the presence of a reliable freshwater spring in the Ras al-Ayn area and a seasonal stream called the Sayl Amman, the location did not enjoy a year-round population until the settlement of Circassians by the Ottomans in 1878. Amman grew when it gained a stop on the Hijaz Railway but was still a relatively small town when the emir settled there in 1921. With the 1928 Organic Law, Amman officially became the capital of the Emirate of Transjordan. That move set in motion a radical restructuring of the political geography of the Transjordanian area, with the rapidly changing capital its new center.

In this chapter, I examine the history of Amman and its major periods of protest. I explore the transformation of the city through population growth and the establishment of refugee camps. Urban planning documents throughout the period convey the colonial spatial imaginaries of a planned and ordered capital. From the massive demonstrations of the 1950s through the pivotal events of Black September in 1970–71, protests shaped and were shaped by the spatial and material features of both the topography of the land and the city's built environment. Those protests, in turn, deeply affected the ways in which the regime would come to assert dominance over the residents and spaces of the city, including making alterations to the built environment aimed at preventing or containing future protests (examined in chap. 8).

We have seen in chapter 2 how the organization of "national" resistance to the state-making project of the early twentieth century helped evoke an East Bank spatial imaginary distinct from those of the Hijaz and Greater Syria. In this chapter, we will see how, by midcentury, those prominent East Bank towns and their powerful tribes became a new kind of periphery. I examine the place-making of both protest and repression, bringing into view the repertoires and meanings that emerge in individual spaces of the rapidly changing urban environment. I then examine the spatial imaginaries of urban planning documents, which envision new infrastructure for government, commercial, residential, and leisure spaces while also redirecting flows of both vehicular and pedestrian traffic. The analysis shows how the capital, its spatially situated class divides, and its relation to geographies of political, economic, and social power at the national scale are central to Hashemite state-making and state-maintaining. But first, let's take a theoretical look at protests, cities, and place-making.

CITIES AS SPACES OF PROTEST

Cities are key spaces for protest, as they are often the seats of government and economic power and home to diverse populations across class divides. As a built environment, cities usually start as smaller towns and expand, adding buildings, infrastructure, and new neighborhoods as needed. Sometimes expansion comes through centralized urban planning, but more often towns expand into cities organically. As they do, different spaces in the built environment come to have different meanings, associations, and characteristics. Some places are recognizable to inhabitants as sites of "wealth" and "luxury," while others are associated with "crime" and "poverty." As we shall see, these symbolisms and associations, embodied in a kind of public knowledge, prove critical for understanding where and how protests take place in the built environment.

Henri Lefebvre pioneered the systematic exploration of the production of space and its meaning for social and political life. Let's pause a moment to flesh out some of the distinctions he made about different kinds of spaces, as they offer considerable traction for theorizing the meaning and political effects of protest. An abstract conception of space entails notions of distance, area, or volume. This sense of space frequently emerges in descriptions of protest events, such as estimates of the number of protesters, the physical dimensions of a specific location, distances traveled to reach a protest, or the movement of protesters and security forces from one location to the next. Largely quantifiable, these dimensions of protest are easily coded in data sets. A concrete conception of space, by comparison, treats space as relational and saturated with meaning. Rather than measurable aspects of material space, it is "defined in relation to human occupation, use, or gaze. Concrete space is a space for some person or collection of persons. It is used, seen, and experienced."[1]

Analyses of concrete space foreground symbolism and practice—meaningful actions that are learned, repeated, and altered. By the 1980s, the term "place" had come into wide use in scholarly debates to refer to concrete conceptions of space, emphasizing the cultural meaning of particular spaces and the various powers embodied in and advanced through the built environment. More than mere locations, places shape and are shaped by people who inhabit, traverse, and utilize them. Transformations of place can be intended by those who build or construct them, but they often result from quotidian uses and ways of traversing them. Protests, therefore, can transform the meanings attached to particular spaces. As Tali Hatuka puts it, "Protesters respond, contribute, negate, or change the story of a place, which has evolved in the collective memory of a society. The physicality of a place and memory should be seen as mutually constitutive."[2] After a major protest or violent repression of protesters, a location can also meaningfully become a different place—the place where X happened.

Notions of (measurable) space and (meaningful) place suggest that material objects can possess agentive capacities.[3] The material aspects of buildings, open squares, winding passages, and transport infrastructure work to direct movement and convey meaning, just as the movements of persons in space can alter those meanings. Spaces can be inclusive or exclusive. Shopping malls, gated communities, and the conversion of public spaces to commercial ones—even if they include ostensibly "public" spaces—all convey a particular sense of place, with attendant expectations about who and what kinds of activities are welcome.

Urban planners and scholars of cities have long recognized how the construction of a road or railroad track can profoundly alter social relations, divide and create communities, and exacerbate economic inequalities. The Hijaz Railway not only increased the speed and efficiency of moving goods and people across the Transjordanian area, it also encouraged the movement and settling of people along its route, turning outposts into towns and towns into cities. Bedouin raids, in turn, created a need for greater defense of the railway. Indeed, infrastructure projects such as ports, roads, pipelines, railways, and energy facilities always evoke an authoritarian impulse in their overseers. Infrastructure must be defended and protected; the practices and competing priorities of diverse peoples raise technical problems for the government to solve, obscuring the politics at work. Thus, the maintenance of order entails a violence enacted by those seeking to preserve it against those objecting to it. As Don Mitchell observes, it is the political authorities who characterize the actions of challengers as violence that threatens public order. The extraordinary violence of the state and its agents, meanwhile, is most transparent only in "extraordinary" circumstances, and primarily when seeking to silence and subdue challengers.[4]

Meanwhile, authorities can harness urban planning and changes to the built environment to do political work in silencing dissent. The iconic example is Georges-Eugène Haussmann's reconstruction of Paris in the 1850s and 1860s, which embodied a martial spatial imaginary of public order and space. The widening of streets and the location of army barracks at arteries at the edges of the city were techniques for controlling and shaping the movements and practices of people occupying and traversing those spaces—not to mention facilitating the rapid movement of troops to quash insurrections.[5]

Protest in the Built Environment

The spatialities of any built environment affect the nature and possibility of social protest. The layout of an urban space—such as the presence or absence of pedestrian areas, an open plaza, and narrow alleys—creates opportunities for protesters to gather and be heard in some spaces but not others.[6] As Hatuka argues in her study of how activists strive to choreograph protest in consideration of space, different kinds of spaces can produce different protest dynamics. A town square with its town hall, for example, represents a certain kind of symbolic state power. By comparison, streets provide space for marching in ways that both disrupt commerce and make the claim-making visible to a wider audience. Protests in leisure spaces like parks, however, are far less disruptive of governance and commerce, and even sometimes have the air of a festival.[7] More than just containers, however, places have histories and reputations or legacies, embodied in a kind of public knowledge that protesters know as part of the repertoire of contention. As we will see in chapter 5, individual protest spaces can also have their own spatial and temporal routine.

People choose where to protest, and thus every protest site is in some way meaningful.[8] Building on Lefebvre, encounters between protesters and security forces are therefore contests over place.[9] Protest itself can be understood as a form of embodied geography, one in which the actions of protesters in material space—marching, destroying property, or trespassing—work to change the meaning of spaces that resonate politically.[10] As Katerina Navickas argues, strategies of resistance are shaped by spatial structures that are not static, and "in struggling for power in those spaces, social movements created their own spaces and forms of spatial practice."[11] In these ways, protests are a key means of producing and shaping meaning and thus place.[12]

Few scholars of the Middle East have brought the concept of place to bear on our understanding of political protests,[13] and most that do examine the role of central squares and symbolic spaces as sites of mobilization during the Arab uprisings, usually focusing on a single square in one country (such as Egypt's Tahrir Square). Most of these scholars echo Lefebvre and the literature on the right to the city to argue that place is not simply "the arena of social struggle; it is a constituent stake in that struggle."[14] Other than my own work,[15] the only examination of protest and space in Jordan is by Pascal Debruyne and Christopher Parker, who show that Jordanians protest about issues related to the construction of neoliberal megaprojects, particularly the spatial and economic exclusions that megaprojects entail. Analyses of protests, they argue, need to attend to the "material contexts of meaning and practice within which protests have been situated." Debruyne and Parker also note that protests can work as a means for imagining solidarities "across cleavages of locality and scale,"[16] as my discussion of the 2018 *Habbit Huzayran* protests in chapter 1 showed.

There is a lot in Debruyne and Parker's analysis that resonates with the analyses developed throughout this book. They discuss, for example, the geographic dynamic of people traveling between the capital and the outlying governorates to participate in protests, actions that allow groups to make connections to those elsewhere. But their analysis stops short of examining the spatialities of protest routines and protest spaces themselves, beyond noting that protests are mounted in symbolic places and work to inscribe meaning into those spaces with their slogans, placards, posters, banners, and songs. I build substantially on this welcome attention to protest and place-making in this and later chapters, presenting an argument with longer historical reach and careful attention to variations across space and geography, and detailing a wider range of spatial dynamics of protest as well as of repression.

FROM OUTPOST TO CAPITAL

The choice of Amman for Jordan's capital radically restructured the political geography of the Transjordanian area in only a couple decades. We have already seen that Amman was inhabited only seasonally until 1878 and gained a stop on the Hijaz Railway in 1902. Although Amman's permanent population was small at the time, a thriving town quickly developed. When the religious scholar Jamal al-Din al-Qasimi visited Amman in 1903, he was impressed by the town's vitality, noting that "the commerce of the town is reaching the highest level of activity as is the construction of buildings, as a result of the numerous people settling there."[17] The new town attracted Palestinians and others from Greater Syria seeking administrative jobs with the Ottoman authorities, but it was also a destination for people from elsewhere in the Transjordanian area.[18]

The first Municipal Council of Amman was established in 1909, although at that time the town was a permanent home to only some three hundred families.[19] New arrivals encountered a small town center at the intersection of three wadis (valleys that seasonally carry streams), the primary of which— Sayl Amman—often carried water year-round from the Ras al-Ayn spring just west. The center was surrounded by seven steep and rocky hills (sing. *jebal*), from which potential intruders could be spotted. Ancient Philadelphia's ruins were scattered among the buildings and a citadel sat atop one hill, indexing that the ancient Roman colonizers had also recognized that the location and its topography were ideal for commercial and defensive purposes.

Construction of homes and businesses expanded along the wadi floor from the Roman ruins west. The railway station was located to the east near the Ottoman barracks that would later be used to house Arab Legion forces. The train passed through twice a week, with camels and horse-drawn carriages congregating at the station to transport people and goods along unpaved streets.[20] As the downtown area became crowded, businesses and residents gradually began to build upward, with steep stairways connecting the central district below.

Hashemite Amman

By the time Abdullah arrived in Amman in 1921, the town was home to some 3,000 year-round inhabitants—a tenfold increase in fifteen years, but still smaller than Irbid and Salt.[21] People began to arrive in search of jobs, favoritism, and subsidies as well as to express grievances toward the new emir's policies. The city was in need of upgrading not only to accommodate the new administration but also in order for the emir's forces to effectively secure it. To control public space, Abdullah invested in improved and extended roads as well as telephone and telegraph services.[22] Compared to elsewhere in the

FIGURE 3.1. Amman circa 1920.

Transjordanian area, Amman and parts of the north enjoyed rapid upgrading of roads and other infrastructure for trade and security in the first two decades of Hashemite rule. New telecommunication connections from Amman to Palestine and Egypt were established by 1928 and to Baghdad by 1935; connections south to Karak, Tafileh, and Ma'an, however, were not completed until 1938.

The first new buildings constructed in Amman under Hashemite rule were the Raghadan Palace, a small prison, and the Grand Husseini Mosque built on the site of the Umari mosque dating from the seventh century. By the mid-1920s, the government had built new offices for the Parliament, the Prime Ministry, and the emir, among others. New hotels welcomed visiting dignitaries and wealthy tourists. An earthquake in 1927 destroyed most of the town, however, save the new mosque and palace. With British money and expertise, new buildings were constructed within a year. The British officer Andrew Park Mitchel, who oversaw the new Department of Land and Survey, produced the first map of Amman, whose new spatial imaginary reflected Western urban planning at the time, with a wide central boulevard along the east-west valley[23]—about the only place that the topography allowed for the construction of a relatively straight road.

Amman was not a historic site for rebellion or protest, but new practices emerged around the time the Hashemite regime had settled there. As Mithqal al-Fayiz of the Bani Sakhr was lobbying for Abdullah to settle in Amman in 1920, the town's residents organized demonstrations against British officials stationed there.[24] When France bombed Damascus for several days in October 1925, Ammani shop owners organized strikes. Then in 1928, people flooded into Amman's main streets (as they did in other Transjordanian towns) in opposition to the Organic Law. Those demonstrations, which lasted several days, began to establish a repertoire for demonstrations in the capital: gathering at the Grand Husseini Mosque. The novelist Abd al-Rahman Munif recalls the centrality of the mosque to all manner of protests, with the balcony of a doctor's office adjacent to the mosque used for addressing the crowds during protests.

As the town expanded, Abdullah encouraged merchants from Salt to move there, particularly after Salti tribal leaders resisted accepting his authority.[25] Efforts to settle Bedouin in the 1930s added additional residents.[26] In response to demand for housing and infrastructure, the British proposed developing a comprehensive urban planning scheme for the capital. The British-supervised

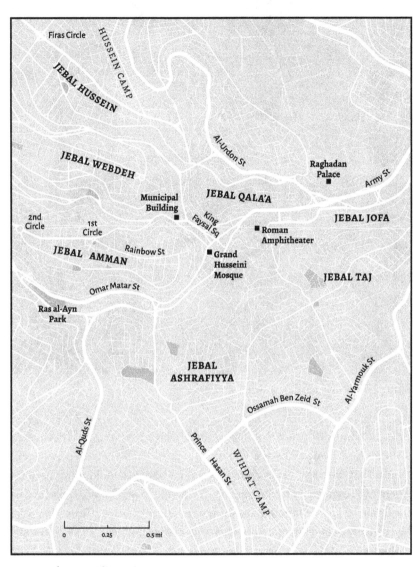

MAP 3.1. Amman city center.

FIGURE 3.2. Protest in downtown Amman in 1933.

Urban Planning Ordinance of 1933 again reflected European modernist sensibilities for widened streets and open spaces. As head of the Department of Land and Survey, Mitchel envisioned a major municipal building at the point where two commercial streets joined to form King Faysal Street, bookended by the Grand Husseini Mosque and government administrative offices. The street had already been widened in the late 1920s to create more space for public gatherings and the easy passage of automobiles,[27] and the reenvisioned site would include a large plaza for official ceremonies.[28] In 1935, the regime organized its first military parade in that space, a celebration of the anniversary of the Great Arab Revolt, orchestrating a show of military power and Hashemite victory that sought to inscribe Hashemite authority into the town's central public space. As a kind of martial place-making, it advanced a narrative of historic Hashemite victory while warning challengers to Hashemite authority in the present and into the future. Celebrations on the anniversary of the revolt continue until today, and they remain occasions for both a display of power and the reproduction of the regime's official narrative about Jordan's past.

The rebellions of the early twentieth century had by the 1930s mostly given way to street demonstrations as a means of claim-making toward the regime. Protests in solidarity with Palestinian and other Arab causes were most common, although domestic issues also brought Jordanians into the streets. In 1933, for example, property owners gathered at government offices in Amman to protest the regime's land confiscation policy, leading the government to ease that policy and show a somewhat more sympathetic attitude to those who had defaulted.[29] Shop owners organized numerous strikes in solidarity with the Palestinian Revolts beginning in 1936. The destruction of property and infrastructure sabotage, however, remained part of the repertoire for expressing dissent. Shops of merchants who traded with Zionists, for example, were often vandalized or destroyed, and demonstrations in the capital and

FIGURE 3.3. Military parade at King Faysal Plaza in 1940 on the occasion of the anniversary of the Great Arab Revolt. Source: Library of Congress.

elsewhere were sustained for several years. When Abdullah expressed his approval of the Peel Commission's recommendation for the partition of Palestine in 1937, massive protests broke out at the Grand Husseini Mosque.[30] The area called King Faysal Plaza—really the wide King Faysal Street connecting the Grand Husseini Mosque to the east and the main municipal building to the west—developed its own spatial routine for protests: gathering at the mosque, listening to speeches, and then marching west to assert claims outside of the government offices. Competing place-making practices at King Faysal Plaza—of state power asserted through military parades and opposition voiced in demonstrations—together marked the area as unquestionably political. Novelist Abd al-Rahman Munif, writing about Amman in the 1940s, beautifully describes the spatial dynamics of protests during these decades:

> The student demonstrations were like small tributaries that flowed into the big river, which was the main public demonstration outside of al-Husseini Mosque. There, the mood of the protests would be determined and the older leaders would emerge. Words that were said took on connotations and signified a stand for which there was a price to pay either immediately or sometime later.[31]

A CITY AND NATION TRANSFORMED

From a population of 3,000 in 1921, Amman rapidly outgrew all other towns in Jordan by 1943; at the time of independence in 1946, it had reached 100,000.[32] With the 1948 war and the establishment of the State of Israel, however, the spatial imaginaries and political geographies of both the nation and the capital were dramatically and rapidly transformed. The influx of Palestinian refugees inverted Jordan's demographic geography from predominantly rural to predominantly urban as some 300,000 Palestinians fled east across the Jordan River. Refugees who were educated professionals, merchants, and artisans concentrated around the growing urban centers of Amman, Irbid, and Zarqa rather than in the United Nations (UN) refugee camps, where peasants and rural Palestinians settled.[33] The influx sparked a construction boom that rapidly changed Amman's built environment. The first wave of refugees, beginning in 1948, ballooned Amman's population to 250,000. In 1949, another 20,000 Palestinians were set up in Zarqa Camp just northeast of Amman. As refugees continued to make their way into Jordan, however, a second camp was established in 1952 closer to the city center, on Jebal Hussein. Initially housing 29,000 refugees, the site abutted the downtown area to the northwest, on one of the city's main seven hills. A third refugee camp in 1955 abutted Amman's downtown area to the south. Officially called the New Camp but known as Wihdat Camp, it housed more than 51,000 refugees. Even larger numbers of refugees settled in Amman outside of the official camps, and new money lenders migrated from elsewhere in Jordan as well as from Syria and Palestine to service them.[34] New roads connected newly settled areas to the downtown area, and Palestinians entered the local economy primarily as merchants and laborers.

The repercussions of the 1948 war were significant for both the political geography and the Hashemite spatial imaginary of Jordan. Just as Transjordanians were developing a more unified national identity, they were flooded with people who clung tightly to the hope of a reunited Palestine. Their arrival would gradually work to solidify the emergent East Bank spatial imaginary, as Palestinians changed the face of the nation while they waited for the opportunity to return home to Palestine. But Abdullah still had expansionist aspirations, and he defied public sentiment and formally annexed the West Bank to Jordan on April 24, 1950, granting citizenship to most Palestinians inside Jordan. With his hope of expanding his Hashemite domain, annexing the West Bank brought him closer to realizing the spatial imaginary of his dreams. Palestinians as well as many Transjordanians were outraged, seeing the annexation as a betrayal of the promise of liberating Palestine. In Amman, demonstrations broke out at the Grand Husseini Mosque and in the camps, as they did across Jordan and the West Bank. Palestinians on both sides of the Jordan River also protested frequently against their poor living conditions as well as to demand the liberation of Palestine from Zionist control.

Meanwhile, Arab nationalism was enjoying a high degree of popularity across the whole of the Arab region, invoking another spatial imaginary with affective attachments. Jordanian Arab nationalists organized regular demonstrations in solidarity with Arabs protesting elsewhere. When Iraqis took to the streets in mass demonstrations against the 1948 Portsmouth Treaty (which renewed the 1930 Anglo-Iraqi Treaty codifying Iraq as a British protectorate), for example, hundreds in Jordan protested in solidarity while as many as four hundred protesters in Iraq were killed in a matter of days.[35] Solidarity protests were particularly strong in Amman, where many had familial ties and affective attachments to Iraq.[36] Furthermore, more Jordanians had gained experience with political protests during their university years in Baghdad, Beirut, Cairo, and Damascus,[37] and the first generation of high school students to come up through Amman's new education system even learned how to protest from their teachers. Seteney Shami recounts the humorous recollection of a Circassian man in Amman who, together with his classmates, marched to the Ministry of the Interior to protest the sorry state of their school, whose roof leaked in the rain. They first chanted "Fix the School!" but then added "Down with imperialism!" The minister met with them and reportedly said, "As for the school, I talked to the Prime Minister, and we will do what you want. As for imperialism, leave that to me."[38]

With Hashemite rule in Iraq deeply shaken, Abdullah—who by all counts was less popular in Jordan than Faysal was in Iraq—faced the likelihood that Jordanian Arab nationalists would soon challenge his rule. British influence remained strong, with the monarchy dependent on British financing and British officers in control of the army. The 1950s proved a troubling period for monarchies in the region more generally, particularly those backed by former colonial powers. In July 1951, Abdullah was assassinated in Jerusalem by a Palestinian angry that he had annexed the West Bank to Jordan. Abdullah's eldest son, Talal, took the throne for a brief period, during which Arab nationalist army officers overthrew Egypt's King Farouk, in July 1952. During Talal's brief time on the throne, he allowed for greater freedom to hold political demonstrations. With Talal suffering from mental problems, however, his eldest son, Hussein, became king when he came of age on his eighteenth birthday in August 1952.[39]

Throughout this period, Arab nationalism and other political ideas spread via multiple new technologies. Nearly all homes now had radios,[40] and King Hussein's expansion of press freedoms allowed for a flourishing of periodicals representing diverse political perspectives. Literacy remained low, particularly outside of the larger cities, but it rose rapidly in the next decades. Crowded cafés and downtown spaces created the kinds of minipublics in which public political discussions flourished. In 1954, Prime Minister Hazza Majali (of the powerful Karaki family) introduced plans to build extensive new roads, develop the port of Aqaba, expand tourist infrastructure, and develop domestic industries including phosphates, potash, and cement.[41] Thousands of new jobs were created. While the regime worked to deliver to its restless citizenry, however, opposition sectors formed political parties, trade unions, and other organizations that together formed the Jordanian National Movement. As Betty Anderson describes from interviews and careful study of memoirs, the movement's members viewed themselves as fiercely patriotic.[42] They fully accepted the spatial imaginary of Jordan as a coherent and unified nation, but they rejected the West Bank's annexation. More importantly, they hoped to end British patronage and reorient the regime toward Arab nationalist solidarities.

Escalation of Dissent

As King Hussein attempted to accommodate Arab nationalist voices, Egypt's Gamal Abdul Nasser emerged as a strong and charismatic Arab nationalist leader, with far more popularity at home and across the region than Hussein enjoyed. Arab nationalism and Israel's violence against Palestinians led to a heightened political atmosphere. When Israeli troops commanded by Ariel Sharon destroyed the Palestinian town of Qibya, killing at least fifty, protests broke out across Jordan and Palestine. Strikes and demonstrations continued for days. When the king dissolved Parliament in June 1954, Arab Legion troops were preemptively positioned across Amman and at the Hussein/Allenby Bridge in order to prevent protests from forming.[43] Hoping to align his regime with Arab nationalist sentiments, the king scheduled new elections for October 1954 and allowed political parties to legally field candidates. While the leadup to the elections was marked by peaceful rallies and vibrant political debate, Jordan's first multiparty national election did not unfold as smoothly.

On election day, October 16, 1954, some popular Arab nationalists, including Suleiman Nabulsi,[44] announced their withdrawal from the election due to government manipulation of the process. Almost immediately, protests broke out in Irbid and on King Faysal Plaza in Amman. Demonstrators in Amman gathered in other locations as well, clashing with armed forces and setting fire to a library run by the United States; at least three protesters were killed by Arab Legion forces as they fought to regain control of the capital. The government declared a state of emergency, and the Arab Legion positioned vehicles and troops at major intersections across the growing city. Foreign embassies, which had also become frequent sites for protest, were carefully guarded.[45] More demonstrations broke out on October 18 after the king blamed communists for the violence. The regime rounded up and arrested leftist and Arab national leaders and accused them of instigating the rioting.[46] In the end, as many as eighteen were killed, 150 wounded, and at least 165 arrested.[47]

Hussein continued to rely on British backing, but he also wanted a place in regional security alliances. In April 1955, Jordan participated in the Bandung Conference, a meeting of twenty-nine African and Asian states to advance economic and cultural cooperation independent of colonial and neocolonial control.[48] But the king's attention was also focused on British efforts to get Jordan to join the Baghdad Pact, a security alliance encouraged by the United States that included Great Britain, Turkey, Iraq, Iran, and Pakistan. The pact was intended to counter Nasser's growing regional power, his efforts to forge a unified Arab political entity, and the spread of Soviet influence in the region.

In November 1955, nationwide demonstrations broke out upon news that King Hussein intended to join the Baghdad Pact; by mid-December, many protests had turned violent. On December 16, Arab Legion troops clashed with demonstrators, resulting in at least forty deaths and three hundred arrests, including two parliamentary deputies. In Amman, crowds again concentrated near the Grand Husseini Mosque and King Faysal Plaza, but thousands spread out along streets in all directions.[49] The government announced a nationwide curfew in the afternoon to clear the streets, and the army again occupied major intersections. Two days later, Arab Legion forces killed one student protester and injured at least seven. As the violence escalated, the Ministry of the Interior issued more warnings against demonstrations. In the West Bank, protesters in Jericho attacked the site of a development project, while in Hebron they destroyed a UN office.[50] Delegates from several of the main towns demanded that the king express opposition to the pact.[51] Student protests in Jerusalem set fire to cars belonging to European diplomats and crashed through the gates of the Turkish Consulate.[52] In Amman, protesters congregated downtown, but by evening Arab Legion forces had again cleared the streets. A general strike continued for five days. Even the Muslim Brotherhood, which enjoyed warm relations with Hussein's regime, called for supporters to join protests and honor the general strike. Women organized demonstrations and participated in others, and according to Nicola Pratt they sought to use demonstrations to try to reshape the dominant gender norms of the time.[53]

On December 19, Majali resigned as prime minister. The king called for Parliament to be dissolved and for new elections to be held, the results of which would determine whether Jordan joined the Baghdad Pact. For a few weeks, Jordan's streets saw relative calm. But by January 8, 1956, large protests broke out in Amman, Hebron, Nablus, and Jerusalem.[54] According to one news story filed from Beirut, "stone-throwing mobs stormed through Amman and burned the United States technical center"; the army killed at least one as it tried to break up the crowds. While a nationwide general strike kept workers home, in Amman a crowd of eight hundred stormed a US government building, setting a fire inside. As that news report notes,

> Rampaging unchecked through the streets, the demonstrators stoned spectators, looted houses and smashed windows and doors with stones and clubs. Arab Legion troops finally moved into action around 5:30 P.M., but not until the streets had been littered with stones and glass and the dusk lighted by blazing buildings.[55]

In Ajloun, demonstrators burned two buildings used by the American Baptist Mission.[56] Across Jordan, the Arab Legion killed or injured at least fifty in January alone.[57] Against this violence, government radio portrayed calm, describing the demonstrations as peaceful save for a few "subversive elements."[58] The regime imposed a curfew on Amman and some other towns, which was relaxed on January 12 and lifted two days later. Hundreds of leftist activists and Arab nationalists were jailed or fled the country.[59]

*　　　*　　　*

By this time, the spatial dynamics and temporal rhythms of Amman's protest repertoire were well established. As a result of the place-making and history of earlier protests, the Grand Husseini Mosque was a known place for contentious claim-making—what Jordanian Communist Party leader Isa Madanat described as the "go-to place" for protests in Amman.[60] Protests were also held at foreign offices in the downtown area and at embassies located in Jebal Amman and elsewhere. Most protests began in the afternoon, often on Thursdays and Fridays, and lasted a couple hours, concluding before the sunset prayer. During more contentious periods, the streets could be packed all week and continue into the early hours of the morning. Protests could be peaceful or violent. As Pratt shows, women were active participants in many marches and demonstrations, including those against the Baghdad Pact but also others advocating for Arab nationalism.[61] Photos from the period, however, suggest that men regularly outnumbered women at protests.

At times, massive demonstrations erupted more as celebrations. On March 1, 1956, for example, Glubb and several other British officers leading the Arab Legion were relieved of their command—a long-time goal of Arab nationalists.[62] Jordanians nationwide poured into the streets. The *New York Times* reported on the events and their affective dynamics in Amman:

> Boisterous, almost frenzied demonstrations of joy went on for three days in the narrow, dusty streets of the city. Genuine enthusiasm is obvious. . . . There was something terrifying in their intensity in spite of the fact that they were so joyous.[63]

Arab Legion soldiers joined the celebrations, engaging in "wild dancing and shouting."[64]

Tensions Peak

In October 1956, Jordanians elected a new parliament dominated by Arab nationalist and leftist voices. Nabulsi—one of the socialists and Arab nationalists who had withdrawn from the 1954 election—did not win a seat but was appointed prime minister by Hussein to form a cabinet. The king's tolerance of the Arab nationalist movement and leftist politics, however, was not long-lived. Nabulsi wanted to sever Jordan's relations with Great Britain and move into the nonaligned Arab nationalist camp led by Nasser. In January 1957, Jordan signed the Arab Solidarity Agreement with Egypt, Syria, and Saudi Arabia, who were to provide financial assistance. The agreement did not sit well with the king, particularly as Egypt broadcast anti-Hashemite rhetoric in the West Bank and Amman.[65] But in March 1957, the twenty-year British-Jordanian security alliance expired and Nabulsi succeeded in blocking its renewal. Jordanians took to the streets nationwide in mass celebrations reminiscent of those following Glubb's departure a year earlier. Amman residents inadvertently damaged infrastructure by firing guns in the air that severed wires and interrupted telephone and electrical services. Indeed, the celebratory discharges caused enough injuries to lead Nabulsi to cancel a large political rally.[66]

On April 10, King Hussein asked Nabulsi and his cabinet to resign. Tensions escalated over the next weeks between the regime's supporters and Arab nationalists, with large competing demonstrations supporting both sides. On April 22, leftists and Arab nationalists convened a "Patriotic Congress" in Nablus, threatening to call for mass demonstrations and a general strike in support of Nabulsi and his resigned cabinet. Smaller protests and strikes took place across the West Bank.[67] The army was divided over whether to use violence to break up protests, but Amman was relatively quiet. The Muslim Brotherhood, now wary (and likely weary) of the leftists, no longer encouraged participation in protests. In Jericho and Nablus, Brotherhood supporters even clashed with Arab nationalist protesters advocating confederation with Egypt and Syria.[68]

Thirty years after rebellious Bedouin were hired to provide the fledgling Hashemite regime an army, they now dominated the Arab Legion as it asserted control over the streets.[69] They occupied all major intersections downtown and patrolled the streets to prevent people from gathering; hundreds were arrested and imprisoned,[70] marking the definitive end of Jordan's first substantive experience with democracy and multiparty politics. The government banned all political parties and forced the closure of their publications. It declared martial law, and Habis Majali—the Karaki military leader born in Maʿan prison in 1910—moved to purge the army of at least fifty perceived anti-Hashemite officers. The Eisenhower administration, keen to pick up regional allies to balance Nasser's influence, encouraged the king to move aggressively against Arab nationalists and provided US $10 million in April and again in June to pay salaries at a time when the regime had only US $2 million in the bank. That summer, it provided US $10 million in weapons, the substantive beginning of the US-Jordanian security alliance.[71]

With martial law came the end of a decade of vigorous protests across Jordan and in the capital, where a rapidly expanding urban landscape saw the emergence and evolution of repertoires for both protest and repression. The downtown area around King Faysal Plaza and the Grand Husseini Mosque was the first meaningful place in the capital for claim-making against the regime;

82   CHAPTER 3

it was also a place for the regime's assertion of authority, from celebratory military parades to forcibly clearing protesters from the streets and militarizing the landscape by occupying intersections with Arab Legion vehicles. Refugee camps also emerged as new spaces of protest, operating as pockets of Palestinian space within Jordanian territory.

JORDAN IN MULTISCALAR POLITICAL GEOGRAPHIES

Zooming out from Amman for a moment, we see that people sometimes traveled from the outlying governorates not only to join protests in the capital but also to act as counterprotesters. Prominent tribes traveled to Amman to support the regime's opposition to the Arab Solidarity Agreement, for example, and at least two hundred Bedouin from prominent families gathered downtown and marched to Raghadan Palace to express their support for the king while crowds were demonstrating against the dismissal of the Nabulsi cabinet.[72] The Bani Sakhr and Adwan tribal confederations even put aside their history of animosity to form a kind of auxiliary proregime paramilitary. Joined by other prominent East Bank tribes, they moved through the streets of Amman, disrupting demonstrations and tearing down posters of Nasser. The group eventually converged on Raghadan Palace, where they rallied in support of the king.[73] In tearing down the posters of Nasser, they were attempting to undo the Arab nationalists' place-making in the downtown built environment while also asserting a kind of East Bank nationalism and its more limited spatial imaginary. Of course, East Bank tribes were not universally behind the king, as many supported Arab nationalism and embraced leftist ideas. In this moment of flux, with the annexed West Bank and Arab nationalists looking outward while East Bank loyalists looked inward, what was Jordan and who was Jordanian?

Jordan's unsettled political geography was not unique in the Middle East. Not only were regimes being overthrown and foreign patrons expelled, but numerous states were experimenting with alternative spatial imaginaries that ranged from formal unification to regional security alliances. In Jordan, the king faced down an alleged coup at the Zarqa military base in April 1957, between Bedouin loyalists and Nasserists who hoped to forge a union of some sort with Egypt. That alleged coup was supposedly quashed when the king rushed out to the base to speak with the officers and troops. Hussein was also hoping to realize the vision for expansive Hashemite rule in the region. Just weeks after Egypt and Syria formed the United Arab Republic in March 1958, Hussein signed a federation with the Hashemite regime in Iraq, a union in which each country maintained individual sovereignty. For a moment, it looked like Jordan (with the West Bank) would become part of a larger Hashemite spatial imaginary.

But challenges to that vision kept coming. In June, the regime arrested twelve Jordanian officers for allegedly attempting to overthrow the monarchy. The streets of the capital were relatively quiet, with protests only in the Hussein and Wihdat camps around Palestinian issues.[74] But then, on July 14, the dream of a unified Hashemite domain was upended when the Iraqi regime was overthrown by a military coup. Hashemite rule in Iraq was over, and with it the federation between Iraq and Jordan.

With a renewed focus on security, the regime restructured the small civil police as the Public Security Directorate, significantly expanding its authority.[75] But Jordan still needed regional allies. Hussein moved to improve relations with Saudi Arabia at a time when Nasser was building alliances with other republican states.[76] The Egyptian-Syrian union dissolved in 1961, but Nasser continued promoting Arab republicanism. Jordanians celebrated Algerian independence in March 1962 with massive demonstrations at the Grand Husseini Mosque, further fanning the flames of Arab nationalism.[77] In September 1962, Imam Yahya of the Mutawakkil Kingdom of (North) Yemen died, and Yemeni military officers with ties to Nasser declared a republican state. Nasser sent thousands of troops to Yemen, and Jordan entered the war on the side of the royalists with a small air force contingent—as did Saudi Arabia and Great Britain.

Nasser remained popular in Jordan, however. Leftists and Arab nationalists opposed Jordan's involvement in Yemen, mounting protests at the Grand Husseini Mosque, the Saudi embassy, and the new University of Jordan campus (established in 1962). Students held strong pro-Nasser sentiments, expressed in campus debates and during many protests. Parliamentary elections in November 1962 returned a diverse parliament that included a significant number of opposition figures. In January 1963, a major strike in Jerusalem during Hussein's visit led him to call the parliamentarians to the Royal Court and announce that the regime was "not prepared to tolerate any opposition that was not 'constructive.'"

He argued that strikes and demonstrations were no way to solve problems: "there is something called the respect for the authority of the government . . . and it is inconceivable that we will allow [strikes] to be repeated." Prime Minister Wasfi al-Tall chastised the Parliament for encouraging oppositional activities, which he deemed outside of Parliament's appropriate role: "it is also not a form of parliamentary freedom to incite [citizens] to demonstrate or to strike."[78]

Elsewhere in the region, instability seemed to be the norm. The next two months saw Ba'athist coups in Iraq (February 1963) and Syria (March), which put Arab unification—this time among Egypt, Syria, and Iraq—back on the table. Tall's rhetoric shifted from the harsh criticism of just months earlier to describing his close friendship with Ba'athists and other nationalists, with whom he claimed to have daily political discussions.[79] But amid domestic unrest and massive demonstrations, the king asked for Tall's resignation, which he submitted on March 27; he was replaced by the notoriously corrupt Samir al-Rifa'i, a long-time regime loyalist who had served under King Abdullah.[80] Anti-Rifa'i sentiment quickly combined with pro-unionist and Arab nationalist views to spark a new round of nationwide demonstrations that lasted for several days. On April 20, protests turned violent in Jerusalem, with police killing four and injuring at least thirty when demonstrators chanted "Nasser, Nasser" and demanded that Jordan join the new union.[81] Protests in Amman and Irbid—the largest on the East Bank—remained peaceful, but the adoration of Nasser was on clear display.[82] Students on the University of Jordan campus were quickly developing their own spatial repertoire for protests, beginning with speeches on campus and then marching off campus where others might see them.

On April 20, parliamentary deputies voted "no confidence" in the cabinet for the first time, forcing Rifa'i's resignation after a month in office. In Amman, people took to the streets to celebrate his resignation, but this time the army's ranks remained united in suppressing the demonstrators and clearing the streets;[83] the king dissolved the lower house of Parliament the following day. A new assembly was elected in July, but without the spirit of liberalization and open political debate that characterized the November 1962 contest.

The 1967 Loss and Black September

The Hashemite spatial imaginary of Jordan as permanently including the West Bank continued to clash with that of Arab nationalists and Palestinians, for whom only a unified Palestine was imaginable. Egypt sought to foment anti-Hashemite sentiment in Jordan in part by establishing the Palestinian Liberation Organization (PLO) in 1964. At its inaugural meeting in Jerusalem's Intercontinental Hotel, the new organization took no formal position about Hashemite authority over the West Bank, but criticism circulated. Egypt broadcast anti-Hashemite rhetoric in the West Bank and Amman and encouraged opposition.[84] The Egypt-Jordan relationship was hot and cold over the next years, with cooperation one moment and tensions flaring the next. When, in November 1966, Nasser criticized Hussein for his passive response to an Israeli operation in the West Bank, both Palestinians and Transjordanians demonstrated nationwide, backing Nasser's assertion. In Amman, Arab nationalist protesters questioned why the king was so unwilling to align Jordan with Syria and Egypt.[85]

In June 1967, Israel gained territory in Syria, Jordan, and Egypt in the Six-Day War. Jordan lost control of the West Bank, and with it the holy city of Jerusalem. Since King Hussein claimed the role of protector of those holy spaces—Jerusalem is the third holiest place in Islam after Mecca and Medina—the loss was as devastating symbolically as it was politically.[86] More troubling for the regime was that Palestinian guerrilla fighters, known as *Fedayeen*, fled the West Bank across the Jordan River, and they escalated their activities both in terms of attacks into the West Bank and organization and recruitment in the Transjordanian area, including in Amman and its refugee camps. Indeed, as the PLO established a base in the Jordanian capital, they radically altered the city's political geography, taking control of entire neighborhoods and gaining considerable support from Palestinian refugees and Arab nationalists. The city's Hussein Camp, Wihdat Camp, and Hashimi Camp all provided powerful enclaves for guerrilla activities. On anniversaries of significant events for Palestinians (such as the adoption of the Balfour Declaration, the 1948 Nakba, and the 1967 war), the PLO mounted massive demonstrations in Amman, in outlying Palestinian camps, and in Salt, Jerash, and Irbid where many new refugees had settled. PLO protests did not follow the established spatial routines, largely eschewing the Grand Husseini Mosque and local spaces of power and instead favoring the embassies of states seen as sympathetic to Israel. At their demonstrations, they would often throw rocks at the embassies.[87] The PLO also encouraged demonstrations at the British oil refinery and strikes by the Jordan Cement Industrial Workers.[88]

The new wave of Palestinian refugees into the East Bank and the capital increased Jordan's demographic shift. No new refugee camps were constructed in Amman, but nine were established in central and northern areas, including Baqaʿa Camp near Salt. As the northern towns and cities expanded again, East Bank identity and its spatial imaginary grew stronger, and not only among the more prominent tribes. Many with long-standing ties to the East Bank worried that the Palestinian refugees in those northern cities threatened not only Jordan's character but East Bank sovereignty. Yet as the *Fedayeen* began launching attacks into Israel and the West Bank from Jordan, their popularity in Amman and areas where most Palestinians settled steadily increased. Numerous protests and demonstrations nationwide, in nearly every town as well as in many locations in the capital, condemned Israel and its occupation of Palestinian lands. Arab nationalist women participated in protests on the university campus and other locations.

Protests continued over the next two years, with massive nationwide celebratory demonstrations in March 1968 when the *Fedayeen*, aided by the Jordanian army, defeated Israeli forces in the Battle of Karama, in a town of that name close to the Jordan River which divides the West Bank from the East

FIGURE 3.4. Women marching in condemnation of Israel in Amman in 1968. Source: Keystone Press/Alamy Stock Photo.

Bank. Students remained active in protests on and off campus; in April 1970, hundreds of students marched to the US embassy with *Fedayeen* members in opposition to the planned visit of a US diplomat.[89]

By the summer of 1970, the *Fedayeen* controlled large neighborhoods in Amman and Irbid, in most refugee camps, and in the Jordan Valley. In September, *Fedayeen* from the leftist Popular Front for the Liberation of Palestine hijacked four airplanes and landed them in Jordan at the largely unused Dawson's Field airport (named for the Brit who developed the plan for taxation and land tenure in Transjordan in 1927). The hijackers removed the passengers and then spectacularly exploded the empty airplanes on September 12; on September 14 they called a general strike. Three days later, *Fedayeen* militias took control of the northern city of Irbid and declared the establishment of a "people's government" there.[90] The state declared martial law, but Hashemite political authority over Jordan was under direct attack.

The repression that came to be known as Black September began when the army launched attacks on the *Fedayeen* strongholds in Amman's camps. The fight for the city became literal, with residents recalling bullets flying over their homes as the two sides exchanged gunfire. The PLO reported more than 3,400 killed in the first eleven days of fighting.[91] On September 27, Nasser—just before his death—arranged for a cease-fire between the regime and the PLO, and Hussein appointed a new prime minister, Ahmad Tuqan.[92] But a month later (October 28), Wasfi al-Tall was reappointed prime minister, having stood by the king's side through the previous weeks of turmoil.[93] Tall sought no compromise. He set about eradicating the Palestinian resistance movement in Jordan, driving the *Fedayeen* first out of Amman and then moving from enclave to enclave, forcing the remaining fighters to retreat north. The last 5,000 retreated north to the Ajloun hills. As Philip Robins succinctly writes, by July 15, 1971, "there was only one state left in Jordan."[94] The new building of the expanded General Intelligence Directorate—Jordan's notorious secret police, known as the *mukhabarat*—had been completed earlier in 1970. Now with a mission to crush all political dissent, it earned nicknames like Blue Hotel, Palestine Hotel, and the Fingernails Factory for its torture of Palestinian dissidents.[95]

While the fighting marked a low point for relations between the regime and the Palestinian national movement, political divisions in Jordan did not fall neatly along Palestinian–East Bank lines. Palestinians in the army did not mutiny during the fighting, and significant portions of the Palestinian bourgeoisie—largely Amman-based—backed the regime in the conflict. Indeed, as Laurie Brand notes:

> Some northern Transjordanians (with a history of hostility toward the Hashemites) and others fought with the Palestinian resistance. Whether these Transjordanians were fighting against the Jordanian regime or with the Palestinians matters less than the fact that they saw their identity and interests in opposition to the state, not in opposition to the Palestinians or the PLO.[96]

After the fighting ended in late 1971, Amman was rebuilt in less than a year. The city expanded in all directions as more people arrived in search of shelter or opportunity. As Janine Astrid Clark argues, the government's move toward hypercentralization also entailed locating all major services in Amman instead of in the outlying governorates where Jordanians of East Bank descent were the majority.[97] The character of the city continued to evolve, gradually developing its own urbanity. Indeed, Yazan Doughan writes that while Jordanians have regional variations in dialect, a distinct Ammani dialect began to emerge.[98] Refugees continued to pour into the kingdom: as many as 50,000 Lebanese fleeing the civil war brought their savings to Jordan and settled primarily in Amman, as did more West Bank Palestinians searching for greater economic opportunities[99] or fleeing repressive Israeli control in the West Bank.[100] Tens of thousands of migrant laborers also came to the kingdom, notably from Egypt, the Philippines, and Sri Lanka, and most of them settled in and around the northern cities. At the same time, thousands of Jordanians emigrated for more lucrative jobs than they could obtain at home. Many found construction jobs in the Gulf, sending remittances that flowed back into the Jordanian economy. The political geography of the Transjordanian area just half a century earlier was entirely inverted, with political power, economic investments, and major services now concentrated in the capital and northern cities. In juxtaposition to the diversity of the capital, tribal authorities were mostly located outside of the capital, in Jordan's oldest settled areas. As we shall see in the next chapter, the regime was about to embrace the East Bank spatial imaginary, including a version of its cultural articulation, as the official state narrative about who and what is Jordanian.

WHITE COLONIAL SPATIAL IMAGINARIES

Let's return to the scale of the city in order to see how this political history unfolded in a historical context of competing spatial imaginaries and the conditions of possibility that they entail. Amman expanded in a haphazard manner, particularly as large flows of refugees created new neighborhoods in a sped-up period of growth. Urban planning does not often anticipate such high-speed change, as it lays out visions that are expected to take years to realize. A closer look at some of the multiple plans for urban development in the capital brings the spatial and political dynamics of centralized planning into view. From the 1950s to the 1990s, fifty-six major planning projects were proposed for Jordan, on scales from the local to the national; four were dedicated to Amman.[101] All were drafted or heavily influenced by British urban planners trained in European modernist ways of seeing and ordering urban spaces. As such, the plans for Amman reflected the white colonial spatial imaginaries of each period. Amman's particular challenge, to be sure, was its topography of steep hills and valleys, which did not readily lend themselves to straight streets and perpendicular intersections.

In 1938, Amman's British mayor proposed a land-use plan to manage rapid development.[102] As we shall see, it and other plans were never fully realized because the rapid demographic changes rendered many of the plans obsolete before they could begin to be implemented. The first large-scale master plan for Amman emerged as British planners worked with King Hussein to create a new vision of what the capital of the nation might look like after the first major flow of Palestinians settled in Jordan. The British authors of the first major plan, in 1955, were Gerald King and Max Lock, affiliated with the United Nations. They were optimistic that their modernist vision could be implemented, noting that "if the scheme has been designed upon the right economic and social foundations, the plan will be judged by its architecture and the relation of this to the landscape and civic design."[103] The "right economic and social foundations," of course, were shaped by a white European colonial spatial imaginary.

First, the city needed updated, expanded, and centrally managed infrastructure, including roads, sewerage, clean water, health facilities, and educational institutions.[104] But the plan also imagined new configurations of residential and commercial areas, with entirely new neighborhoods providing services and leisure sites such as parks. As the document reads,

> The Plan is based upon a conception of self-contained mountain neighbour-hoods, grouped around the valley, along which the original city has extended, and linked by a series of inter-mountain roads which also give access to the city centre.[105]

Travel between these neighborhoods, made difficult by the steep cliffs of the seven hills, would be facilitated by the construction of "road bridges" linking the steep hills, eliminating the need to travel down into the city center before ascending another hill.[106] Many of the existing buildings and residential housing were to be cleared, particularly around the Great Husseini Mosque, to make way for restaurants, cinemas, ground-floor shops, new office buildings, and parking facilities.[107] New housing would extend the city significantly to the south.[108] The plan envisioned order at a time during which massive demonstrations were regularly bringing Amman to a standstill. Advanced during a period when Arab nationalists were questioning Hashemite rule, the plan was never implemented.

The next major plan for the capital was 1968's *A Masterplan for Improving Visitor Services and Activities in Amman.* The draft team was led by British planner Vernon Newcombe but this time included Jordanian planners, although they had also been trained in European ways of seeing and ordering the built environment. But the addition of Jordanian voices increased local knowledge of the city and perhaps influenced the plan's attention to Amman's rapidly growing poor neighborhoods. Like the 1955 plan, traffic and housing were central concerns, but the 1968 plan now proposed decentralization of the commercial activities from the downtown area and the construction of a new industrial zone to the southwest of the city.[109] Whereas the 1955 plan envisioned residential expansion to the south—where the Wihdat Camp was located—Newcombe envisioned expansion west, following the existing trend.[110]

The new plan also envisioned Amman as a tourist destination, with its Biblical, Roman, Nabatean, and Islamic heritage sites. The contemporaneous *Seven-Year Program for the Economic Development of Jordan, 1964–1970* likewise discussed Jerash and Petra as major tourist attractions. Meanwhile, the 1968 city plan focused on making Amman's city center more attractive for tourists. It included features designed explicitly to serve foreign (and particularly European) visitors, including pedestrian malls, open spaces, and minibuses that would shuttle tourists between the heritage sites and up to citadel ruins. The new downtown would include a stadium, national theater, public library, and national museum, all within close proximity to the Roman amphitheater.[111] The area would be the kind of space that would direct attention away from contemporary politics and toward a heritage past juxtaposed to a visual and distinctly European urban "lifestyle" politics, not a place projecting a Jordanian national imaginary as suggested in the 1955 plan. As the 1968 plan states:

> The distinguishing elements of this proposed lineal park are the open spaces and the separation of the pedestrians from vehicular traffic. Through this specialization and separation of functions of streets from open space, the life of the city can be brought into focus. This life is mostly in the open in the urban spaces where crowds gather and people participate in *the activity and excitement of urban living*. This is the sidewalk café and the museum, the library, the theater and nightclub, the pageantry of the public city and the commerce of the shops.[112]

In the 1960s, wealthy Jordanians were already creating new neighborhoods that sought to emulate this kind of lifestyle. Built on former farmland or empty plots, the construction of new enclaves did not need to accommodate an existing built environment or its residents. The neighborhood of Shmeisani, for example, was primarily home to wealthy merchants and foreign diplomats, and a number of foreign embassies also relocated there. As the area became crowded, the elite continued to relocate west and southwest, creating the luxury neighborhoods of Sweifiyya and Abdoun.[113] For residents with the means to build larger villas with gardens and fountains, relocating out of Shmeisani became appealing, with more open spaces and wider roads to accommodate private cars and provide adequate parking. Thus, while the 1968 plan imagined new leisure spaces catering to the tastes of largely European tourists, portions of western Amman were already embracing European ways of seeing and organizing both public and residential urban spaces.

Finally, the 1968 plan envisioned a large municipal center for the western portion of the Abdali neighborhood abutting Shmeisani. A new complex would include offices for multiple ministries, including the prime minister, a headquarters for the General Intelligence Directorate (the one where political dissidents would be tortured), an enlarged Parliament building (relocated from Jebal Amman), and a large state Abdullah Mosque. The new Parliament included a secretariat (opened in 1969) and a general assembly hall (opened in the late 1970s).[114] With this cluster of buildings, a core of the government's administrative center was relocated out of the downtown area to Abdali, which some three decades later would be chosen as the site of a megaproject (see chap. 9).

But Amman continued to expand in all directions with little regard for the spatial imaginaries of the planning documents. As new neighborhoods appeared, the economic divide between the east and west portions of the city grew increasingly stark. As Najib Hourani argues about the growth of Amman in the 1970s:

> The petrodollar surge and the networked production of space deepened and solidified today's stark division of Amman into wealthy and poor halves. While poor Jordanians continued to migrate from rural villages and secondary towns into the dense city center and the eastern industrial districts, the wealthy expanded the city westward into spacious luxury suburbs.[115]

Banks moved or established their main offices in Shmeisani, marking it as Amman's new financial district. The old neighborhoods of Jebal Amman and Jebal Webdeh—the ones Munif describes so beautifully in his memoir—gradually declined, their crowded historic villas and narrow streets no longer desirable for the elite.

Place-making in Amman therefore was shaped by the manner of the city's expansion as well as by major political events. Protests, repression, and military parades marked the area around King Faysal Street as avowedly political, even as it was surrounded by commercial areas. Waves of refugees and migrants made and remade entire neighborhoods. Expansion westward deepened the stark class divide that Munif had noticed by the late 1940s, wherein the rich and the poor inhabited the increasingly separate spatial imaginaries of West Amman and East Amman. Most government offices were also relocated out of the downtown area. The Grand Husseini Mosque continued to be a meaningful place to gather for protests—its spatial routine largely intact—even as its symbolism as the seat of government power was mostly gone by the 1970s. And the *Fedayeen* establishment of enclaves across the city turned neighborhoods into conflict zones, just as the violent repression during the 1970–71 Black September period stood as the definitive statement of the staying power of Hashemite authority. A diverse set of public political claim-making protests shaped, and were shaped by, the built environment, as were the meanings and symbols embodied in particular spaces.

Finally, "seeing" Amman and indeed Jordan at multiple scales brings into view different political geographies—from the emerging class divides of the changing city to evolving affective connections with other towns and regions, to the nation-level geography of the regime's tribal support base largely outside the capital. Indeed, this period saw the solidification of an East Bank spatial imaginary, one that marked Palestinians as outsiders even as they became integral to Amman's urbanity, private sector, and built environment.

CONCLUSION

The relatively rapid inversion of the geography of power between the towns of pre-Hashemite Jordan and the Hashemite capital in Amman invites theorization about the political periphery. Most often, peripheries are conceived in relation to centers of power, often but not always in spatial terms. Hiba Bou Akar and Pascal Menoret, for example, conceive of peripheries as spaces of urban displacement, often produced through different kinds of planning processes and urban growth.[116] In their studies of Beirut and Riyadh, respectively, the urban periphery is created out of the center and its excess. Such displacements would characterize Jordan's urban centers only beginning in the 2000s.

But another kind of periphery operates in Jordan, one in which the tribal East Bank areas, which predate the centralized state, have become a new periphery to the economic and demographic weight of the capital. We have seen how the capital itself was built in what was once a space that was both economically and politically peripheral, a choice that spatially located "Hashemite power" in spaces apart from spaces of East Bank tribal authority. But as Amman emerged as Jordan's central financial and administrative center, it did so while remaining encircled, metaphorically if not quite spatially, by the regime's East Bank tribal support and its expectations based on the social contract.

The radical and rapid transformation of Jordan's political and economic geographies did not go uncontested. Prominent tribes in the outlying governorates deeply resented that wealth was being concentrated in Amman, even as many of them enjoyed privileged government positions. But they were particularly angry because they perceived that Palestinians, who became a majority in the capital, benefited from the city's upgraded services and infrastructure. The newly peripheral East Bank areas, then, pushed back at the center, at times even forcing it to concede. The resentment toward Amman reached such levels that, in the 1970s, the cabinet began holding its meetings in the capitals of the other governorates to demonstrate interest in developing those areas while marking them as local sites of power worthy of tribal-regime consultation.[117] As Clark argues, East Bank tribal communities were not concerned with hypercentralization per se but with hypercentralization at the expense of their areas.

The next chapters, particularly chapters 4 and 9, show how the Hashemite regime sought to shore up its power beginning in the 1970s by insuring that East Bank areas were not politically peripheral, even as Amman continued to develop as Jordan's economic engine. To respond to East Bank demands, for example, the regime created new subnational bodies, reorganizing local administration without weakening centralized Hashemite control.[118] This pattern of center-periphery relations continues today, with Jordanians of East Bank descent demanding that the regime honor the social contract established in the 1920s. When East Bankers are angry about state policies, this economic periphery converges on and makes claims against the center—a spatial technique for claim-making that will be detailed in chapters 7 and 9.[119]

Meanwhile, after Black September the Hashemite regime craved stability and set about beefing up its various security agencies with crucial assistance from the US armed forces and the Central Intelligence Agency. Seeking to construct a narrative that superseded the *Fedayeen* challenge to Hashemite authority, King Hussein sought to project the regime's stability and endurance through a project advancing a very specific national identity for Jordan. Before we zoom out in the next chapter to explore this project at the scale of the nation, let's take a look at how this new vision for Jordan played out in the capital.

To construct a narrative of Jordan as a modern and stable nation, the regime needed to project an image of Jordan that conformed to largely Western expectations. For Amman, that vision required that the capital be perceived as a modern, world-class city. But if English-language tourist guides are any indication, Westerners were not even close to seeing Amman in that light, even by the 1980s. The 1987 Lonely Planet *Jordan and Syria,* for example, begins its section on Amman by noting that the city "is certainly never going to win any prizes for being the most interesting city in the world and in fact has very few attractions." It does note the emergence of upscale areas, even describing Shmeisani as a "swish neighborhood."[120] But overall the capital felt to outsiders (and to many locals as well) more like a dusty, boring town than a thriving modern city.

The regime must have been thrilled just a few years later, however, with the description of Amman in the 1994 *Spectrum Guide to Jordan*, which presented a starkly different representation:

> Modern buildings blend with the remnants of ancient civilisations. The profusion of gleaming white houses, kebab stalls with roasting meat, and tiny cafés where rich Arabian coffee is sipped in the afternoon sunshine, conjure a mood straight from A Thousand and One Nights. . . . For businessmen Amman offers the most up-to-date convention and communication facilities. Its strategic position and cosmopolitan atmosphere make it one of the foremost centres of finance and trade in the Middle East today.[121]

That description feels overblown, however, as Amman at that time was far from a metropolis with world-class infrastructure. The capital's primary luxury hotel, the Intercontinental, was decades old and showed it. Even the most upscale restaurants like Romero, with its male waiters in full suits, felt rundown and tired; periodic electrical blackouts did not help, leaving diners in the dark as waiters scurried to light the candles ready at hand.

But perhaps what is most telling about descriptions of the city in tourist guide books is that they convey the capital's competing spatial imaginaries—of affluent and modern West Amman and impoverished East Amman—by focusing exclusively on the former. Indeed, the guides include city maps that cover only spaces in West Amman, with the downtown historic district—spatially the center of the city—positioned on the right edge of the map. The 2003 edition of *Lonely Planet Jordan* similarly focuses exclusively on West Amman, describing the capital as cosmopolitan with elite neighborhoods reminiscent of global cities like Paris.[122] We will see how crowded, poor East Amman seems to have value primarily as a heritage backdrop to the modern, Western capital. Meanwhile, East Amman and its majority of the city's residents are entirely erased from the picture.

Chapter 4

JORDANIZATION, THE NEOLIBERAL STATE, AND THE RETREAT AND RETURN OF PROTEST

STATE-MAKING AND STATE-MAINTAINING ARE DIALECTIC processes, as we have seen, shaped by acts of public claim-making and state efforts to repress or control them. We have also seen how the built environment both shapes and is shaped by geographies of economic and political power. But how does an existential challenge to state rule shape processes of state-maintaining? The Hashemite regime faced such a threat from the Palestinian *Fedayeen* militias in the late 1960s, ended only through state violence during the 1970–71 Black September period that killed thousands. In the aftermath of such violence, to what techniques of repression and domination does the state turn, and how are those techniques spatially and rhetorically deployed, from the local to the national scale? How do those techniques constrain what the state can do when it is threated by economic collapse, and when nationwide protests break out in opposition to the adoption of economic reform policies?

To answer these questions, this chapter traces the state's actions following Black September and into the neoliberal periods under King Hussein and then King Abdullah II following the former's death in February 1999. These events provide rich empirical material for developing three main theoretical interventions. First, state-maintaining in the face of armed insurrection can entail techniques including the distribution of material goods, the expansion of repressive capacities, and the advancement of a narrative portraying

98 CHAPTER 4

those who challenge the state as outsiders. While these moves facilitate state-maintaining, they also change the state's character. After Black September, the Hashemite regime deepened its repressive capacities while also advancing a project of "Jordanization," one that anchored national identity in a mash-up of East Bank, tribal, and Bedouin history, thus discursively rendering citizens of Palestinian descent as outsiders.[1] This process, as we shall see, entailed an official narrative of Jordan's history that elided critical distinctions between "East Bank," "tribe," and "Bedouin."

The second theoretical intervention of this chapter is to explore how neoliberal economic policies affect state-maintaining and the exercise of power in such a context. Austerity and privatization lead not to a retreat of the state but to new kinds of state interventions that matter for our thinking about space. We have seen how the emergence of Amman as Jordan's primary urban and economic center "peripheralized" East Bank tribal communities, but the tensions it produced really came into view when the economy began to falter in the mid-1980s. With encouragement from the Reagan administration in the United States, Jordan turned to the International Monetary Fund (IMF) to support its faltering economy in 1988. The agreement required the state to gradually lift subsidies and downsize its bloated public sector—that is, to reduce the number of jobs to which East Bankers felt entitled. During this early neoliberal period, Hussein remained reluctant to privatize state industries, a project his son would undertake in the 2000s.

The third theoretical intervention explores how protests figure into these two processes—the Jordanization of the state and neoliberalization. Despite an escalation of violence against all forms of political dissent in the 1970s, public claim-making returned, first from within the ranks of the army and then with student protests on campuses. Large-scale nationwide demonstrations broke out in solidarity with the Palestinian Intifada in December 1987. But it was the state's implementation of the first IMF-mandated economic reforms in April 1989 that ignited a massive "rage" against the regime's policies. Those protests were particularly disconcerting for the state because East Bankers—those who were the primary beneficiaries of the Jordanization project—were the first to rebel. The moment indexed another existential threat for the regime, with its support base leading the nationwide protests.

In the remainder of the chapter, I first examine misconceptions about divisions between and among Jordanians of East Bank and Palestinian descent. Doing so complicates the portrayal of "East Bankers" as the regime's loyal support base, and it lays the groundwork for my examination of the kind of nativism that views only some citizens as "true" Jordanians. I examine the process of Jordanization and then the state's turn to neoliberal economic reforms in a time of fiscal crisis. Next I examine the reemergence of widespread protests, with particular attention to anti-austerity protests in 1989, bringing into focus the repertoires of resistance and repression in the East Bank governorates. I then return to the scale of the now burgeoning capital city, outlining the new patterns and spaces of protest that will be examined in coming chapters. Finally, I summarize the chapter's theoretical contributions.

THE POLITICS—AND FICTIONS—OF NATIONAL IDENTITY

One technique for state-making and state-maintaining is to construct and advance a notion of national identity, one that establishes which citizens have the right to make certain kinds of moral and material claims on the state. This insight is hardly new, and the literature on the topic is vast and does not need to be rehearsed. Let's turn instead to how this process unfolded in Jordan in the aftermath of the Black September violence. The state project of Jordanization centered East Bank, tribal, and Bedouin identity in the official national narrative; any claims about issues relating to Palestine (or other territories outside of Jordan) were rendered "external" to Jordan. The move was fascinating not only for what claims were rendered "foreign" but also because it conflated important distinctions to project an uncomplicated "Jordanian" tribal identity.

Who Is Jordanian and What Does "Tribal" Mean?

We have seen how the diverse people living in the Transjordanian area prior to the start of the colonial state-making project had multiple and imbricating affective connections to people and lands elsewhere, and they did not share a single identity, not even something as loosely encompassing as "tribal." Not all people living in the Transjordanian area were or are tribal, and for those who have a tribal affiliation, what that means in practice varies considerably. To give just a few examples: some tribal authorities manage the distribution of tribal land, some secure employment for members, and some adjudicate conflicts within and across tribes. In the past, as we saw, they also waged wars and raids. Not all tribes have unified or agreed-upon leaders. Many Jordanians with tribal affiliations do not feel strong affective connections to their tribe or clan (the latter being smaller subunits within a tribe), although those attachments might be activated during periods of heightened conflicts between tribes. Tribal affiliations may be interpolated by others, including the state. Localized communities in many areas invoke distinct histories, and many retain strong local identities and even dialects.[2] The point, as we shall see here and later, is that "membership" in a tribe has never entailed a consistent meaning or set of obligations, and tribal attachments vary across space and time. And while Bedouins are tribal, most tribes are not Bedouin.

In its expansive use inside Jordan, then, the label "Jordanian" (*'Urduni,* or *'Urduni-'Urduni,* literally "Jordanian-Jordanian") brings all of these people from the Transjordanian area under one umbrella. The label can even accommodate families with roots outside of the area, as long as they have been settled and integrated for some perceived adequate period of time. Take the powerful Majali family of Karak, for example, whose forefathers migrated from Palestine in the eighteenth century. The Majali have been established in the region for a substantial period and have been prominent in Karaki leadership for centuries as well as in national government under Hashemite rule. In the eyes of most of my Jordanian interlocutors, the Majali are now Jordanian (although two activists reminded me of their Palestinian roots), a prominent family but not really tribal. The Majali seem to have earned their attachment to the land through time as well as through their bravery in rebelling against the Ottomans alongside other East Bank communities; recall that Habis was born in prison during one such rebellion. Although the Circassians and Chechens settled in Amman by the Ottomans in the late nineteenth century arrived more recently than families like the Majali, they are often included under the expansive use of "Jordanian," and they are not tribal in the sense of either the settled tribes of the older towns or the nomadic and seminomadic Bedouin.

Jordanian opinion during my research showed more ambivalence toward whether other families should be considered Jordanian. The Rifaʿi family, for example, emigrated from Palestine in the early twentieth century, and the family has been prominent in the Hashemite regime, holding high government offices. Branches of the Rifa'i family are also established in Lebanon and Syria, however, so while some of my interlocutors described them as Palestinian bourgeoisie, others framed them more negatively as opportunistic outsiders with financial and political ambitions but little affective attachments to any particular place. Still others saw them as staunch Jordanian nationalists with strong anti-Palestinian views. Curtis Ryan writes that during the 1989 *Habbit Nisan* protests, some of his East Bank interlocutors criticized Zayd Rifa'i, who was then prime minister, dismissing him as Syrian. During the period of the Arab uprisings in 2011, however, he heard Zayd's son Samir, who was now prime minister, dismissed as a neoliberal and bourgeois Palestinian businessman.[3] Ryan asked, "What would he be if he shifted away from the king's neoliberal agenda?" The response was both funny and telling: "Then he would be Jordanian again."[4]

Against this expansive view of who is Jordanian is the notion advanced by the more radical and chauvinistic "nativists." Their narrower definition sees only those with long-standing affective connections to the Transjordanian area as the "true" sons of Jordan. Long-established families like the Majali seem to make the cut, but not perceived opportunists like the Rifa'i; Chechens and Circassians are not Jordanian, but neither are they treated with hostility as long as they do not make political claims to rule. Here the main point is that Jordanian citizens do not agree on who is Jordanian. In many uses, "Jordanian" (and "Transjordanian" and "East Bank" in English) merely indexes a residual category, its primary meaning being a citizen of Jordan who is not Palestinian. At times, the parameters of these categories are used to call into question who has the moral right to rule, and in the narrowest, radical nativist formulation the Hashemite are reminded that they are latecomers to the region.

In terms of political orientations, it is a mistake to assume that "tribal" Jordanians are necessarily politically conservative, although of course many are. Some support communist and other leftist ideas, for example, while others are Islamist and even hold sympathies for more radical salafi ideas and movements. During conflicts like Black September, as we have seen, some East Bankers expressed support for the Palestinian *Fedayeen*, some for the regime, and some were largely ambivalent. Places like Karak might better be described as neotribal, because various other affinities, solidarities, social networks, and forms of nontribal local leadership have evolved over the decades. And, of course, East Bank areas are marked by significant class and generational divides.

East Bankers also diverge on their positions regarding Palestinian issues. Most strongly support the Palestinian national movement. They regularly protest alongside Palestinians against Israeli military actions and other regional and international developments affecting issues like the right of return or an independent Palestinian state. But opinions diverge around issues related to the rights and future of Jordanians of Palestinian descent, as we will see in chapter 6.

Who Is Palestinian?

Jordanians of Palestinian descent are likewise not homogenous. We saw earlier how some Palestinian bourgeoisie aligned with the state against the Palestinian *Fedayeen*. But while Palestinian–East Bank tensions were high in the wake of Black September, the flush economy brought the Palestinian bourgeoisie in line with the regime despite the Jordanization process that primarily benefited Jordanians of East Bank descent. In an influential article, Laurie Brand identifies four distinct groups among the Palestinians residing in Jordan: the poorer camp dwellers; small merchants and lower-level government employees; regime loyalists who achieved success through business or the upper levels of bureaucracy; and those who migrated to the Gulf states for employment and have "little attachment to or understanding of Jordan as a nation."[5] I would add two additional distinctions. We have already seen that some Jordanians with ancestral roots in Palestine are not really considered Palestinian any longer; although my interlocutors periodically referenced those roots, so they are not entirely forgotten. We also see some divides between refugees from the wars of 1948 and 1967, the latter of whom tend to hold more uncompromising views toward issues like the right of return. In this book, I have used the terms "Jordanians of Palestinian descent" and "Jordanians of East Bank descent," and both in their expansive sense.

POLITICAL DISSENT UNDER EXTREME REPRESSION

The Jordanization project advanced an official narrative of the nation as having a "tribal" and "Bedouin" past—in scare quotes because we know those concepts are complex and not congruent—and the regime sought to shore up its East Bank tribal support base through a combination of patronage and jobs. The General Intelligence Directorate (known popularly as the secret police or *mukhabarat*) and the Jordanian Armed Forces (the renamed Arab Legion) were significantly expanded, creating more jobs and more divisions for East Bankers. Those new sectors also (conveniently) worked hard to quash all opposition movements. In addition to Palestinian activists, the directorate closely monitored labor and union activities, particularly at the Professional Associations Complex in Amman.[6] Dozens of localized labor strikes were held until a harsh crackdown in 1974, with leftist and union activists increasingly arrested, tortured, and deported.[7] All manner of activist or oppositional political organization was illegal. The Muslim Brotherhood, however, had sided with the regime in crushing the *Fedayeen* during Black September, viewing the Palestinian Liberation Organization as too leftist, secular, and radical while also currying favor with the regime. Prominent Brotherhood leaders were rewarded with government positions, including at the cabinet level, and the ability to organize "social" activities locally with little impediment from the government.[8] This all worked with the Jordanization project because the Hashemites also descended from the Prophet Muhammad, providing a useful counterweight to leftist and Arab nationalist challenges.

One significant protest came surprisingly from within the government's own East Bank–dominated security sector—the Fortieth Armored Brigade, the army's elite combat unit.[9] Troops and officers from the unit mounted a demonstration on February 3, 1974, that lasted for two days. Described in a CIA document and the English-language press as a "mutiny," officers and some hundred troops paraded around the streets of Zarqa (where they were based) in trucks and armored personnel carriers.[10] They chanted for higher wages, the restoration of some recently lifted subsidies, and the dismissal of several "corrupt" government officials, including Prime Minister Zayd al-Rifaʿi and Armed Forces Chief of Staff Zayd bin Shakir. They declared that they intended to march on Amman if their demands were not met.[11] The king responded by raising wages and restoring some subsidies through the new Ministry of Supply, which had recently been established to ensure that the population had access to basic commodities.[12]

At the time, increasing wages to placate dissent within the army was an easy decision, as the Jordanization project was in full throttle and Jordan's

104   CHAPTER 4

economy was strong. Tens of thousands of Jordanians—many of Palestinian descent—departed for employment in the Gulf, returning significant remittances to their families back home to help fuel a construction boom. As much as a third of the labor force had migrated to the Gulf for work by the early 1980s, sending an average of US $918 million home to Jordan. Remittances peaked at US $1.2 billion in 1984, an amount equal to around one quarter of Jordan's total Gross Domestic Product.[13] Inside Jordan, the expansion of government jobs through the Jordanization project meant that more than half of the population was employed by the state in some capacity.[14]

The Return of Protests

During the 1978–79 academic year, students at the University of Jordan in Amman and Yarmouk University in Irbid mounted demonstrations over a range of political and economic issues, including economic problems, the lack of democratic participation, university involvement in student governance, and the Israeli occupation of Palestine. Engineering students were further outraged at the ongoing crackdown on activism—including the targeting of engineers—at the Professional Associations Complex in Amman.[15] In March 1978, students at the University of Jordan were particularly intent on reviving a culture of political expression. They mounted large demonstrations against the peace treaty between Egypt and Israel and demanded the creation of a free student union that would enable students to play a more active role in campus governance. Those protests, which lasted for eleven days, were put down by security forces clubbing students to break up the demonstrations; several students were killed, and dozens and perhaps hundreds were arrested. The university administration punished students who had participated with suspensions, expulsions, and the denial of student aid.[16]

Five years later, on February 5, 1984, hundreds of students at Yarmouk University protested proposed changes to the curriculum, bringing university operations to a standstill for five days. The students succeeded in pressuring the university administration to suspend the proposed curriculum and the new standards for grading and advancement.[17] But when protests broke out at the university again in May 1986, the regime response this time was severe.[18] A student conference had voted in late April to demand the creation of an independent student union, and members of many student associations had collectively resigned in solidarity. On May 11, thousands walked out of their exams and assembled on campus for a demonstration.[19] Multiple security agencies entered the campus to violently disperse the protesters, resulting in at least three deaths and hundreds of injuries.[20]

Having crushed the student protests, the government led a rapid reorganization of the university that utilized a spatial tactic: creating a second campus away from the main one in the city of Irbid. Named the Jordan University of Science and Technology (known by the English acronym JUST), the new campus was located some 124 miles east of Irbid near Ramtha, a small town near the Syrian border. The move effectively isolated activist students (from the schools of engineering, dentistry, medicine, nursing, and pharmacy) from the rest of the student body. Along with the reorganization of the various academic programs, the new campus also allowed for increased state penetration of student activism and organization.[21] Isolated and no longer visible to the residents of a surrounding large city, protests on the new campus would have no outside audience.

Beyond the campuses, Jordanians mounted protests over issues such as housing. Amman had continued to expand rapidly in the 1980s, with remittances joined by the flight of capital from Iraq (during the Iran-Iraq War of 1980–88) to fuel construction.[22] Lebanese fleeing their civil war also invested in new neighborhoods in Amman. The government was most concerned with controlling the expansion of informal housing in poor neighborhoods, however, and sought to limit construction or destroy emerging poor neighborhoods. Residents resisted these efforts at every turn. On July 17, 1983, for example, demonstrators in East Amman protested the demolition of what the government termed illegal buildings that were homes for the city's growing population.[23]

Jordanians of both East Bank and Palestinian descent also demonstrated in support of the Palestinian national movement, and many of those events were also met with violence. In March 1982, hundreds of protesters in Amman carried PLO flags and denounced King Hussein for his failure to recognize the group. Police violently broke up the demonstrations, killing several and injuring at least sixty.[24] Then with the outbreak of the Palestinian Intifada in December 1987, Jordanians nationwide mounted protests and marches of solidarity. For several weeks, crowds of several hundred each demonstrated

106 CHAPTER 4

in refugee camps, in downtown Amman at the Grand Husseini Mosque, and in predominantly East Bank areas in the outer governorates. Facing down an economic crisis, the regime finally relinquished Jordan's claim over the West Bank in 1988. The government tried to quiet the growing economic unrest by reaching out to business leaders and promising them a greater role in the country's economic policies.[25] But Palestinians living in the West Bank sold off their Jordanian dinars amid uncertainty, contributing to the dinar's drop in value against the US dollar.[26] When the dinar's value plunged, the United States urged Jordan to begin negotiations with the International Monetary Fund for debt relief and economic assistance. In late 1988, Jordan signed an agreement and the state cut the value of the dinar in half.[27]

THE 1989 HABBIT NISAN PROTESTS AND THE
MAKING OF THE NEOLIBERAL STATE

In 1989, the Hashemite regime reached a critical juncture in state-maintaining. Most scholars estimated that half of Jordan's citizens were of Palestinian descent, concentrated largely in the greater Amman area and in other northern towns and cities. But the Jordanization project counted on East Bankers outside of the capital as the regime's primary support base, exchanging regime loyalty for not only the material benefits of government jobs and patronage but for their moral authority embodied in the official narrative of nation and East Bank heritage. Although spatially peripheral to the economic growth of the capital, the welfare state slowed the economic peripheralization of some East Bank communities. But tensions between some areas and the regime had been simmering for several years, particularly in Ma'an, a major hub in Jordan's trucking industry. Ma'anis had benefited economically from the construction of the north-south Desert Highway in the 1960s as well as the development of the Red Sea port of Aqaba. While the area's Bedouin from the Huwaytat tribal confederation found employment primarily in the security services, and some town-dwellers found jobs in government, a large portion of Ma'an residents worked in the trucking industry, the mineral industries, and services for tourists and pilgrims headed to the holy cities in Saudi Arabia.

As we have seen, the Jordanization project was made possible by the boom of the 1970s, which increased trucking traffic from Iraq to Aqaba.[28] But Ma'an began a steady decline after 1982, when upgrades to the Desert Highway moved the road east and out of town, along with the area's primary pilgrimage rest station. Then passenger traffic on the Hijaz Railway was indefinitely suspended, and the government administratively detached Ma'an from Aqaba and Petra, further lessening the town's importance. Bedouin in the areas around Ma'an, however, retained more access to the regime through their centrality in branches of the security services. This town/Bedouin divide illustrates how categories like "southern" or "tribal" make little sense for understanding political motivations. The town residents who relied on trade saw themselves become economically and politically marginalized.

Meanwhile, the government's investments in Amman and its infrastructure exacerbated the resentment felt by towns that were becoming increasingly marginalized as economic investment and development in the capital expanded. Inflation in the late 1970s led to anger over higher prices, and the cost of living increased by as much as 200 percent during that decade.[29] In the mid-1980s, truck drivers staged a protest in Ma'an to express their frustrations over their deteriorating economic situation during a visit to the town by the king.[30] But with the oil price collapse in the mid-1980s, maintaining the flow of state jobs and payments to East Bank communities proved difficult. Jordan faced growing debt and dwindling reserves, and remittances from Jordanians working in the Gulf declined sharply, with some 35,000 returning home in 1987 alone.[31] The flush years were over, and the state's Jordanization project left it with a bloated bureaucracy and a massive security apparatus but with little ability to continue to fund them. As one leftist activist put it, the time was ripe for the return of protests: "The party [state largesse] was over, and they didn't have any plan to deal with [the economic collapse]."[32]

And with that, the state entered its first neoliberal period, encouraged by Reagan to sign an agreement with the International Monetary Fund for loans and aid to mitigate the economic crisis. Let's pause here for a moment, as the term "neoliberalism" needs some discussion. What scholars (and the World Bank) today call neoliberalism refers to a broad set of economic policies adopted beginning in the 1970s, marking a definitive end to Keynesian economic policies in which the state plays a role in keeping unemployment low and supporting the economy. David Harvey elegantly defines neoliberalism as

> a theory of political economic practices that proposes that human well-being
> can best be advanced by liberating individual entrepreneurial freedoms and

skills within an institutional framework characterized by strong private property rights, free markets, and free trade. . . . It optimizes conditions for capital accumulation no matter what the consequences for employment or social well-being.[33]

Neoliberalism is not, of course, a monolithic or single process or set of policies. It is a complex set of practices for extracting wealth by what Harvey calls "accumulation by dispossession"—not by producing goods to market, but by finding ways of acquiring capital through any (legal) means possible. Lisa Wedeen identifies four distinct political economy processes that are indexed by the term neoliberalism:

1. Macroeconomic stabilization (via "austerity policies" encouraging low inflation and low public debt, and discouraging Keynesian countercyclical policies)
2. Trade liberalization and financial deregulation
3. The privatization of publicly owned assets and firms
4. Welfare state retrenchment[34]

Others like Mitchell Dean have approached neoliberalism more as a "thought collective," stressing the "contingent sources, multiple forms, and heterogeneous and apparently contradictory elements of neoliberalism, which means that it is irreducible to a simple and coherent philosophy or ideology."[35] For Wedeen, however, neoliberalism's ideological components can be reduced to the way in which the state is no longer the primary addressee of people's moral and material entitlements. Neoliberalism suggests a shift in risk-bearing, away from governments and onto individuals and families. This does not mean that there are not contingent forms and contradictions, as every ideology has contradictions. But neoliberalism's logics are recognizable and distinct.

The challenge for Jordan, then, was that the Jordanization project—the expansion of government jobs and the provision of subsidies through the new Ministry of Supply—did the exact opposite of what neoliberalism required. And Jordanians refused to turn away from the state as the primary addressee for making moral and material claims. After Hussein agreed to the IMF conditions, Jordanians were appalled to watch the value of their savings plummet with the 1988 devaluation of the dinar. Tensions came to a head when, on April 16, 1989, the government raised prices on cigarettes, fuel, and some beverages.

Two days later, Ma'ani truckers encouraged local residents and students to join them in demonstrations against the lifted subsidies. Private taxi drivers, many of whom were not East Bankers, joined the protests over worry that they would not be allowed to raise the government-regulated fares to offset the fuel price increases. The demonstrations escalated in a matter of hours, and Ma'ani residents renewed a tactic from their protest repertoire by blockading the main north-south road through town. They threw eggs and tomatoes at government vehicles and at cars known to be carrying government officials.[36] As they called for the resignation of Prime Minister Zayd al-Rifa'i—who some disparaged as Syrian—demonstrators began attacking government buildings. Police attempting to break up the protest killed two protesters, and the crowds responded by overtaking government vehicles and setting them on fire. Outside of Ma'an, large protests broke out that same day in Shoubak, Naqab, Jafr, and Wadi Musa. In nearby Hussayniya, demonstrators set fire to an oil tank. The crown prince traveled to Ma'an to ask local leaders to stand down, but his procession was stoned, forcing it to turn back.[37] Protesters in impoverished Ghor Safi (in the southern Jordan Valley) burned government buildings and exchanged gunfire with the police. Within three days, tens of thousands demonstrated and rioted nationwide, blocking roads everywhere and bringing the country to a standstill.

The geography of these *Habbit Nisan* (April rage) protests thus began in the south and quickly spread nationwide. While many analyses portray the protests as confined to East Bank areas,[38] my research and interviews with more than a dozen who participated in them reveals a more complex picture. First, the protests did begin in the East Bank economic periphery, but Ma'an has a significant number of residents who do not have East Bank roots. The protests also spread to northern urban areas where Jordanians of Palestinian descent are a majority. In Irbid, rioters set fires and blocked the main north-south highway. In Amman, Jordanians of both Palestinian and East Bank descent demonstrated at the King Husseini Mosque. Students of all backgrounds protested in Taybeh and Deir Abu Sa'eed and at the JUST campus in the northern desert, Yarmouk University in central Irbid, and the University of Jordan in Amman. The absence of significant protests in the Palestinian refugee camps does not mean that Palestinians refrained from joining protests in other locations; the camps were simply not the usual places for protesting around issues unrelated to Israel/Palestine.

Second, much of the worst violence took place between East Bank protesters and East Bank–staffed security forces. These deep divides within and between some of the East Bank communities reflect resentments about perceived and real favoritism as well as differing patterns of employment and economic prosperity. These cleavages also underline the aforementioned misconception that "East Bank" is a single category of belonging. Grievances exist within as well as between tribes, clans, and families, and among town dwellers and Bedouin.

And third, claim-making during the protests was not limited to restoring the subsidies that sparked the first protests. Many of the protests expressed demands for substantive political reforms, including the restoration of elections and increased political freedoms. In Karak, political leaders and trade unionists drew up a comprehensive list of demands, including free elections, reduced corruption, the cancellation of the price increases, the resignation of the prime minister, the creation of a government that would be accountable to the people, and greater support for the Palestinian Intifada. Curtis Ryan recalls being told in 1989 by students who had mounted protests at Yarmouk University that they included pro-Palestinian slogans and provocatively cut the Hashemite star out of Jordan's flag[39] to wave at demonstrations.[40]

In terms of the localized spatial dynamics of the protests, demonstrators drew directly from the existing protest repertoires, gathering in known spaces for protest and using familiar tactics. In doing so, they also engaged in new forms of place-making or -remaking, carrying affective memories of past protests and grievances into the present and creating new events to be commemorated by new generations. Because of their symbolism, government buildings were frequently targeted. In Salt, protesters threw stones at the police and demonstrated in Ayn Square. In Tafileh, they set fire to a village council building. In other places, protesters gathered at locations associated with political dissent, as they did in Dhiban where hundreds assembled at the local Union of Professional Associations office. In Amman, the largest crowds were downtown near the Grand Husseini Mosque. All of these places were sites of government authority, political dissent, or known places where protests had occurred.

One long-standing spatial tactic, besides targeting government property and officials, was to use fires, herds of sheep, and all manner of material objects to block roads and sabotage infrastructure. Blockades nationwide brought transit to a standstill in many areas and slowed the arrival of security forces. On April 20 alone, protesters in the north blocked the Amman–Iraq highway, the main highway leading both north and south of Irbid, the Jerash–Amman highway in the town of Mustada, and the highway leading from Salt to Amman. Security forces, trying to clear roads that had been blocked with burning tires, killed several Bani Hassan tribe members. In central Jordan, roadblocks were mounted in Dhiban and other Madaba towns. In the south, the main north-south highway was blocked in Karak, Tafileh, Wadi Rum, Ma'an, Hussayniya, and Aqaba. In Amman, demonstrators in the Hayy Tafayleh neighborhood—an area whose residents have roots in the town of Tafileh—blocked local roads with fires. Blockages came and went, expanding the network of obstructions to transport as security forces struggled to clear them.

The regime eventually turned to the Jordanian Armed Forces to put down the protests and clear the streets. They did so via spatial tactics such as occupying Ma'an and Karak with tanks for at least five days and replacing the protesters' road blockades with military checkpoints. Two army battalions in Ma'an imposed a curfew and searched houses for weapons—an aggressive violation of private space that was repeated in 2002 and which Ma'anis still recall today.[41] In Madaba, troops cleared the streets and arrested unionists and professional association organizers from their homes. In the end, security forces killed at least sixteen protesters and arrested hundreds.[42] Those arrests, however, led to an innovation in the protest repertoire: mounting protests in front of jails and prisons where protesters were being detained. For much of the summer, crowds held peaceful sit-ins in front of governorate offices nationwide—including at the Council of Ministers offices in Amman.

Legacy

The political implications of the protests, beginning in southern East Bank areas before spreading nationwide, were not lost on King Hussein. During the days of rioting and demonstrations and in the months following, pamphlets authored anonymously as well as under the names of prominent East Bank tribes and powerful families circulated widely. As with claim-making during the protests themselves, these pamphlets articulated moral and material demands concerning both political and economic issues. Some pamphlets read like primers on the economic situation or tensions over Jordanian identity that had escalated after Black September, while others read like mini-manifestos.[43] Residents of Ma'an and Karak boasted of their willingness to confront the regime and bring routine life to a standstill; other areas spoke about the *Habbit Nisan* as a movement, or *hirak*—a term that would reemerge during the 2011 protests. Ma'anis emphasized that solidarity and courage were among their core values and that the protests provided an opportunity to demonstrate those qualities and "revive a local sense of self-worth." One Ma'ani activist argued that with every violent protest, Ma'anis came to see themselves as the most politically courageous Jordanians. "In the past two decades most Jordanians have become afraid of the state and its security forces—except for Maanis."[44]

Hussein sought advice from a group of loyalists who had served the regime in various capacities. Should he respond with repression or appear responsive to outrage from his East Bank tribal base? He opted for the latter, sacking Rifa'i as prime minister and announcing a political opening that he hoped would allow the state to channel dissent into institutions it could manage.[45] His decision to hold free elections was widely welcomed, although Jordanians of both East Bank and Palestinian descent expressed doubt that the state would ever become a democracy. But free and fair elections indeed were held in November 1989 for a new lower house of Parliament, conducted through an entirely new electoral map.[46] (The previous system, which allotted half of the seats for the West Bank, obviously had to be abandoned when Jordan relinquished its claim to the West Bank in 1988.) The new electoral system created a new geography of electoral or parliamentary power, providing stronger representation for the governorates outside of Amman where East Bank communities were a majority. In a way, it worked as a noneconomic technique for continuing the Jordanization project, allocating more constituents per district (and thus lesser representation) for the districts in Amman, Zarqa, and Irbid, where Jordanians of Palestinian descent were concentrated. In a sense, the protests that began in the economic and spatial periphery (to the capital) worked to solidify a political geography in which East Bank populations in governorates outside of Amman and Irbid were more tightly connected to the centers of political power than those in the rapidly expanding capital. As such, the geography of electoral representation worked both to accommodate East Bank demands and repress Palestinian representation, all while adding to the veneer of Jordan as a moderate and democratizing nation.

In sum, the state-maintaining of the Jordanization period (expansively including East Bankers in the welfare state) and the onset of the neoliberal period (expansively including East Bankers in the new electoral geography) each changed the character of the state. Austerity and privatization led not to a retreat of the state but to new kinds of state interventions. After the 1989 *Habbit Nisan* protests, state-maintaining now took the form not only of cash payments and employment but of extending the perks of parliamentary participation. While the bloated public sector remained dominated by East Bank employees, Jordan continued its agreements with the IMF, and thus new cuts to subsidies and downsizing for the welfare state were on the horizon. Indeed, the regime established its own repertoire for responding to nationwide protests: If massive demonstrations in the outlying East Bank governorates spread nationwide, the king would dismiss the prime minister, appoint a new one, and call for a national dialogue. If the protests were against austerity measures, the state would reverse parts of the subsidies, often through a workaround that technically maintained the cuts while providing alternative means of offsetting the impact of price increases.[47] If the claim-making was about political reforms, the king would task the new cabinet with studying and implementing them. This pattern would be repeated so often over the coming decades that it became a national joke.

THE NORMALIZATION OF PROTEST?

In addition to the resumption of parliamentary elections, the 1989 *Habbit Nisan* protests ushered in a return to the political freedoms of the mid-1950s. Jordan held elections for the lower house of Parliament in November 1989, which returned an assembly dominated by leftists and Islamists.[48] In 1990, it launched a National Dialogue to outline the new political vision and the obligations of the government and its citizens, and martial law was canceled.[49] Political parties were legalized in 1992. In many ways, the results of the 1989 protests were a revelation, invigorating Jordanians with the possibilities that nationwide protests might realize. The state continued its commitment to both the Jordanization project and neoliberal reforms, however, even as the expansive welfare state and the maintenance of state-owned industries were at odds with

CHAPTER 4

neoliberal logics.[50] Indeed, many East Bank grievances were little alleviated as Hussein slowly restructured the state in the service of neoliberalism.

The new era saw a return of routine street politics, including periodic nationwide demonstrations as well as sometimes hundreds of small and localized protests each year. But while protest was legalized under a new public gatherings law, reforms stalled as Jordan moved in earnest toward signing a peace treaty with Israel. The problem for the government was that the 1989 Parliament was dominated by Islamist and leftist parties unlikely to ratify the treaty. The king needed the 1993 elections to return an assembly that would pass a treaty, and it announced changes to the election law four months before the November 1993 poll. The new law further increased the representation of East Bank areas at the expense of the diverse northern urban areas, where opposition political parties were also the strongest. The new law advantaged prominent East Bank tribal leaders with local reputations and support bases, supplying the regime with East Bank loyalist deputies. Spatially, restructuring the districts to ensure East Bank dominance also brought prominent East Bank voices from the periphery into the spaces of the capital, where they established local residences for when Parliament was in session. Expectedly, the 1993 elections returned an assembly in which East Bank loyalists comprised a majority, and the Wadi Araba peace treaty with Israel was signed in 1994. But the streets were far from quiet.

Anti-Austerity Protests

Nationwide anti-austerity protests broke out again in 1996 when the state lifted subsidies on wheat and the price doubled overnight.[51] On August 13, Karakis took to the streets, targeting government buildings and constructing roadblocks (with rocks and barrels) to prevent entrance into the city from both main roads. Government buildings were vandalized and set ablaze. Newspapers reported that crowds chanted "Long live the king, down with Kabariti." Abd al-Karim Kabariti was the prime minister at the time and had pushed for the latest IMF package to be passed in Parliament, and most protesters directed their anger toward the prime minister to avoid crossing the red line against criticizing the king. Unreported in the newspapers, however, were some protest chants criticizing the king for neglecting East Bank areas while the capital flourished.[52] Protesters expressed other grievances as well, such as demanding the lifting of sanctions on Iraq. That first day, the police used tear gas to dispel the crowd of more than a thousand.

The demonstrations quickly spread to other locations. Protesters were peaceful in Salt, while those in Tafileh chanted and threw rocks at police forces, who retaliated with tear gas. In Ma'an, police teargassed a demonstration of more than three hundred. In Amman, protesters in Hayy Tafayleh mounted a peaceful march that was dispersed when it encountered a contingent of riot police. Elsewhere in Amman, the army moved troops and soldiers to prevent protests from forming, particularly around refugee camps suspected of harboring antiregime sentiment.[53] Large protests broke out daily at the Grand Husseini Mosque.

But Karak remained the epicenter for the 1996 protests, bringing the normal functioning of the city to a halt and expressing some of the most direct and harsh criticism of the government. On the fourth day of protests, August 16, the state made a massive show of force: two dozen armored military vehicles and dozens of troop transporters entered the city while helicopters circled overhead. Demonstrators withdrew from the streets but threw stones at troops from windows and balconies. The king traveled to Karak and expressed his determination to prevent more protests, but he returned quickly to Amman and demonstrations resumed the next day. Kabariti finally announced a curfew on Karak, which the army imposed and maintained until August 25, departing only after a full week of calm.

All told, more than two hundred Karakis were arrested, three-quarters of whom were released within a month; the remainder were released in October. The Majali and other prominent Karaki families pressured the government for the releases, and in the end no one was charged. Government officials vacillated on who was to blame. Because Karakis chanted against the sanctions on Iraq, the government suggested that foreign agents were behind the unrest rather than Jordanians themselves: first blamed were members of the Arab Socialist Baath Party in Jordan and then the Iraqi government itself. One Iraqi official in Jordan was accused of being an Iraqi intelligence officer and forced to leave the country.[54] Karaki activists, however, scoffed at the claim that foreign elements had orchestrated or even fueled their protests. They noted that they had carefully chosen the government buildings symbolizing specific grievances, such as the local office of the Ministry of Education, which had recently raised school fees.[55]

FIGURE 4.1. Routine protests returned to the Grand Husseini Mosque after the 1989 *Habbit Nisan* protest. Source: Dana M. Moss.

Protests around Regional Political Developments

Jordanians of both East Bank and Palestinian descent maintained affective connections beyond Jordan, particularly to the Arab world. For many, those attachments included the embrace of Iraq's president Saddam Hussein for his anti-imperialism, strident opposition to Israel, support for the Palestinian national movement, and criticism of US interventionism in the region and globally. When Iraq invaded Kuwait in August 1990, it was unsurprising that tens of thousands of Jordanians took to the streets nationwide to demonstrate in support of Iraq. Although tens of thousands of Jordanians had previously worked in the Gulf (or had family members who still did), many Jordanians viewed the Gulf regimes and their citizens as arrogant and morally hypocritical. As the protests continued for weeks and then months, the state did not try to clear the streets, and indeed at least some protests were organized or authorized by government employees, including teachers who led schoolchildren to join demonstrations.[56]

But the protests put King Hussein in a bind: Jordan desperately needed financial support from the United States, but allowing the US-led coalition to stage in Jordan could spark protests on a scale that threatened the regime, particularly coming so soon after the 1989 *Habbit Nisan* protests. He opted instead for a "neutral" position, which tempered domestic criticism but led to devastating cuts to foreign aid by the United States and the Gulf states aligned behind Kuwait. The Gulf states further retaliated against Jordan by expelling most of its tens of thousands of workers remaining in the Gulf; no more than 10 percent of the workers retained employment compared to the levels of the early 1980s. The return of those workers led to an 8 percent increase in Jordan's total population.[57] Jordanians protested throughout the war into early 1991. Over the next years, Iraq continued to be a topic around which Jordanians protested, particularly concerning the postwar sanctions that brought devastation and suffering to the Iraqi people.

Following the fallout from Jordan's neutrality, the king sought to rehabilitate Jordan's relationship with the United States by pursuing a peace treaty with Israel; he also hoped to play a prominent role in the Oslo peace talks. But when the Wadi Arab peace treaty was signed in October 1994, many Jordanians of both East Bank and Palestinian descent were outraged that the king had made peace without any provisions for the return of Palestinians who had been driven out by the wars. One particularly vocal critic was the independent Islamist Layth al-Shubaylat, who had a history of arrests for his political speech.[58] In 1995, another frequent critic of the Hashemite monarchy, Mahmoud al-Awamleh, was fatally shot during a police assault. Opposition voices took the shooting as a warning against crossing the red line of criticizing the king, but Shubaylat was undeterred. He called the king a traitor during a speech against the peace treaty in Irbid in December 1995 and repeated the accusation at a lecture in Tafileh some days later. In March 1996, he was convicted of *lèse-majesté* and sentenced to three years in prison. But Shubaylat—whose father served as a minister and as head of the Royal Court in the 1950s—was pardoned in November 1996 on the king's birthday (an annual tradition).[59] The king personally drove him from Swaqa prison to Shubaylat's mother in Amman, a testament to both the prominence of the family and the need to be perceived as acting fairly and justly toward East Bank communities.

But then in 1998, Shubaylat publicly condemned the United States and defended Iraq at a speech in Ma'an's main mosque as Ma'anis were in the streets protesting US missile attacks on Iraq. When government officials arrested him, Ma'anis were furious and poured into the streets in large numbers, again blocking the main north-south road through town. The police killed eight people and arrested hundreds as they worked to clear the streets of protesters. In a form of collective punishment, the state even cut off water and electricity to the town.[60] When Shubaylat was released some days later, the army was called in to enforce a curfew for forty days.[61]

King Hussein died in February 1999, and his eldest son, Abdullah II, took the throne. Small and single-sector protests continued under his tenure, but the new king faced nationwide protests as the Second Palestinian Intifada in fall 2000 brought Jordanians to the streets for months. A year later, the September 11, 2001, attacks brought demonstrations first in solidarity with the United States people, including a candlelight vigil at the US embassy (relocated to the posh Abdoun neighborhood). But when the United States launched retaliatory military actions against the Taliban in Afghanistan in November 2001, tens of thousands protested for weeks nationwide, with large gatherings in downtown Amman and outside the US embassy.

In Ma'an, tensions with the regime were particularly high, as some Ma'anis had demonstrated in support of Osama Bin Laden and showed sympathy with other salafi extremists.[62] Then in January 2002, a Ma'ani youth was detained by the police and died in custody, officially of kidney failure.[63] News of the death brought Ma'anis to the streets for days; some set a police station on fire and destroyed government vehicles. In the melee, a police officer was killed and at least a dozen on both sides were seriously injured. The army put the town under siege, imposing a curfew for five days. Then in March and April, large demonstrations broke out nationwide—including in Ma'an—against Israel's invasion and destruction of Palestinian villages and cities, including Jenin and Nablus.

Amid these heightened tensions, and with considerable frustration with the new king among East Bank communities, US Agency for International Development (USAID) official Lawrence Foley was assassinated in Amman on October 28, 2002; the regime suspected Islamist extremists. The United States was gearing up for the war on Iraq, and the Jordanian state already anticipated major protests because the country was unlikely to remain neutral this time. Acting preemptively, the army's Special Forces entered Ma'an in early November, ostensibly to root out local support for drug dealers, arms smugglers, and suspected Islamist extremists.[64] Angry residents clashed with the troops, even exchanging gunfire from windows. Three days of fighting were followed by five days of relative calm, but clashes resumed on November 17. The next few days saw the largest-scale fighting in Jordan since Black September, with state forces firing machine guns into the windows from whence gunfire came. In the end, seven Ma'anis were killed and more than a hundred were arrested. The clashes ended only when the army arrived to lock down the entire town and enforce a curfew. Helicopters circled the skies for days, as troops conducted house-to-house searches, which local activists likened to the tactics used by Israeli Defense Forces against Palestinians.[65] The state cut telephone and radio communications, and the curfew lasted five days.

AMMAN'S NEW GEOGRAPHY OF PROTEST

Let's zoom in to the level of the capital to see how protest spaces and routines had changed. Picking up where chapter 3 left off, Amman under King Abdullah II's rule was a major metropolitan area with a population of 1,014,000 in 2000.[66]

The city was changed in two fundamental ways that would come to significantly shape political protests in the capital over the next decades. First, the built environment had sprawled in all directions, with government buildings as well as commercial spaces across the diverse and disconnected neighborhoods of West Amman. Protesters continued to gather downtown near the Grand Husseini Mosque, but they also convened in other locations. Buildings in parts of West Amman were increasingly larger and taller, which created buffers from the sounds of downtown as well as blocking sight lines. Until the 1970s, for example, few buildings in Amman were taller than eight floors, with most four floors or less. Taller buildings began to appear first in Shmeisani in the 1960s. By the 1990s, however, high-rise buildings were common, embraced by many as a welcome sign of Amman's "modernity" despite their destructive effects on the existing urban fabric.[67] The hilly geography of the city always made it difficult to see the downtown protests from all but the nearest edges of the hills, but protests that could be heard from the neighborhoods of Jebal Amman and Jebal Webdeh of the 1940s and 1950s were now muffled by distance, urban noise, and the structures of the built environment. The road and highway infrastructure had also been improved and expanded, facilitating the flow of traffic in and out of downtown and between the newer neighborhoods.[68]

The class divide between East Amman and West Amman that began emerging in the 1940s[69] had become even more dramatic. Indeed, most of the scholarship on Amman emphasizes the increase of this divide since the 1980s.[70] While poor and working-class neighborhoods sprawled to the south, east, and north of the downtown area, a disproportionate share of investment was concentrated in West Amman: high-rise luxury hotels, new embassies, and the headquarters of many regional and international banks and businesses. The US embassy, as noted, had relocated from the crowded Third Circle area on Zahran Street to a fortress-like compound in West Amman's affluent Abdoun neighborhood. Abdoun itself had evolved from an outlying cluster of villas in the 1960s to a vibrant neighborhood by the early 1990s, with restaurants, cafés, shops, and eventually malls. The Abdoun Circle intersection, flanked by restaurants and clubs, attracted people on weekend evenings who wanted to see and be seen. New spatial repertoires for protest emerged around symbolic spaces in affluent West Amman, while older repertoires were largely maintained downtown and in East Amman.

FIGURE 4.2. Typical vista of central Amman and its hilly topography. Source: Eliana Abu-Hamdi.

Downtown/City Center

The Grand Husseini Mosque remained a central space for protest. Massive demonstrations during the Gulf War of 1990 and 1991 expressed popular support for Iraq and against the US-led coalition. As Queen Noor recalls those protests, the streets of Amman were "filled with placards extolling [Saddam Hussein's] virtues," expressing anger at Washington's hypocrisy in condemning Iraq's occupation of Kuwait but not Israel's occupation of Palestine.[71] Amman's residents filled the downtown streets routinely, with many of the largest demonstrations focused on regional political developments. For example, when an Israeli settler massacred twenty-nine Palestinians praying at the Ibrahimi Mosque at the Cave of the Patriarch in al-Khalil/Hebron in February 1994, the downtown filled with protesters within hours of the news. People returned to demonstrate for days when Israeli troops killed some twenty-six Palestinian protesters in the West Bank. The mosque was again the epicenter of protests in Amman during the 1996 anti-austerity protests that began in

CHAPTER 4

Karak, the Second Palestinian Intifada in 2000, and the Israeli invasion of Palestinian towns in March 2002.

While many downtown protests were undisturbed by the police, at other times the state struggled to control large-scale demonstrations. In January 1998, for example, protesters against the sanctions on Iraq filled downtown Amman and other towns. As the late activist Aida Dabbas recalled the scene:

> What was supposed to be a peaceful expression of opposition to the pending military strike against Iraq became a violent attack against unarmed citizens. I was present as an independent human rights observer and witnessed the police bullying people before the march had even begun. I was one of dozens who were beaten with billy clubs, shoved into vans and taken to the police station, but I was released without being charged.[72]

Hundreds were arrested, with many detained for days.[73] The violence against these protests was surprising, but the regime had decided to silence such widespread outrage against the actions of its most important ally, the United States. Unable to continue protests in the streets, Ammanis began posting antiwar signs in their office and automobile windows; others flew black flags to signify opposition to the government's repression of free speech.

During this period, downtown Amman was suffering economic decline. As a commercial district, its low-end retailers now attracted working-class residents and immigrants, with the area becoming rundown particularly after the financial collapse of the 1980s. Cheap hostels attracted international backpackers, and small bustling restaurants catered to them and working-class Jordanians. A few bars and cafés were still known as gathering points for leftists and Arab nationalists, some in operation since the heady days of Arab nationalism. Refugees found cheap housing in antiquated buildings with poor facilities. Upper-middle-class and wealthy Jordanians no longer frequented downtown, gathering instead at new restaurants, leisure sites, and shopping areas in West Amman.

But the government talked of reviving downtown Amman, in the context of discussions about turning Amman into a "modern" capital. Those ambitious plans were embodied in the Greater Amman Comprehensive Development Plan of 1988, which sought to assert a government planning role in the city.[74] Downtown areas were to be rehabilitated with the intention of creating sites of leisure as well as symbols of the nation. The large Hashemite Plaza, for example, had been inaugurated November 13, 1986, adjacent to the Roman amphitheater. Queen Noor characterized the plaza as a symbol of the nation and "the original heart of the city,"[75] but downtown remained largely unchanged. In 1995, the king talked again about making Amman a "modern Arab cultural capital." One of the new projects was a large complex for municipal government buildings, replacing the old municipal building on the northwest end of King Faysal Plaza. The new site in Ras al-Ayn included a multibuilding complex with gardens and public spaces. But the location was neither centrally located nor easy to reach. The original plans were adjusted to provide for better traffic flow, but in the process easy pedestrian access was eliminated. Rather than a symbol of a modern capital welcoming to pedestrians as a leisure site, the new Municipal Complex that opened in 2000 was an island surrounded by asphalt. As Raed Al Tal writes, "Amman's citizens and workers go about their business barely acknowledging the complex's presence. For them, it is an unseen part of their daily lives and difficult to navigate by foot or by car."[76] But the new complex did, however, alter the spatial routine of downtown protests. While people still assembled at the Grand Husseini Mosque, they now marched west to the new Municipal Complex, a longer distance that could also accommodate more protesters.

The Professional Associations Complex

The Professional Associations Complex in Shmeisani emerged as a space for protests beginning in the 1990s, including larger gatherings in the complex's parking lot as well as events organized in its auditorium. During the repressive 1970s and 1980s, the regime targeted leftists and Arab nationalists in the professional associations, but the building remained known as a place where political debate took place, even in hushed tones. Jordan's professional associations and unions are mostly government organized, and membership is mandatory to practice one's profession (if a relevant union or association exists). Most members have little engagement with their union beyond paying their required annual dues. With the political liberalization following the 1989 *Habbit Nisan* protests, the Union of Professional Associations organized numerous political events and protests, many of which were held at the complex itself. Beginning in the mid-1990s, political freedoms were rolled back, and new election laws every cycle gradually diminished the ability of opposition parties to win seats in an electoral geography constructed to overrepresent East Bank communities. Activists talked of the union and its complex as the only meaningful remaining place for public political dissent. As the location became known as a space for protest, however, the state increasingly shut down protests and marches organized by the union on the complex's grounds as well as elsewhere. Violent repression increased under Abdullah II, as we have already seen in Maʿan in 2002. At the complex in Amman, the state used riot police, dogs, batons, tear gas, and water cannons to disperse the hundreds who periodically assembled to protest in the complex's parking lot. During a protest on May 12, 2001, for example, Abd al-Latif Arabiyyat—former speaker of Parliament and secretary-general of the Islamic Action Front—was injured by an officer swinging a baton.

In spring 2001, Abdullah II dissolved Parliament and delayed the scheduled November 2001 elections. Without a parliament in session, the cabinet began to pass temporary laws. While such laws are supposedly only for purposes of national security, more than a hundred temporary laws imposed new limits on free speech and freedom of assembly. The Penal Code was extended to encompass criticism of "friendly nations" like Israel and the United States. Some of the leaders of the Union of Professional Associations—particularly members of the Anti-Normalization (with Israel) Committee—were arrested for criticizing friendly nations and organizing demonstrations at the complex. The committee and its activities were declared illegal. Al-Jazeera reporters were detained by police and later expelled from Jordan for attempting to cover the protests. But the union leadership at that time was unintimidated and eager to maintain the main complex as a place for political dissent. In November 2001, a rally there expressed solidarity with the people of Afghanistan, despite having failed to receive the newly required protest permit. According to Abd al-Hadi Falahat, president of the union's governing council at the time, police approached him during his speech with orders to stop the event. "We went ahead with the rally [without a permit] because we believe we have the right to express our opinion on crucial matters," said Falahat.[77] But in the end, the police shut down the event.

In June 2002, I was present as police entered the complex and broke up an event that included a film and speakers expressing criticism of Jordan's peace treaty with Israel. Later that month another protest at the complex called for the boycott of Israeli and US products. This time, police used a new spatial tactic: they cordoned off the complex to prevent protesters from assembling; even those seeking to conduct routine business were prevented from entering until after 8:30 p.m.[78] The government formally banned the Anti-Normalization Committee in November 2002 for organizing unauthorized protests and posting blacklists of Jordanians conducting business with Israeli counterparts.[79] Then in spring 2003, the union repeatedly tried to organize events to express solidarity with Iraq as the US invasion loomed, but police mostly kept protesters from assembling. Finally, in March 2005, the government introduced a bill to Parliament that greatly restricted political freedoms, including a provision that the professional associations were not allowed to engage in political debate of any kind. In protest of that bill, numerous civil society groups organized sit-ins and demonstrations, including at the complex; police routinely broke up those events and arrested protesters.[80] Under state pressure, the union leadership grew increasingly accommodating of the government, particularly as new leadership was groomed and elected. The union continued to organize rallies at the complex, but primarily around issues that the regime supported, such as the May 31, 2010, rally honoring the fifty Jordanians who were on the Turkish-organized Freedom Flotilla that sought to deliver aid to Israeli-blockaded Gaza.

New Protest Spaces across Amman

With the relocation of major government buildings out of the downtown area, Amman's urban geography of protests shifted, and these new protest spaces developed their own spatial routines. People mounted protests on a space opposite the Parliament complex built in Abdali in the 1960s, particularly when the assembly was debating laws relating to elections, public gatherings, and other rights and freedoms. In 1997, for example, journalists protested there for weeks to demand that Parliament rescind restrictive changes to the press and publication law such as an increased capital requirement for newspapers and the monetary punishment for violations of the law. In 1999, another protest at the Parliament advocated for changing the laws that allowed for lenient sentences for some acts of violence against women.

Protesters also began to gather in front of other government offices. In 1996, a group demonstrated outside the court of cassation in support of judges who were inside striking against the detention of other judges and lawyers. Foreign embassies are also common sites of political demonstrations. And the Fourth Circle, an intersection of Zahran Street in West Amman, emerged as a frequent new place of protest, due to the location of the Prime Ministry directly on the circle. The first documented protest at the Fourth Circle was on March 13, 1990, when more than a hundred gathered to protest the dismissal of government employees for political reasons. In the 1990s and 2000s, the location was also a more (symbolically) safe space to engage in claim-making against the state. Given laws criminalizing direct criticism of the king, protesters mostly directed their claim-making toward the prime minister. In 1989 and 1996, for example, anti-austerity protesters gathered at the Fourth Circle, directing their outrage at the prime minister for pushing the IMF reforms through Parliament. As we will see, the Fourth Circle would become one of the most contentious places for protesting in the capital.

CONCLUSION

The case of Jordan illustrates how state-maintaining can work through techniques such as the distribution of material goods, the expansion of repressive capacities, and the advancement of a national narrative portraying challengers as outsiders. These techniques, however, can change the state's character. King Hussein's pivot to neoliberal reforms in the late 1980s threatened the Jordanization project, and the massive 1989 *Habbit Nisan* protests forced changes to the state to try to accommodate both neoliberalism and the maintenance of the regime's East Bank tribal support base. The retreat and return of protests over these decades demonstrate how claim-making and state responses to them shape state-maintaining. We also saw that Hussein's brief toleration of some protests gave way to efforts to constrain the expression of political dissent, with the state under Abdullah II moving quickly and harshly to silence political dissent—and not very successfully. Finally, we zoomed in from the national level to the scale of the capital city, seeing how urban growth altered the places and routines of protest in the built environment. In the next chapter we zoom in even closer, to examine the spatial and temporal routine of protests in a single space, the Kalouti Mosque in West Amman.

Chapter 5

AN ETHNOGRAPHY OF PLACE AND THE POLITICS OF ROUTINE PROTESTS

PROTESTS ARE MOUNTED IN SPACES THAT HAVE OTHER USES AND meanings, as the very purpose of protest is to disrupt the normal to attract attention for claim-making. Even sustained occupations are mounted in spaces that have other uses and meanings. Here an ethnography of place is illuminating. In addition to examining the materiality of a particular location and how it is structured (Henri Lefebvre's sense of abstract space), an ethnography of place explores how it is used, by whom, and what kind of place it is (concrete space, or "place")—its meanings, its history, its affective dynamics, its location in spatial imaginaries, and how it embodies and conveys different forms of power. Lived and embodied spaces are produced and reproduced through their daily usage as much as through the disruptions created during moments of protest. Building on Michel Foucault, Farha Ghannam argues that all spaces are heterotopic spaces, in that they have "changing uses, and meanings that could be invested in a particular space during certain times but that could be redefined and appropriated."[1] Attention to the rhythms and practices of spaces during nonprotest times—including their affective dimensions—can deepen our understanding of how protests alter those spaces.

Take the protests that begin at the Grand Husseini Mosque in downtown Amman. For more than a century, the mosque has been known as the go-to place for demonstrations in the capital. But the location has many other

128   CHAPTER 5

meanings and uses, and those have changed over time. For decades it was the center of commerce in the city as well as the site of government administrative offices. But as Amman expanded, those offices and many businesses relocated westward in diverse locations. As shown in map 9.1, upscale hotels, restaurants, and shopping areas also emerged in western neighborhoods, creating the new spatial imaginary of "West Amman" associated with affluence, government power, and global connections. The Royal Court and Municipal Complex are still located downtown, but the area gradually deteriorated into a low-end shopping and dining destination for the lower classes and tourists visiting historic sites like the Roman ruins. Now considered by some as part of impoverished "East Amman," the old city center is dusty, dirty, and loud. It has rhythms and energy that some find welcoming and lively, but that many West Amman residents avoid as trashy and dangerous.

How does understanding this atmosphere of the downtown area expand our understanding of protests there? For one thing, examining the rhythms and activities of the area in periods when there are no protests can help us understand precisely how protests disrupt those normal routines and how those disruptions are experienced. When a large demonstration has been announced to commence at the Grand Husseini Mosque, for example, shop owners and customers who arrive that morning may encounter police vehicles or barricades. Some people will choose to leave the area to avoid inconveniences caused by the protest—such as detours necessitated by crowds and closed streets—but others will go about their routines even as the police presence steadily increases over the next hours. The atmosphere is typically not one of anxious anticipation of violence, however, but of mild curiosity if not outright indifference. Shop owners do not rush to board up windows; indeed, many stay open throughout protests, perhaps even hoping the crowds might bring a spike in business (see fig. 4.1). Some downtown protests are exceptions, as the next chapter will show, but most are routine and even boring. This affective response to impending protests downtown tells us that people are accustomed to protests in that space, and that they expect both protesters and the police to follow a familiar and nonviolent routine.

This chapter examines routine protests as they are situated in the built environment. The scale of analysis zooms in on a single location, an area adjacent to the Kalouti Mosque in the affluent neighborhood of Rabia in West Amman.[2]

Built in the late 1990s, the mosque became a place for protest during the Second Intifada in 2000 because of the location's proximity to the Israeli embassy. After those first massive protests—thousands strong for months—the Kalouti protests over time developed their own spatial and temporal routine, mostly unfolding in a predictable manner and in an atmosphere lacking tension or anxious anticipation. What are the political effects of such routine protests, given their ritual character, the repetitiveness of their demands, and the fact that they are seldom disruptive? In this chapter, I first examine how protests become routine and why protesters often adhere to informal rules specific to a location. I then provide an overview of Palestinian solidarity protests in Jordan to establish patterns that bring the particularities of the Kalouti protests into focus. Next, I examine the spatial and temporal routine of protests at the Kalouti Mosque in the 2000s through an ethnography of place, including how protests, police, and those not protesting move in and across the area before, during, and after protests. Finally, I show that while protests make claims on authority structures, the spatial and temporal routines of certain protests can simultaneously work to shore up the regime's power.

RULES, ROUTINES, AND REPERTOIRES

In June 2009, I sat in a taxi on my way to a protest in West Amman, directing the driver to a nearby landmark without mentioning that a protest was my destination. As we sat ensnarled in traffic, the driver complained about political demonstrations causing congestion. This affective response of annoyance rather than nervousness reminded me of my time living in Washington, DC, when taxi drivers similarly complained about closed streets and slowed traffic caused by protests. It is surprising, however, that localized protests are as normal a part of the urban environment in Amman as they are in Washington, DC, because the Jordanian state is authoritarian. Protests in Jordan thus challenge scholarly assumptions about differences in the expression of political dissent between democratic and nondemocratic contexts.

That many Jordanians are astonished to learn how widespread protests are attests to their normalcy—most protests simply are not news. Many scholars are like Jordanians in this regard, in that they seem to take note of protests only when they are "big events" that hold the possibility of upending existing power structures. The Arab uprisings attracted such attention not only because of the spectacle of massive demonstrations in multiple countries simultaneously but also because they brought down regimes and sent others scrambling to survive. As the alternately outraged and elated masses in multiple countries asserted their collective agency, they created the kind of moments in which new worlds suddenly seem possible, even within reach.[3] But such "eventful" moments are relatively rare.[4] Most protests hold little possibility of realizing the claims they are making, if they register at all. Indeed, as Dina Bishara shows, states may entirely ignore protests to deflate their impact.[5]

Outside of rare eventful moments, most protests are shaped by established repertoires, the known forms of protest and the kinds of police responses they will likely elicit. The informal rules of these repertoires can be violated, of course, albeit typically with greater consequences for protesters than for the police.[6] Indeed, repertoires evolve precisely because participants—police as well as protesters—innovate or test red lines. As Sidney Tarrow argues, even the rare eventful moments do not immediately change the established protest repertoire, but they "contribute to its evolution through the dynamic evolution of larger cycles of mobilization in which the innovations in collective action that they produce are diffused, tested, and refined in adumbrated form and eventually become part of the protest repertoire."[7]

The "rules" of the repertoire can also differ depending on who is protesting—whether they are known activists, political elite, first-time protesters, laborers, or members of a prominent family or tribe, to give just a few examples. Environmental activist Basel Burgan, for example, has been harassed for years for his leading role in the campaign against nuclear power in Jordan. But, as he bluntly put it, he has no leverage to pressure the regime to stop harassing him because he is "from a shit Christian tribe" that holds little political influence.[8] Meanwhile, outspoken critics such as Parliament member Hind al-Fayiz (from both the powerful Fayiz family and the Bani Sakhr tribal confederation) routinely push boundaries and criticize the regime.[9] And the informal rules are not only discursive but also spatial and temporal; red lines are drawn not only around what can be said and done and by whom, but also where one can do it and for how long. In this sense, spaces in which protests are repeatedly mounted develop spatial routines specific to them, even as they are instances of more general events such as a "march."

Protests at the Kalouti Mosque are ideal for a theorization of the spatial and temporal dimensions of routine protests. How did these protests become routine? What are the spatial and temporal dimensions of that routine, and what are the red lines whose crossing might invite escalated repression? How can an ethnography of place at the Kalouti protests help us understand the atmosphere and disruptive potential of the Kalouti protest routine? The next section locates the Kalouti protests within a nationwide geography of protest against Israel and in solidarity with the Palestinian struggle before turning to the Kalouti protests themselves.

ANTINORMALIZATION AND PALESTINIAN SOLIDARITY PROTESTS

Palestinian solidarity protests are among the largest nationwide mobilizations in Jordan. They first emerged in the 1930s with the Palestinian Revolts and continued through the 1970–71 Black September period. While East Bankers have divergent views about the proper place in Jordan for citizens of Palestinian descent, most Jordanians are critical of Israel, sympathetic to the Palestinian struggle, and supportive of an independent Palestinian state. With the outbreak of the first Palestinian Intifada in December 1987, large-scale demonstrations erupted across the country despite a ban on public gatherings under martial law. The leadership of the Union of Professional Associations—at the time in the pocket of the regime to root out leftist or Arab nationalist activism—mounted numerous strikes and demonstrations in support of the uprising. They formed the Committee for the Support of the Palestinian Uprising and hung banners on the Professional Associations Complex's exterior walls, widely visible to the busy thoroughfare and adjacent commercial district of upscale Shmeisani.

Palestinian solidarity protests continued sporadically for the next two years, marking a gradual return of street politics that would explode with the 1989 *Habbit Nisan* protests. In December 1989, nationwide demonstrations marked the second anniversary of the Intifada, with major road blockades and large-scale turnout. A few months later, on April 13, 1990, at least five hundred protested outside of the US embassy against Israel's efforts to disperse a peaceful protest in Jerusalem. A month later, however, on May 14, police dispersed thousands of protesters who had joined Jordan's first large-scale (Palestinian) Right of Return march from Amman and Baqa'a Camp (northwest of Amman) to the Allenby/Hussein Bridge in the Jordan Valley—then the only land crossing into the West Bank and one closed to civilian traffic. Protests continued across Jordan through early summer, with large demonstrations in Amman, Irbid, and Baqaʻa Camp, where police killed two Palestinian protesters on May 22. At least one additional protester was killed in the coming weeks.[10]

In the months before Jordan signed the Wadi Araba peace treaty with Israel in October 1994, protesters in Amman assembled at the Parliament, the Grand Husseini Mosque, and the Professional Associations Complex. Smaller protests took place in the outer governorates, including in Karak, Tafileh, and Maʻan. Islamists, leftists, and Arab nationalist figures from various political parties formed an antinormalization movement called the Popular Arab Jordanian Committee for Resisting Submission and Normalization.[11] Former prime minister and General Intelligence Directorate (*mukhabarat*) head Ahmad Obaydat joined the executive committee, and another former prime minister, Taher Masri, publicly expressed support. While Masri is of Palestinian descent, he is usually seen as a regime loyalist; Obaydat hails from a powerful East Bank tribal family. Support for the committee from such powerful regime loyalists initially provided some political cover for its provocative activities.

The committee first focused on boycotts of Israeli and US goods rather than protests. By 1996, however, antinormalization demonstrations at the Professional Associations Complex and elsewhere were common. The Union of Professional Associations even tried to expel any member who did not oppose normalization, but many members complained that expulsion went too far.[12] In January 1997, the committee organized a protest against the first Jordanian-Israeli trade fair, at the Marj al-Hamam convention center just outside Amman. Thousands turned out for demonstrations over several days, effectively shutting down the grand opening despite police use of water cannons and dogs to disperse the protesters.[13] With the outbreak of the Second Intifada in fall 2000, massive protests again broke out nationwide, with at least two protesters killed in clashes with the police.[14] In Amman, more than ten thousand gathered at the Grand Husseini Mosque and numerous other locations (including the Kalouti Mosque), blocking major intersections and bringing the city to a standstill. Outside of the capital, protesters occupied central squares and blocked roads, including in Maʻan, Karak, Ghor Safi, Irbid, and in the refugee camps; students mounted demonstrations on their campuses. Many protests ended with the singing of *Mawtini* (My Homeland)[15]—a sort of unofficial Palestinian national anthem. *Mawtini* is sung at protests across the Arab world, and in Jordan particularly at Palestine-related protests. It is taught in Jordan's public schools as a patriotic reference to the Hashemites' role in the Great Arab Revolt and is often sung by students daily following the national anthem.[16]

The Second Intifada protests peaked in October 2000, when the government reported 203 marches and 73 demonstrations in a single week.[17] The antinormalization committee announced more boycotts of US and Israeli products, tossing those goods, along with Israeli and US flags, into bonfires at demonstrations. At the complex, committee members painted an Israeli flag on the floor so that anyone entering would have to walk on it. Protests continued for three months, with one sit-in in Ma'an lasting at least ten days in December. When police arrested many of those protesters, other Ma'anis mounted sit-ins against the detentions. They set up a tent opposite the local courthouse where the detained were being held, and they returned daily for more than a week.

While Palestinian solidarity and antinormalization sentiments were high, Jordanians were divided about blacklists. Some expressed concern that the lists could unfairly punish Jordanians who were forced to deal with Israel in the course of their jobs. But the committee posted names at the complex anyway, and those listed suffered threats and physical attacks. After someone on the list was killed in Amman, public opinion turned against the blacklists. The regime used that shift in public mood to move against the committee, and in the next weeks arrested at least twenty activists, including seven executive committee members.[18] When six activists and human rights advocates from Amman attempted to join the Ma'an sit-in for a solidarity *iftar* (the sunset meal for breaking the fast during the holy month of Ramadan), the army and police stopped their vehicle just south of Amman, put guns to the heads of three of them, and then arrested all six.[19]

Some eighteen months later, nationwide demonstrations again erupted when Israel launched Operation Defensive Shield, which lasted from March 29 to May 3, 2002.[20] In Amman, some ten thousand gathered in multiple locations on seven consecutive Friday afternoons, and armored vehicles occupied intersections. In June, activists planned to have artists paint large pro-Palestinian solidarity posters in a vacant lot on Gardens Street in West Amman, in hopes of attracting the attention of passersby without mounting an event the government would find contentious. Even that event was prevented (see chap. 8).

This partial overview of Palestinian solidarity protests establishes two points that will help us understand the Kalouti protests and the regime's response to them. First, Palestinian solidarity as well as opposition to the peace treaty is widespread, including among many East Bank Jordanians. The regime's manipulation of the electoral law before the November 1993 parliamentary elections succeeded in returning sufficient proregime votes to pass the peace treaty in 1994, but solidarity with Palestinians against Israel remains a uniting issue. Each new Israeli military campaign brings large crowds to the streets, as it did again from December 27, 2008, to January 18, 2009, when Israel's brutal siege of Gaza, Operation Cast Lead, killed 1,400 Palestinians. Second, the regime unevenly represses antinormalization and Palestinian solidarity protests. It allows protests in some locations and at certain times while violently dispersing others. At times, it even encourages protests against Israeli actions when politically expedient. The regime's sensitivity to criticism over its relations with Israel also shapes police responses to protests. When public opinion against the blacklists and boycotts increased in spring 2000, for example, it used the opportunity to arrest antinormalization activists and break up their protests. But at the 2009 protests at the Kalouti Mosque, it used violence to disperse the protesters.[21]

The next section turns to the Kalouti protests, organized by antinormalization activists throughout the 2000s. After the Second Intifada in 2000 and Operation Defensive Shield in 2002, protester turnout at that location diminished from thousands to sometimes only a few dozen. The protests developed their own routine, specific to the spatial configuration of the location and with informal red lines or rules limiting how far protesters could go before inviting repression. Those limits were discursive (do not criticize the king), spatial (do not deviate from the protests' spatial routine), and temporal (do not attempt to establish an ongoing encampment—a tactic discussed in chap. 7).

THE KALOUTI PROTESTS

The Kalouti Mosque is located in the affluent neighborhood of Rabia, part of the spatial imaginary of affluent West Amman. It has wider and cleaner streets and intersections than much of East Amman, and they are lined with newer model cars. The immediate area around the Kalouti Mosque is a mix of mostly four-story apartment buildings with some businesses and office buildings. A large lot just north of the mosque is largely vacant save for a few garden plots of cabbage. The lot is not entirely flat, with the north and east portions leading uphill. A small convenience store abuts the north end. The mosque is located at the bottom of a hill near the busy intersection of Ahmad Suleiman al-Najdawi Street and Omar bin Abd al-Aziz Street— the latter known locally as "the street that leads to the Zionist embassy." The latter road, which has a concrete median dividing traffic, does not, however, lead to the Israeli embassy. Heading northeast from the Kalouti intersection and past the vacant lot, the road curves to the right and up a steep hill. The Israeli embassy is located several blocks north, reachable by turning left onto one of the smaller roads that are often blockaded during larger protests.

With the Israeli embassy about a half-mile away, the newly constructed Kalouti Mosque emerged as a new location for protests during the Second Intifada in 2000. The mosque itself played no facilitating role in the area's association with antinormalization protests; it was merely a landmark for those traveling from areas outside of the Rabia neighborhood. It is worth stressing, too, that the Kalouti protests are not necessarily "Islamist," as adopting the mosque's name might imply; protests at the Grand Husseini Mosque, similarly, are not necessarily Islamist in substance or composition (although some are). Place-making at Kalouti protests is exclusively about Israeli-Palestinian issues; there is no other reason to protest there.

During the Second Intifada, thousands came for months to Kalouti protests. Teachers brought students from nearby schools, while activists, political parties, the Muslim Brotherhood, and the antinormalization committee rallied their followers to turn out. During those protests and again during the seven weeks of Operation Defensive Shield in April 2002, some of the protesters called for the crowds to march on the Israeli embassy, and many pushed up the street in its direction. They were stopped by riot police blocking their path, and the police arrested hundreds. Most of those arrested were taken to police stations several kilometers away, where they were detained and released hours later; others were held in administrative detention for up to two weeks, often without being charged.[22] This spatial and temporal technique of policing

CHAPTER 5

worked to separate known activists from the crowds and each other, scattering them across the city and detaining them until the protests had died down.

Although large-scale protests waned by summer 2002, the antinormalization committee, oppositional political parties, and some independent activists continued mounting protests at the site over the next years. They announced protests as "marches on the Israeli embassy" and used Union of Professional Associations text messaging lists to notify tens of thousands of members. Most often, however, only a few hundred turned out. Regular participants included the Jordanian Communist Party, the leftist Jordanian Democratic Popular Unity Party,[23] the Muslim Brotherhood, and the Islamic Action Front Party. Opposition figures like Layth Shubaylat also occasionally turned up. Many of the elected leaders of the professional associations were also Islamists, so their coordination with the union around antinormalization came easily.

An Ethnography of Place of the Kalouti Routine

Conventional accounts of protest focus on the details of the event itself, particularly the actions and interactions of the protesters and police. These details are essential for theorizing about protests, but they present an incomplete picture. An ethnographic account, by comparison, aims to also capture affective dimensions such as the mood of the crowd, the level of hostility of the police, when the atmosphere changed and why, and of course what the various actors make of the events themselves. An ethnography of place, as discussed above, further considers the materiality of a particular space, how it is used and by whom both during and between protests. It seeks to reveal a place's meanings, affective dynamics, location in spatial imaginaries, and how it embodies and conveys different forms of power. The following ethnography describes the spatial and temporal routine of Kalouti protests during much of the 2000s, constructed not from a single protest but from nearly two dozen. It begins well before protesters assemble in order to assess to what extent the protests disrupt the area's other rhythms and how those in the vicinity anticipate and experience the protests. The photos are from a single protest on June 2, 2010.

The intersection near the Kalouti Mosque is often congested with traffic, particularly when everyone is trying to get home around lunchtime. On days of announced protests, some state security vehicles move into place in the morning, but they do not otherwise affect normal activities, nor do pedestrians avoid walking near them. The atmosphere remains relaxed and casual as protesters begin to assemble. Some people exit the mosque after prayer and gather next to the mosque and on the adjacent field, milling around and chatting. But most of the protesters do not reside in the area and thus also do not regularly pray at that mosque. In this sense, the Kalouti protests are not predominantly "local" protests of people living in the Rabia neighborhood. These are destination protests, much like those at the Grand Husseini Mosque.

Multiple branches of Jordan's security forces are present, and in numbers that well exceed those of the protesters. The Public Security Directorate (police) handles most of the routine policing in Jordan (at least until the late 2000s) and is always present at protests. As protesters gather, the police cluster in groups of two or three and stand off to the side or across the street, at times conferring with other forces present. They sometimes interact with protesters, seemingly familiar with those like the leaders of the Muslim Brotherhood and Islamic Action Front. During one Kalouti protest, a police officer told me that they watched known activists and party leaders to assess the mood of the crowd, the level of tension, and whether it was increasing.[24]

The second security forces, and the ones who will most directly engage the protesters, are the riot police, who were originally a division of the Public Security Directorate.[25] In 2008, the Interior Ministry created Jordan's gendarmerie (*quwat al-darak*) following disputes between East Bank tribal leaders and military leaders. Police from the Public Security Directorate sometimes express frustration with the gendarmerie, which they feel can escalate tensions at protests. The gendarmerie's riot gear, military style, and distinct armored vehicles convey an ominous warning that it is prepared to use force if any red lines are crossed. At the Kalouti protests, the gendarmerie stations its forces in two locations. The first is opposite the field, near the far end from the mosque in the direction of the embassy. Most of the gendarmerie troops are clad in riot gear, but they are directed by uniformed officers without helmets or shields. As protesters assemble, these troops move to the sidewalk on the west side of the road, across from the field. Some leave their helmet shields raised and hold their shields casually, even as the protests get underway. A second contingent of gendarmerie is stationed on the far side of the field, clustering up a hill on a road, with some eight to ten or more armored vehicles. They also present a menacing image, even at a distance from the protesters.

A car or van pulls into the mosque parking lot, and three or four people unload a dozen green Muslim Brotherhood flags. Leftists arrive with the red flags of the Unity party and the Communist Party. Protesters gather in various locations—near the mosque, on the sidewalks, in the vacant lot. They look for and chat with friends. More people arrive carrying Palestinian flags and, less commonly, Jordanian flags; placards and banners might be hand drawn or printed. After about an hour, someone from the Islamist camp begins reciting passages from the Quran and leading a prayer over an amplifier. Some of the leftists start a call and response, antagonistically shouting over the Quranic recitation or prayer. On some occasions, younger Brotherhood supporters get into fights with leftists chanting over the prayers, with shouting escalating to shoving and even punching. After the prayers, the Islamist contingent gradually joins the other protesters toward the west side of the field and eastern edge of the street. The protesters come together into a single assemblage for a period, visible by the mingling of red and green flags from the different political parties. On some occasions, the Islamist and leftist camps remain distinct, even if immediately adjacent to each other.

Gradually, the assemblage moves off the curb and into the street. As more bodies join, some step out in front of oncoming vehicles, blocking traffic and launching a chorus of horn honking. Police officers assist angry drivers in backing out of the area. Some protesters wear the black-and-white keffiyeh symbolizing Palestinian nationalism and resistance; a few cover their faces "Hamas-style" (as one protester described it to me)—with only the eyes visible—while most drape the scarves around the neck. A few protesters wear the red-and-white checkered scarf that in Jordan symbolizes Transjordanian or East Bank identity, but far fewer than at protests about domestic issues. Some women are dressed in conservative Muslim attire, such as a loose *jilbab* robe and a hijab; some cover their faces to reveal only the eyes. Other women wear jeans and t-shirts, with no head covering. Women are a considerable and diverse contingent, from 10 to 30 percent of the crowd. Most men wear slacks and button shirts; a few wear graphic t-shirts with images such as the Marxist revolutionary Che Guevara or musicians whose lyrics convey progressive political messages, such as Bob Marley, Green Day, and Rage Against the Machine. Bystanders can sometimes exceed the numbers of protesters, and those who linger are mostly men.

FIGURE 5.1. Protesters with the flags of Islamist and leftist political parties mixed as the street is partly blocked to traffic and onlookers stand on the median to watch. Source: Jillian Schwedler.

Once the protesters move into the street, the gendarmerie troops begin to assemble in the road, donning helmets and standing shoulder to shoulder. The timing is important to the routine, signaling that the various police present know that the protesters are not going to come at them quickly. Two or three gendarmerie officers move around the line giving orders. The gendarmerie line assembles in approximately the same spot at every protest, perpendicular to the building marked "114" with the city's bright blue building numbers. But this "march on the Zionist embassy" is not at all a march. The protesters are mostly stationary, with people facing inward toward whoever is leading call and response. Protesters also mill about and move in and out of the protest, at times joining chants and at other times chatting with friends. The chanting is not always unified, although some chants dominate for a while until others rise up. A dozen or more journalists and photographers move through the crowd as well as stand on the street's median, monitoring the protest and its progress.

In 2008, several leftist activists pointed out to me that the Islamists always leave after about an hour, a pattern I saw repeated. "Watch the green flags disappear, the Brothers are afraid of actually confronting the police," said one. Independent and leftist activists have long criticized Islamists as co-opted or else afraid of real confrontation with the regime. One leading organizer of the Kalouti protests noted, too, that the Islamists also brought a photographer to document their participation in protests.[26] Indeed, the pages of the Islamist paper *Al-Sabeel* feature images of Islamists at protests, with articles extolling their courage and commitment without mentioning their early departure.

In 2003, Islamic Action Front leader Hamzah Mansour offered a different explanation. He told me that the Front and the Brotherhood viewed advocating on behalf of the Palestinian cause as among their core missions. To that end, they regularly worked with other political parties on related events and were active in the antinormalization campaign. But they avoided confronting security forces during protests because they feared instigators who sought to give the police a reason to respond harshly or to later blame the Islamists for any violence or property damage. As discussed in the next chapter, his fears were not unwarranted. The kind of thugs Mansour was referencing are now known as *baltajiyya*, but that term was not yet used in Jordan in 2003. Mansour called them instigators (*muharideen*). "When we see people that we do not know," he said, "we are concerned that they will try to disrupt the event by throwing stones or damaging property."[27] Thus while leftists see the Islamists' caution as evidence of their unwillingness to really challenge the regime, Islamist leaders see it as a tactic for protecting their reputation as peaceful opposition.

Back at the Kalouti protest, the chants stop while a speaker articulates the protesters' demands and grievances through a bullhorn. These speeches can last a few minutes or more than half an hour. Then chanting resumes and the crowd inches slowly up the street. During this entire period, people walk in and out of the protest—journalists, foreign observers, and even protesters themselves. It is as if the Kalouti routine has an established performance "stage" (defined by the chanting crowd in the street) while everywhere else is "offstage." The police and gendarmerie appear concerned only with what happens in the assemblage itself, "onstage"; even known activists and party leaders are of little interest when they depart from the crowd.

FIGURE 5.2. View from behind the gendarmerie line shows the "on stage" part of the protest and the ability to easily walk in and out of the crowd. Source: Jillian Schwedler.

The protest thins considerably with the departure of the Islamists. As the distance between the protest and the gendarmerie gradually decreases, women move to the front and take the lead in the chants. One female activist told me that this tactic allowed them to direct their grievances directly at the security forces while reducing the likelihood that their actions would be met with force because photographers could capture images of troops beating women.[28] This confrontation is the only tense moment of the afternoon, with protesters addressing the gendarmerie directly, accusing them of defending Zionist authorities and thereby betraying their brethren. But even at this juncture, one can easily walk out of the crowd and move around and behind the gendarmerie line; one seems to be marked as a "protester" only when actively participating with the crowd in the street. The protesters do not attempt to push past the gendarmerie line; the march is purely symbolic. This confrontation, the penultimate stage in the protest, can continue for thirty to ninety minutes, depending on the size and energy of the crowd.

FIGURE 5.3. Women in the "march" move to confront the gendarmerie. Source: Jillian Schwedler.

Most Kalouti protests end with the singing of *Mawtini*, the patriotic Arab nationalist song. Eventually a car is successful in nudging the thinning crowd to the side so it can pass. The remaining protesters step back onto the sidewalk and the protest is over. As people disperse, some hang off to the side and talk. Others return to their cars or flag a taxi, heading home or else planning to meet later. The police and gendarmerie gradually disperse as well, although the last troops do not depart until well after the last protester has departed. Long before then, however, the rhythms of the immediate area return to normal.

The temporal and spatial routine of these smaller Kalouti protests is not particularly contentious or disruptive. The biggest effect on the atmosphere and activities of the location is the blocking of vehicular traffic and the anger and frustration of the drivers whose path is blocked by the protest. But all other activities continue, and passersby do not seem concerned that either the protesters or the police and gendarmerie will resort to violence, even when they are face to face. Pedestrians move up and down the sidewalks just as they did before the protest began, and the cashier from the convenience store—which is only a few meters from the gendarmerie line—sometimes stands at the door to watch when he is not serving a customer.

CONTENTIOUS PERFORMANCES AND BREAKING ROUTINE

Not all protests are contentious, or contentious in the same ways. Protests that cross known red lines, deviate from the established rules, or call for upending the existing structures of power are *transgressive*; those that seek a specific policy change without calling for the overthrow of those in power—even if the demand is as significant as canceling a peace treaty—are *nontransgressive*.[29] Except for the largest mobilizations during Israeli military campaigns into occupied Palestinian areas, the Kalouti protests are nontransgressive, with protesters and police largely adhering to the known spatial and temporal routine. Protesters assemble in their expected location with security services already present; leftists shout over the Islamists' prayers; the assembly moves onto the street; the gendarmerie lines up to block the path up the road; the Islamists depart; the protesters begin to move toward the gendarmerie; women move to the front; the remaining protesters continue chanting for some period after reaching the gendarmerie line; the protesters sing *Mawtini* before departing; and the rhythms of the area return to normal as protesters and then security forces depart.

The routine and its rules appear known to all; even bystanders appear unconcerned, stopping only occasionally to watch or take a photo. These rules are written collectively over time. At the first large-scale protests from 2000 through 2002, some of the crowd did hope to march on the Israeli embassy. But as the numbers of protesters decreased and then dwindled, the remaining activists reproduced the spatial patterns of the larger protests—gathering at the vacant lot, moving into the street, and then pressing up the street toward the embassy. With smaller numbers, however, they had little hope of pushing past the line and so they no longer even tried; the confrontation became purely symbolic. The Kalouti protesters understood that if they deviated from routine, they risked severe repression. As one activist put it to me (in English), the police would "beat the shit out of us" if they tried to push past their line.[30] In adhering to the spatial and temporal regime, the protesters as well as the police worked to reproduce it.

But innovations are always possible, on both sides, although deviations from routine tend to hold greater risk for protesters than for the police. The

144   CHAPTER 5

greatest opportunity for innovation by protesters comes from numbers—when crowds swell from fifty to hundreds or even thousands. During Israel's brutal 2008 Operation Cast Lead, for example, Israeli forces bombarded Gaza and killed some 1,200 to 1,400 Palestinians.[31] Thousands of Jordanians took to the streets for nationwide demonstrations for much of the campaign, which lasted from December 27, 2008, until January 18, 2009. At the Kalouti site, protesters established an encampment, erecting tents with many remaining at the site overnight, only to see the crowds swell again the next day. Activists created a "graveyard" with tombstones symbolizing the death toll. On Friday, January 9, 2009, larger than usual crowds gathered in the afternoon, and the gendarmerie tried to keep the protesters off the streets and contain them on the lot. As many as a thousand turned out, chanting and periodically charging but not breaking the gendarmerie line. Some threw objects at the gendarmerie—including small rocks and at least one shoe[32]—and others burned an Israeli flag to great cheering. Some demonstrators even shot firearms into the air in front of the gendarmerie line.[33] This was not routine, on either side, and the gendarmerie violently broke up the protest that night. It is worth quoting at length an account of the events detailed in the progressive online magazine, *7iber* (*hiber*, or "ink"), because it describes well the contest over space as well as the atmosphere:

> The event seemed like a game of cat and mouse. The protesters would push forward, and the police would push back . . . [until] protesters and police collided one too many times. Tear gas was the velvet curtain descending, as protesters scattered out of harm's way. People were chased down the main road and past the side streets. Within minutes, this section of the Rabia district was quarantined, with police at every corner, blocking paths of entry. Within the hour, water cannons were unleashed on the tents of the main protest site that had occupied the space behind the Kalouti Mosque for over ten days.
>
> Tear gas canisters rolled down the streets and the cold wind blew their smoke in every direction. Protesters took to the side streets, approaching the main road every so often before fleeing once again at the sight of the police. Protesters continued to linger in the area, while many fled the district entirely. In the end, the police had moved their trucks in to the tent-area, with the municipal workers brought in to sweep the streets as well as throw the tents, and

the Styrofoam tombstones that had been based there for days, all in the garbage. Everything was swept away in an instant.[34]

The massive assembly empowered the crowd, with the usual Islamists, leftist parties, and antinormalization activists far outnumbered by "average" Jordanians of both Palestinian and East Bank descent—that is, those who were not otherwise politically organized. Did they know or care about the established routine? Those who brought and fired weapons were not among the usual activists, but they, too, broke from routine. People also remained on the site for more than a week in a tent encampment. As the next chapter shows, these protests came as other protests were escalating nationwide, including among the East Bank tribal communities central to regime support.

After the Israeli incursion ended in mid-January, crowds at subsequent Kalouti protests diminished again to a hundred or so. Both the police and protesters largely returned to the established routine—until the police itself introduced an innovation. During a protest on June 2, 2010, events largely unfolded according to the established spatial and temporal routine. But as the protesters inched closer to the line of gendarmerie blocking the road, a group of men entered the street and began talking to the gendarmerie officers in charge. These men were what are known as *baltajiyya*—either plainclothes officers or else regime loyalists—and this was the first time they had appeared at a Kalouti protest. After a few of them spoke with the gendarmerie officers, they clasped hands and stood shoulder to shoulder, forming a tight second line with their backs to the gendarmerie and facing the protest assemblage. They glared menacingly at anyone who approached, including those (like myself) who were photographing them. One protester affiliated with the leftist Unity party surmised that this new line was intended to give the gendarmerie cover if things turned violent. Although violence did not escalate that day, we will see how plainclothes loyalists and counterprotesters often seek to violently disperse peaceful protesters. Their appearance instantly changes the atmosphere regardless of location, heightening the tension and leaving protesters to confer about their next moves.

Therefore, routines specific to individual protest spaces are likewise shaped by protest and policing practices at larger scales. As *baltajiyya* emerged with greater frequency at other protests, for example, new spatial patterns of protest policing emerged, and not all of them mundane. In some instances, these

FIGURE 5.4. Plainclothes *baltajiyya* line up in front of the gendarmerie, with one clearly unhappy that I was taking photos. Source: Jillian Schwedler.

plainclothes thugs work in tandem with the police and gendarmerie, while in other instances the police strive to separate them as counterprotesters. The key issue here is that certain spaces develop their own protest routines, and that established routines at places like the Kalouti Mosque are produced and reproduced through the actions of both the police and protesters, and those routines are always subject to innovation.

THE WORK OF ROUTINE PROTESTS

Given that routine protests have repetitive demands, are ritual in character, and are seldom disruptive, what are their political effects? I argue that even highly routinized, nontransgressive protests can have political effects in at least five ways. First, routine protests are a form of place-making that ensures that certain locations in the built environment will be associated with dissent—spaces where protests have been held in the past and *will likely be held in the future.* And individual spaces can be associated with specific issues. The Kalouti Mosque became associated with protests relating to Israel, the Parliament with legislation, the Fourth Circle with the Prime Ministry, and so on. The Grand Husseini Mosque is a generic protest location, not associated with any particular issue.

Second, routine protests can work to *maintain* access to certain spaces, places where demonstrations are known to be tolerated so long as they adhere to the established routine. The routine must be maintained through practice— that is, if protesters stopped protesting, restarting them in the future could prove more difficult because the regime might have less confidence that they would be contained by an established routine. Nontransgressive protests thus keep open the possibility of transgressive contention in the future, as the place-making around routine protests ensures that people know where to go in the event that they want to collectively assemble to express dissent.

Third, routine protests can affect public political discourse by putting or keeping issues active in public debate. In this sense, the objective is not only successful claim-making (e.g., cancel the peace treaty), but also to ensure that an issue is taken up or continues to be discussed. One antinormalization activist, for example, said that the Kalouti protests were aimed both at demonstrating and sustaining public opposition to the normalization of Jordan's relations with Israel. Given that the regime considers the peace treaty as nonnegotiable, opposing the treaty is contentious even if the protests are not. Indeed, as Paola Rivetti shows, activists often engage in protests with little expectation of realizing their demands; rather, those protests help activists show others that alternative possible futures can be imagined; we need only wait for the right opportunity to realize them.[35]

Fourth, routine protests can convey information to different audiences. Islamists at the Kalouti protests, for example, focused on demonstrating their support for the Palestinian movement and opposition to Israel and the peace treaty, but without really challenging the regime. Their performance is directed largely at their own constituents, by way of the extensive coverage in the Islamist newspaper *al-Sabeel.* That coverage never mentions their early departure from protests or their efforts to avoid transgressive protests. But the timing of their departure also signals to the regime their wish to avoid antagonizing the regime. This tactic is demonstrated, too, by Islamists' preference for holding their own protests at the Grand Husseini Mosque downtown, even providing their own parade guard.

And, fifth, routine protests can also do political work for the regime. They produce tangible "evidence" for domestic and international audiences of Jordan's declared commitment to democratization; protests index freedom of speech and assembly. King Abdullah II routinely boasts that Jordan is a moderate regime working to implement democratic reforms, while in practice political freedoms have steadily declined since the early 1990s. Protests in which the security forces do not use violence or attempt to disperse those assembled allow the regime to perform its own tolerance of political dissent. Particularly in the capital, where foreign audiences are present, most protest policing is far less violent than in the rebellious East Bank towns, where protests also more commonly include the destruction of government property and the blocking of major transportation routes. Police in the capital make no efforts to stop photographers from documenting routine protests, as those photos provide evidence of their restraint as they circulate in other spaces. With the innovation of the of *baltajiyya*, violence against peaceful protesters might also be plausibly attributed to private individuals acting on their own— despite obvious coordination with the gendarmerie. Finally, scholars have long shown how governments can gain valuable information by monitoring protest activity, particularly changes in their size, participants, claim-making, locations, and intensity. With the routine Kalouti protests seldom numbering more than a hundred, any escalation provides valuable information about the broader atmosphere of political dissent to both the regime and those organizing protests.

CONCLUSION

This chapter began by urging scholars to consider protests not as events but as sets of behaviors in material spaces that embody meaning through their routine practices as much as their disruptions. Locating protests in the built environment brings into view the materiality of a particular location as well as its meanings, history, affective dynamics, location in spatial imaginaries, and how it embodies and conveys different forms of power. Focusing on protests in a single location—at the Kalouti Mosque in West Amman—I have shown how lived and embodied spaces are produced and reproduced as much through their daily usage as through disruptions created during protests. Examining the rhythms and practices during both protest and nonprotest times—including their affective dimensions—can deepen our understanding of how protests alter those spaces.

Routine protests come into view not as events that either succeed or fail to achieve their goals but as repeat encounters among police, protesters, and others living in and traversing the material spaces in which protests take place. Those encounters have political effects, and they can do different kinds of political work. Understanding the landscape of routine protests in a case like Jordan can also help us make better sense of more eventful moments, like those examined in the next chapter.

Chapter 6

JORDAN IN THE TIME OF THE ARAB UPRISINGS

REPERTOIRES OF PROTEST AND REPRESSION STRUCTURE PROTESTS because they give everyone some idea of what to expect, even if those expectations are not always met. Few protests entail the kind of eventful moments when everything seems up for grabs. The period of the Arab uprisings in 2011 was such an eventful moment, made more shocking because mobilization happened on a regional scale and brought down several long-standing authoritarian regimes. As regimes flailed about in response to the unprecedented scale of protests happening simultaneously across the region, citizens toggled between rage at the regime and elation at their power in numbers. How are we to understand repertoires and routines during such exceptional periods? What innovations emerged to the established repertoires? Why did Jordan's protests during this period not escalate to revolutionary levels (or did they?), despite having a far richer history of protest mobilization than most authoritarian regimes? How does attention to space, geography, and competing historical narratives help us to better answer these questions?

The preceding chapters together suggest that to fully understand the meanings and dynamics of the protests during the Arab uprisings of 2011, we need to consider three factors, all of which entail attention to spatial and temporal dimensions. First, the uprising protests need to be situated historically within each state as well as regionally, with particular attention to established techniques for state-maintaining and repertoires for protest and repression. Histories of protests and how they are remembered also matter, as do different communities' self-understandings as rebellious or quiescent. Knowing these histories and their patterns enables us to recognize innovations on all sides. Although individual states have their own histories, those histories are also connected to regional and global histories, structures, and processes, as we saw with Jordan's colonial state-making project. People also have complex affective attachments within and beyond the territorial state, and those attachments and the spatial imaginaries they invoke shape the actions of protesters as well as states responding to them.

Second, we have already seen how even routine protests are implicated in state-maintaining, but eventful protests are even more so because repertoires for protest and repression may rapidly change when regime survival is at stake. Decisions about how to deploy state violence or accommodation in response to protests have long-term consequences for the composition and exercise of state power. As with historical anchoring, we also need to resist the impulse to draw quick conclusions about what the uprisings meant or what they accomplished in their apparent aftermath—"apparent" because "end points" can be analytically elusive and empirically deceiving. Life-cycle temporalities abstract the uprising period from longer historical anchoring, disconnecting them from earlier periods and obscuring diverse forms of contention that continue after the largest crowds have dissipated.

Third, we can learn a lot from the kind of ethnography of place explored in chapter 5, focusing our attention not only on the size, location, and composition of protests but also on atmospheric dynamics at the local, national, and regional scales.[1] The affective dimensions of protests not only help explain the actions of protesters and state actors, they also can help us identify, for example, when small protests are contentious and large-scale mobilizations are not. For Jordan, attention to the content and affective dimensions of claim-making reveal how seemingly conservative and nonrevolutionary claims—calls for reform and not the fall of the regime—can also be the source of the greatest threats to Hashemite authority.

The remainder of this chapter is organized as follows. I first present an overview of the multisectoral protests that emerged in the five years before the uprising period alongside growing grievances within some East Bank tribal communities. The bulk of the chapter examines nearly two years of protests during the Arab uprising period of 2011–12 under five prime ministers, along with counterprotester violence and regime efforts to quash dissent and divide the movements. I draw attention to innovations in the repertoires of both protests and repression, including the evolution of established spatial routines in specific locations. I move between local, national, and regional scales, showing how local protests and the regional uprisings (and their spatial dynamics) together coproduced Jordan's uprising at the national scale. Finally, I examine the political implications of escalating rhetoric against the regime and the increasing willingness of some East Bank tribal communities to publicly criticize the king. The overall analysis offers a corrective to political scientists who are fixated on questions of success and failure; instead it attunes us to ongoing processes of protest and what meanings they hold for those witnessing or participating in them. Jordan also undercuts much of the social movement literature's orientation toward life-cycle analysis of waves of protest by showing us how that temporality obscures subnational variation, affective connections across time and space, and everyday experiences of contention.

LABOR PROTESTS AND EAST BANK GRIEVANCES

In the decade after King Abdullah II's ascent to the throne in 1999, not a year passed with less than a hundred protests. Many were small, localized demonstrations, such as sit-ins of no more than a dozen workers. Regional events, in contrast, brought tens of thousands to the street: the Second Intifada, the Iraq War, and Israeli military interventions into Palestinian-controlled areas. The nontransgressive routines that emerged around the protests at the Grand Husseini Mosque and the Kalouti Mosque stood in stark contrast to the state's violent repression of other protests.

Abdullah II was not popular among portions of the East Bank tribal communities. He spoke poor Arabic and sat stiffly among them. The violent crackdown on protests in Ma'an in 2002 kept southerners relatively quiet for a few years, but anger about that state violence simmered, and not only among Ma'anis. Complaints that the regime was not honoring the social contract also steadily grew. When the king launched an accelerated privatization drive—deepening the neoliberal state in a manner King Hussein had avoided—many East Bankers saw only corruption. Large areas were impoverished, and they watched in dismay as billions poured into gleaming megaprojects and up-graded infrastructure in Amman, Aqaba, and the Dead Sea resort area. Privatization per se was not a problem, but many perceived that the Amman-based Palestinian bourgeoisie was disproportionately benefiting from it. Jordan's agreements with the International Monetary Fund also required it to lift subsidies and cut the very government jobs to which East Bankers felt entitled. The collapse of portions of the agricultural sector further devastated many East Bank economies, escalating a decades-long trend of migration to Amman in search of jobs. With wealth increasingly concentrated in a small number of spaces, growing regions of the country struggled with unemployment, low income, and inadequate water, housing, and electricity. Government subsidies were not a matter of perks but survival, and numerous antipoverty programs could not keep many areas from struggling.[2] In this context of growing economic dissent, new activist movements emerged in multiple sectors as conflict within and among tribes escalated.

Day-Wage Labor Protests

The largest new sphere of activism emerged around labor grievances. One movement was organized by day-wage laborers who worked years in the same positions without the security or benefits of permanent employment. In 2006, day-wage agricultural workers agitated for permanent employment in Dhiban, a town and agricultural area of some 15,000 Jordanians of East Bank descent located in the central Madaba governorate southwest of Amman. Government figures put unemployment in Dhiban among the highest in Jordan at around 40 percent,[3] and activist Ali Brizat estimated the real figure as closer to 60 percent.[4] Local agricultural workers created an informal union to strategize how to get their jobs made permanent. In 2006, thirteen of them, including seven women, organized a sit-in outside the Ministry of Agriculture in West Amman. Reviving a spatial repertoire for claim-making established in the 1920s, they traveled to the capital to demand jobs and benefits instead of protesting at their place of work. Two weeks later, they staged a second protest at the same location, this time with sixty-eight workers, including twenty women. Muhammad Snayd emerged as the group's spokesperson, and early talks with the prime minister were promising.[5] But whenever talks failed to make progress, the workers traveled to Amman to demonstrate. Dhiban is relatively close to the capital;

the forty-five-mile trip can be made in ninety minutes, allowing for an easy day trip. The laborers had hoped to stage weekly protests in Amman, but most could not afford the cost of the trip, and certainly not on a weekly basis. Some asked their parliamentary representatives to cover the cost of transportation to the protests or sold personal possessions to be there.[6]

On May 1, 2007, 750 Dhiban workers mounted a protest in front of the Parliament building on International Workers' Day. When the parliamentarians inside refused to acknowledge them, they marched to the Prime Ministry at the Fourth Circle and called for the resignation of the prime minister and cabinet, blocking traffic and demonstrating until a deputy prime minister invited them inside.[7] Despite repeated promises from the government, however, the workers failed to secure permanent employment. In 2010, women in the movement argued that they needed to escalate their tactics, and they organized an overnight sit-in outside the Royal Court in downtown Amman on March 29. The move was a bold innovation to the established protest repertoire because it both established an overnight encampment and addressed their grievances to the monarchy (via the symbolism of the Royal Court location) and not the government. Day-wage laborers from across the governorates joined the encampment in Amman, with women's numbers exceeding those of men.[8] The encampment was brief, however, lasting only one night. Two Amman-based activist movements—the Social Left Forum and the Democratic Youth Movement—provided tents for the women to shelter overnight, while a nearby mosque allowed them to use the toilet. Then on May 1, they held another demonstration at the Professional Associations Complex to demand the rehiring of 256 workers who had been fired. At that event, the group's spokesperson, Snayd, learned that he had been fired from his job at the Ministry of Agriculture. Undeterred from his activism, he was arrested two weeks later at a sit-in. His detention led to weekly protests in Dhiban for the much of the year,[9] which continued even after his release, until the last of the 256 were rehired on February 1, 2011.[10]

Aqaba Dockworker Protests

In 2001, the Aqaba Special Economic Zone Authority (ASEZA), built and financed by the US Agency for International Development, began modernizing the rundown port. In 2005, preparations to move the port south to deeper waters were overseen by Al Maabar, an entity of the government of Abu Dhabi. When dockworkers and local residents learned of the plans—which included the destruction of entire neighborhoods—they took to the streets in protest. Dockworkers saw their affordable in-town housing as part of their compensation. In the Shalaleh neighborhood, locals demonstrated for months throughout 2005 against their forcible relocation to new housing outside of town.[11] Residents not forcibly displaced found themselves unable to afford the skyrocketing rates for real estate. Locals were further angered that many of the workers in the ASEZA projects were foreign workers from Sri Lanka, Egypt, and the Philippines.[12]

Dockworkers at the port continued their periodic protests over the next years, with some described as riots. In 2009, they began mounting weekly demonstrations, demanding that the Jordanian government resume control of the port from Al Maabar. They organized the protests on Fridays in order to not lose time at work.[13] The turnout varied from a few hundred to thousands, peaking on July 31 when as many as three to four thousand joined a sit-in.[14] While the vast majority of the protests were peaceful, this one was broken up violently by the gendarmerie, leading to sixty-five arrests and one serious injury.[15] Tareq Tell reports that the army commander in Aqaba intervened to protect dockworkers who had sought refuge from the violence in a nearby military hospital.[16] While military officers have historically expressed little sympathy with labor struggles, Tell—himself a retired Special Forces officer as well as an Oxford-trained historian— argues that the incident also marked the beginning of an alliance between East Bank labor movements and their sympathizers in the military.[17] Several long-time activists, however, scoff at Tell's suggestion that the efforts of a couple army officers marked a substantive change in their long-standing disinterest in labor activism. At stake in this disagreement over the role of military officers in Aqaba is the centrality of radical nativist voices in mobilizing activism among impoverished East Bank communities (more on this in a moment). Regardless, the state violence that day did not dissuade the dockworkers from continuing their weekly protests throughout 2010. But to preempt a repeat of that violence, they invited international media and independent Jordanian journalists to observe and document their peaceful protests.[18]

Other Labor Protests

In 2010, Jordan Labor Watch reported 139 labor protests, the first year it began documenting them.[19] The economic downturn coincided with the privatization of several public assets, leading Jordanians to blame government policies for rising costs, unemployment, and stagnant wages. Teachers began organizing for better pay and the right to unionize. They formed the Committee for the Revival of the Teachers' Professional Association and mounted at least twelve protests that year.[20] A general strike in April shut down parts of the national school system for several days. Students joined their teachers in the strike, most significantly in Karak, Ajloun, and Salt.[21] In Karak, so many teachers went on strike that it shut down local schools. The regime tried to get current and former ministers, parliamentarians, military officers, senators, and Karaki tribal leaders to pressure their friends and family to not participate, but some responded by stating their support for the teachers.[22] In an effort to break the strike, the government forced some of the more prominent activists into early retirement, including Adma Zurayqat, a teacher from Karak. On her behalf, activists and teachers in the capital organized a solidarity march from Amman to Karak, after which the "retired" teachers were reinstated.[23]

Escalating Tribal Violence

In 2009, the Public Security Directorate reported 229 violent incidents between and among East Bank tribes and families, which it said marked a significant increase from previous years. Incidents included road blockades and the destruction of property, tactics from the old East Bank repertoires for expressing grievances. An example from Ajloun in August is instructive. Ashraf Momani was stabbed to death by his ex-brother-in-law, a member of the local Simadi family. In revenge, the Momani set fire first to the home of the killer and then to homes and businesses owned by other Simadis. For nearly a week, the police and gendarmerie blocked the main roads into town while government officials met with local leaders to work out a means of restoring calm. Then, in spring 2010, two university students of different clans in Salt fought over a bus seat until one struck the other enough times to kill him. Both clans took to the streets, and roads into Salt were cut off for two days until the police and gendarmerie could restore order.[24] Violence emerges not only among tribes and extended families but also between them and state security forces.[25] The next November, for example, a police lieutenant allegedly beat to death Fakhri Anani Kreishan in Ma'an.[26] In response, locals fired guns at police and set a police booth ablaze.[27] Prominent tribal elders called for peace through tribal arbitration or truce (*'utwa*),[28] but younger Ma'anis continued to protest anyway, blocking the Aqaba–Amman highway for more than twenty-four hours.

These grievances and political dissent among Jordan's East Bank communities were not limited to the outlying governorates, and tribal affiliations remain important to parts of life in Amman. Certain tribes and families are associated with neighborhoods in the capital dating to at least the 1940s,[29] and the spike in tribal violence of the late 2000s also reached Amman. In November 2010, for example, a twenty-year-old peddler in the Hayy Tafayleh area in East Amman was beaten to death by police after an altercation with a city official. Local residents responded by burning down a police building and several local shops. After six officers were wounded by gunfire, the police broke up the crowds with tear gas.[30] Nor is violence limited to Amman's more impoverished eastern neighborhoods. In May 2010, for example, a supposed drug bust in the upscale Khalda neighborhood of West Amman ended in the death of Abd Salam Nu'aymat—a wealthy businessman and prominent figure in the Nu'aymat family, which has long-standing ties to the neighborhood. After police shot Nu'aymat seven times and killed him on the spot, as many as a hundred of his kin took to the streets, burning a police kiosk and damaging two police cars.

This spike in tribal violence captures a range of grievances surfacing in late 2010 and contributing to the general atmosphere of heightened contention across the country. Mariam Ababsa argues that the escalation of such conflict indicates not a resurgence of tribalism but rather its breakdown. "Clan members who have become wealthy," she argues, "free themselves from tribal hierarchy and deal out justice themselves, until the conflict becomes so intense that traditional clan leaders are forced to intervene to arbitrate the situation."[31] Janine Astrid Clark presents a different take, arguing that tribal tensions escalated in the 2000s because some smaller tribes had lost local power as a result of the government's amalgamation of municipal councils. Dozens of protests broke out in 2010 and 2011 demanding "better municipal services and the redrawing of municipal boundaries to reverse the amalgamation."[32] Those protests were in opposition to what many perceived was a concentration of influence (*wasta*[33]) and services in fewer hands.[34] In her interviews, Clark found that some people directly related tribal violence on university campuses to the increased tensions in the municipalities due to amalgamation.[35]

The Veterans' Manifesto

On April 1, 2010, the National Committee of Retired Servicemen—normally a core institution of support for the regime—issued a manifesto (*bayan rasmi*, or official statement) signed by seventy prominent veteran officers. Manifestos and other "black papers" (unsigned manifestos) circulated among East Bank tribes in the wake of earlier protests, but they were not widespread. With growing dissent in multiple sectors by 2010, however, the number of these statements increased along with labor protests and tribal violence. Often issued in the name of a tribe or prominent family, manifestos are frequently followed by counterstatements, often from within the same tribe or family. Manifestos became part of the repertoire for protest, a means of expressing political dissent that circulates in public. They are passed from hand to hand, published by online outlets, and—with the rise of social media over the next decade—posted directly to Facebook and Twitter.

The veterans' manifesto of May 2010 was authored by Tariq Tell and Nahed Hattar. It echoed the grievances of many Jordanians of East Bank descent about the "Zionist project to liquidate the Palestinian cause at the expense of Jordan." It further expressed concern about the "soft transfer" of Palestinians into Jordan and the resurrection of the notion of Jordan as an "alternative homeland" for Palestinians.[36] Some leftist activists of both Palestinian and East Bank descent took issue with these passages, seeing them as advancing anti-Palestinian demands that they saw as exclusionary and bigoted. The veterans' manifesto was also highly critical of the regime, saying that "government policies show extreme weakness." This weakness resulted from economic problems stemming from privatization, the inflation of public debt, and the spread of poverty, hunger, and unemployment among Jordanians. The statement also captured underlying concerns about protecting the privileges of current and former military officers and safeguarding the institutional channels through which their relatives and communities had been incorporated into the regime.[37] Neoliberal reforms put that privilege under strain, however, and it did not help that Abdullah II was far less popular than his half-brother Prince Hamzah. Hamzah had been named crown prince at the time the new king took the throne in 1999, and he was said to be the favorite of their father, King Hussein. When Abdullah II named his own son Hussein as crown prince in 2004, many East Bankers were unhappy with the decision. Hamzah continued to visit with them regularly at a time when Abdullah II and the cosmopolitan Queen Rania remained focused on Amman. While the royals were advancing their vision for a new Jordan, they were seen as neglecting East Bank tribal areas and disrespecting tribal authority and prestige. The parts of the manifesto condemning neoliberalism and high-level corruption may have also been about perceptions that Jordanians of Palestinian descent were benefiting from those reforms at the expense of East Bank tribal interests.[38]

The audacious veterans' manifesto was the talk of Jordan throughout 2010, along with a second manifesto on corrupt privatization and a third on neo-liberalism.[39] Economic hardship—the Jordanian economy had also suffered from the 2008 global financial collapse—combined with the perceived neglect of the old social contract to fuel a rising and radical East Bank nativism. As discussed earlier, Jordan's radical nativists emphasize their longer history in the Transjordanian area, distinguishing themselves not only from various refugee communities but also from others with familial ties outside the spatial imaginary of East Bank Transjordan. They describe themselves as indigenous Jordanians (*ahl al-balad* or *'abna' al-balad*)—in essence, "true" Jordanians. Tell argues in his scholarly writing that from the late Ottoman period on, the merchants and bureaucrats who made their way into Transjordan were identified by locals as *aghrab*, strangers or foreigners.[40] Nativists who follow this line of thinking narrow the field of "true" Jordanians to exclude those with attachments to Greater Syria, Palestine, Iraq, and elsewhere outside of the Transjordanian area. Nativists consequently lay claim to special rights vis-à-vis political authority. One contentious implication of this form of nativism is that it portrays the Hashemites as outsiders.

In response to the first veterans' manifesto, former prime minister and General Intelligence Directorate (*mukhabarat*) head Ahmad Obaydat circu-lated a countermanifesto signed by a wide range of voices, including Arab nationalists, independent and party-affiliated leftists, the Muslim Brother-hood and Islamic Action Front, and numerous former government officials.

Recall that Obaydat had forged similar cooperative ties with the opposition activists and political parties in the antinormalization committee. For him and many others, and despite their criticism of the peace treaty and Israel, the radical nativism conveyed in the veterans' manifesto went too far. Their countermanifesto emphasized that the East Bank and West Bank were historically connected, and that Jordan should remain engaged in pushing for a resolution of the Israeli-Palestinian conflict that included the right of return for all Palestinians.

The veterans' manifesto and the countermanifesto churned national political debate, uniting some voices while alienating others. Tell reports that in the last quarter of 2010, a group that called itself the Progressive Democratic Jordanian Tendency was formed by some of the nativists in the National Committee of Retired Servicemen, the leaders of the teachers' movement in Salt and Karak, the day-wage labor movement, and the nativist writer Hattar.[41] Other activists dispute Tell's narrative, arguing that this group was united in name only and never cohered as a movement. But as a highly contentious parliamentary election approached in the fall, the regime faced heightened criticism from all directions.

The November 2010 Parliamentary Elections

The November 2010 election provided a target for many Jordanians' growing frustrations. The king had dissolved Parliament on November 24, 2009, halfway through its four-year term. A new election law, announced May 18, 2010, did not address many complaints, such as the overrepresentation of East Bank areas. The Islamic Action Front and the leftist Jordanian Democratic Popular Unity Party boycotted the election, reiterating their long-standing demand (with other opposition voices) that Jordan become a constitutional monarchy in which the Hashemites would reign but not rule. The National Committee of Retired Servicemen endorsed the boycott, and together with other nativist allies called for convening a sixth Jordanian National Congress, invoking the oppositional gatherings from 1928 to 1933 that challenged Hashemite rule.[42] In the two months running up to the elections, tens of thousands protested across Jordan, and even the veterans organized demonstrations.[43] The elections were held amid accusations of widespread fraud, many of which were substantiated. Violence broke out among tribes and families backing competing candidates, and between security forces and those protesting the electoral results. Serious injuries were reported in Karak, Salt, and Ma'an. In December, the Progressive Democratic Jordanian Tendency organized a demonstration in front of Parliament criticizing the newly elected speaker, Faysal al-Fayiz, a former prime minister and member of the powerful family of the Bani Sakhr. Fayiz had strongly opposed the creation of an independent teachers' union, and Jordanians of both Palestinian and East Bank descent viewed him as a figure of corruption.

JORDAN'S PLACE IN A RESTIVE REGION

As protests spread across Tunisia in late December 2010, aggrieved Jordanians were capping off a year that saw hundreds of protests across multiple sectors. In early January 2011, Ali Brizat, Muhammad al-Snayd, and five other activists from the day-wage laborer movement formed the Dhiban Youth Committee and called for weekly protests against the government. Although some Dhiban residents had been active in leftist and Islamist groups since the 1970s or had participated in the day-wage labor protests in Amman, the town was not a hot spot for protests and thus had no established local protest routines.[44] At their first protest, on Friday, January 7, as many as a thousand joined the original seven demonstrators in front of the central Dhiban mosque,[45] a turnout that surprised even the organizers.[46] The protest turned into a march, and they paraded through the streets of Dhiban.[47] Proud of their success—weeks before Egyptians took to the street—some jokingly invoked a new spatial imaginary in declaring an independent "Republic of Dhiban."[48]

Following the surprisingly large January 7 turnout, Dhiban activists joined others to form the Jordanian Campaign for Change. In its early days, this movement primarily included activists from the various labor movements nationwide. The group became known as *Jayeen Min Ajl al-Taygheer*—"We are coming to bring change"—an ominous message with a spatial dimension: we are not only demanding change, we are literally coming to Amman to demand that change (as had the day-wage laborers). As Snayd put it,

> The Rifai government waged war on unions. Union leaders were imprisoned, fired or relocated to distant sites for having organized strikes. These transfers made us think of new ways to struggle for change: using protests and echoing people's grievances about the government, such as economic policies that

raised the prices of basic goods used by the poor, increased unemployment, and poverty. So, we founded the *Jayeen* movement. We organized demonstrations all over the country, calling for a new national unity government.[49]

The group was diverse, and it included Jordanians of both East Bank and Palestinian descent. It called for a "Day of Rage" on January 14, announced in group text messages, via activist and labor networks, and advertised on Facebook and other social media. The slogan connected Jordan to protest movements in the region and indeed globally, invoking the global protests of the 1960s as well as the current uprising in Tunisia. The rage was apparently to be contained, however, as *Jayeen*'s Facebook announcement stated that protests were to remain peaceful and that only the Jordanian flag should be raised.[50] In Amman, it called for people to assemble downtown at the Grand Husseini Mosque. Likely in an effort to undercut turnout, the king announced on January 10 some modest cuts to fuel taxes and caps on the prices of some foods. No one knew whether the upcoming protest would attract a large turnout.

On January 12 in Tunisia, however, the main union (the UGTT) backed a strike in Sfax under the same "Day of Rage" slogan. Demonstrations there were so large that many Tunisians felt it was the turning point that signaled the eventual fall of the Ben Ali regime. The next day, Tunisians descended on their capital, and Ben Ali's regime fell the third day.[51]

Despite this dramatic turn of events, in Amman it looked like the January 14 protest might be a bust. The event was boycotted by what activist and writer Hisham Bustani calls the "official opposition" in Amman—the leftist and nationalist political parties, the Muslim Brotherhood and Islamic Action Front, and the Union of Professional Associations.[52] But some five hundred protesters still turned out, a sizable crowd without the participation of the established opposition. Initial chants of "Down with the Government Price Increases" on January 7 in Dhiban were replaced with slogans like "Down with the High-Priced Government."[53] The state did not seek to break up the peaceful protest, with police even serving more as parade guards who handed out water and juice boxes.[54] But even as news of Ben Ali's departure from Tunisia reached Jordanians in the streets, they remained modest in their demands. "The people want the reform of the regime," they chanted, drawing an affective connection with the familiar chant of the Tunisian uprising[55] but also deviating from it by replacing "fall of the regime" with "reform of the regime." Crowds also chanted, "the King is the only constant in Jordanian politics."[56] The slogan worked both to reaffirm Hashemite rule but also perhaps to slyly criticize it, as it indexed that Jordanian politics was all about the king himself, perhaps indirectly implying his neglect of the people. It also served as a way of safely mentioning the king during protests, opening space for later critique, first through word play and later directly, as we will see below. Although the Muslim Brotherhood and Islamic Action Front had refrained from calling their supporters to the January 14 protest, they announced a demonstration to be held two days later. A few hundred turned out for their sit-in in front of Parliament, which called for a constitutional monarchy and canceling Jordan's agreement with the International Monetary Fund.

With the fall of Ben Ali's regime in Tunisia, the atmosphere began to change as people began to buzz about what might happen, in Jordan and regionally. Jordan's protests had not reached a massive scale, nor had the smaller protests that began in Oman on January 17. The "Arab uprisings" were not yet a regional event, although the horizon of political possibilities seemed to have changed. But *Jayeen's* second protest, on Friday, January 21, attracted at least three thousand to the Grand Husseini Mosque, with crowds filling the road for nearly two miles northeast toward Parliament. Leftist activists gathered at the Fourth Circle in front of the Prime Ministry, calling for the fall of Samir al-Rifaʿi and his cabinet. In a stunning coincidence not lost on Jordanians, Rifaʿi's father Zayd was the prime minister sacked in 1989 as a result of the *Habbit Nisan* protests. This time, military veterans joined protesters in calling for the removal of Rifaʿi, who was disparaged as a corrupt and bourgeois Palestinian.

On January 25, Egyptians took to the streets to protest police violence, and their January 28 protests escalated to revolutionary levels. Egyptians beat back police violence across Cairo and elsewhere nationwide, achieving the region's second major uprising that looked like it could possibly depose President Hosni Mubarak. On January 27, Yemenis also began to protest, although not yet in large numbers; in Djibouti, small protests broke out on January 28. It seemed that people across the region were trying to join Egypt and Tunisia in achieving nationwide mass mobilizations, and Jordan was part of that crest. Indeed, Jordan's January 28 protests were massive, with as many as ten thousand in Amman and perhaps another ten to fifteen thousand in other locations

164   CHAPTER 6

nationwide.[57] The Muslim Brotherhood encouraged its supporters to turn out,[58] and protesters in Amman gathered across the city, in neighborhoods as well as in familiar protest locations including Parliament, the Fourth Circle, and the Grand Husseini Mosque. In Karak, opposition parties and the Union of Professional Associations joined hundreds of protesters to demand reform and express solidarity with protesters in Egypt and Tunisia.[59] In Aqaba, hundreds of dockworkers joined demonstrations of more than a thousand. Separate labor protests were organized during this period in every sector except the security forces, including teachers, bank tellers, imams, university employees, journalists, taxi drivers, and nurses and doctors at state-run hospitals.[60] But Jordanians still called only for reform.

On January 30—as protests broke out in Sudan—five friends called for a demonstration outside of the Egyptian embassy in Amman. More than two thousand showed up, and the press called the organizers the Movement of Jordanian Youth, although they may have meant merely that it was a movement of Jordanian youth rather than an organized group with that name. The *Hirak* (movement) label stuck among journalists and Jordanians alike as a generic name for a wide range of new activist movements.[61] Then on February 1, King Abdullah II responded to the protests in the familiar way—by sacking the prime minister. Rifa'i was replaced by Ma'rouf al-Bakhit, who had served in the position from 2005 to 2007. The teachers' movement withdrew from protests, opting to give Bakhit a chance.[62] Their decision paid off, as he quickly granted them permission to form a union. In an effort to quiet protests in East Bank communities, the government poured $500 million into government salary increases and cash payment to prominent tribal leaders believed to command their communities. These efforts may have worked, as the next Friday protests, on February 4, were diminished in size. In Amman, no more than a thousand turned out, with Islamists dominating protests at the Grand Husseini Mosque and a smaller contingent of leftist activists demonstrating at the Fourth Circle. The Muslim Brotherhood and Islamic Action Front continued to call their supporters into the streets, not least because they had lingering animosities with Bakhit from his earlier tenure.[63] The next Friday, February 11—the day that Egypt's Supreme Council of the Armed Forces removed Mubarak from office—protests were smaller still. The only large protest in Amman was at the Grand Husseini Mosque, where hundreds were dominated by the Islamists and their constituents.

Meanwhile, the "Arab uprisings" or "Arab Spring" was becoming a region-wide phenomenon, as more protests broke out following Mubarak's ouster. Many journalists and even scholars focused their attention on countries with major mobilizations, excluding from regionwide analyses cases with lower-level protests, like Jordan, Djibouti, and others to come. That focus not only works as a kind of political silencing, but it obscures how people across the region saw themselves engaged in a common movement against their repressive regimes. They adopted or adapted the same slogans and watched the uprisings on al-Jazeera television, the screen divided into squares with live coverage of the simultaneous protests in different countries. Iraqis began demonstrating on February 12; Bahrainis on February 14. On February 17, Libyans took to the streets. But despite the heightening atmosphere of anger and exhilaration across the region, Jordan's crowds continued to diminish. The February 18 protests saw no more than three hundred at the Grand Husseini Mosque and none at the Fourth Circle. In Amman, the gendarmerie stood by as 150 loyalist counterprotesters attacked the downtown protesters with metal rods and sticks, injuring at least eight.[64] Not a single counterprotester was arrested, nor did a promised inquiry into the events materialize. The next Friday, February 25, the police reverted to handing out water and juice boxes to the crowd of a few hundred.[65] The changing state response to the protests—alternating between violence (or at least not stopping counterprotesters' violence) and acting like friendly parade guards—illustrates how these eventful moments left the state uncertain how to respond, with repertoires and routines in flux. Protesters, too, were more unsure of what to expect, even as they likewise innovated.

Meanwhile, protests continued to spread at the regional level, with new protests in Kuwait on February 19, Morocco on February 20, Mauritania on February 25, and Lebanon on February 27. In early March, residents of Daraʻa, Syria, took to the streets, with major protests reaching Damascus and Aleppo on March 15. In Jordan's northern border town of Ramtha, crowds gathered for weeks, chanting "One and one, Daraʻa and Ramtha are one!"[66] The chant invoked the affective connections both of northerners as historically people of Greater Syria and of the former Ajloun domain, which historically included Daraʻa. In the coming weeks and years, the Syrian uprising (and later war) would spill into Jordan, as thousands and then hundreds of thousands of Syrians would flee in search of refuge.

Mobilization outside Amman

Jordan's major protests were multisectoral during these first months, but issue-specific protests also continued. The dockworkers restarted their weekly protests in February and continued throughout the year. On one occasion, they blocked the entrance to the port for more than a week.[67] And contrary to many analyses, Jordanians of Palestinian descent joined East Bankers at protests, particularly in Amman, Zarqa, and Irbid. Only one protest was recorded in a Palestinian refugee camp, in Baqa'a Camp northwest of Amman.[68] But East Bank tribal communities were both most willing to criticize the regime directly and to be a primary source for counterprotesters and *baltajiyya*, the violent thugs who sometimes coordinated with the police in protests.

On February 5, a new manifesto signed by thirty-six members of prominent East Bank tribes accused Queen Rania and other high-ranking government officials of corruption. It expressed disgust with a 2010 decadent party hosted by the queen in Wadi Rum and attended by global celebrities like Nicole Kidman and Ivanka Trump. That lavish affair left the regime looking woefully out of touch with the economic plight of its citizens. The "Coalition of 36" manifesto also claimed that tribal lands had been inappropriately given to members of the queen's family. It declared a "crisis of governance" and called for political reforms, an elected prime minister, an end to corruption, and a reversal of neoliberal projects, particularly privatization. The manifesto created a stir nationwide not just for its content but because many signatories—which over the next year grew to more than a thousand—were from prominent East Bank tribes, including the Bani Sakhr, Abbadi, Shoubaki, and Manaseer. As Tell puts it, the manifesto "gave notice that the compact between Jordanians and the Hashemite dynasty, once based on a mutual partnership, was being violated."[69]

Many East Bank tribes also began voicing long-standing grievances over land-use agreements with the government. Hashemite and British authorities formally recognized tribal rights to access the lands of their traditional domains (*wajihat 'asha'ir*) in the 1920s and 1930s, but the state had seized land for various projects over the years. The Bani Sakhr, for example, still felt aggrieved that the state forced the sale of some land in the late 1970s to build the Queen Alia Airport south of Amman. Now during the uprising period, tribes were escalating their expression of those grievances, perhaps wagering that the regime was vulnerable and might be more responsive. A crowd of several dozen in Zarqa blocked the Zarqa–Mafraq highway on February 4, demanding that the government allow them to use the lands east of the road that they believed had been given to them decades earlier. They put up tents along the road and stopped a minibus carrying police and threw stones at it.[70] On February 13, three thousand members of the Zawahra and Khalayla tribes blocked a main road near Amman to demand the return of lands that they believed belonged to them. Two days later, at least five hundred protesters from the Bani Sakhr staged a sit-in across a main road for similar reasons; they remained encamped there overnight for two days.[71]

On campuses across the country, students protested in numbers not seen in decades. At Yarmouk University—where police had killed student protesters in 1986—students demanded reduced tuition, greater freedoms, and less of a security presence on campus.[72] On other campuses, the gendarmerie intervened in clashes between students of different tribal and clan affiliations, including at Zaytouna University and at Balqa Applied University in Salt.[73] And in a movement coordinated across multiple campuses called "You Slaughtered Us" (*dabahtuna*), students called for political freedoms on campus, free student elections, and an end to the tribe-based violence.[74]

The Hirak

Among the most significant developments of the uprising period was the emergence of new youth-led organizations, with at least forty groups nationwide.[75] They included both seasoned activists and first-time protesters from across the political spectrum.[76] Many were members of prominent East Bank tribes, but Jordanians of Palestinian descent also participated, particularly in Amman, Zarqa, Irbid, and Jerash. Most of the group names included a location, the word "movement" (*haraka* or *hirak*) and either "popular" (*sha'abi*), or "youth" (*shabab* or *shababi*). Many also labeled themselves "free" (*ahrar*). Some were organized around family or tribal affiliations, such as the Khalayla Youth Movement and the Group of Bani Sakhr Tribal Sons for Reform.[77] Collectively, these groups came to be known as the *Hirak*. Although individual *Hirak* groups often communicated with each other and with Amman-based activists and movements—such as coordinating slogans for each Friday's protests—they otherwise remained largely independent. Contrary to many scholarly portrayals,[78] many of them gradually lost their youth-dominated character; indeed, even in early protests, participation in *Hirak* protests was intergenerational.[79] Yazan Doughan argues that many identified "youth" not as an age group, but as

> a generational category of Jordanians who seek to construct a different relation to their elders and to the state by claiming a new historical past. In doing so, they constitute themselves as autonomous political actors unencumbered by the narratives of their elders' generation and the latter's relation to the monarchy.[80]

Many focused on labor and economic grievances,[81] anticorruption, and criticism of the failures of local tribal leaders. The first two prime ministers after the uprisings—Ma'rouf al-Bakhit from the powerful Abbadi tribe of the Balqa region and Fayez Tarawneh of the Tarawneh family of Karak—both faced harsh criticism from the *Hirak* groups of their home constituencies.[82]

The *Hirak* held weekly protests nationwide.[83] In Irbid, early protests were organized by local branches of political parties, but the independent Irbid Popular Movement emerged to focus on a reform agenda that was broadly shared. The Free Tafileh Movement shifted its focus from local development projects to demanding broad political reforms, using the Ottoman fortress in Tafileh as its headquarters. The *Hirak* in Karak emerged from existing activist networks and maintained the long-standing local practice of coordinating among those affiliated with political parties. The Ma'an and Shoubak movements likewise included a mix of participants, but with religious conservatives more prominent in the Ma'an group than in many others.[84] The East Amman neighborhood of Hayy Tafayleh also had an active movement that organized in part to counter the perception that the neighborhood was a primary source of counterprotesters and *baltajiyya*.[85] A group of unemployed youth from that neighborhood protested at the Royal Court in March 2011, demanding jobs and university scholarships. When they were each given a JD 200 check (US $280), they tore them up and stepped on them, declaring that they "had not come to beg."[86]

The character of the *Hirak* movements, however, evolved quickly in these first months of 2011. In January and February, for example, the *Hirak* saw cooperation among individuals with leftist, Arab nationalist, radical nativist, and Islamist orientations, without any one group dominating. But by the spring, *Hirak* activists complained that the Muslim Brotherhood had begun to dominate their coordinating committees in Tafileh, Hayy Tafayleh, Salt, Jerash, Ajloun, and Shoubak.[87] One activist from Karak described the Muslim Brotherhood and Islamic Action Front as claiming to spearhead the protests nationwide, pushing a reformist agenda rather than calling out corrupt individuals, as many *Hirak* activists preferred. Many of these new activists were excited by the new movements precisely because they were distinct from preexisting political movements and parties. According to one *Jayeen* activist, the movement remained strongest in East Bank tribal areas outside of Amman where Islamists were less able to dominate.[88] Whole communities and even families were divided on whether to support the regime or calls for reform, and how far those reforms should go.

THE FIRST MAJOR TURNING POINT

By March, the composition of groups organizing protests had evolved, and the *Jayeen* coalition of labor activists, leftists, and their allies expanded to include a number of other organizations and movements.[89] Protests continued nationwide, although many new sectors asserted narrow claims. In Irbid and Amman, for example, downtown landlords and tenants organized a strike in their respective souks on March 8 to protest changes to the rent law, and they continued similar strikes over the next year.[90] The *Hirak* continued mounting protests nationwide, sometimes in creative new ways. In Hayy Tafayleh in East Amman, for example, the local *Hirak* organized a "people's court" in which mock trials were held to convict corrupt government officials.[91] The progressive online news outlet *7iber* organized "hashtag debates" as forums for exchanging ideas on a range of social, political, and economic issues.

At the regional level, protests in Yemen, Syria, Bahrain, and Libya reached revolutionary levels and their regimes responded with violence. The context of violence led Abdullah II to redouble efforts to divide and deflate Jordan's protests through a combination of repression and accommodation. It granted concessions (such as allowing teachers to form a union) and distributed largess (cash payments and salary increases), while pushing loyalist East Bank tribal elites to condemn activists and dissuade people from joining protests. As Malika Bouziane and Katharina Lenner show, the king and other government officials also made repeat visits to key East Bank constituencies. The

Kura district (in Irbid governorate) received JD 40 (US $56) million to create income-generating projects; in Karak, JD 4.7 (US $6.6) million cash went to assist poor families. After the king promised millions for infrastructure and development projects in Ma'an during one personal visit, protests the next day commemorating the 1989 *Habbit Nisan* brought scant turnout.[92]

In March, the government announced that the Public Gatherings Law would be amended so that the protesters no longer needed to obtain a permit. It also announced the creation of a National Dialogue Committee, a move that many saw as a meaningless prop in the regime's routine response to large-scale protests. The committee included former ministers, civil society leaders, and representatives from some opposition political parties and was chaired by former prime minister Taher Masri. It was tasked with proposing amendments to the laws for elections and political parties within three months, and a separate Economic Dialogue Committee was charged with proposing economic reforms.[93] The Islamic Action Front refused to participate, just as it had refused to participate in the Bakhit cabinet. Without Islamist buy-in, the committees were unlikely to win widespread support for any recommendations. As the king seemed to be succeeding in dividing Jordan's movements, other regional regimes were turning increasingly to violence. On March 14, for example, Saudi troops entered Bahrain, beginning a period of brutal repression of protesters and the medical professionals who treated their injuries.[94] While Jordan avoided that level of violence at home, it sent gendarmerie troops to Bahrain. But some of Jordan's protests were violently dispersed, while others were left alone. What explains the uneven deployment of state repression?

March 24 Youth

The symbolism of certain spaces, along with innovations in protest routines, drew clear connections to uprisings that had reached revolutionary levels elsewhere in the region. One protest in Jordan proved more than the state or its loyalists could tolerate, resulting in deadly repression by only the second day. On March 24, some five hundred Jordanians staged an open-ended sit-in at a major traffic interchange in West Amman known colloquially as the Interior Circle (for its proximity to the Ministry of the Interior, not located directly at the roundabout).[95] A group calling itself the March 24 Youth announced the protest on Facebook and YouTube: "We, the youth of Jordan, male and female,

are free and are fed up with postponements, promises, and corruption. . . ."[96]
One participant described the group as

> a mixture of free Jordanian young men and women, who are tired of delays
> and the promise of reform, who see the spread of corruption, the deterioration
> of the economic situation, the regression of political life, the erasure of free-
> doms, and the dissolution of the social fabric.[97]

Organized on Facebook and via personal networks, the group included mainly
independent activists, most of whom were left-leaning but also including some
Islamists. *Jayeen* activists participated in the planning and the protest but were
not the sole organizers.[98] The prominent East Bank Abbadi tribe sponsored a
large banner that bore a picture of the king and made clear that the demands
of the group were for reform and not the fall of the regime.[99] The location
was a new one for protest, however, and the assembly was Jordan's the first
planned ongoing encampment of the uprising period. Although the planners
went to great lengths to call for reform while expressing support for the king, a
sustained encampment would connect Jordan's protests to the encampments
of Tahrir Square in Cairo and Change Square in Sana'a, and to the protests
targeting the interior ministries in Tunis and Cairo.

The organizers chose March 24 for its symbolism, near the anniversary of
the Battle of Karama on March 21, 1968. As discussed in chapter 3, the Jordanian
Armed Forces and the PLO fought together during that battle to repel an Israeli
incursion, and the anniversary is celebrated as a national victory that united
Jordanians of all backgrounds against Israel. The organizers hoped to frame
their protest for reform around patriotic themes, and their chants, banners, and
slogans did not challenge the monarchy itself. Flags associated with political
parties were not displayed, and many sported the red-and-white checkered
scarf associated with East Bank identity. As the protesters assembled, the police
and gendarmerie positioned barricades and blocked traffic from some areas.
For hours, they stood to the side without intervening. Men and women milled
around the area, chatting with the protesters, taking selfies, and moving on.
The protesters displayed posters in English and Arabic and had a truck with a
sound system. They gave speeches, engaged in chants, and sang *Mawtini*, other
popular Arab songs, and the Jordanian national anthem.[100] In addition to tents
and sleeping gear, they brought cleaning supplies to keep the area tidy.

172 CHAPTER 6

As the first afternoon wore on, some protesters criticized the General Intelligence Directorate and called for parliamentary elections to adopt proportional representation (which would diminish East Bank representation). These claims deviated from those that had been agreed upon in advance. One poster, for example, showed two fists, one gripping flowers labeled "the hand of the people" and the other gripping screaming people with their arms flailing labeled "the grip of the mukhabarat." Khalid Kalaldeh, a *Jayeen* activist, blamed the Muslim Brotherhood participants for introducing the new slogans. "For us these demands were too divisive, as they suggested support for the idea that the regime should fall."[101] Meanwhile, a group that described itself as a loyalty march arrived and took up position in counterprotest.[102] A proregime demonstration of as many as twenty-five thousand had been held earlier in the day at King Hussein Gardens in West Amman, organized by a group called Homeland's Call (*nida' al-watan*). With many of them now at the Interior Circle, the gendarmerie separated them from the March 24 Youth, with barriers creating a corridor between them. The evening passed with little incident; both groups remained on the circle overnight. Protesters positioned candles in the shape of Jordan's territory, with a Jordanian flag in the middle along with one red- and one black-checkered scarf entwined to symbolize Jordanians of both East Bank and Palestinian descent. Sometime in the night, the power to the roundabout was cut off, and the darkness engulfing the encampment heightened fears among protesters about what was coming next.[103] Counterprotesters started hurling rocks at the encampment, and as many as thirty-five were injured.[104]

In the morning, when members of the March 24 Youth camp began their morning prayers, the counterprotesters—whose numbers had grown significantly from the night before[105]—began blaring patriotic music over loudspeakers. Shouting back and forth created an increasingly tense atmosphere as police worked to contain the counterprotesters, who periodically threw stones at the protesters (and were not arrested for doing so) behind the barricades. Someone on the loudspeakers repeatedly asked the protesters to ignore the counterprotesters and not throw stones back, saying "peacefully, peacefully," a slogan that was used in Tahrir Square. Counterprotesters continued threatening the protesters, even self-describing as *baltajiyya*.[106] When the counterprotesters breached the barricades sometime around midday, they charged the March 24 Youth with sticks and metal rods. As the protesters knelt and held hands to show that they were not provoking the attack, the gendarmerie seemed to join the counterprotesters in breaking up the encampment. Indeed, the loyalists may have even been *baltajiyya*. Human Rights Watch reported that the gendarmerie and police stood aside as "a group of thugs wearing civilian clothes, holding sticks and batons, [came] out of the official *darak* [gendarmerie] vans, and [moved] toward protesters running away from the circle."[107] Protesters trapped by barricades and fences endured the most severe beatings. The violence was captured on videos uploaded to YouTube, and some videos clearly show the counterprotesters coordinating with the gendarmerie.[108] In the end, one protester, fifty-seven-year-old Kahiri Sa'ad, was killed, and dozens were seriously injured.[109] Some hundred were arrested, some of whom were tortured and, in at least one case, told to leave the country.[110] Those with powerful East Bank tribal connections, however, were quickly released. Sixteen members of the fifty-two-member National Dialogue Committee resigned over the violence, declaring that the dialogue was a sham.

In the following weeks, *Jayeen* gradually disbanded over disagreements about the direction of the movement. Many activists shifted their energies to mounting or joining protests outside of Amman.[111] Meanwhile, loyalists created Facebook pages that spread rumors about who had really organized the March 24 sit-in, denying the strong East Bank affiliations of many of the core organizers and instead portraying the group as dominated by Islamists and Jordanians of Palestinian descent. Prime Minister Bakhit latched onto this false characterization, which is still repeated by government and security officials as a point of fact.

New and Old Sectors of Protest

Protests continued to emerge in new spaces, around new sectors, and by groups with no history of activism. In Zarqa, for example, some 350 salafi protesters gathered in front of a mosque on April 15, dramatically waving knives and demanding the release of some two hundred salafi prisoners. The group had been holding protests for weeks, including at the Fourth Circle, but this was the largest. They, too, clashed with loyalist counterprotesters, but the salafi fought back with clubs and daggers as well as their fists, and both sides threw whatever loose stones and broken concrete they could find. In the end, eighty-three total were injured, including four officers with serious stab wounds inflicted by the salafi protesters.[112]

That same month, four phosphate workers, experienced in protest through their professional associations, organized a sit-in in front of the Amman headquarters of the Jordan Phosphate Mines Company.[113] They were frustrated not by low wages or long hours, however, but because they felt that their assigned jobs underutilized their skills and experience. When the company had been privatized in 2006, workers complained that Walid Kurdi, who is connected to the royal family through marriage, played a corrupt role in the transaction. The company's privatization, it seemed to them, merely transferred control from the state to a member of the royal family—a common complaint about Jordan's privatization process.[114] The group gathered thirty phosphate employees, both women and men, and staged a three-day sit-in. They denounced corruption and mismanagement and demanded new bylaws, a transparent personnel system, and fair treatment for employees. But when negotiations produced a deal that disappointed the workers, they announced on May 1 the creation of an independent union (distinct from their official union) and organized strikes in multiple locations in June.[115]

Other protests also continued around Israel/Palestine, with large demonstrations in Baqa'a Camp to mark the May 15 anniversary of the 1948 *Nakba* (catastrophe) and 1967 *Naksa* (setback). Antinormalization protesters organized a Right of Return demonstration in the town of Karama near the Israeli border. While the police and gendarmerie observed the Baqa'a protests without intervening, at Karama they were joined by counterprotesters to violently disperse the crowd.[116] By early summer, however, most protests had fallen into routines. *Hirak* groups organized small protests outside of Amman, and one southern *Hirak* group stamped bank notes with "The people want the reform of the regime."[117] As Ziad Abu-Rish argues, "what remained [of the protests] was much more diffuse and isolated in nature, taking the form of a combination of disparate public sector employee strikes, university campus violence, and confrontations between security forces and either tribal or Islamist groups."[118] The atmosphere resembled that of 2010—pockets of violence and protest across the nation—but not the revolutionary fervor of other Arab uprisings.

In the heat of the summer, however, state violence returned. The Muslim Brotherhood coordinated with some *Hirak* groups, labor activists, and other leftist activists to mount an event at the Grand Husseini Mosque on July 15.[119] Some two thousand protesters gathered with hundreds of security forces.

At least twenty veiled women joined the initial march, behind hundreds of male protesters who followed a slow-moving truck from which chants were broadcast from loudspeakers. The assembly moved from the mosque toward the Municipal Complex, following the location's established spatial routine. The police and gendarmerie, however, moved to block their path, and the confrontation escalated from shouting and shoving to beating protesters with batons.[120] Dozens of loyalist counterprotesters, initially positioned on the far side of the police line, joined in beating protesters and journalists alike until they scattered. Troops remained throughout the area into the next day. Some of the protesters regrouped nearby, but they danced and sang a Bedouin wedding song and were left alone by the security forces.[121] In the wake of the violence, the police issued a rare apology and offered compensation to injured journalists. Four officers were even arrested for beating peaceful protesters, although the government blamed the protesters—and the Muslim Brotherhood in particular—for provoking the police to violence.

FIGURE 6.1. Police block the progress of a march at the Grand Husseini Mosque in July 2011, just moments before counterprotesters attacked the peaceful crowd. Source: Tally and Samuel Helfont.

176 CHAPTER 6

Tensions remained high when protesters organized a sit-in at the Municipal Complex two days later. As police broke up the protest with wooden clubs, a traffic officer grabbed a small barbecue grill (*manqal*) from a nearby shop and started chasing protesters, swinging it like a bludgeon.[122] At a smaller protest later that week, counterprotesters tried to clash with the protesters, but this time were prevented by the gendarmerie, which had erected metal fences and used their vehicles to keep the groups apart. At the end of that protest, police escorted the protesters safely past the loyalists. Another protest at the Interior Ministry (the building, not the circle) on July 20 called for the government to investigate the police response, with one sign reading, "I'm human, not a barbeque!"[123]

Back to Routine at the Kalouti Mosque

Meanwhile, Jordanians continued to mount protests around issues related to Israel/Palestine. An antinormalization alliance—now referring to itself as the Kalouti Group—organized weekly protests at the Kalouti Mosque throughout most of 2011, but none attracted more than a few hundred. Retired generals and others from the National Committee of Retired Servicemen demonstrated in front of the US embassy on September 14, angered when a Wikileaks cable confirmed suspicions about heavy US meddling in the Palestinian struggle.[124] But the Kalouti Group was inspired by events in Cairo in early September, where protesters breached the Israeli embassy by breaking apart a security barricade with sledgehammers, climbing through a window, and then tossing stacks of Hebrew-language documents out the window.[125] Elated by the Cairo embassy breach, the Kalouti Group announced on Facebook a "March of a Million" on the Israeli embassy in Amman, planned for Friday, September 16. Israeli officials evacuated all but a skeletal staff from their embassy,[126] and hundreds of security forces took up positions at the Kalouti Mosque and at other locations around the embassy.[127] The organizers hoped that the buzz around the Cairo embassy breach would provoke a massive turnout, and the size of the state show of force suggested it feared the same. But only a few hundred protesters turned out, chanting familiar slogans and burning an Israeli flag. Although the organizers were disappointed, they counted the preemptory evacuation of the Israeli officials as a success.[128] Kalouti protests continued periodically throughout the fall, with security forces outnumbering the protesters.

INCREASINGLY DIRECT CHALLENGES TO THE REGIME

The geography of dissent during this period saw the largest protests in the capital but the most worrisome protests for the regime in East Bank tribal areas. While *Hirak* protests diminished in size following the violent repression of the March 24 Youth encampment, the regular arrest of activists sparked ever more protests. When some Dhiban activists were arrested on May 10, for example, *Hirak* activists from nearby regions made their way into the building where the activists were being detained and staged an open-ended sit-in, demanding that either the prisoners be released or the police arrest them, too.[129] Here a spatial dynamic new to the uprising period comes into view, particularly the extent to which activists moved quickly to join protests in other regions. The detained activists, including day-wage-labor activist Snayd, were released pending charges.[130] When he was sentenced to three months in prison, *Hirak* activists organized more protests against his conviction.

Meanwhile, the state kept distributing largess to these communities, and the king regularly visited the governorates to personally listen to grievances. He met primarily with tribal elders, however, snubbing the *Hirak* groups. On June 12, the king gave a nationally televised speech in which he promised reforms including a transition to an elected prime minister. The following day, however, as his motorcade was headed to meet with tribal leaders in Tafileh, angry crowds reportedly threw stones and chanted slogans against the king. Government officials claimed that the crowds were overzealous supporters hoping to meet the king, but independent news sites reported that crowds burned government buildings and clashed with the gendarmerie. Precisely what happened remains unclear, and some residents suspected that counterprotesters were sabotaging their peaceful demonstrations by attacking people in the streets and setting fires.[131] Whatever happened, dozens were injured that afternoon, and rumors spread nationwide that Tafileh was revolting against the regime. When Agence France-Presse reported on the incident, some dozen loyalists protested outside its office in Amman for reporting what they believed was a false rumor of an attack against the king.[132] Jordanian journalists quickly responded by organizing their own demonstration in support of Agence France-Presse and press freedoms in general.

Violence against *Hirak* protests escalated in late summer. Counterprotesters attacked a proreform protest in Karak with sticks and knives on August 5, injuring at least eight; police again watched without intervening.[133] The following day, Karakis demonstrated against gendarmerie violence, chanting and throwing eggs at government buildings. Then they escalated their rhetoric, with "We want to throw out the king, too!" Dana M. Moss writes that one activist recalled the moment as the first time that protesters explicitly called for overthrowing the monarchy.[134] In other East Bank areas, tribes were putting aside historic grievances to make claims against the regime. In the village of Salhoub near Jerash, for example, representatives from the Bani Hassan, Bani Sakhr, Da'ajna, Bani Hamida, Ajarma, and Hajaya tribes mounted demonstrations in October calling for political and economic reforms. The gathering was significant because the Bani Sakhr leaders hosted the event in a Bani Hassan area—a symbolically significant action given the history of animosity between them—and the various tribes coordinated their calls for reform. Counterprotesters attacked some of the Bani Hassan protesters with guns, batons, and rocks, injuring thirty-five, and they sabotaged the protesters' sound system and smashed twenty-seven vehicles in the vicinity.[135] Some of the protesters then organized a press conference and accused the government of trying to stir up intertribal conflict as a strategy of divide and rule. On October 14–15, protesters in Ma'an, Irban, and Sahab were also violently attacked by loyalist counterprotesters.

Undeterred, tribes continued coordinating their protests, including elders and not just the younger *Hirak* activists. In November, new groups were formed among the Bani Sakhr, Bani Hassan, D'aja, Ajarma, and the *Hirak* of the northern Badia (desert) district, calling for government reform and creating the Jordanian Tribal Coalition Movement for Reform.[136] But on December 23, a protest in Mafraq organized by the Muslim Brotherhood that included Bani Hassan and Bani Sakhr leaders was again violently attacked by counterprotesters.[137] Originally planned as a march, the police ordered a change in the route that redirected the protesters toward counterprotesters armed with rocks and sticks. Some protesters sought shelter in a mosque but were chased inside and assaulted.[138] The local Islamic Action Front office was burned to the ground, and the gendarmerie used tear gas to break up fighting between protesters and counterprotesters. Government-owned media portrayed the clashes as Islamist-tribal conflicts, but Bani Hassan members issued a statement declaring, "the deplorable incident . . . was not the work of the tribe to which we proudly belong, but the work of a few individuals who held and still hold private agendas, who manipulated the youth in the name of loyalty and allegiance."[139] Bani Hamida members denounced the use of violence against protesters, but no investigation into the events materialized. Coordination among powerful tribal families and other political groups (including Islamists) now extended beyond the *Hirak* groups.

Meanwhile, the government tried to appear responsive to demands for a crackdown on corruption by arresting two prominent government officials. The first was former Amman mayor, Omar Ma'ani, who was charged with corruption and fraud; dramatically, he was also denied bail. Many believe he was scapegoated, however, as his arrest was tied up with powerful Amman landowners who objected to his efforts to create zoning restrictions for the Greater Amman Municipality plan.[140] The second was former General Intelligence Directorate chief Muhammad al-Dhahabi, who was arrested for laundering Iraqi money. He was banned from traveling abroad and his personal assets were frozen.[141]

With parliamentary elections scheduled for December, the government announced new electoral districts for areas with five thousand residents or more, a move intended to placate East Bank areas.[142] But many complained about how the districts were drawn and demanded their own districts. When the government said that reforms could not be implemented before the elections, protests broke out in many East Bank areas.[143] In the town of Northern Mazar, for example, locals organized a sit-in that shut down the municipal building by preventing employees from entering. As the number of these protests increased, the king again sacked the prime minister, replacing Bakhit with Awn al-Khasawneh on October 24. Khasawneh postponed the elections to 2012 and promised to resolve districting problems.[144]

Meanwhile, Jordanians continued expressing solidarity not only with protests across the Arab region but also with anticapitalist protests globally. A coalition of youth groups, political parties, and the Union of Professional Associations demonstrated on October 15 in front of the US embassy in solidarity with the Occupy Wall Street movement, which was itself inspired by the Arab uprisings and particularly the Tahrir encampment.[145] While they did not attempt to establish their own encampment, their solidarity with the sustained Occupy encampments rattled the regime. Even small encampments drew harsh responses from security forces. In December 2011, for example, unemployed youths from the Free Tafileh movement erected protest tents in front of a government building, refusing to leave until they were given jobs. Noting that routine protests produced diminished results, one of the leaders reflected on their tactics:

> We had already been demonstrating for more than a year. At that time the demonstrations had become a weekly routine, and the impact of the demonstrations seemed to go down. We wanted to do something new to show the government and other people that we are serious. So, we decided to set up the tent camp.[146]

The gendarmerie moved in and tore the tents down, beating protesters and dispersing them with tear gas. As many as two dozen were arrested, sparking solidarity protests in other towns and outside of the prison where they were being held.[147] One of the organizers in Tafileh estimated that eight hundred people regularly participated in weekly protests there, of a population of some 80,000.[148] Some other reform-minded protesters distanced themselves from the Free Tafileh movement. In Irbid, for example, *Hirak* activists argued that the Free Tafileh actions were too radical.

Despite the winter weather turning bad, protests still escalated nationwide around a wide range of issues. In Salt, Mafraq, Irbid, and Amman, protesters demonstrated against changes to the new landlord and tenant law passed in 2000. The new revisions had been slated to convert all forms of rent into "market rents" on December 31, 2010, but amid the escalating dissent the regime announced a delay for one year, and the law finally went into effect on January 1, 2012.[149] After incensed landlords gathered on January 29 to protest in front of Parliament, Prime Minister Khasawneh promised to review the law.

Dockworkers also went on strike in December, setting up a tent in front of the Aqaba Special Economic Zone Authority headquarters and disrupting port operations.[150] Their protests finally bore fruit: 757 day-laborers at the port, all employed before January 1, 2006, were granted permanent jobs.[151] Protesters in Karak, Ma'an, and Tafileh railed against corruption. One chant raised questions about the process of privatization, demanding "Where did the phosphates go?"

Southern leftists called for an end to the central US role in Jordanian affairs—a "Rejection of Subordination"—reiterating concerns over Jordan becoming the alternative Palestinian homeland.[152] In Amman, the gendarmerie and counterprotesters both used violence against protesters calling for reform. On December 25, for example, a Muslim Brotherhood protest at the Fourth Circle was violently dispersed after demonstrators allegedly tried to push into the Prime Ministry compound. On January 13 and 20, 2012, protesters at the Grand Husseini Mosque and the Fourth Circle clashed with counterprotesters. On January 27, some two thousand turned out for a Muslim Brotherhood protest downtown, where counterprotesters attacked not only the protesters but also the vehicle of Islamic Action Front Secretary-General Hamzeh Mansour as he departed. And after two proreform bloggers were anonymously stabbed in January and February, protests erupted around freedom of speech and the demand that the regime do something to stop such violence.

Abdullah II was more than frustrated. On February 12, he complained in a public speech that protests were scaring off potential foreign investors. Outraged that this was what the king was most concerned about, more protests were mounted against the state's economic policies. A poll from the University of Jordan's Center for Strategic Studies found that most Jordanians continued to view protests as the most viable means of affecting political change.[153] The new phosphate union, which still had no legal status, called for a second general strike, which completely shut down the operations of the company[154] until the workers reached an agreement with management.[155] In March, landlords from the downtown Amman souk again camped out in front of Parliament. Some activists tried to commemorate the anniversary of the March 24 Youth movement at the Interior Circle, but they found the location heavily guarded by the gendarmerie.

Outside of Amman, East Bank women organized a women-only protest to shame the regime for arresting protesters for demanding democracy and basic freedoms.[156] Hundreds of women also protested in Tafileh for the release of six protesters. The mother of two of those arrested said, "Women have been left out of the protest movement because Jordan is a traditional society. But just as people want to reform the regime, we want to reform women's role in political life."[157] As the ongoing protest environment led to more open political debate, more Jordanians were emboldened to criticize the royal family and even the king. In mid-March, six protesters in Tafileh were arrested for criticizing the king, as were thirteen others protesting at the Fourth Circle. After prominent Tafileh leaders expressed anger, the king released an eighteen-year-old who had burned a photo of the king at a protest.[158] In Ajloun, people openly discussed not only the king's failings but whether Abdullah II should be Jordan's "last king." Others debated whether perhaps a different Hashemite might be preferable on the throne. The name that circulated was Prince Hamzah, the half-brother of the king and whom King Hussein had designated as crown prince on his deathbed. Hamzah was seen as more in touch with, and respectful of, tribal customs and authority. East Bank communities wanted a restoration of the social contract, and they were musing about which Hashemite might better deliver it.

Amid ongoing protests, the king sacked Khasawneh in May 2012 and appointed Fayez Tarawneh, the third premier since Rifaʻi was sacked in February 2011. But Jordanians remained frustrated, and they continued mounting protests around new issues and in new spaces. Beginning in June 2012, for example, a coalition of activists organized demonstrations against Article 308 of the Penal Code, sometimes called the Rape Law.[159] On June 25, some two hundred protesters, primarily women, linked arms at the Interior Circle, and they continued gathering in that manner throughout the summer. They also organized demonstrations on Rainbow Street near the First Circle, a location with no prior history of protest.[160] Everyone seemed to be protesting something, but not in coordination or with a united message.

THE TEMPORALITIES OF JORDAN'S "UPRISING" PROTESTS

What did these diverse protests mean for Jordan as well as for the protesters themselves? By the fall of 2012, Jordanians had been protesting weekly and sometimes daily for some twenty months. Many activists saw their protests as part of the regional Arab uprisings and as aligning with those uprisings temporally. But while many labeled the other Arab uprisings as "revolutions" (*thawrat*), they did not label their own protests as such. Of course, the regime, government officials, and loyalist counterprotesters would be loath to grant the protests status as a revolution. But even activists and opposition groups did not talk about Jordan's protests as revolutionary. Indeed, one of the most interesting insights gleaned by viewing the period of the uprisings from the standpoint of Jordanian activists is that the protests in early 2011—when tens of thousands were demonstrating in all parts of the country—have not been given a name. This namelessness seems surprising because many of Jordan's other major protests and rebellions, such as *Habbit Nisan* and *Hayyat Karak,* have names. Some speak of *Hirak* 2011 or the *Hirak* protests (*ihtijajat al-hirak*), but the period is often just referred to as the 2011 protests (*ihtijajat* 2011). The attempted March 24 Youth encampment retains its own name (and anniversary), but others do not. In fall 2012, however, new massive nationwide protests would ultimately serve as a kind of bookend to the uprising period, and they would receive their own name. And like their namesake, the protests broke out in response to the lifting of subsidies, as mandated by the International Monetary Fund.

Earlier, in June 2012, Prime Minister Fayez al-Tarawneh had announced the cancellation of several food and fuel subsidies. Demonstrations broke out in all parts of the country, many organized by local *Hirak* groups. In Tafileh, protesters chanted, "The people are the red line!"[161] In Karak, they waved shoes during a visit by the prime minister, who was also from Karak.[162] These summer protests, however, remained small and localized. In September, Tarawneh announced the need to reduce fuel subsidies by around 10 percent. This time the response was massive, and protests brought the nation to a standstill. In a tactic not seen before, taxi drivers in Amman clogged a major street, abandoned their vehicles, and marched to the Ministry of Transportation to protest the price hikes. A few days later, police used tear gas to disperse protesters in Tafileh who were chanting against the king. After days of nationwide protests, Tarawneh restored the subsidies. At Interior Circle protests in Amman, two dozen were charged not only with unlawful assembly but also with defaming the king.

Tensions continued to escalate around multisectoral protests as well as narrow grievances. On October 3, the Muslim Brotherhood, Islamic Action Front, and some *Hirak* groups organized a large demonstration at the Grand Husseini Mosque under the title "Save the Homeland." The group was met by counterprotesters declaring "We Are with You," meaning with the king. Then, on October 5, Abdullah II dissolved Parliament before the end of its term, and thousands took to the streets nationwide demanding reforms. Five days later—shocking no one—the king sacked Tarawneh, appointing Abdullah Ensour as the fourth new prime minister since the start of the uprising period.

184   CHAPTER 6

Even the National Committee of Retired Servicemen was mounting protests, demanding better retirement benefits at the Royal Court in October and at the Fourth Circle on November 10.[163]

But a new prime minister could not undo Jordan's agreements with the IMF, and on November 13, Ensour announced that the subsidies on fuel and electricity had to be reduced. The public response was immediate and explosive, and Jordanians flooded into the streets nationwide. In Amman, they gathered in multiple locations, including at the Interior Circle, where some two to three thousand hoped to establish an ongoing encampment. The gendarmerie inexplicably had not anticipated a protest at that location and was concentrated in the downtown area two miles away. As troops and armored vehicles tried to make their way uphill on the snaking streets to reach the Interior Circle, public transit workers created obstructions on the roads. Protesters threw rocks at the gendarmerie, which retaliated with tear gas and clubs. Some protesters managed to regroup in neighboring Jebal Hussein on Jalil Street, but the gendarmerie used tear gas and armored vehicles to block them from reaching the crowds assembled downtown.

Elsewhere in Amman, smaller protests erupted in poor neighborhoods where people felt neglected by the state.[164] Protesters from Hayy Tafayleh marched downtown toward Raghadan Palace and joined others assembled there. They chanted and gave speeches for several hours, after which they moved back toward the Grand Husseini Mosque in what were now the early hours of the morning.[165] Muslim Brotherhood members openly called for the fall of the regime for the first time.[166] Violent confrontations at the Interior Circle and Jebal Hussein continued, with the gendarmerie only able to fully disperse the protesters in the early hours of November 14.[167]

Outside of Amman, protests were also violent. Several gendarmerie officers were injured when shots were fired during protests in Taybeh and Irbid, where demonstrators set a gas station on fire. After an Irbid protester was killed outside of a police station, angry crowds set fire to government cars and burned down a municipal building.[168] In Salt, protesters blocked the main Salt–Amman highway and set six police vehicles on fire. A crowd tried to break police lines to reach Prime Minister Ensour's home, which was empty at the time. They threw rocks and smashed two nearby cars, and the police retaliated with tear gas. In Baqaʻa Camp protesters clashed with the police. In

Ajloun, hundreds demonstrated in the central square. In Jerash, police shot a protester, who died sixteen days later. In Dhiban, hundreds blocked a major intersection. In Karak, protesters set a court building on fire, blocked the highway with burning tires, and assembled in front of the governorate offices. In Tafileh, they blocked roads, attacked government buildings, and set three police vehicles on fire. In Mazar, they burned down the main courthouse. In Ma'an, they erected tents, vandalized government buildings, and blocked the Desert Highway with burning tires.[169] Within twenty-four hours, the police had arrested hundreds of protesters. Teachers called a strike and the Union of Professional Associations called for a three-hour work stoppage for the following Sunday. At least two people were killed and hundreds were arrested in the four days of unrest.

These nationwide protests, which saw tens of thousands in the streets and considerable destruction and burning of government property, came to be known as the *Habbit Tishreen* (November rage) protests. The name invokes an emotional ("rage") response to the anti-austerity 1989 *Habbit Nisan* protests that led King Hussein to embark on limited political liberalization. But this time, protesters nationwide crossed the red line against direct criticism of the king. For several days, it appeared that Jordan might have a revolution after all. Outside the Grand Husseini Mosque in Amman, protesters even chanted, "Revolution, revolution, it's a popular revolution!"

Contentious Temporalities

The eventfulness of these moments lies in the fact that the future seems suddenly up for grabs. The Arab uprisings were such a period, and indeed, some of them effected change at the national and regional levels. But the uprisings must also be situated historically, and the case of Jordan is illustrative. While its nationwide protests drew affective connections of solidarity and common struggle with protesters elsewhere in the region and even globally, the 2011 escalation and its patterns both emerged from and introduced innovations to existing repertoires for protest and repression. The failure of multisectoral protests to cohere into a united call for the fall of the regime is explained by the existing geographies of political, social, and economic power, where privatization and neoliberal investments concentrated wealth in a geography inverted from that of the regime's East Bank tribal support base. The state-maintaining that took place through the regime's scramble to placate loyalist areas combined with demands for restoring the social contract and abandoning some neoliberal economic policies. As we shall see in coming chapters, the state's decisions during this period about where and how to deploy state violence or reach accommodation in response to protests would have long-term consequences for the composition and exercise of Hashemite power. Careful attention to the content and affective dimensions of claim-making during protests also helps reveal how the seemingly conservative and nonrevolutionary claims of most protests during this period—mostly calls for reform but a shift toward calls for the fall of the regime—bring into focus the greatest challenges to Hashemite authority. In this final section I probe an additional dimension of the period, namely, a shift in the temporal dimensions of the content of public political claim-making. What is said at protests, in manifestos, and among East Bank tribal communities brings forth new imagined futures. Debates about these hypothetical futures suggest that not all Jordanians embrace the regime's narrative about Jordan's past, present, and future.

In the context of claim-making at protests, even small changes to the words or phrasing of slogans and chants can reveal shifts in how Jordanians view political authorities and what political futures they imagine or hope to realize. By the time of the *Habbit Tishreen* protests in November 2012, a growing number of Jordanians were no longer afraid to cross the red line and criticize the king. Some chants called for him to step down, and others imagined someone else in power. Some of these criticisms of the king were conveyed subtly. For example, Jordanians would understand "We are speaking Arabic, clear Arabic, leave!" as a reference to the king's poor command of Arabic. The joke is that the protesters want the king to understand their demands, but the message is conveyed without naming an addressee. Other savvy protesters saw opportunity in the fact that Prime Minister Ensour's first name is Abdullah, creating ambiguity as to whether the king or prime minister was the addressee. Large banners held by the crowd outside the Grand Husseini Mosque, for example, declared, "Freedom is from God, in spite of you, Abdullah!"[170] Protest chants included variations on "Step down, Abdullah, step down!" and "Freedom, Freedom, Down with Abdullah!" But which Abdullah?

A more obvious crossing of the red line was "Qaddafi, Ben Ali, and Mubarak all left, Abdullah, go, go!"[171] Since the first three were the heads of state ousted in 2011, one can reasonably conclude that the Abdullah here is the king. Other chants and slogans, however, were unmistakably direct. At Firas Circle in Jebal Hussein, protesters chanted, "Oh Abdullah, son of Hussein, where is the people's money?" Similarly, "Rania and Abdullah stole Jordan!" leaves no ambiguity. On November 16, after three days of nationwide protest, large crowds in multiple locations finally chanted the slogan of the Arab uprisings, "The People Want the Fall of the Regime!" Although the phrase had been heard sporadically at protests since the beginning of the uprising period, this was the first time that large crowds in Jordan adopted it.

The "Corruption Dabke" (*dabka al-fasad*) also became popular during the uprising period, performed in Hayy Tafayleh in summer 2011 and in multiple locations during the 2012 *Habbit Tishreen* protests. Here protesters repurpose the dabke—a traditional dance of the Greater Syria area usually performed at weddings and celebrations—as a vehicle for political claim-making. Men form a circle, hold hands, and perform the dabke's repeated sequence of steps while chanting verse. Multiple versions of the Corruption Dabke are in circulation, but one captured widespread attention during the *Habbit Tishreen* protests. It begins by naming the story of Ali Baba and the Forty Thieves, a well-known tale from *One Thousand and One Nights*. Whereas in the original tale, Ali Baba discovers the den of treasures belonging to the forty thieves, here the forty thieves are *with* Ali Baba. In the second line, "Ali Baba" is replaced with "Ali Baba II"—a more transparent reference to King Abdullah II—who is then named as the individual directly responsible for corruption. The third line references "your palace," indicating that Ali Baba II is royalty. In the fourth line, however, the metaphor gives way to a direct attack on the king when "Ali Baba II" is replaced with "Abdullah II."

> Forty thieves with Ali Baba, forty thieves
> Ali Baba II is the sponsor of corruption, Ali Baba II
> We will not stand in front of your palace begging for your benevolence, we
>   will not stand in front of your palace
> Your epoch has gone Abdullah II, your epoch has gone
> Our sustenance is in the hands of God not in yours, our sustenance is in the
>   hands of God
> We're the slaves of God, we're not your slaves, we're the slaves of God.[172]

CHAPTER 6

In no uncertain terms, the verses directly inform the king that his era is over. It indexes a turning point in the plot, that from here on they would only serve God, not the king. The verses are repeated numerous times, with the dance lasting ten to fifteen minutes and as long as half an hour. Over the course of a protest, the Corruption Dabke may be performed several times.

As shown in this chapter, the old East Bank social contract had been under strain well before the uprising period began in late 2010. The king drew ire from many East Bank circles when he removed his half-brother Hamzah as crown prince in 2004. But Hamzah continued to visit tribal leaders, and it was common knowledge that many believed he would be the better king. By 2012 his name was invoked in *Hirak* protests, most commonly outside the capital. Some held up pictures of Hamzah and called for him to replace Abdullah II as king. "This king can't reform himself," one protester told a reporter, "So let him bring in his brother."[173]

The invocation of Hamzah's name reveals the strain on the social contract that East Bankers believe gives them the right to assert moral and material claims on the Hashemite regime. It signaled a moment of precarity for Abdullah II. But the details of alternative hypothetical futures have not before been brought into focus. We have already seen how the Hashemite claim their legitimacy to rule in part as a notable Hijazi tribe with blood ties to the family of the Prophet Muhammad and as leaders of the Great Arab Revolt of 1916–18. East Bank tribal communities are therefore assumed to accept Hashemite authority as legitimate, and the regime goes to great lengths to cultivate this narrative.

But the legitimacy argument does not hold up on close inspection. First, legitimacy has many possible meanings. As Lisa Wedeen argues, it could entail widespread popular support, moral authority to rule over others, adherence to established practices, or just a general appropriateness to rule.[174] Measuring legitimacy (however defined) is problematic if not impossible, because evidence such as expressions of fealty tell us only what people are willing to do publicly and not what they believe. As Wedeen shows in her study of political authority in Syria, people may feign their adoration of the regime because they fear retribution if they fail to do so. As the case of Syria demonstrates, the maintenance of rule has less to do with legitimacy than with other techniques of power. Even more, because European colonial powers helped establish many Arab monarchies, including Jordan's, significant portions of the population—particularly leftists and Arab nationalists—have always questioned the authority of those colonial regimes.[175] Monarchies across the region were violently overthrown in the twentieth century, and earlier chapters show that the Hashemite monarchy has not gone unchallenged. Indeed, such challenges are the very reason that many scholars questioned the regime's stability in the early period of the uprising.[176]

Second, the legitimacy argument assumes that protests are a response to a deficit of legitimacy produced by grievances. The sequencing of this argument, however, obfuscates the contingency and the logics of the protest environment, such as how people become political activists and even revolutionaries through their participation and as a consequence of their participation. Activists organize protests, but protests also produce activists. In this sense, a crisis of legitimacy is—more convincingly—a *byproduct* of large multisectoral protests rather than its cause. Yet during the period of the uprisings, the legitimacy argument resurfaced among journalists and scholars who observed that with only one exception (Bahrain), the other monarchies had survived the uprisings. Monarchies are assumed to have greater legitimacy, but convincing evidence is never given. It is precisely this argument that is seen to explain why Jordan was a null case during the uprising period. But as I have shown here, Jordan did see a massive escalation of protests and an unprecedented willingness to criticize the king. This "monarchical exceptionalism" argument about legitimacy is repeatedly debunked by scholars who showed how individual monarchies quelled their protests,[177] but it never seems to go away.

But Jordan's protests did bring forth debates about the Hashemite regime and who should hold political authority, articulating the moral and material obligations of the regime. Claim-making during the period from 2006 to 2012 sees East Bank communities imagining and debating Jordan's political future, from loyalists who steadfastly back the king to those calling for the fall of the regime. I have already shown that the long history of East Bank protest upends the conventional view of East Bankers as a unified and universally loyal support base. Long-standing economic grievances combine with complaints about the unevenness of patronage, both perceived and real. And with the rise of a radical nativism in the years leading up to the uprising, some have not hesitated to criticize the regime. Consider six distinct possible political futures for Jordan that are articulated at protests:

1. The Hashemite monarchy and King Abdullah II will continue to rule with absolute authority.
2. The Hashemite monarchy and King Abdullah II will continue to rule but must adopt significant policy changes.
3. The Hashemite monarchy will continue to rule but with a different king.
4. The Hashemite monarchy and King Abdullah II will continue to rule, but he will be the last king and some other form of East Bank tribal authority will replace the monarchy upon his death.
5. The Hashemite monarchy will continue, and King Abdullah II will remain on the throne, but the state will become a constitutional monarchy and the king will reign and not rule.
6. The Hashemite monarchy will be replaced by a democratic republic.

The regime prefers the maintenance of the status quo, as do loyalists like the counterprotesters and many in the security forces willing to use violence to maintain the king's authority. Hypotheticals 2 and 3 invoke futures in which the Hashemite authority is ongoing, but in 2 it is conditional on adopting policy changes and in 3 the personhood of the king is open for discussion; Hamzah is currently invoked as that possible alternative. In hypothetical 4, the Hashemites remain in power only through Abdullah's lifetime, after which the monarchy would end, and presumably some other form of East Bank tribal authority would come into power. Hypothetical 5 calls for a constitutional monarchy, which would mean that Hashemite rule would convert to an exclusively ceremonial role. Hypothetical 6 imagines the monarchy dissolved entirely, replaced by a democratic republic. As we will see below, the radical nationalist version of a democratic republic envisions that only certain East Bank tribes would have the full rights of citizens.

Each of these hypothetical futures was invoked during the uprising period. Most analyses of Jordan's uprising, however, focused only on how Jordanians conservatively changed the slogan common to the Arab uprisings, swapping out the "fall" of the regime for its "reform." Not attending more closely to the content of slogans, chants, and manifestos during this period misses a significant shift in public political discourse, and one that we shall see has affected politics in the kingdom for years to come. Hypothetical 2 was undoubtedly the most common claim heard during the protests prior to the 2012 *Habbit Tishreen* protests, with most calling for reforms but drawing a line at calling for the fall of the regime. The East Bank manifestos that emerged in 2010 and 2011, however, also expressed alarm over Queen Rania and the place of Jordanians of Palestinian descent in Jordan's future. Nativists in particular imagine that all Jordanians of Palestinian descent will return to their own homeland, and the regime should be working aggressively to that end. Some also imagine a future without the monarchy, such as the discussions in Ajloun about whether Abdullah II might be Jordan's last king. Others openly suggested that Hamzah might be a better king, a view that burst into public view during the *Habbit Tishreen* protests. But hypotheticals 3 through 6 each invoke a future at odds with the official state narrative projecting Hashemite rule into the future. Islamists, leftist activists, and other opposition figures frequently call for hypothetical 5, a true constitutional monarchy.

The most radical of these scenarios—hypothetical 6—not only imagines a future in which the Hashemite regime no longer wields political authority, in its nativist version it also invokes the past as a means of calling into question whether the Hashemites should have authority to rule Jordan at all. Prominent among those explicitly voicing this view is Ahmad Uwaydi al-Abbadi, a leader in the Abbadi tribe. He has been repeatedly arrested since 2012 for characterizing the Hashemites as outsiders and calling for East Bank tribes to assume political leadership of the country. He advocates for a democratic republic, but as a nativist he invokes "Jordanian" identity in its narrowest sense, one in which eligibly for citizenship would be "negotiated" among East Bank tribal leaders.[178] At protests, he refers to a large map showing the areas controlled by the main tribes in 1917, advancing a narrative whose temporality is at odds with that of the regime: those who arrived after the Great Arab Revolt (including the Hashemite) are simply not Jordanian. When asked by a reporter during a protest in 2019 what would happen to the majority of Jordanians who do not belong to the major East Bank tribes, he responded, "this will be subject to negotiations" among the real sons of Jordan.[179] This nativist narrative calls the present and future of Hashemite rule into question by relegating its status in Jordan's past to that of an outsider or interloper. Jordan's protests thus work as spaces of vibrant public political debate in which people both invoke and consider hypothetical futures. Given that this debate is anchored in the regime's supposed East Bank tribal support base, it reveals that the king's authority and perhaps even the fate of the Hashemite regime remain very much open for discussion.

Chapter 7

THE TECHNIQUES AND EVOLVING SPATIAL DYNAMICS OF PROTEST AND REPRESSION

REVOLUTIONARY OR EVENTFUL MOMENTS MAY BE FLEETING, BUT challenges to state power are less the exception than the rule. After exceptional moments of unrest (like the Arab uprisings), states work hard to (re) assert their power, just as activists and opposition groups struggle to keep alternative futures alive and destabilize the state's assertion of stability. These ongoing engagements receive less attention than "big event" moments, but they are critical moments for state-maintaining.[1]

The November 2012 *Habbit Tishreen* protests ended with the security forces clearing the streets, and hundreds were arrested nationwide. Activists were divided over a number of issues, including the utility of trying to restart protests. The uprisings in Libya and Syria had devolved into civil wars, and Islamists had swept Egypt's elections—outcomes that neither the leftist activists nor the *Hirak* wished to see for Jordan. Some activists started thinking of Jordan's own Muslim Brotherhood—with whom they had coordinated in antinormalization and uprising-era protests—as a greater enemy than the regime. As one leftist activist put it, many at the time thought "Now is the time for an historic reconciliation with the regime, because Islamists are the real enemy."[2] Jordan's mainstream Islamists, however, were themselves splintering. One faction created a new centrist Islamist group, leaving behind two others that both claimed the Muslim Brotherhood title. Then in the aftermath of

Egypt's bloody countercoup in July 2013, enthusiasm for major political reforms further diminished.

My activist interlocutors were also deeply divided over Syria.[3] Many of them had long appreciated the Syrian regime's staunch anti-imperialist and anti-Israeli positions. With the onset of the Syrian civil war, some still defended the Asad regime. Others could not bring themselves to take the side of a regime that was committing unspeakable atrocities against its people; but neither could they comfortably throw their support behind an opposition increasingly riddled with Gulf-funded Islamist militias. The Syrian conflict ended friendships among activists and splintered the antinormalization movement, with one long-time Kalouti organizer leaving Jordan to reside in Damascus. As late as 2016, many who had been highly active in the 2011–12 protests remained reluctant to return to the streets.[4]

Activists continued to mount protests over these years, but most events remained small and localized and none called for widespread political reform. The first new large-scale nationwide protests were sparked by another violent Israeli campaign in Gaza in summer 2014.[5] But in winter 2018, the small anti-austerity protests outside of Amman were followed in May with the nationwide *Habbit Huzayran* protests against a draft new tax law and austerity policies (chap. 1), likely the largest protests in Jordan's history. More protests broke out later that year over the revised new tax law, and much of 2019 saw aggrieved East Bankers protesting not only in the outlying governorates but also by traveling hundreds of miles to protest in the capital. Multiple sectors organized protests into 2020 until the coronavirus pandemic brought a weeks-long lockdown. When restrictions were eased, however, Jordanians slowly returned to the streets over issues related to the pandemic, more Israeli atrocities, and to commemorate the tenth anniversary of the March 24 Youth encampment.

This chapter examines the decade of protest after the uprising period, further developing the theoretical interventions introduced earlier about techniques for state-maintaining in the face of continued challenges. I examine Jordan's post-uprising repertoires of protest and repression and show how and why the regime deploys its coercive apparatuses unevenly. As part of the process of state-maintaining, political authorities make decisions about how to contend with resistance, and those choices shape the institutions and practices of governance. That is, protests work to structure the political terrain on which the regime seeks to produce and maintain its power. In the next section, I provide an overview of the sectors of ongoing protest, summarizing familiar movements like labor and examining new protests around such issues as citizenship, water scarcity, nuclear energy, and a gas deal with Israel. I then examine protest repertoires and their spatial dimensions, highlighting innovations to the established routines. I examine the regime's hostility toward protest tents, theorizing about why encampments are so threatening to the state. Finally, I return to Jordan's repertoire for repression and examine its techniques and tactics, including their spatial dimensions, for responding to public expressions of political dissent.

SECTORS OF PROTEST

In the post-uprising period, Jordan's protests fell into four clusters that sometimes overlapped: those organized by Amman-based activists, political parties, and the Union of Professional Associations; those organized by East Bank and *Hirak* activists; those organized around a single issue by individuals immediately affected; and nationwide protests in which activists were joined by large numbers who did not normally participate in protests. In the latter, large protests broke out primarily around economic issues (e.g., taxes, austerity) and international issues (e.g., Israel/Palestine, the Iraq War). The hundreds of protests that were mounted between those massive waves of protest were much smaller in size, from a few dozen to hundreds or perhaps a few thousand participants in the downtown Amman area. This section examines some of the new and ongoing protests to show how they map geographically and spatially. The picture that comes into view is one in which most of the more violent protests took place in East Bank governorates or in East Bank neighborhoods in the capital. Blocking roads was common everywhere outside of Amman but destroying government property was more common to the south. In the capital, most activists worked hard to avoid the damage of public and private property that was common in East Bank towns like Ma'an, Tafileh, and Karak.

Single-Issue Protests

Most of the new locations for protest were small, mounted near government offices, and policed by only a handful of regular police officers (not the gendarmerie) who seemed more interested in observing than interfering in the

196   CHAPTER 7

demonstrations. One ongoing set of protests concerned Jordan's law on citizenship, which prevents Jordanian women from passing their citizenship to their children, even those born on Jordanian soil; only the children of men who are Jordanian nationals gain citizenship. In opposition to this law, Nima Habashneh created a Facebook page in 2009 under the slogan, "My mother is Jordanian, and her citizenship is my right." Habashneh and her group began to organize protests and sit-ins at various government offices in Amman each year, and their protests include mostly women silently holding signs unless passersby stop to ask questions. In February 2013, they joined eleven other small groups to form a coalition, "My Nationality Is the Right of My Family."[6] Palestinians from Gaza, who, unlike refugees from the West Bank, were never granted citizenship rights in Jordan, have also protested periodically since 2006 for citizenship rights.

Other protests sought to press claims around internet censorship, press freedoms, and laws limiting freedom of speech.[7] Students demonstrated on campuses about issues like tuition increases, such as in November 2016 at Hashemite University. After one student activist was expelled, hundreds of students demonstrated for days, demanding the expulsion be reversed. Small protests are also held annually on International Earth Day and International Women's Day, and in solidarity with any number of protests and movements happening around the globe. In 2019, for example, the Jordanian branch of the international environmental movement Fridays for Future began holding marches at the King Hussein Gardens in West Amman. Some small protests have also been organized periodically against temporary government closures of bakeries. José Ciro Martínez reports small protests in which the police stand around smiling and not interfering as bakers give speeches and those in the crowd wave bread.[8]

Outside of Amman, dozens of protests were mounted annually in East Bank areas over water shortages. While wealthy Jordanians are able to purchase water from private suppliers, many Jordanians endure several days each week without water. The government has drained nonrenewable water tables over the decades—in large part to service urban and resort areas—and hundreds of unlicensed wells have made water even more scarce. In East Bank towns suffering from chronic shortages, residents regularly mount protests by blocking roads and demonstrating in front of local municipal offices. The king or

TECHNIQUES AND DYNAMICS OF PROTEST AND REPRESSION   197

other government officials then travel to meet with locals and promise them water. During one 2013 protest in a town near Mafraq, the king personally assured the townspeople that water tankers would arrive soon. They refused the offer, however, extracting from the king instead a promise to provide the area with piped water.[9] In 2014 in the town of Beit Ras (north of Irbid), a man was killed when he tried to pass through a blockade created by water-shortage protesters.[10] Protesters in many nearby villages, belonging to the Bani Kinana tribe, proceeded to attack government offices, disrupt work on water lines, and compel the workers at gunpoint to stop working until government representatives arrived to negotiate.[11]

A new environmental movement emerged in 2009 in opposition to nuclear energy. The Jordanian Friends of the Environment opposed the Jordan Atomic Energy Commission's announcement that it planned to build nuclear power plants in the kingdom.[12] According to antinuclear activist Basel Burgan, the movement was initially made up of middle-class environmentalists, who organized events in many East Bank tribal areas to educate them as to the economic, political, health, and environmental consequences of nuclear energy.[13] Some tribal leaders were persuaded by the toxicity concerns and in turn took their grievances to Amman. A group from the Bani Sakhr tribe, for example, protested at the Fourth Circle against plans to build nuclear plants on their land.

While many protests remained small, labor activism was the first to regain its vibrancy in the post-uprising period, often demonstrating against government failures to honor promises made following earlier protests. Phosphate workers mounted another strike in May 2014,[14] and teachers mounted demonstrations as union negotiations with the government continued. The teachers reached a new agreement with Prime Minister Abdullah Ensour concerning wage increases in 2016, but when those increases had not been implemented by the start of the school year 2019, hundreds of teachers marched on the Prime Ministry on September 5.[15] The gendarmerie blocked their path to the Fourth Circle, dispersed the crowd with tear gas, and arrested fifty-seven teachers, who were later released without being charged. Many Jordanians were outraged by such an extreme response to a peaceful march, and the union called for a nationwide general strike on September 8, the start of the school year. In Amman, the main demonstration assembled at the Fifth Circle of Zahran Street, a half-mile west of the Fourth Circle because the latter had been blocked

198 CHAPTER 7

FIGURE 7.1. Man holding two photos of his son, who was imprisoned for throwing stones during a visit to the West Bank. Source: Jillian Schwedler.

by gendarmerie troops and armored vehicles. Large demonstrations continued nationwide for weeks, with the teachers receiving widespread support from all sectors of society.[16] Although the government relented and offered wage increases that fall, in July 2020 police stormed the offices of the teachers' union, arrested its officers, and declared the union disbanded. Teachers continued to organize protests into 2021, demanding that their union be reinstated.

Finally, while most protests are organized by groups or movements, some protesters make highly personal claims within the context of broader issues. One man with a poster bearing two photos of his son—one as a young boy and one as a teenager—appears at protests in Amman about a wide range of issues. Israeli Defense Forces had arrested the son during a visit to the West Bank and sentenced him to fifteen years in prison for throwing stones.

Large-Scale Protests
The lifting of government subsidies and issues relating to Israel/Palestine continued to bring the largest crowds to the streets nationwide. The 2018 *Habbit*

Huzayran protests against the proposed tax law and austerity measures led Abdullah II to—yet again—sack the prime minister, now Hani Mulki, and replace him with the reformist Omar Razzaz, formerly a World Bank director in Lebanon and the CEO of Ayla Oasis, a US $1 billion tourist resort in Aqaba built around a man-made lagoon.[17] To shore up support for a revised version of the tax law, the king traveled around the governorates throughout the summer to hear grievances directly from East Bank tribal elites. In November, the revised tax law was published in the *Official Gazette,* clearing the path for it to take effect on January 1.[18] A week later, on November 30, protesters assembled near the Fourth Circle under the slogans *Ma'anash* ("we have nothing") and *Mish Sakitin* ("we will not be silent"), which were hashtagged on Twitter and Facebook. As with the massive protests six months earlier, claim-making around unemployment quickly expanded to condemn corruption and neoliberalism in general. Crowds increased in size over the next four weeks, peaking at some two thousand on December 13. Angry Jordanians traveled from all parts of Jordan to join protests in the capital, reproducing the spatial routine adopted by the day-wage labor movement in 2006. While some of the protesters told journalists that they were loyal to the regime, others chanted "No loyalty or affiliation, except to the Lord of Heaven."[19] Protesters in Karak, Irbid, and Dhiban established small, tented encampments and mounted prolonged sit-ins, sometimes remaining at their sites overnight. Over the next months, weekly demonstrations became routine but numbers diminished to a few dozen, and they were often outnumbered at least five to one by security forces. Even a protest commemorating the thirtieth anniversary of the 1989 *Habbit Nisan* attracted only some two dozen protesters.

As we saw in chapter 5, deadly Israeli military campaigns bring Jordanians to the streets in large numbers. In July 2014, Operation Protective Edge and its large-scale invasion of Gaza lasted for seven weeks, killing more than twenty-three hundred Palestinians and injuring ten thousand, including three thousand children.[20] More than ten thousand Jordanians protested nationwide throughout the campaign. Several marches in Amman began at the Grand Husseini Mosque, but protests at the Kalouti Mosque attracted at least a thousand. Protests also broke out in the Wihdat, Baqa'a, and Jerash camps, but many Jordanians of Palestinian descent traveled across Amman and from outlying areas to join the Kalouti and Grand Husseini protests. With large crowds come heightened tensions as well as the increased possibility of crossing red lines or making innovations to the established routine. At one Kalouti protest during that period, for example, some dozen protesters broke from the spatial routine and pushed past the gendarmerie in the direction of the Israeli embassy. They were arrested and detained for days but were released without being charged.

A new movement emerged around an issue relating to Israel/Palestine. Jordan had begun exploring an agreement for the purchase of natural gas from Israel's Leviathan fields—land that most Jordanians view as stolen Palestinian land. In 2014, the National Electric Power Company (NEPCO) announced it would begin importing gas from Israel when the facilities were ready in several years. Some antinormalization activists organized a new movement to contest the deal under the slogan, "The gas of the enemy is occupation."[21] The spatial imaginary of the slogan was intended to invoke two senses of occupation: Israeli occupation of Palestinian land, but also the extension of Israeli occupation into Jordan via purchase of "occupied" gas. The movement brought together a diverse collection of Islamists, leftists, *Hirak* groups, trade unions, pan-Arab nationalists, professional associations, women's rights groups, and youth organizations; the National Committee of Retired Servicemen also endorsed the movement.[22] In order to keep the message focused, only anti-gas slogans were used, and no flags of political parties or other flags were carried at protests. Demonstrations were held in diverse locations: at the Grand Husseini Mosque, Parliament, the Fourth Circle, and the NEPCO building adjacent to the Ministry of Energy. To ensure that the movement was not Amman-centric, protests were also organized in Irbid and Zarqa. Turnout varied from less than a hundred to as many as a few thousand. At the protests outside of Parliament, parliamentarian allies sometimes emerged to address the protesters and journalists. Smaller protests continued through winter 2015, but one downtown protest, on March 5, attracted some three thousand. Invigorated at the turnout, the march broke the established spatial routine and continued past the Municipal Complex in Ras al-Ayn until it reached the Fourth Circle. When the deal was signed in September 2016, protests again broke out in multiple locations, and more rounds of protests were held in March and May 2019.[23] While those were relatively small, nationwide protests broke out with the June 2019 announcement of the US plan to resolve the Palestinian-Israeli conflict, the so-called "Deal of the Century."[24]

When the gas deal went into effect on January 1, 2020, thousands joined protests over the next four weeks. The final one was on January 24, when the coalition called for protesters to meet near the NEPCO offices and Ministry of Energy. Less than a hundred protesters were well outnumbered by security forces. The protesters were blocked from proceeding along Zahran Street, diverted down a side street but allowed to assemble at the rear of those buildings. The demonstration continued for an hour, with the usual chants interrupted by some speeches. Activist and writer Hisham Bustani articulated their demands over a bullhorn, but he also addressed the security forces as fellow Jordanians, saying that they should be defending Jordan by opposing the gas deal, since "the gas of the enemy is occupation" of Jordan as well as Palestine.

REPERTOIRES FOR PROTEST

How do protests work to structure the political terrain on which political authorities produce and maintain power? In what ways did the repertoire for protest evolve during and after the uprising period? Protests in Jordan during this period can by classified into four main types: those in the outlying East Bank governorates organized by angry tribes and *Hirak* groups; those in the capital and cities organized by the political parties, professional unions, and other independent and organized activists; protests specific to narrow issues like labor, water, or citizenship; and spontaneous nationwide protests in which Jordanians of all backgrounds pour into the streets in anger over issues like Israeli military operations. How these protests unfold is subject to a variety of factors, including spatial routines for specific locations.

In many ways, the tactics as well as the spatial routines for protesting in the outlying East Bank tribal areas, particularly in the south, have changed little over the decades. Protests in those areas are also more violent than elsewhere, often seeing the destruction of government property and vehicles. Infrastructure sabotage, the destruction of government property, and the blocking of roads are the key techniques for drawing the state's attention. As we will see in a moment, however, the increasing use of tents is an innovation that has become highly contentious.

Protests organized by independent and organized activists, political parties, and the Union of Professional Associations, by comparison, largely seek to avoid violence. They adhere to established protest routines and spaces, and

202   CHAPTER 7

they seek to avoid damaging property. While Amman has multiple known spaces for protest, not all spaces are equally contentious. The largest protests in the country continue to be those at the Grand Husseini Mosque, and yet those marches invite some of the least aggressive policing as long as protesters adhere to the established spatial routine of marching from the mosque to the Municipal Complex.

Often what explains the state's uneven use of violence is not the content of the claim-making but who is protesting and where they are doing it. Protests in January 2015 again demonstrate this dynamic. That month, protests erupted across Jordan against the publication of cartoons in the French satirical weekly, *Charlie Hebdo*, depicting the Prophet Muhammad in ways that many Muslims deemed to be a great offense to Islam. The Muslim Brotherhood and Islamic Action Front organized a large march from the Grand Husseini Mosque to the Municipal Complex that met no obstruction from the gendarmerie and police on site. But when a small contingent of leftist activists attempted to demonstrate in front of the French embassy—an obvious symbolic place but not a usual location for protests—the gendarmerie blocked roads to prevent the protesters from assembling there.[25] At other times, the location matters less than either the claims being made or who is making them. The day-wage labor movement, for example, repeatedly protested with no major incident at the Ministry of Agriculture. But when some three hundred protested there on July 5, 2009, in opposition to the import of Israeli goods into Jordan, the gendarmerie surrounded and beat them, allegedly for not having received permission to hold the protest.[26]

Artist Nidal Elkhairy captures this spatial dynamic in his drawing titled "Cute Darak at the Fourth Circle." In Arabic, *gendarmerie* is *quwat al-darak* (or *darak* for short). The title of the drawing is a play on the similar sound of the words *quwat* in Arabic and *cute* in English. "Cute Darak" is a reference to the crown prince's comments during a visit to the Fourth Circle during the 2018 *Habbit Huzayran* protests, when he commended gendarmerie officers for their restrained behavior in honoring citizens' right to protest.[27] The gendarmerie officer in the drawing is hugged by a small child and saluted by a higher-ranking officer. But in the background, we see a city in flames, with batons beating protesters and rocks thrown by unseen *baltajiyya*. Amman was not literally burning, of course, but the flames represent the high level of

FIGURE 7.2. "Cute Darak at the Fourth Circle." Source: Nidal Elkhairy.

conflict between protesters and the state. A speech balloon shows the protesters chanting, "Down with the rule of the [International Monetary] Fund!" And the writing on the left side of the drawing identifies East Amman's Hayy Tafayleh neighborhood as the location of some of the gendarmerie's violent suppression of demonstrations. Thus, while the gendarmerie was on this occasion relatively well behaved at the Fourth Circle, where both government and media attention were focused, it was brutal in its treatment of protesters in other areas. Strikingly, the ranking officer faces away from the violence, ignoring it or just seemingly not noticing it.

Protests organized by the Muslim Brotherhood and Islamic Action Front also bring the dynamics of different locations for protest into view. Jordan's mainstream Islamists have a long record of organizing protests for their own constituency as well as demonstrating alongside leftists and other political parties, particularly around issues of democratic reforms and in response to violent Israeli military campaigns. When Islamists organize their own protests, however, they favor adhering to the nontransgressive routine at the Grand Husseini Mosque. As shown earlier, the sprawl of Amman from the 1960s onward changed the character of downtown in ways that gradually made protests there less disruptive. When all roads passed through downtown, large demonstrations literally brought the city to a standstill. But the construction of numerous bypass roads and new neighborhoods meant that most people could avoid the area and thus protests there are far less disruptive than they were in previous decades. People still know to find protests at the Grand Husseini Mosque, but the location's geography, at the base of steep hills, renders even thousands of protesters difficult to see or hear outside of the immediate vicinity. The vast majority of downtown protests are uneventful, and, as shown in figure 4.1, shop owners do not even close during protests, as they have no fear of violence or damage to their goods.

Recalling the early departure of Islamists from the Kalouti protests to avoid confronting the gendarmerie, we can infer that protests downtown work for the Islamists by providing occasions that mobilize and invigorate their constituencies without the risk of inviting a repressive response from the regime. Indeed, they even provide their own parade guards with bright yellow vests to ensure that their events proceed as planned. Those protests also provide dramatic images, taken from high places like the citadel or other surrounding

FIGURE 7.3. Muslim Brotherhood parade guards in their vests manage a march outside of the Grand Husseini Mosque in Amman. Source: Dana M. Moss.

hills, that appear in the Islamist *Al-Sabeel* newspaper. Those images work to reproduce the political relevance of the Islamists by demonstrating their ability to turn out large crowds; the choice of location and adherence to the spatial routine, however, simultaneously signal to the regime their willingness to avoid real disruption or contention.

From Periphery to the Center

Traveling to mount protests was not new, but new spatial practices emerged before and during the uprising period. In the 1920s and 1930s, we saw how tribal groups traveled from their home areas to the new capital to demand jobs or assert other claims to the fledgling Hashemite regime. That spatial practice fell out of favor, however, until it was renewed by the day-wage labor movement to increase pressure on the government in 2006. The *Hirak* groups during the period of the Arab uprisings also traveled to join or mount protests outside their home areas. They rented buses to reach the Fourth Circle *Habbit Huzayran* protests in 2018, and they traveled regularly to protest the detentions of *Hirak* activists outside their home areas. The 2018 *Ma'anash* and

Mish Sakitin protests that erupted in late November also marked a dramatic increase in people traveling from the outlying governorates to join the protests in Amman. Local activists in Aqaba, for example, were frustrated that their protests were making few gains, so they decided to go to the Royal Court in Amman as a more visible and dramatic means of claim-making.[28] In these "Marches of the Unemployed," men sometimes walked without shoes, joined by other unemployed workers along the way but at times arriving a handful at a time, or even alone. They receive tremendous sympathy along their route, with townspeople offering food and shelter during the evenings. They continue to camp for sometimes weeks outside the Royal Court, often hanging banners announcing their home region and their desperation for jobs. Protesting in that location—rather than outside Parliament or the Prime Ministry—signals that they hold the regime and not just the government responsible for their plight. These marches continued throughout 2019 and into 2021, halted only temporarily by the coronavirus shutdown.

With all this moving around to join a variety of protests, the *Hirak* activists in closest proximity to Amman became more connected to each other, sometimes even more than they were to *Hirak* groups in the south. Some networks were more tightly connected simply because Amman could be reached in an hour. That proximity factored into what Charles Tilly calls the time-distance costs that create opportunities and constraints for public claim-making.[29] Protesters from Dhiban, Madaba, Irbid, and Jerash, for example, were by 2019 familiar with each other and with Amman-based activists because they regularly saw each other at protests. People from Ma'an, Karak, and Tafileh are sometimes present at the same protests, but most often in much smaller numbers and without seeming to be personally acquainted.[30] Activists in Amman also sought to forge connections and travel to protests outside of Amman, efforts the regime seemed intent on preventing. In chapter 4, I discussed the Amman-based activists who were arrested and detained for several days when they tried to join a sit-in in Ma'an during the Second Intifada in 2000. Some of those same activists helped form the anti-gas deal movement in 2014, and they introduced new geographic dynamics in how they organized their protests. When the gas deal went into effect on January 1, 2020, weekly protests over the next month moved from the capital to the outlying governorates and back again. At the first protest, on January 3, some three thousand marched from the Grand Husseini Mosque to the Municipal Complex. On January 10, protests were held in Zarqa, Irbid, Karak, and Aqaba, specifically to show that the movement was not limited to Amman-based activists.[31] But when Amman-based activists tried to join those protests outside the capital, security forces blocked their convoys of vehicles and forced them to turn back to Amman.[32] The January 17 protest returned to the capital and the Grand Husseini Mosque, again seeing thousands turn out. This strategy of organizing protests to move in and out of the capital, rather than mounting protests across the nation simultaneously, was a dynamic innovation.

Virtual Spaces

Jordanians have been using virtual spaces to organize protests much longer than many realize. Indeed, by the 1990s, Jordan was leading the Arab world in internet connectivity[33] and cell phones were ubiquitous and affordable. In 1996, Minister of Information Marwan Muasher launched a feature on a new government web page called "Ask the Government." Jordanians could post questions to a running feed, and Muasher would try to respond to queries such as why a street was torn up or how to get speed bumps installed in a particular location. Realizing that the posts were not moderated, activists used the live feed to share information during the protests against Jordan's first joint trade fair with Israel in early 1997. Activists communicated with protesters by text message and posted to the public feed such information as the location of police blockades and what tactics the police were using to disperse demonstrations. They would also gather information from other posts and text it back to their networks in the streets.

When the combination of smartphones and social media came into wide-spread use—particularly after Facebook and Twitter launched in Arabic in late 2009—virtual spaces quickly became part of protest repertoires, with activists posting to various social media platforms as well as uploading videos to You-Tube, in real time and in Arabic.[34] By 2015, most protests were announced on social media, on personal or group pages (such as the anti-gas deal coalition) or on dedicated events pages. People used social media to publicize and condemn the arrest of protesters, and they changed their profile pictures in solidarity with those arrested or killed. When the popular nativist author Nahed Hattar was murdered in Amman in September 2016, for example, many East Bank youths changed their own Facebook profile photos to his photo.

Activists also livestream their demonstrations and name them with hashtags. Derek Gregory argues that it was the combination of physical space and virtual space that enabled Egypt's uprising to be so successful, giving protests spaces to extend their messages while also coordinating in-person activities.[35] And the virtual and physical spaces were interconnected as well: when Egypt's internet was shut down on January 28, people took to the street to find out what was happening; when curfews were imposed, they had usually turned to the internet for connections and information. In Jordan, the March 24 Youth encampment of 2011 was broadcast live, and Dhiban and other *Hirak* protesters have likewise livestreamed their events. These uses of social media amount to a new means of occupying space, and it vastly expands the geography of dissent by making public claim-making visible, audible, and accessible to those beyond the immediate vicinity. Virtual spaces allow protest events not merely to refract but also to expand and deepen.[36]

Of course, virtual spaces also make protests and those who participate in them visible to the regime and its repressive security forces. Indeed, Jordanians are increasingly arrested for what they say or post in virtual spaces, and the regime has passed a harsh Cybercrimes Law to facilitate that repression. As we have seen, however, many Jordanians, particularly those of East Bank descent, have become increasingly bold in their willingness to criticize the regime in virtual spaces, in ways that are at once less ephemeral and more visible than only speaking out at protests. Finally, virtual spaces have been used by loyalists to slander protesters. The photos of female protesters, for example, have been altered and then posted on Facebook, shaming them and questioning their honor, motives, and integrity.[37] In a country where women are still murdered for real or imagined acts deemed to be "dishonorable," such slander can have grave consequences.

Creative Claim-Making

Activists have also innovated the repertoire for protest by turning to creative forms of political expression less likely to draw violent repression. Art has always been a form of public expression, with graffiti, installations, and public performances of various sorts being central to claim-making. Charles Tripp provides a rich look at these "symbolic forms of resistance" in his sweeping examination of protest in the Middle East.[38] Jordan has seen many of these forms and more. In April 2002, for example, activists organized a Palestinian "Right of Return Quilt," which included hundreds of panels stitched together to form a quilt so large that it covered the entire stage of the Royal Cultural Center. The quilt was so big that it had to be transported in segments and sewn together on location. At least seven thousand people came to see it over a period of several days. Another event, organized in solidarity with Palestinians and Iraqis suffering war and occupation, saw thousands of Jordanians across Amman fly kites on an afternoon in spring 2003.[39] Following the US invasion of Iraq that same spring, activist artists produced a huge mural in Amman, "No to Arab Silence."[40] We have already seen in chapter 5 how in 2009 antinormalization activists erected tombstones at the Kalouti protests to signify the murder of Palestinians by Israeli forces. The anti-gas deal movement handed out t-shirts with their slogan at a Women's World Cup game in Amman in the fall of 2016.[41] It also called for weekly one-hour nationwide "blackouts" that fall, during which Jordanians were urged to shut their lights off at an appointed time in the evening. The action had its own spatial effect, taking the protest out of the streets and making it readily visible across Amman's built environment—place-making across the whole urban landscape. Even more, people who would not likely participate in street protests could register their dissent with the flick of a switch in the safety of their homes.

Music and dance are also common at protests, whether by singing *Mawtini* or by performing the Corruption Dabke. Indeed, both practices are common elsewhere in the Arab world, and their performance connects Jordanian protest with the spatial imaginary of the Arab world, across time and space.[42] And protesters are not the only ones to resort to song and dance at demonstrations. At the 1997 protests against the Israeli trade fair, for example, lines of security forces performed traditional Bedouin songs and dances following taunts by the protesters that the police were defending Israel.[43] As a form of reply to those accusations, their traditional Bedouin dances signaled their long attachment to the Transjordanian area, a kind of nativist temporality that put their loyalty beyond rebuke.

Another innovation and creative means of voicing dissent is the holding of a mock trial or "People's Court." These theatrical performances serve as occasions for expressing explicit political claims while also signaling a lack of confidence in the actual judiciary's willingness or ability to prosecute cases of malfeasance or corruption. They create a kind of parallel sense of justice, where one can publicly "prosecute" the corrupt and illegal. Mock trials have "convicted" individuals associated with privatization who are believed to be corrupt, such as Bassam Awadullah and Walid al-Kurdi. Mock trials were held during the uprising period, and they occurred in the capital as well as in the East Bank governorates. Those being prosecuted, however, were not only individuals. On September 5, 2015, the anti-gas deal movement held a public "trial" at the Professional Associations Complex, at which the gas deal was the defendant and the cases both for and against the deal were presented. The government put heavy pressure on the leadership of the Union of Professional Associations to cancel the event, but because union leadership was in disarray, no decision was made. The governor of Amman also tried but failed to pressure activist organizers via telephone calls to call off the event. The "trial" attracted some five hundred observers, and after the gas deal was found guilty, they carried a large placard with the "court's" decision to the Prime Ministry at the Fourth Circle.[44]

Contentious Spaces and Practices

As I have shown, states deploy coercive apparatuses at protests unevenly, depending on not only the claims being made, who is making them, and how they are being expressed, but in what spaces they are located. We have seen how protests at the Grand Husseini Mosque became less contentious as the city grew, while the Fourth Circle location—a space for nontransgressive protests through much of the 1990s and 2000s—became increasingly contentious. In nontransgressive protests, the regime is sometimes eager to show that it is tolerant of protests, at least those that adhere to established routines. We have seen that police passed out water or juice boxes at some of the winter 2011 protests, as they did at a June 2010 rally in support of Jordanians aboard the Freedom Flotilla—the ships that departed Istanbul in an effort to bring aid to Gaza. Activist Naseem Tarawneh reflects on the atmosphere at many protests, with "families with their kids wandering between the riot police."[45] He laments that when the police are handing out water, it lessens the con- frontational atmosphere and protests are deflated of the potential to bring substantive change. "It's not just soft-containment and crowd management," he writes, "they're also providing refreshments for the act."[46]

Some spaces, however, are simply off limits, and spaces can become more or less associated with contention as protest and repression shape place-making in particular locations. The changing meaning of the Fourth Circle is exemplary of such evolving meanings. Anti-gas deal activists marched there from the Municipal Complex in 2014 without interference, despite it being a deviation from the established downtown routine. But in September 2016, they aimed to again reach the Fourth Circle but were arrested by gendarmerie officers (no protesters were charged). During the 2018 *Habbit Huzayran* protests, thousands of police and gendarmerie forces prevented protesters from reaching the Fourth Circle, and the location was subsequently off-limits, a new spatial red line. Activists were allowed, however, to organize "Fourth Circle" protests a half-mile away, in a parking lot adjacent to the Jordan Hospital (see fig. 7.1). This was the location for the *Ma'anash* and *Mish Sakitin* protests in late 2018, and the ongoing Thursday evening protests that continued through early summer 2019. During one antinormalization protest at the space, protesters painted "Death to Israel" and an Israeli flag on the pavement for protesters to walk on, a form of place-making that left the space marked as "protest" and "anti-Israeli" well after the protest ended.[47]

The new location developed its own spatial routine, not as a "march to the Fourth Circle" but as "Fourth Circle protests." Demonstrators assembled in the parking lot with security forces lined around the perimeter. After weeks of protests the numbers participating diminished, and the atmosphere eased as the protests became routine. These protests were discursively transgressive (in their direct criticisms of the king) but spatially nontransgressive (permitted by police in that location). The relocation from the actual Fourth Circle also moved protesters off the streets and sidewalks and into a contained lot, where their stationary demonstrations were also less disruptive of traffic. The wall of security forces also served to limit the visibility of the protests and the placards from the main street.

One fascinating new dynamic at these "Fourth Circle" protests was that people sometimes traveled to the location to observe but not join the protests on their way out to meet friends. One activist described it as a kind of "date night" routine. In a literal sense, East Bank protesters traveled to the capital from the economic periphery to make public political claims, their protests declaring "impoverished East Bank" smack in the middle of affluent West Amman. But even with many of these protests feeling routine, the "Fourth Circle" was understood by activists to be one of the more contentious locations for protests in Amman. As one anti-gas deal activist said while discussing where they planned to protest in January 2020, "We aren't ready for the Fourth Circle."[48]

The second place that became a contentious location for protests after the uprising period was the Interior Circle in West Amman. As detailed in chapter 6, the violent dispersal of the March 24 Youth encampment in 2011, in which a protester was killed, also marked the location as a place for transgressive claim-making. We saw that during the 2012 *Habbit Tishreen* protests, the Interior Circle was the epicenter for the most contentious claims against the regime. Crowds there chanted the Arab uprising slogan, "The People Want the Fall of the Regime!" The gendarmerie dispersed those protests with considerable violence and worked hard to prevent the location from emerging as a routine place for protests. Since then, the site has become largely off-limits for protests, with a spatial fate similar to that of the Fourth Circle and the Kalouti Mosque; that fate is the subject of chapter 8.

Tents and Encampments

Encampments entail a hostile occupation of space, more aggressive in their temporality because they create visible disruptions that last not for hours but are ongoing. They deviate from the temporal routine of most protest events, leaving the state with no knowledge of how the events will play out or when they will end. Indeed, open-ended encampments dare the state to do nothing at its peril. In this sense, encampments create a kind of sustained "crisis" time, one that severs public space from the regime.[49] Encampments also "subvert the older, Western, and profoundly colonial sense of order and occupation," as Derek Gregory puts it, the kind of order that was supposedly a relic of a bygone era but that in practice has been continued into the "postcolonial" period.[50] Crowds and encampments therefore do not merely occupy space; they work rather as "space-in-progress," a kind of ongoing yet liminal place-making.

The tent is the symbol of encampments, and the Hashemite regime hates tents. Its violent response to tents is reminiscent of David Graeber's "Fear of Giant Puppets," his article that examines how US police were bizarrely obsessed with destroying giant puppets carried in global justice protests.[51] Tents in Jordan—like queer pride flags in Egypt[52]—are giant puppets to the gendarmerie—they must be stopped/prevented/erased at all costs. Activists have erected tents at protests in Jordan since at least the Second Intifada in 2000, but the regime did not always view them with hostility or try to remove them. The tents of the day-wage labor movement at the 2006 protest outside of the Royal Court, for example, were left alone, perhaps because the protesters camped out for only one night.[53] Those tents may also have been permitted because they worked to reproduce a kind of patriarchy, in which even activist women need shelter and protection. At the Kalouti protests in winter 2009, however, police tore down tents and violently dispersed the protesters after more than a week. The fear of tents and encampments escalated during the period of the Arab uprisings, particularly after the encampment for eighteen days in Egypt's Tahrir Square led to the fall of Hosni Mubarak. Long-term encampments of any size, particularly those involving tents, were a new red line. The March 24 Youth encampment, as we have seen, was violently cleared after only one night; the attempted July 15 encampment later that year was also met with violence on the first day. Another encampment emerged in July 2012, when Jordanians whose parents were unknown and thus had no legal status staged an open-ended sit-in at the Fourth Circle.[54] In this "orphans' protest," participants slept in the center of the roundabout without shelter for nearly two weeks. They were undisturbed until they became part of public political debate, after which the gendarmerie received orders to forcibly disperse them.[55]

But perhaps precisely because encampments and tents became so contentious, they also became more common, particularly outside of the capital. Water shortage protests in the north, for example, routinely pitch protest tents outside government offices or adjacent to their road blockades.[56] The struggle over protest tents in Dhiban illustrates how they have developed outsized meaning as hostile and transgressive. Between 2013 and 2016, local activists erected tents during many protests, including those demanding employment, condemning corruption, and opposing the arrest and detention of other activists. A tent in April 2016 was up for nearly two months before the gendarmerie tore it down and forced the twenty-two protesters to vacate the location. About fifty days into that protest, the Dhiban protesters gathered supporters and erected a tent at Salam Square in Madaba, the main city of the governorate. During that protest on June 13, the gendarmerie tore down the tent and arrested five protesters, including day-wage labor activist Muhammad Snayd. The activists were released only after promising not to reerect the tent, but they broke that promise only two days later when negotiations with the government still failed to bear fruit. Three of the protesters were summoned to the security center in Dhiban, transferred to Madaba, and sent to Marka prison. Back in Dhiban, the gendarmerie fired tear gas at the protesters, arrested twenty of them, and again tore down the tents.[57]

Dhiban activist Sabri Masha'aleh saw those 2016 protests as part of a long history of bold protest from Jordan's East Bank community, even proudly recalling the Yarmouk University student protests in 1986. After the period of the Arab uprisings in 2011–12, he argued that "the tent became a symbol for the protests in Jordan. We were eating, sleeping, and making statements in it. We also did a live stream via Facebook and turned the tent into a TV studio where we did interviews."[58] When Dhiban activists were again arrested in April 2019, protesters in the neighboring town of Mleih erected a tent to protest in solidarity. Then in August, Snayd was arrested yet again, this time under the Cybercrimes Law for accusing former prime minister Hani Mulki and his family of corruption. Local activists erected a tent next to Snayd's house in Mleih throughout his two-week detention.[59] As Anne Marie Baylouny shows, tents have also been used in much of the north as alternative housing: for some who have been kicked out of housing by landlords who can obtain higher rents from refugees, tents provide shelter while also working as a form of space-in-progress.[60] Whether used as temporary housing or during protests, tents across the landscape create a form of built environment, a visible geography of sustained dissent.

In the state's zeal to prevent tents from being erected, the gendarmerie has become hostile to any cloth that might potentially be a tent. At one of the anti-gas deal protests, the group unfurled a 35 x 7-meter banner in an empty lot opposite the NEPCO headquarters' tall offices, where officials would see the banner if they looked out the windows. The gendarmerie saw the size of the fabric, assumed it was a tent, and refused to let the activists unfold it until they were convinced it was a banner and not a tent. Tents at protests are so

FIGURE 7.4. Banner reading "The Gas of the Enemy Is Occupation" is displayed as part of a demonstration. Source: The Anti-Gas Deal Campaign.

contentious that some activists avoid them because they know that tents invite violent repression. At protests in Salt in early 2018, for example, hundreds gathered daily against anti-austerity policies, but without tents despite bad winter weather. According to one of the organizers, Hani Azab, they had considered putting up a tent but decided against it, as it would likely have led to violent clashes with the gendarmerie. If that happens, he said, "everyone will lose."[61]

REPERTOIRES OF REPRESSION

Jordanians turn to protest so frequently because it works as a direct channel to draw the attention of the government. Indeed, we have seen consistently that protests are a means of entering into dialogue with the state, which for the state can diminish the more radical possibilities of protests.[62] We see this through calls for "national dialogue" following large-scale protests as well as when protesters articulate relatively narrow claims—"get us water or we will continue to block the road and disrupt trade." In many cases, the regime can best reproduce its support base and thus its authority by at least appearing responsive if not always acquiescing. During the winter 2018 protests,

216 CHAPTER 7

for example, Salti protesters spoke of feeling abandoned by the regime, their voices unheard. Local first-time protesters included retired high-ranking security officers who had failed for more than decade to obtain salary increases through other channels.[63]

Much of the analysis thus far has focused on where and how security forces engage with protesters. But repression takes place through a variety of other techniques. This section examines the Jordanian regime's repertoire and techniques for repression, from the use of various legal provisions to punish or harass activists to various means of threatening, intimidating, and co-opting them.

Use of Legal Provisions

The Public Gatherings Law, the primary legal provision governing protests, has been amended repeatedly over the past decades. Beginning in 1990, organizers were required only to notify the municipality of plans to hold a protest. From 2001 until just after the outbreak of the uprising in 2011, organizers were required to obtain a permit but could apply only within three days of the event. Those who did obtain a permit were personally responsible for any damage to property that might occur. In practice, the permit system was used to control the types of protest, their size and locations, and who was allowed to organize them. While the governorate was responsible for processing protest applications, it only implemented decisions made through the Ministry of the Interior.

Groups eager not to run afoul of the regime, such as the Muslim Brotherhood and the Islamic Action Front, carefully adhered to established protest routines. When permits were required, Islamist leaders often consulted informally with their government contacts to discuss protest events before applying for the permit. But they also knew what kinds of events were likely to be approved. Many leftists, independent activists, and labor organizers, however, never applied for permits or else did so only selectively. The Union of Professional Associations vacillated in its willingness to protest without a permit, largely depending on its rotating elected leadership. East Bank activists in the governorates, however, organize when and where they like, often with little advance planning and without seeking permits. During periods of large-scale protest, people simply pour into the streets and central squares nationwide without permission. As we saw in chapter 6, the government suspended the permit requirement in spring 2011, as thousands of protesters were flaunting it anyway.

While the Public Gatherings Law has obvious relevance for constraining protests, protest organizers are seldom charged with violating its provisions.[64] More commonly, activists are charged under laws like Article 164 of the Penal Code, which prohibits gatherings of more than seven people with the intention of committing a crime or disturbing public order. Other laws used against protesters include the Telecommunication Law, the Information Technology Law, and the Prevention of Terrorism Law, all of which contain provisions that criminalize acts of sedition, slander, defamation, and incitement. In 2002, for example, activist and former parliamentarian Toujan Faysal—Jordan's first elected female parliamentarian, in office from 1989 to 1993—was arrested for accusing Prime Minister Ali Abu Ragheb of corruption in an open letter to the king published in the Houston-based *Arab Times*.[65] She was convicted under the Prevention of Terrorism Law of harming the Jordanian state. Activists organized protests at the Fourth Circle and Parliament demanding her release as she embarked on a hunger strike, after which she was released by royal decree but not pardoned.

The Prevention of Terrorism Law also has been used repeatedly over the decades to prosecute activists engaged in protests. Protesters against the so-called Deal of the Century, for example, gathered on Friday, June 21, 2019, at the Taj Mall traffic circle in the Abdoun neighborhood of Amman, about a half-mile from the US embassy. As they marched toward the embassy, they were surprised to be stopped by the gendarmerie a few blocks from their destination, as they had previously been allowed to protest there peacefully. Three activists who led the chants were arrested five days later. Activists felt that the blockade and arrests amounted to inappropriate harassment because the march had adhered to the known routine for protests at the US embassy.[66] The three were charged under the law with "carrying out actions that would expose the kingdom to the risk of hostile acts or disturb its links to foreign states." That is, criticizing a foreign ally amounts to an act of terrorism, and the detainees had led chants against Muhammad bin Salman, the crown prince of Saudi Arabia. Two of the detainees were Jordanians of Palestinian descent living in Baqa'a Camp, including one who had been previously arrested for participation in a protest. Students and members of the leftist Jordanian Democratic

Popular Unity Party from Irbid, who participated in the embassy march, were later summoned to the General Intelligence Directorate (*mukhabarat*) office in Irbid, where they were threatened and asked to inform on other activists.[67] A particularly extreme (and absurd) use of the Prevention of Terrorism Law occurred in August 2020, after the popular Jordanian cartoonist Emad Hajjaj posted a satirical cartoon to his website and social media depicting a dove carrying an Israeli flag and spitting in the face of the United Arab Emirates's de facto ruler, Muhammad bin Zayed. Hajjaj was arrested and held in detention for four days, released only following a massive global Tweet storm calling for #Freedom4EmadHajjaj.

The newest legal tool for repressing claim-making in both material and virtual spaces is the Cybercrimes Law passed in 2015 and amended in 2019.[68] According to the state's official justification, the amendments were intended to criminalize hate speech: "each writing and every speech or act intended to provoke sectarian or racial sedition, advocate for violence or foster conflict between followers of different religions and various components of the nation."[69] But the law is so broadly worded that it forbids any speech that could create anxiety (*qalaq*) among the people. Any criticism of a public official can be considered criminal, as can sharing rumors or "fake news." Antinuclear activist Basel Burgan was arrested under the Cybercrimes Law in the summer of 2019 for posting to Facebook a statement by a former engineer in Jordan's nuclear program. The engineer's document seemed to confirm a rumor—one that was already in wide circulation—that one of Jordan's nuclear plants had a radiation leak. Although Burgan erased the post the next day after learning it was false, the prosecutors charged that his post had created anxiety and he was jailed for two weeks. His ongoing case (more than two years as of this writing) and years of harassment show how the state uses these broad laws to silence and intimidate activists.

Other articles in the Cybercrimes Law stipulate that "anyone who deliberately sends, forwards, or re-shares information or data that entails slander or defamation or libel using the Internet, websites, or any information systems could be imprisoned from three to six months," along with paying a fine. The law gives the government the right to search any electronic device, computer, or phone.[70] By including apps (applications) in the category of information systems, the government has legal standing to search private messages sent through popular message services like WhatsApp. The wide reach of the law has grave consequences for political speech: nearly every *Hirak* group, political party, social movement, and protest group has a Facebook page; half of the Jordanian population is on Facebook.[71] Protests are announced with event pages and activists livestream protests as well as posting videos and images of them, so the law is a powerful tool for the regime to silence dissent.

In March and April 2019 alone, the government arrested more than a dozen activists for their posts. Ahmed Tabanja, for example, traveled from Irbid to Amman to protest in front of the Royal Court with other unemployed Jordanians. He was arrested on March 17 and detained for two days for livestreaming the protest on Facebook; he was arrested again on March 29 for additional Facebook posts. He was sentenced to two months in Ma'an prison, 185 miles from his family in the north. This repressive use of spatial dynamics seeks to keep activists as far as possible from the communities that might protest their imprisonment or give them solace through regular visits. Dhiban activists Sabri Masha'aleh and Muhammad Snayd were among those arrested during this period. Masha'aleh was charged for four Facebook posts, one of which directly criticized the king.[72] Dhiban activists organized a protest condemning his arrest. One of the men at the protest said that he had been inspired to join the demonstration by those who had walked to Amman to demonstrate in front of the Royal Court for jobs and economic relief. Later in April, he marched to the Royal Court and protested alone, at one point encircled by gendarmerie.[73]

To give one final example, two journalists were arrested under the Cybercrimes Law in 2019 for reporting on the protests near the Fourth Circle. Reporter Rana Hmouz hosted a weekly fifteen-minute segment titled *The Fourth Circle* on the Jordan Today television station. She and the director of the station, Muhammad Ajlouni, were charged with criticizing the head of the gendarmerie, who had spoken against military veterans for joining the protests.[74] Both Ajlouni and Hmouz were found guilty. Ajlouni was forced to close the station permanently later in 2019, when he found that advertisers were facing pressure to withdraw their contracts, leaving the station without a viable revenue stream.

From Harassment to Co-optation

In addition to charging activists and protesters under various elastic laws, the state engages in widespread harassment and intimidation in an effort to silence critical voices. Television journalist Hmouz said in April 2019 (prior to her arrest) that she anticipated being arrested because she was receiving anonymous threatening phone calls. In one instance, the caller referenced her status as a single mother. Such warnings to "take care" hint at not only one's physical safety but also the potential spillover effects on one's family and loved ones. Intimidated family members may pressure individuals to stop their activism.

Activists also receive "invitations" to have a "friendly chat" at the General Intelligence Directorate offices.[75] Some meetings are initially friendly—tea may be served if one is of high enough importance—but the tone by the conclusion is subtly, or not so subtly, threatening. Others describe long waits after arrival and interrogation-style questioning. One activist joked that the more pleasant the exchange and higher ranking the officer, the more the *mukhabarat* saw you as a problem. And the threats are real. In addition to surveillance and arrest, activists have lost their jobs, and they and their organizations have had their assets and computers seized for bogus reasons. Other companies find their employees quitting and their business clients suddenly canceling contracts, as happened with the advertisers to the Jordan Today television station. Antinuclear activist Burgan likewise faced numerous canceled contracts for his pharmaceutical business after a contentious exchange with the *mukhabarat*.

Co-optation is another strategy for derailing activism and protest. These conversations are sometimes initiated during *mukhabarat* "interviews," and at other times they come via a direct phone call from a government official. Two executive committee members from the antinormalization committee were co-opted in 1995: Kamel Nasser (then president of the lawyers' association) was named Minister of Political Development, and Mustafa Shunaykat was named Minister of Agriculture. Khalid Khalaldeh, an outspoke regime critic and *Jayeen* activist in 2011, became Minister of Political and Parliamentary Affairs. Mothanna Gharaybeh, another activist from the uprising period, became Minister of Digital Economy and Entrepreneurship. Numerous other activists report being offered government and ministerial positions, with harassment resuming after they declined.

Changing the Conversation

Not all attempts to co-opt or redirect protests for regime purposes are successful. During periods when protests erupt nationwide, the regime and government struggle to contain the protests while appearing sympathetic to popular opinion. Such has been the case during nationwide demonstrations against Israel's violent military campaigns. During the nearly two months of protest that brought the nation to a standstill in March and April 2002, the regime tried to redirect Jordanians' anger toward sympathy for Palestinians in need of humanitarian aid. Abdullah II announced a fund-raising initiative and a telethon that included politicians, local celebrities, and prominent tribal leaders. Jordanians were encouraged to send a text from their mobile phones to donate JD 10 (US $14) to the humanitarian relief effort. Then the regime mounted its own protest event. The Jordan River Foundation—a royally affiliated organization—announced that Queen Rania would lead a march in support of humanitarian relief for Palestine. The group assembled at the Fifth Circle on Zahran Street, a site that held zero symbolism for the Israeli-Palestinian conflict. Independent activists even mocked the choice of location, noting the West Amman intersection was the site of luxury five-star hotels and their exorbitantly expensive restaurants and bars. The queen was joined by prominent businessmen, parliamentarians, and other powerful individuals including prominent leaders from East Bank tribes.

Here the spatial dimensions of the queen's march expose the regime's efforts to redirect protesters' focus by switching locations in the built environment. The largest protests in Amman were mounted in familiar protest spaces (downtown) and near buildings associated with those directly responsible for the violence (the Israeli embassy) or supportive of the State of Israel (the US embassy and the Prime Ministry). The queen's march, however, assembled near luxury hotels and concluded at a UN office of humanitarian affairs a half-mile away. The route entirely avoided contentious symbolism or spaces associated with Israel, invoking instead the maternalism of a caring mother seeking to provide comfort. During Israel's bloody winter 2009 invasion of Gaza, the regime similarly organized solidarity marches, this time beginning at several mosques in West Amman (including the King Abdullah Mosque adjacent to Parliament and the Grand Husseini Mosque downtown) and converging at the stadium of the

CHAPTER 7

Sports City complex. As in 2002, none of these spaces held any symbolism or relevance to the conflict at hand.[76]

Co-opting Protests

At times, the regime has sought to take over a protest initiated by activists to serve its own purposes. One stunning example was a protest organized by the Campaign Against So-Called Crimes of Honor, formed in the late 1990s by a group of left-leaning independent activists. The campaign launched a massive petition drive in early 2000, stunningly accumulating tens of thousands of signatures. It then sought permission to hold a march on Parliament, where it would deliver the petitions and demand the laws be revised. The group's requests for a permit, however, were denied. Some of the organizers reached out to Queen Rania for support, as she had moved among some progressive circles before becoming queen. Following intervention from the Royal Court, the march on Parliament was granted a permit.[77]

But the campaign was surprised when a rally was announced in its name but without its knowledge. Some five thousand turned out for the "protest" at the Parliament on February 14, 2000, including prominent East Bank tribal leaders who arrived from out of town. Another fleet of buses—also not arranged by the organizers—transported to the site hundreds of people who had assembled at the nearby Sports City complex. The organizers knew that the event had been co-opted when the protesters showed little interest in amending the laws that enabled honor crimes. Many chanted "Long Live King Abdullah!" and some even expressed support for honor crimes.[78]

MAKING PROTESTS WORK FOR THE REGIME

What did the regime gain by co-opting an event for a cause it supported? And how can a regime benefit from protests that are critical of its policies or even its existence? I have shown how negotiation and co-optation can work to deflate the radical potential of protests while also serving as occasions for state-maintaining. But states can use protests to their advantage in other ways, even when claim-making is critical of the regime. The scholarly literature on protests has long acknowledged that protests can provide regimes with valuable information. The varying size of the turnout, for example, allows the regime to gauge support for an issue at a given moment. Similarly, allowing most protests to proceed peacefully allows the regime to portray itself as democratic-minded, if not yet fully democratic.

King Abdullah II and Queen Rania have courted Western audiences since ascending to the throne in 1999. In co-opting the Campaign Against Crimes of Honor, the "protest" not only put pressure on the more conservative elected lower house,[79] it was a good international public-relations move, displaying for Western allies the then-new regime's commitment to advancing women's rights and introducing the cosmopolitan queen as a secular progressive. The king, meanwhile, comes across to Western audiences as a serious but down-to-earth and likable guy. He speaks English with an American accent (due to his prep-school days in Massachusetts's Deerfield Academy), and he is at ease in public forums like Comedy Central's *The Daily Show* with Jon Stewart.[80] Stewart, normally a smart and critical interviewer, repeatedly fell under the king's spell, parroting the false claim that Jordan is a constitutional monarchy and that it is doing its best given its "bad neighborhood." Washington think tanks and US government officials also buy into this narrative. Of course, US hypocrisy concerning democracy promotion is infamous, and we shall revisit the US role in Jordan in chapter 9. But showing relative restraint in policing protests—particularly compared to the August 2013 massacre of hundreds of peaceful protesters in Egypt—allows Abdullah II to burnish his credentials as a moderate and Western-friendly reformer.

The regime can also use large-scale protests to do other political work. Nationwide anti-austerity protests, for example, are of course unsettling for the regime, particularly the angry claim-making coming from its East Bank support base. The 1989 *Habbit Nisan* protests even forced the regime into a political opening. Large protests have repeatedly led to the fall of prime ministers and forced the state to find work-arounds from fully lifting subsidies, particularly on basic goods such as bread and fuel. But large protests also allow the government to argue that certain reforms demanded by foreign governments and international agencies are untenable because they could trigger further massive protests. To move forward with those reforms, therefore, the regime will need continued support to produce a kind of stability and security that will project Hashemite rule into the distant future. As activist and writer Hisham Bustani writes of the 2018 *Habbit Huzayran* protests,

The protests were used to sustain the regime as the only entity able to control and deal with them in a manner that would ensure the implementation of the required functional conditions (such as the economic requirements accompanying the IMF loans, or the political requirements related to American aid, etc.). The political authorities also used the protests to bring in grants and financing from other sources (such as the Gulf states), and to extend the time for the implementation of the financiers' requirements.[81]

The argument is that the king leveraged the scale of the 2018 protests—at the same time that the regime touted the large number of Syrian refugees it had received—to call for increased foreign assistance in keeping Jordan stable, which requires the maintenance of the Hashemite regime. In a sense, then, the "forever on the brink" narrative of long-term stability in the face of ever-present precarity is essential to Hashemite state-maintaining.

Finally, protests can also provide political cover for the regime to make a significant policy change that would otherwise anger an important ally. In October 2018, for example, Jordanians protested Jordan's leasing of land to Israel in Baqoura (in the northwest) and Ghumar (south of the Dead Sea). The lease, included as part of the 1994 peace treaty, was set to expire after twenty-five years, in 2019. Following the October 2018 protests, Abdullah II announced that he would not renew the lease.[82] He may well have already decided against it, but the protests provided an opportunity to allow the lease to expire while appearing to be responsive to popular sentiment. These international connections to Jordan's domestic politics are further examined in chapter 9.

CONCLUSION

This chapter has shown how states struggle to create "normal" times and project stability through a wide range of techniques, and how people challenge state power through their choices about how and where to protest. State-maintaining is an ongoing process, and protests show how state and society are mutually constituted through these struggles. The decade after the uprising period in Jordan saw continued protests in a wide range of sectors, including several massive and nationwide protests. It saw spatial innovations such as increased travel to participate in protests, which in turned deepened networks among protesters in the vicinity of the capital. And we have seen how tents have become the "giant puppets" in Graeber's sense of objects so saturated with contentious symbolism that they invite violence from the gendarmerie. Tearing down tents is an act that aims to erase their presence, to remove them from the built environment as a means of asserting state power. In the next chapter, we take a close look at how the state affects changes to the built environment in ways that create obstacles to protest, and how protests in turn shape the built environment.

Chapter 8

PROTEST AND ORDER IN MILITARIZED SPACES

AFTER THE VIOLENT CLEARING OF THE MARCH 24 YOUTH EN-campment in 2011, Prime Minister Maʿrouf al-Bakhit insisted that the government was not trying to prevent people from protesting. He even encouraged Jordanians to express their grievances publicly, so long as they did so without disrupting traffic. His concern about traffic seemed disingenuous, however, as demonstrations and car parades through Amman by regime loyalists were ignored by the police, even when they blocked major intersections.[1] The problem was clearly not traffic disruptions per se but disruptions by people making claims against the regime. Loyalist disruptions were welcome because they worked to reproduce rather than challenge the regime's authority and thus its desired political order.

Order is a set of relationships, an arrangement of things organized to serve some purpose or end. Order must be constantly maintained, as we have seen with state-maintaining. Those in power thus seek to arrange things—to create their desired order—in ways that refine, reproduce, or expand their power. Among the things that might be arranged are infrastructure, trade routes, where people reside, and how economic resources are distributed. Abdullah I, for example, established his capital in small-town Amman in the 1920s as one means of arranging things to facilitate the creation of a colonial territorial state. The control of space, therefore, is central to the creation and maintenance of state power. In addition to space, states wield temporal regimes that provide justification for the actions they take to reproduce their power. Analytically, we need to move beyond the conceptual binary of "normal times" of "order" and "crisis times" of "upheaval" to bring into view the numerous and often violent techniques deployed to maintain "order."

As we have repeatedly seen, the political order that is produced and reproduced over time is deeply shaped by those either resisting it or demanding to benefit from it. In similar ways, the built environment of a city is shaped as much by upheavals and challenges to the established order as it is by urban planning and the visions of those in power. As Don Mitchell shows, protests and other forms of disruption affect the circulation of capital and state investment decisions. They shape laws governing people and activities in urban spaces, and they produce new strategies of and institutions for policing and repression.[2] In French colonial Algeria, one of the first acts of the colonial administrators was to assign numbers to buildings and name the streets of the Casbah.[3] In these ways, the militarization of the city—via the deployment of techniques for both controlling dissent and imposing a particular vision of order—is built into the urban landscape.

Urban planners are, of course, directly implicated in the militarization of cities. The very act of designing an object, city, or building, as Léopold Lambert argues, works in the same way as an army, in that both "anticipate and encourage specific behaviors."[4] Georges-Eugène Haussmann's reconstruction of Paris in the 1850s and 1860s stands as the iconic example. As David Harvey writes, the structure of Paris's new system of avenues "surrounded the traditional hearths of revolutionary ferment" and allowed security forces to freely circulate in those areas as needed.[5] Paris reminds us that the political arrangement of things created through urban planning does not prevent violence by creating order; rather, it requires violence to create one kind of order to discourage or prevent any other. "The violence of the military organization of the city," Lambert argues, "does not come from outside: the architecture of the city contains this very violence within itself. Its militarization is merely the process by which this violence reveals itself in an explicit manner."[6]

The militarization and violence of Amman is readily visible in the built environment, and it has been shaped by earlier moments of conflict and contention. During the Black September violence that saw the army defeat the

Palestinian militias in 1971, for example, whole neighborhoods were bombarded and at least half of Wihdat Camp was destroyed. During reconstruction, some roads were widened to enable the transport of armored vehicles, particularly along the hills where the *Fedayeen* guerrillas had strongholds.[7] Over the next years, other narrow streets were widened to facilitate policing and surveillance. Infrastructure upgrades, meanwhile, have been disproportionally located in affluent West Amman, speeding travel across some parts of the city while movement remains slower and more restrictive within the camps and narrow streets of poorer neighborhoods.[8]

Beyond the location of buildings, roads, and other material features of the built environment, techniques for militarizing the city include the use of "temporary" blockages, road closures, and checkpoints. Use of these techniques increased dramatically following the coordinated suicide bombings of three hotels in Amman on November 9, 2005. Al-Qaeda in Iraq claimed credit for those attacks, which killed fifty-nine (including thirty-eight attending a wedding) and injured 115. In their wake, security around hotels visibly increased, as it also did for malls, hotels, embassies, foreign businesses, and government buildings. Metal detectors were installed at entrances and concrete roadblocks limited how close vehicles could get to buildings. These "temporary" walls of movable concrete slabs have become permanent and visible blockages.

Techniques of blocking and controlling movement in the city, however, are not merely inconveniences in "crisis" times of heightened threat. Their irregularity also works to disrupt the routine movement of people and thus announces the state's ability to do so. Mona Fawaz et al. draw attention to the affective dimensions of these blockages and disruptions. Their discussion of post-reconstruction Beirut is worth quoting at length. These securitization techniques, they argue,

> ultimately consolidate in the formation of an anxious cityscape with varying levels of intensity: "hot" spots—the symbolic centers of political control—where the map reflects an intense concentration of security elements, and "diffuse" areas—where the presence of the security apparatus becomes comparatively diluted—[are] nonetheless almost always present. Security is furthermore a dynamic and continuously changing concept. It operates within temporal regimes of "crisis time" and "normal time" as well as night/day, weekday/weekend, etc., during which the cordoned-off areas spill over to their

surroundings, including in their bunkers' additional streets and blocks, while additional "hot spots" are created, and neighborhood-level organization of security patrols and surveillance are deployed.[9]

In Amman, the locations of hot spots are likewise in flux. Armored vehicles may be stationed at one location for days or even weeks and then disappear. In some locations, like the Fourth Circle, movable concrete barricades seem to be a permanent fixture, at times pushed to the sides but at other times blocking circle entrances and exits for nonobvious reasons. Parked security vehicles also routinely create blockages along traffic circles and at overpass entrances. Despite the government's expressed concern about traffic congestion, it is itself directly responsible for most blockages and tolerates others created by loyalists.

The unpredictability of blockages is part of the militarization of the city, fostering an atmosphere in which people are unable to know at any given moment where blockages will appear or disappear. That unpredictability, or "anxious cityscape," can be a central factor in the functioning of state power over movement

FIGURE 8.1. Concrete barriers at the Fourth Circle prevent vehicles from using the U-turn lane. Source: Jillian Schwedler.

and space. The militarization of the city thus entails a range of techniques that are always potentially present, even in their absence. As with the antiterrorism legislation adopted in many countries following the September 11, 2001, attacks on the United States, ostensibly temporary "crisis" times can become permanent, structuring routine or quotidian politics that have nothing to do with existential threats. Along with Jordan's annual Army Day military parades, therefore, the changing landscape of security vehicles and concrete barricades puts the regime's stability and precarity on display simultaneously, while also asserting its power to affect the most routine of daily movements. Ironically, this temporality of ongoing "crisis" time works in the service of producing the kind of "normal" time: that is, it projects regime authority and stability both now and into the future, enabling it to attract foreign investment as well as reassure regional and global allies of the state's security.

The remainder of this chapter examines the militarization of Amman as it pertains to protests in different locations across the city. I show how the state uses various techniques for militarizing the built environment before, during, and after protests, and I present an original typology for theorizing about material obstacles to protest in the built environment. Just as the Hashemite political order and state-maintaining project are deeply shaped by challenges to them, so the militarized built environment both shapes and is shaped by protests. I zoom in from the scale of the city to examine specific locations, expanding on earlier discussions about the uneven deployment of security forces by situating protest spaces in larger geographies of power across the city. I draw comparisons with the militarization of other cities and the ways in which similar techniques are used in both democratic and authoritarian countries.

THE MATERIAL OBSTACLES TO PROTEST IN THE BUILT ENVIRONMENT

The built environment of a city is constantly changing. New neighborhoods emerge, the character of existing ones evolves, and those in power seek to shape the city to reflect their vision of order. In addition to the militarization of a city, states exert power by directing the flow of capital and determining the location of sites of power, as we have seen with the emergence of the West Amman spatial imaginary of affluence, privilege, and global connection. While states have these powers at their disposal, activists and other insurgents are relatively resource-poor. As William H. Sewell has argued, insurgents also have far less spatial agency than power holders. States and corporations can build roads, ports, factories, industrial zones, new neighborhoods, and so on, engineering sometimes major changes to the built environment to suit their needs. Those making claims against them, however, have little recourse but to accept the physical environment as given and work instead to inscribe new and contentious meanings into specific locations across the city.[10] How has the state militarized Amman's built environment to suit its needs? How have state projects affected the potential for protests to be visible and disruptive, and how have protests in turn shaped Amman as well as other cities?

Urban Sprawl and Infrastructural Upgrading

I have already discussed the impact of urban sprawl on protests in the capital, but I summarize those arguments here to provide context for the coming discussion. Amman evolved from a small town with a population of a few thousand in the 1910s to a sprawling metropolis of more than five million in 2020. The geography of the location, with steep hills reaching up from the valley floor where three wadis (seasonal valley streams) once came together, meant that until the 1960s, most roads passed through the downtown area. A few dozen people could easily disrupt traffic and commerce, cutting off goods from reaching the railway station. It was nearly impossible for anyone trying to move through the city to not be aware when a protest was happening, because the gatherings were visible and disruptive. Even those working or residing up the steep hills surrounding the wadi could look down and see streets crowded with protesters, with chants echoing as they bounced between the hills. Downtown protests brought the city to a standstill during the many protests of the 1950s, but the imposition of martial law in 1957 kept the area relatively quiet for a time. The 1960s saw marches in the capital against Israel and in solidarity with Nasser, but no large-scale demonstrations. Following Black September, repression of protests was swift and harsh.

When large protests returned to the Grand Husseini Mosque in the late 1980s, the city was dramatically changed. Government offices and high-end commerce were spread across affluent West Amman, rendering downtown protests far less disruptive to the routine functioning and flow of political and economic power. Bypass roads enabled vehicles to avoid the congested downtown entirely, and not only during times of protest. Yet groups like the Muslim Brotherhood and the Islamic Action Front still favor protests commencing at the Grand Husseini Mosque, where police seldom interfere with marches that adhere to the established spatial routine. Large crowds can assemble while Islamist parade guards maintain order, and these marches seldom draw the ire of the regime because they are not disruptive.

Beyond urban sprawl, other changes to the built environment structure the opportunities and possibilities of protest without that being the intended effect. As states decide where to undertake infrastructural development, for example, those projects advance the militarization of the city as they seek to structure how and where people and vehicles move and where there are spaces to assemble. Alterations to Zahran Street in West Amman—which intersects with Queen Rania Street at the Fourth Circle—offers a clear example of these effects.

In the late 1990s, the state initiated a massive, multiphase infrastructure development plan for the capital. These changes included efforts to ease the congestion at many of the traffic circles along Zahran Street, where residential buildings, government offices, and high-end hotels were crowding in areas that were farmland but a generation earlier. Over the next decade, all but the first two traffic circles (closest to downtown) were reconstructed with high-speed underpasses. Through-traffic could now pass underneath the circle at high speeds, while only those making turns would enter the circle itself. The unintended consequence for protesters was that the underpasses undermined one technique of Fourth Circle protests: bringing traffic to a halt by clogging the intersection with demonstrators. Of course, protesters could still stop traffic on the circle in front of the Prime Ministry—as they periodically did—but the underpasses rendered those demonstrations far less disruptive, and the protesters were entirely invisible to vehicles passing underneath. These changes to the built environment downtown and at the Fourth Circle are but two examples of the ways in which urban growth and infrastructure projects have rendered protests in some locations less visible, audible, or disruptive. But other development and infrastructure projects have also had consequences for the regime's ability to respond rapidly to protests or prevent them from being mounted in the first place.

The military capabilities of infrastructure are not always obvious. The improvements to Amman's main roads since the 1990s, for example, have militarized capacities beyond increasing vehicular flows. Some widened roads

FIGURE 8.2. Underpass at the Fourth Circle. Source: Jillian Schwedler.

in and out of the city, for example, have long, straight stretches and removable medians to facilitate emergency use as an air strip or parade ground. Overpasses and underpasses similarly increase the speed with which security forces and armored vehicles can move around the city. Even the Abdoun Bridge—which connects affluent Abdoun with the Fourth Circle across Wadi Abdoun, eliminating the need to traverse down and up steep narrow and winding streets—also enables the rapid deployment of armored vehicles and security forces to the Prime Ministry and elsewhere in West Amman.

While urban expansion and infrastructure development have had negative consequences for protest, many of the changes they brought were not enacted with that intent. At times, however, states do alter the built environment to prevent protests from being mounted, to break up protests that do occur, and to undo any place-making that the protests might have accomplished. They do this through a variety of techniques, such as rendering spaces inaccessible or increasing surveillance to intimidate protesters. At other times, they seek to strip places of their symbolic association with past protests or as places for

234   CHAPTER 8

political claim-making. In the remainder of this section, I provide an original typology for theorizing five spatial techniques of protest repression: exposures, erasures, enclosures, exclusions, and containment.[11]

Exposures

States create exposures in order to increase the visibility of a place or population, and thus to more fully exert state power over them. Exposures are common following massive protests, typically justified in terms of surveillance and security. They entail alterations or even the removal of aspects of the built environment that obstruct vision and render those inhabiting or traversing those spaces more exposed and thus more vulnerable to state penetration and violence. The new urban "order" of Haussmann's reconstruction of Paris exposed rebellious areas of the city and facilitated the rapid movement of troops to quell any unrest. Following the 2014 sustained protests against Michael Brown's death by police in Ferguson, Missouri, state utility workers removed a large number of trees in the neighborhood where the protests were mounted.[12] Their removal worked as both a warning and example of the state's ability to inflict violence on the community, while also increasing the state's ability to see directly into residents' homes.

In Jordan, the state has used exposures in poorer neighborhoods in Amman, particularly in refugee camps, as a means of establishing order and extending its power. Following Black September, when the Palestinian militias established bases in several refugee camps, the state gradually widened narrow alleys and boulevards that opened them to militarized access.[13] A prominent example is Sumayya Street in Wihdat Camp.[14] Formerly a dirt road, Sumayya Street cuts through the heart of the camp from northwest to southeast. The street was widened in the early 1990s to facilitate policing of the camp's residents and the movement of security vehicles into the camp. After large protests broke out there following the start of the Second Palestinian Intifada in 2000, the state dramatically expanded the police station located just outside the camp on Madaba Street. The resulting structure more resembles a fortress, with elevated observation spaces from which the police can look down into the camp as if it were a prison.[15] A similar approach was implemented in Baqaʿa Camp northeast of Amman, where many Palestinian activists reside. These aggressive exposures convey a dual message: while those populations are

PROTEST AND ORDER IN MILITARIZED SPACES   235

exposed to state surveillance, state power looms in a manner that is impossible to miss, and the widened streets slice a form of militarization through the heart of the camps.

This is not to suggest that affluent West Amman is not subject to surveillance and exposure. With wider roads and far lower population density than East Amman, militarization is at once less obvious in residential neighborhoods and yet visible in the ubiquitous concrete blockades around hotels, embassies, malls, and the like. Many establishments have security cameras and security guards at the entrances, as do embassies and the residences of diplomats, government officials, and other elites. State power is more seamlessly woven into the built environment, whereas in East Amman and poorer neighborhoods, the state visibly exercises its violence, slashing exposures into neighborhoods and surveilling their residents from on high.

Erasures

Erasure is a technique for undoing place-making that aims to remove from the built environment anything that symbolically marks it as a place of protest. The most obvious efforts at erasure are attempts to break up protests or encampments and remove signs, banners, and other items that identify the place as a location for contentious claim-making. But when contention becomes associated with particular locations—whether a single protest like the 2011 March 24 Youth encampment or with protests in general, like the Fourth Circle—another technique used by the state is to attempt its own place-making, that is, marking the location with the symbolism of state power and/or the regime's narrative of its authority to rule. A variety of techniques can be used for erasure and place-(re)making, some of which are aimed at reconstructing areas damaged by the protest, and others of which serve as warnings and reminders to people to consider the consequences before engaging in such protests again.

One of the most dramatic state efforts to erase revolutionary symbolism in a physical location associated with insurgency was the removal of the Pearl Roundabout in Manama, the epicenter of Bahrain's uprising. At the center of the traffic circle stood a large sculpture with three white brackets holding a white sphere at the top—the eponymous pearl. The sculpture was widely recognized as a symbol of the city, even represented on a Bahraini coin. After the brutal repression of the hundred thousand protesters in spring 2011, the government sought to erase the symbol because it was now associated with the uprising. It disassembled and removed the sculpture, replacing the traffic circle with an intersection—what Amal Khalaf aptly calls "squaring the circle."[16] The regime even went so far as to remove from circulation the coin with the image of the roundabout sculpture. The intersection was renamed Farouk Junction, honoring a Sunni caliph contested by Shiʿa. In choosing that name, the Bahraini regime sought to engage in place-making by marking the intersection in a manner that invoked the government's anti-Shiʿi stance.[17] Indeed, during the uprising there in 2011, the regime falsely portrayed the uprising as instigated by foreign Shiʿi agitators, despite overwhelming evidence that Sunnis were also protesting at the circle.

But Bahraini activists found another means of keeping the symbol in circulation spatially. Unable to assemble without the state resorting to violent repression, some activists began stenciling the image of the roundabout sculpture on walls across Bahrain, and not only in the capital. The regime would quickly whitewash over them, usually within a day. But activists photographed the images and posted them on social media, allowing the image to circulate virtually, and well beyond Bahrain's built environment. A few activists have even gotten tattoos of the sculpture. Here the marking and erasing across the built environment is a form of struggle for the right to the city, a contest between the state and the people over its use and meaning. Indeed, as Thomas Fibiger argues, Bahrain's attempt at erasing the "bad memory" of the Pearl Roundabout may have had the opposite effect, elevating the importance of the monument in ways that have led to its ongoing commemoration.[18]

In Cairo, too, first the Supreme Council of the Armed Forces and later the regime of Abd al-Fattah Sisi sought to clear Tahrir Square of the evidence and markings of the revolution. As Asef Bayat writes, the removal of the symbolism was first followed by neglect of the area, allowing garbage and construction debris to pile up in the area, marking it more as a "dump" than the triumphant place of the revolution. A later "monument" to the revolution, mocked and vandalized by activists, was then replaced by an Egyptian flag on a very tall pole—a generic symbol of the nation with no specific association with the uprising.[19] Similar processes played out across the region, with states removing any banners, graffiti, and other symbols of the uprisings from public squares and spaces.

In Jordan, the state has not done anything as dramatic as Bahrain's removal of the Pearl Roundabout, but likely because no symbol from the built environment is associated with calls for overthrowing the regime, as was the case in Bahrain. The state does, however, routinely remove any detritus that remains after protests end (whether peacefully or by force). At times, they are replaced with Jordanian flags and/or large banners bearing images of the king, his father, and the crown prince. These symbols and images announce both state power and continued Hashemite rule over Jordan. Billboards with slogans of national unity also dot the urban landscape and, indeed, appear at major intersections nationwide.

As suggested with the Pearl Roundabout stencils, artwork and graffiti are another means of place-making in the built environment, a visual technique for expressing political dissent in public space. The spectacular artworks created in and around Tahrir Square during Egypt's uprising in 2011, for example, were gradually removed in the months after President Hosni Mubarak's deposition, and the last remaining ones were entirely erased following the July 2013 countercoup. Artists widely documented their work, however, expecting it to be removed. Indeed, art and graffiti were already established forms of place-making in Egypt before the uprising. As Samuli Schielke and Jessica Winegar argue, political, religious, commercial, and intimate messages painted and stenciled onto walls appear and disappear, often at a rapid pace, making the walls "a site of ongoing and unfinished discussion and debate."[20] Certain neighborhoods in Cairo were even known for different kinds of graffiti: pro-Brotherhood, opposition voices, soccer Ultras, and so on. As they write,

> Immediately after Husni Mubarak left office, citizens adorned Cairo with large portraits of martyrs. The Supreme Council of the Armed Forces (SCAF) just as quickly painted them over. Pro-SCAF youth whited out the famous image of a tank facing a panda, by the graffiti artist Ganzeer, under a bridge near a government-run youth center on Gezira Island. Ganzeer and his crew returned and drew a SCAF figure with a forked tongue over the pro-junta graffiti. This well-known graffiti battlefield has been covered up with paint and scrawled upon again and again.[21]

While Amman is not known for political murals or graffiti—let alone this kind of back-and-forth place-making and -remaking—artists do mark public spaces with unauthorized political messages. As Kyle Craig found in his ongoing research, political graffiti and public artwork in Amman that is not sanctioned by the state (such as an NGO-sponsored mural) or the building's owner is routinely painted over or defaced, usually within days.[22] A graffiti (fig. 8.3) on a wall in Jebal Amman, for example, is titled, "The Sectors Are Mixed Up for Us," showing a tic-tac-toe game between NATO and the Islamic State (with the words in red and the hash lines in black). The image suggests that one no longer knows who (of the players) is right and who is wrong, since both forms of interventionism were killing people. One activist suggested to me that the graffiti also implied a certain "coordination" between the two, in that the game is one of making alternate moves. The piece was quickly defaced with red paint blocking out the words "NATO" and "Da'esh" (the Arabic acronym for the Islamic State), but it was not entirely painted over. This kind of erasure also functions as a redaction, with the blurred words signaling that

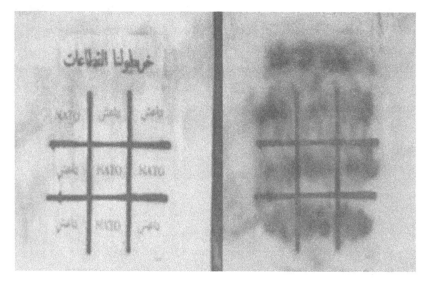

FIGURE 8.3. Political graffiti of a tic-tac-toe game and its redaction on a wall in Jebal Amman. The title says, "The Sectors Are Mixed Up for Us" and the players are NATO and the Islamic State. Source: Kyle Craig.

something is being hidden or removed. What lies beneath, this technique of violence announces, is not for your eyes.

Even when such erasures are not done by the state, the production and removal of political art still indexes the struggle over public space and place-making. After Egyptian LGBTQ activist Sarah Hegazi died in June 2020 by suicide while in exile in Canada, a mural of her face with a rainbow background appeared in West Amman's upscale neighborhood of Jebal Webdeh. Hegazi had been tortured by the Egyptian government for waving a gay-pride rainbow flag at a concert in Cairo in 2017, marking the concert as a space and assembly of "queer pride." A large black square was painted over Hegazi's portrait within days, a redaction of the artist's attempt at marking Jebal Webdeh—with its galleries, bars, restaurants, and other secular spaces—as a queer-friendly neighborhood. Like the examples from Bahrain and Cairo, the marking and removal of graffiti and artwork across Jordan's built environment are part of the struggle over the right to the city and the place-making of particular places for and by those who inhabit it.

Enclosures

Another militarized technique for preventing protests is to enclose spaces with fences or barriers to render them inaccessible for protests. Closing spaces in such a manner can serve a dual purpose for the regime: preventing protests at that location and announcing that the state has the ability to control access to space. Farah al-Nakib writes about how opposition groups in Kuwait planned to use Safat Plaza, an established place for political gatherings in the past, for a large demonstration in January 2011 during the period of the Arab uprisings. But the state immediately boarded up the site and declared it was under renovation. Protesters were forced to restrict their activities to what Nakib describes as a "smaller, historically neutral and more easily controllable park" adjacent to the National Assembly. They named it "Determination Square" and, for the next two years, it was the "official" location for both opposition protests and loyalist rallies.[23] In Cairo, a plaza at the north end of Tahrir Square was fenced off for decades, supposedly for the excavation of a new parking lot. But when the fence was dismantled by protesters during the 2011 uprising, they found no construction and realized that the empty space had been closed off to prevent large crowds from assembling.[24]

In Amman, the state has adopted this fencing technique since at least 2012, rendering many known sites of protest entirely inaccessible. Following the 2012 removal of the orphans' encampment at the Fourth Circle, the regime caged off the circle's plaza with a tall metal fence that left little room for either leisure activities or assembling for protests.[25] Benches were replaced with trees and other plants, a kind of exclusion-through-landscaping technique. The remaining sidewalk space around the circle is frequently occupied by gendarmerie troops, announcing the state's repressive capacities even when protests are not anticipated. Concrete barricades, as noted above, are ever-present at the Fourth Circle, a militarized blockage on standby. Thus, a public space that formerly belonged to the people for leisure as well as periodic claim-making against the government was altered to announce state power and the potential for violence. But even with these foreboding fences, caging, and military vehicles, Jordanians continued to protest at the Fourth Circle. Small protests utilized the wide sidewalk area in front of the ALICO (later MetLife) building, as during the anti-gas deal protest there in April 2015; even that area now has a fence around it. And then, in late 2019 or early 2020, another lot just southwest of the Fourth Circle along Zahran Street, which protesters had also used to assemble, was enclosed with a tall ornate fence.

Other known spaces for protest in the capital have met similar fates. We have seen how the Interior Circle became known as one of the most contentious locations for claim-making in the capital with the violent clearing of the 2011 March 24 Youth encampment and as the epicenter of angry claim-making during the 2012 *Habbit Tishreen* protests. This is where Jordanians finally chanted the slogan of the Arab uprisings, "The People Want the Fall of the Regime!" In an effort to prevent future protests there, the state fenced off and landscaped that circle, too, around 2012 when the Fourth Circle was enclosed. The field adjacent to the Kalouti Mosque, where protests against Israel had been held since 2000, suffered the same fate. Sometime after the massive protests there against Israel's deadly July 2014 campaign into Gaza, a six-foot chain-link fence was erected around the field, bearing a "For Rent" sign (although why one would "rent" a field is a mystery). The symbolism of the location endured, however, and the Kalouti Mosque remains the primary place to protest against Israel. During Israel's brutal May 2021 campaign into Gaza and seizure of private Palestinian homes in Shaykh Jarra (in East Jerusalem), massive crowds again assembled to protest daily for weeks at the location. But because the large field was fenced off, they demonstrated instead on the opposite side of the mosque, on its main plaza and spilling into the street and a smaller lot nearby.

In late 2017 or early 2018, the state fenced off the open space opposite the offices of the members of Parliament that was sometimes described as Amman's "Hyde Park,"[26] a reference to Speaker's Corner there in London. Following the 2019 unemployment marches from the outer governorates to the Royal Court on the north side of Hashemite Plaza in downtown Amman, the plaza was entirely fenced off, with turnstiles at narrow points of entry overseen by guards. Protesters were relocated to the back of the Royal Court, where they were, unsurprisingly, less visible and less disruptive.

FIGURE 8.4. Turnstile entrance to Hashemite Plaza in downtown Amman. Source: Jillian Schwedler.

242   CHAPTER 8

Activists speculate that, similar to the sudden fencing of the privately owned lot near the Kalouti Mosque, the state had pressured the owners to fence the location by telling them that they bore liability for any property damage that might occur during the course of protests. And yet another new space for Fourth Circle protests, discussed below, met with a similar fate in early 2020.

Exclusions

Both erasures and enclosures work to exclude, but here I wish to explore how exclusions can happen through other techniques for the militarization of the built environment. One means is to seek to control the movement of people across particular spaces, explicitly excluding them from accessing certain spaces or else using a variety of techniques to make certain groups feel unwelcome. We have already seen, for example, numerous cases in which the state works to prevent protesters from assembling by blocking roads, erecting fences, and preventing caravans of protester vehicles from reaching their destinations. Here I examine other techniques for excluding people from assembling for protest.

In locations without established protest routines, the police and protesters are often unsure what the other will do, and thus both draw from more general repertoires for protest and repression. In scrambling to outmaneuver each other, activists and the police seek to adapt other routines to the spatiality of the new location. Each tries to anticipate what the other will do and where they will do it, with police blocking expected march routes and activists seeking to evade them. On January 3, 2010, for example, activists called for people to gather at the Egyptian embassy to demonstrate against Egypt's construction of a wall along its border with Gaza. Gendarmerie forces blocked the main roads to the embassy, but protesters arrived from all directions via unpaved side roads and alleys.[27] And we saw in chapter 7 how police blocked protesters from reaching the French embassy to protest over the *Charlie Hebdo* cartoons in 2015. This cat-and-mouse dynamic between protesters and police plays out spatially, as it did during the first day of the Egyptian uprising on January 25, 2011. The organizers of those protests in Cairo announced on a Facebook page some twenty locations for protesters to assemble across the city, from which each group would march to Tahrir Square, the final destination.[28] They aimed to divide the police and force them to block multiple marches. But the plan posted on Facebook was also intended to mislead the police, and additional marches began in locations not publicly announced. With no police ready to block their paths, some of those marches were among the first to reach Tahrir Square,[29] which was also a known location for protests.[30]

In Jordan, the state has used additional techniques for rendering particular locations inaccessible for activists. In 2002, for example, an Art for Palestine event was planned for a location on Gardens Street in West Amman. On the morning of the event, the artists and organizers arrived to discover that the empty lot—an open space on which artists planned to produce works of art all day and display them for passersby—was now rubble. The organizers had visited the space the previous day, so workers must have torn up the pavement the previous night. In rendering the lot unusable for the event, the state again also demonstrated its power through a violent reshaping of the built environment.

Exclusions at the Fourth Circle took a turn beyond fencing and landscaping on February 1, 2018, when the governor of Amman announced that the location—including the few remaining sidewalks—was now off-limits for protests because the area was vital for traffic as a major artery and interchange. His announcement came after the end of a small sit-in by *Hirak* activists from outside Amman, who had traveled to the capital to protest price hikes and held a sit-in encampment that lasted for three days.[31] When the *Habbit Huzayran* protests broke out a few months later, by the second day the gendarmerie had blocked the streets in all directions to prevent protesters from reaching the circle.[32] Later that fall, the *Ma'anash* protests were also prevented from assembling at the Fourth Circle, but they were allowed to assemble instead in a parking lot adjacent to the Jordan Hospital a half-mile north of the Fourth Circle, on Queen Noor Street near the Abdali interchange—another major traffic intersection with multiple overpasses. Security forces easily surrounded and monitored these new "Fourth Circle" protests, using the adjacent pedestrian overpass as a base for surveillance from above. They also usually outnumbered protesters by a magnitude of five or more, surrounding the parking lot, blocking nearby streets, and preventing the demonstration from disrupting traffic or turning into a march. Activists, however, sought to hold on to the contentious symbolism of Fourth Circle protests. They continued to call protests in the new location "Fourth Circle" protests, indicating that the Prime Ministry was the addressee while also evoking a connection to earlier Fourth Circle protests. Figure 7.1 is a protest at that new location, with the large placard reading "Ramadan is sweeter at the Fourth [Circle]."

In addition to moving protests from a busy intersection to a parking lot, the new "Fourth Circle" location had an additional spatial effect on protest and protest policing. The actual Fourth Circle is location on Zahran Street, which traces the top of Jebal Amman, one of the city's main seven hills, following it west from the downtown city center. The underpasses at the roundabout give the location an additional a sense of height, with the Fourth Circle intersecting Queen Noor Street, which descends north toward the Abdali interchange and south toward Ras al-Ayn. The new location exchanged the elevation of the actual Fourth Circle for a downhill location between the neighborhoods of Jebal Webdeh and Shmeisani. Instead of commanding the heights of the traffic circle, protesters now saw tall buildings, a pedestrian bridge, the neighboring hills, and the imposing Abdali interchange overpasses looming above them. During the *Ma'anash* protests on December 13, 2018, the regime decided even surrogate "Fourth Circle" protests were too threatening, and a thick line of multiple security forces blocked the protesters from reaching the lot.[33] Some protesters tried and failed to push through the police lines several times, and others tried to reach the lot through side streets. But the heavy forces prevented their advance, blocking the streets with armored vehicles and thick lines of security forces.

A week earlier, the municipality had also installed an iron fence on the median in Queen Noor Street on which the "Fourth Circle" parking lot is located, further militarizing the street by preventing pedestrians from crossing between intersections and thus further limiting access to the "Fourth Circle" protest site. *Hirak* activists who had traveled from the outer governorates tried to assemble at the nearby Abdali interchange with the intention of marching as a group to join the protest. But they were prevented from assembling as a group and forced to move individually to the "Fourth Circle" location, where they were then able to join the crowd.[34]

Containment

A final spatial technique for militarizing the built environment to repress protests is containment: confining protests to a particular space (that can be surrounded and controlled) or else keeping people from protesting at all

FIGURE 8.5. Heavy security forces at the Abdali interchange block protesters from reaching the "Fourth Circle" for a demonstration. Source: Muhammad Zakaria for *7iber*.

through such techniques as the imprisonment of activists or curfews of entire towns, regions, or even the nation. The first form of containment is a technique common to places like refugee camps, university campuses, and the qualified industrial zones (QIZs). We have already seen how some locations are surveilled almost in the manner of prisons, with elevated observation areas facilitating the monitoring of movements inside for suspicious activities. Some areas, like campuses, are surrounded by high walls and have checkpoints to enter, but even refugee camps without walls are monitored through visible surveillance towers and police patrolling the streets. Residents protesting in the Baqa'a Camp, for example, are sometimes prevented from leaving to join demonstrations in Amman. We have already seen how the expansions to the police surveillance station outside of the Wihdat Camp approach policing with a prison mentality. Protests in camps are often permitted to proceed as long as the crowds do not attempt to leave those spaces.

Similarly, students demonstrating on college campuses are often prevented from marching off campus into the surrounding neighborhoods. In the spring of 1999, for example, Islamist student leaders organized numerous campus protests against a controversial new policy by the University of Jordan administration.[35] The police sealed off the campus and pressured senior party leaders from the Islamic Action Front to instruct the student leaders to stand down. Those in the vicinity of the campus could see the heavy police presence at campus entrances, but not the protesting students contained inside. Other campus protests met similar fates, with student demonstrators allowed to march on campus but confronting heavy security forces when they tried to exit.[36] In the QIZs, the dozens of strikes and protests since the mid-2000s were fully contained in those closed-off spaces, where mostly foreign workers do not even have the right to exit.[37]

Even Fourth Circle protests have been subject to containment, after seeming to suffer every fate. First underpasses made them less disruptive, and then they were relocated to the less visible parking lot where they could hardly be seen. For much of 2019, protests in the new spaces saw heavy security forces on the perimeter, with the protesters mostly able to engage in claim-making so long as they did not attempt to leave the parking lot. (But, as noted above, when those protests grew too large, security forces would at times prevent them from even assembling.) Sometime in early 2020, however, a concrete wall more than six feet tall was erected around two sides of the parking lot where "Fourth Circle" protests were mounted. A third side abuts a building, so only the far side was open. Although protesters could still access the space— unlike the fences along the full perimeter of the "exclusion" spaces discussed above—protests would not be visible to anyone outside the lot. And if they did assemble, they would be easily trapped should security forces choose to move against them. With the state effectively preventing even symbolic "Fourth Circle" protests, activists may well try to return to the actual Fourth Circle in the future. Given how intent the state has become on preventing protests there, the Fourth Circle has become—perhaps even more than the Interior Circle—the most contentious location to mount a protest in all of Jordan.

Imprisonment of activists is an obvious technique of containment, but so are the arrests and detentions of activists who are never charged. This latter technique combines the spatial techniques of both containment and dispersal, as activists are held in jails for hours (or longer) at multiple locations away from the protest location as well as each other. Curfews are another technique for

FIGURE 8.6. The new concrete wall at the "Fourth Circle" protest site would contain any protests there and block their visibility to outsiders. Source: Kyle Craig.

controlling bodies in space by confining people to their homes and allowing them to move only at designated times.[38] The state has repeatedly imposed curfews in towns like Ma'an, Tafileh, and Karak following protests that lasted for days or weeks, particularly when locals blocked major roads and destroyed government property. Most spectacularly, the state enforced a near-absolute nationwide lockdown for several weeks during the coronavirus pandemic of 2020–21, with curfews continuing for much of the next year and a half. While those curfews were not intended for the purpose of quelling protests, activists told me that they believed the state was exploiting the pandemic-related restrictions to silence political dissent. Indeed, the arrest and interrogations of activists continued through the lockdown even as protest activities were minimal. Creatively, hundreds of Islamists found a work-around against the pandemic restrictions that prohibited gatherings of fifteen or more—a rule that activists believe was meant to curtail protests as well as the spread of the coronavirus—by protesting in the unfinished rapid-transit bus lane in West Amman, socially distanced in a long line.[39]

One final containment technique is to allow people to exercise public expression of political speech only in designated locations. In December 2005, during his first tenure as prime minister, Bakhit announced plans to create a "Freedom Square" where people could freely express their political views without fear of repercussion. The proposed location was to be somewhere in Amman's Hashemite Plaza adjacent to the Roman amphitheater, a space geographically in the center of the city but one located outside the spatial imaginary of affluent West Amman and its many sites of government, economic, and foreign power. Several parliamentarians expressed skepticism, one branding the proposal as unfeasible.[40] Progressive and liberal voices were likewise dubious that people would travel to that location just to express their views. Activist Naseem Tarawneh wrote about the proposal in his blog, arguing that "professionals and intellectuals who reside in West Amman won't go downtown to rant, and those who live there will be too afraid to do so."[41] Some activists dismissed the effort as a joke, while others worried that free speech would be limited to only that location,[42] an idea that would be antithetical to the very notion of free speech.[43] The square was never realized, however, the idea abandoned within only a few months of its proposal.

CONCLUSION

In this chapter, I have shown how the state uses a variety of spatial techniques for militarizing the city, undoing (or attempting to undo) the place-making work of protests and creating material obstacles in the built environment that inhibit the mounting of protests and contain their political impact. As Doreen Massey puts it, "For the future to be open, space must be open, too."[44] Perhaps one of the most striking spatial dynamics is the uneven deployment of these techniques across the city, with policing practices varying from neighborhood to neighborhood. We have seen that while the state allows protests in certain places to proceed with little interference, it strives to prevent protesters from ever assembling in other places. When it breaks up protests, it aims to scatter them in multiple directions. That spatial technique of dispersal can take the form of breaking up the protest as well as arresting activists and transporting them to police stations across the city. On campuses and in some poor neighborhoods, by comparison, protests are encircled by security forces and allowed to proceed—as long as they remain contained. Even in the downtown area, protests at the Grand Husseini Mosque are partially contained by the spatiality of the location—surrounded by seven steep hills—as well as by protesters adhering to the spatial and temporal routine of marching from the mosque to the Municipal Complex and later dispersing. When crowds are in the thousands, however, the downtown area is packed solid, with protesters snaking up the main roads out of the area like the arms of an octopus.

In focusing on the spatial and geographic dimensions of protests across Jordan and within Amman's urban built environment, the foregoing chapters have also shown how economic inequalities are spatially situated. Many East Bank communities in the governorates outside of Amman turn to protest because they feel that they are neglected, that they are excluded from the state's geography of neoliberal investment and development. In the capital, affluent West Amman receives the preponderance of domestic and foreign investment. As we shall see, the regime's decisions about where capital flows go hand in hand with the enforcement of private property, both of which are complicit with the militarized management of the city.[45] In the final chapter, I tie together the pieces of the argument: geographies of economic and political power, competing spatial imaginaries of the city as well as the nation, nationwide repertoires for protesting and repression, and ongoing debates about who is truly Jordanian.

Chapter 9

PROTESTING GLOBAL ASPIRATIONS

ECONOMIC INEQUALITIES ARE SPATIALLY SITUATED, AND BOTH real and perceived inequalities are central to public claim-making. Very few Jordanians reside in spaces of neoliberal investment and development, and those outside them find protests the most effective means of getting the state's attention. The regime's state-maintaining, however, means that it cannot simply ignore East Bank grievances. It sometimes cedes to demands from East Bank tribal communities, but it also deploys a wide range of techniques to deflate challenges to its authority. In this way, as we have seen, protests shape how the state reproduces its power, which in turn shapes who takes to the streets to engage in claim-making. Protests both challenge and structure nationwide and local geographies of power, and they are central to the processes by which state and society are mutually constituted. And as we have also seen, protests both shape and are shaped by the built environment.

In this final chapter, I bring together my analyses of Jordan's repertoires for protests and repression, its incongruent geographies of economic and political power, and competing narratives of Jordan's past and future. I examine King Abdullah II's vision for a new Jordan and the ways in which many Jordanians are protesting either that vision itself or their inability to access its promises. I show how that vision directs capital flows in ways that combine to undermine East Bank support for the king, and how neoliberal urbanism not only embodies the king's vision but also fails it. I zoom in to revisit urban development in the capital, this time with a focus on two projects that aim to inscribe the king's narrative about Jordan's past and future into the built environment. These projects are made possible by connecting Jordan to global capital flows and creating the environment necessary to attract foreign investment, which in turn require the regime to project the stability of the nation under Hashemite leadership. To secure that stability, Jordan leverages its connections to regional and international security arrangements, and it privileges US and Gulf security priorities while relying on their economic aid. Zooming out to bring into view these uneven geographies of financial and security commitments, we can also understand why Jordanian security forces have participated in repressing protests elsewhere in the region.

Finally, my analysis zooms in again to the scale of the urban built environment, this time the Aqaba neoliberal zone and the impoverished communities protesting their exclusion from it. The analysis then turns on its heels and looks back at the Transjordanian area from the perspective of the economic periphery, with workers walking to the capital to assert moral and material claims on the king. We follow their slow march north, moving through different spatial imaginaries and their affective connections and seeing past episodes of protest and repression inscribed in the built environment. After reaching Amman, we finally descend into the valley between the original seven hills to join the workers' weeks-long sit-in at the Royal Court, and we see that the king's vision for a new Jordan is far from being realized. What does all of this tell us about Jordanian politics? What broader theoretical insights do we learn from this close analysis of the spatial and temporal dimensions of protest?

A NEW VISION FOR JORDAN

The production of history is not only backward-looking but also forward-looking, a kind of political storytelling central to state-making and state-maintaining. Narrating the past always entails the selection of certain "facts" and the erasure of others, as it opens possibilities for the current state to discursively secure its authority. Nation-states always strive to be seen as both "new" and "historical," as Benedict Anderson observes, looming out of an immemorial past and gliding into a limitless future.[1] This process has been observed in many parts of the world, but perhaps nowhere as dramatically as in the Arab Gulf states. As Ahmad Kanna argues, those regimes have sought to position themselves as guardians of noble and moral traditions as well as modernizers who are already leading their states into exciting futures. The juxtaposition of the "traditional" and the "modern" selectively elevates "traditional" symbols while inscribing "modernity" into spaces of the capital cities through the monumentality of major urban projects.[2] As Farah al-Nakib shows, that exaggerated contrast between the traditional and the ultramodern works to "emphasize the magnitude and magnificence of the present" under the current state leadership.[3]

But Nakib takes the argument further, noting that there was a substantial period of modern state development in the Gulf between the so-called traditional and the ultramodern, roughly from the first state-making projects of the 1930s and 1940s through the neoliberal era beginning in the 1980s or 1990s. Acknowledging this true modern era of the mid-twentieth century, however, renders the contrast between past and present less dramatic. The accomplishments of the present appear more impressive if the true modern period is "erased into obscurity in official, popular, and scholarly discourses of the region's political, social, cultural, and urban development."[4] Nakib's words are worth quoting at length:

> When a renovated pre-oil mudbrick courtyard house or a reconstructed "traditional" *suq* foregrounds a hypermodern skyscraper made of glass and steel designed by an international starchitect, the shift from one life world to the other becomes more rapid, more heroic, more consensual. False starts and mistakes, conflicts and oppositions—all of which occurred in those "in-between" decades—are erased.[5]

The erasure of the midcentury modernist period does more than just glorify the achievements of the present; it also erases the struggles of state-making as well as decades of political protests and strident opposition.[6] And the exaggerated juxtaposition of the traditional and the ultramodern only work by caricaturing the "traditional period," because in reality people for centuries had been engaging with and adopting ideas, customs, and practices from their exposure to other cultures and regions. Rosie Bsheer similarly shows how the Saudi state manipulates not only the built environment to advance a territorialized national history but also a wide range of archives. The objective is to strengthen the Saudi family's authority by first unraveling and then erasing its historic alliance with Wahhabi Islamist authorities. As that alliance was embodied in the symbolism of the built environment as well as archival documents, both needed to be altered to advance the regime's new official narrative.[7]

We have already seen how the Jordanization project following the Black September conflict in 1970–71 invented and advanced a narrative for Jordan's history as having a noble Bedouin past with the Hashemite regime leading the nation into the modern, independent period. Abdullah II is deepening this narrative, constructing both that traditional past and the gleaming future in the built environment, conveying Jordan's exciting future under Hashemite leadership. National symbols are visible across the country, including a huge flag in the capital that looms over the cityscape. Images of the royal family are also ubiquitous, with up to five generations of Hashemite kings plus the current crown prince gazing across generations into the future.[8] The narrative connecting the Hashemite regime to Jordan's past and future is also woven into the built environment, with some locations conveying "tradition-heritage" and others "modern-global." Even as parts of West Amman are in decline—such as the once-shiny Shmeisani[9]—the middle decades are erased in service of a traditional-to-ultramodern narrative. In Jordan's past—as reflected in the Jordanization project—citizens are reimagined to be homogenous and political authority to be consensual, erasing (in Nakib's sense) the decades during which Hashemite rule was repeatedly contested. Gone are violent Bedouin raids and the early revolts and the British aerial bombing necessary to crush them. The massive protests for Arab nationalism and the planned military coups are all erased. And, most importantly, the violence of Black September is conveniently skipped over, the most serious threat to Hashemite rule erased from the narrative. In its place, a noble Bedouin past of a diverse tribal heritage (nevermind that the Hashemites were never truly tribal) led into the exciting future by Abdullah II and his forefathers.

As we have already seen, however, many Jordanians remember and talk about those contentious decades, from the revolts of the early Hashemite period to challenges to the regime's rule midcentury to Black September. Still fresh in their memories, too, are the large-scale nationwide protests, from 1989's *Habbit Nisan* to 2018's *Habbit Huzayran*. Some younger generations, of

254 CHAPTER 9

course, do not remember Jordan's earlier large-scale protests, let alone the revolts of the state-making era. Some of my younger interlocutors have told me that the 2018 *Habbit Huzayran* was Jordan's first massive protest and that the general strike during that period was also Jordan's first. But some newspaper articles and recent books have sought to renew those memories and even alter them, such as Abdullah Mutlaq al-Assaf's book on the Adwan Revolt, which he exaggeratedly calls a *thawra* to liken it to the Great Arab Revolt.[10] One of the messages his book seeks to convey is that Jordan is ruled by a Hijazi family and not a Jordanian one only as a result of the military assistance provided by the British in those early years. Yazan Doughan fascinatingly found that some of his young activist interlocutors from Hayy Tafayleh were not able to narrate their own history as distinct from the official narrative, and yet they realized its falsity: "Our history is all lies!" was a refrain he heard often.[11]

Meanwhile, the Hashemite regime deploys its narrative of Jordan's past through museums and other heritage sites that celebrate Jordan's connection to the ancient Nabatean civilization (especially at Petra and Wadi Rum), events in the Bible (including at Mount Nebo, where Moses was shown the Holy Land and later died), and the Jordan River (where Jesus was baptized at the spot where Joshua led the Israelites across the river to Jericho). The royal family also emphasizes its connection to an Islamic past as descendants of the Quraysh tribe of the Prophet Mohammad and as the guardians of the holy spaces in Jerusalem.[12] Meanwhile, megaprojects, gleaming skyscrapers, luxury residences and resorts, and a new "world-class" airport are just a few of the ways in which the vision of a high-speed and global future are made manifest in the present through the built environment. Rama Al Rabady and Shatha Abu-Khafajah call this juxtaposition "oriental urbanism," a regional but still generic process that precludes local politics of identity to play a central role in urban planning and design.[13]

Take one site for the production of this narrative: the Royal Automobile Museum, located in the King Hussein Memorial Gardens in West Amman. The museum projects Abdullah II's vision of modernity with Amman as its center. Photographs chronicle the city's evolution from the 1920s into a major metropolitan area transformed with modern buildings and wide streets. As Christopher Parker shows, the museum conveys not only a periodization that locates the monarchy as the driver of that developmental and modernization narrative but also a temporality of increasing speed. The historic and orientalized spatial imaginary of Bedouins on horses or camels slowly crossing the desert recedes as Amman emerges as a major metropolitan center from the dusty plateau between the Jordan Valley and the desert to the east: the high-speed and globally connected heart of Jordan's present and future. The intervening decades of state-building, challenges to Hashemite rule, and of course British and later US patronage are erased. Parker notes that even the arrangement of cars in the museum advances a narrative of Hashemite modernization, "one that illustrates the taming of the Transjordanian frontier (and, by extension, the frontiers of contemporary globalism) with the resources of ever-increasing speed."[14] The official narrative of a "nation" emerging from Jordanians' tribal heritage and ancient civilizations following the Great Arab Revolt not only suggests justification for Hashemite rule but also seeks to bolster the king's vision for the future. That romanticized past, however, is easier to (re)construct than it is to bring a limitless future into being—particularly without the kind of financial resources that the Gulf states enjoy. The failure to realize the king's vision is indexed not only by half-built projects across the capital's cityscape but also by the tens of thousands who take to the streets over economic grievances every few years. As we have seen, these acts of public claim-making expose moral as well as material claims about Jordan's past, the king's vision for a new Jordan, and who is benefiting from the neoliberal projects and reforms.

Islands of Economic Development

Upon ascending to the throne in 1999, Abdullah II sought to address poverty and unemployment by quickly launching the Plan for Socioeconomic Transformation. While Jordan's neoliberal period began under Hussein with the 1988 International Monetary Fund agreement, Abdullah II accelerated those policies and began the process of privatizing state industries, a move his father was reluctant to undertake. The plan's primary strategy was to direct excess income from privatization and foreign aid to alleviate poverty-related issues.[15] Abdullah II's newly created Economic Consultative Council advised that Jordan attract foreign direct investment for large projects, altering the nation's economic geography by creating an archipelago of neoliberal spaces in Aqaba, West Amman, and the autonomous economic zones. Export-oriented industries and businesses were prioritized to the detriment of domestic ones. The largest investments passed over many East Bank areas entirely, deepening the incongruity of Jordan's political geography of East Bank favoritism (via the electoral system and government employment) and the concentration of capital in neoliberal spaces.

The notion of neoliberalism entailing a withdrawal of the state from certain economic spaces through privatization, austerity, and the dismantling of the welfare state is shown to be a fiction. Instead, the neoliberal state decides where capital flows, what projects to adopt, and how they will be located spatially.[16] It creates incentives to attract foreign investment to certain places in the built environment, through tax cuts, upgraded infrastructure, and the kinds of services expected by the global elite. And it seeks to ensure not only the stability of the regime but the security of those foreign investments and megaprojects. As forms of state intervention, these decisions, projects, and policies are treated as apolitical and technical solutions to practical problems. The king has argued that this path is the only way forward for Jordan economically, but alternatives to neoliberal reforms have always been at hand.[17] These policies, as we have seen, are a major topic of claim-making during protests. While protesters demand jobs and the restoration of subsidies, they also explicitly name neoliberalism, the International Monetary Fund, and Abdullah II as responsible for choosing their path.[18] I have already given numerous examples of such slogans and chants, but another from the 2018 *Habbit Huzayran* protests is particularly direct: "You know who rules us? The damned Monetary Fund! Take your money and leave us alone!"[19]

Development projects, of course, are always unevenly distributed across space. The state dedicates considerable resources for East Bank development programs, but communities feel those projects are trivial compared to investments in the port, resort, and capital areas. *Hirak* activists in the governorates outside of Amman not only decry insufficient investment in their areas, but they have also criticized what they see as the state's poor choice of programs and its unwillingness to engage them in determining priorities for projects. Dhiban farmers, for example, opposed a project by the royally affiliated Jordan River Foundation—the Happy Farm almond tree farm—launched in the early 2000s. Locals welcomed government development initiatives but recognized that almond trees required more water than the area could sustain.

The endeavor went forward anyway and failed within two years; fields of dead almond trees still stand as monuments to the poorly conceived initiative, only adding to Dhiban grievances.[20]

Spaces that fall within the regime's neoliberal spatial imaginary often function as exceptional spaces outside of the administrative and legal structures governing most of the country. Amman and Aqaba are effectively extraterritorial entities to the governing scheme elsewhere in Jordan, and neither falls under the authority of the Ministry of Municipalities nor their respective governorates. The governor of Aqaba delegated his duties to the Aqaba Special Economic Zone Authority, and the Greater Amman Municipality reports directly to the Prime Minister.[21] Other spaces are similarly neoliberal exceptions in Ayhwa Ong's sense, functioning under different rules and legal regimes than "normal" spaces.[22] In this sense, Jordan's qualifying industrial zones are exemplary of neoliberal spatial and legal logics. While these zones are touted as providing much-needed jobs, in practice the turnover of employees is high. Only eight thousand Jordanians work in them, out of a workforce of thirty-eight thousand.[23] Government claims about the benefits to Jordanians are also overblown, with many rarely learning new skills. While anyone can legally open a zone with the right permission—which includes from Israel and the United States—in practice people close to the regime receive quick permission, and their zones have been the most successful.[24] Conditions for foreign workers are particularly terrible, which has led to dozens of employee strikes.[25] But those workers are isolated in compounds that most of them are not even able to leave, so they have struggled to gain wider attention for their cause.

Sites of economic investment, of course, have spillover effects on surrounding communities, but not always in positive ways. Locals are sometimes hired into jobs, but there are never enough jobs to go around. In other instances, residents have been forcibly relocated to areas outside of new neoliberal spaces. The residents of the Shalaleh neighborhood in Aqaba protested against their forced relocation during the expansion of the port. This spatial restructuring of neighborhoods is not a byproduct of neoliberal projects but part of their very logic: the absence of working-class residents increases the value of affluent spaces. In the case of Aqaba, the removal of nearby "undesirable" communities is even a selling point for the Amman elite looking to invest in vacation property. As Mariam Ababsa argues,

> Residents of Tala Bay, a seaside resort of 400 luxury villas and apartments, ten swimming pools and a two-kilometre-long private beachfront, pride themselves on living in an "ideal community" (made up of the Jordanian elite that has benefited from neoliberal reforms), which gets together for the weekend, without visible religious differences; the resort has neither a mosque nor a church.[26]

Class segregation and the erasure of poverty are precisely what make luxury exclaves desirable. The utopian Tala Bay even boasts of overcoming the sorts of internecine religious conflict that (apparently) plagues the rest of the nation. This intersection of secularism and wealth is desirable for the regime because it evokes the ideal neoliberal and cosmopolitan consumer-citizen, one whose aspirational politics do not raise questions about either the Hashemite regime's authority to rule or the king's vision for a new Jordan.[27]

With historic and heritage sites central to the regime's narrative of the past, state control over them expanded in the 2000s, negatively impacting many local communities. Ecotourism was launched in places like Wadi Dana and Wadi Mujib, and the facilities in high-traffic locations like Wadi Rum, Aqaba, and Petra were overhauled and updated. Barriers were erected to control entrance to the sites, and only state-licensed tourist guides can usher visitors through the areas. Independently owned small local cafés and souvenir shops were removed, with the remaining ones licensed by the state. Small local businesses suffered as tourists retreated to upscale guest houses, luxury hotels, and gated resorts, with their posh bars, restaurants, and swimming pools. These upgrades, along with state control of the tourist sector, have left many locals beholden to the state for wage employment—when they can secure it—at the same sites where for decades their families had succeeded as entrepreneurs providing services directly to tourists. And locals have lost not only their businesses but also access to lands on which many of them had lived and worked for generations. Writing about Aqaba, Mayssoun Sukariah shows how locals in tourist zones are disparaged by the government and Amman-based NGOs as having outdated ideas and customs that are off-putting to tourists. But these elite voices see "culture" as a commodity to be sold to tourists (heritage and authentic encounters) while also being an obstacle to development. Displaced residents lose their jobs and small shops, but NGOs tasked with "retraining" them lecture them about both preserving their "culture" and abandoning the parts of it that object to the consumption of alcohol and women tourists in bikinis.[28]

The exclusions around Hammamat Ma'een illustrate how the state prioritizes economic projects over local needs. The site southwest of Amman is the location of Jordan's largest hot springs, where the Bible's King Herod reportedly bathed. When the state licensed a hotel there to a foreign-owned chain,[29] it granted it exclusive control of prime parts of the springs. Locals were relegated to a smaller area out of sight of the most dramatic waterfalls pouring over the cliffs into the narrow valley. Like the neoliberal spaces in Aqaba, the removal or erasure of the poor and working-class creates exclusivity that generates greater profits, often for foreign investors. These kinds of practices are typical of neoliberal development (and of other forms of gentrification in general), but the largest effects are often those of clearing entire neighborhoods for megaprojects. To see how megaprojects restructure the built environment, we bring the scale down to examine oriental urbanity through two locations in Amman and their different forms of erasure and exclusion.

AN ASPIRING COSMOPOLITAN CAPITAL

Urbanization and the expansion of cities are key features of the modern era as people migrate in search of economic or political opportunity. As cities grew more unequal and neighborhoods became differentiated by wealth, urban dwellers began protesting around what Henri Lefebvre called the "right to the city."[30] Key to the right to the city are struggles over space—how spaces are constructed, used, and by whom. As Lefebvre put it famously, "The city and the urban space are thus the setting of struggle; they are also, however, the stakes of that struggle."[31]

The geographies of neoliberal luxury and consumerism clash with working-class needs starkly in Amman. We have already seen how Amman expanded in the twentieth century and saw explosive growth beginning in the 1980s. Luxury neighborhoods continued to swell despite signs of a looming property market crisis, with owners of periurban lands subdividing them, selling the plots, and then demanding the government provide infrastructure and rezone them for luxury development.[32] Powerfully connected landowners opposed any efforts to impose limits on what they could do with their land. As Eliana Abu-Hamdi argues, both urban planning and unplanning worked to shore up the regime's power while weakening the independent power of the tribes. In areas around Amman, for example, the regime attempted to build public

260   CHAPTER 9

housing to create citizens affectively tied to their new communities, providing benefits directly to residents who would thus not need to turn to local tribal councils.[33]

In 2006, Abdullah II called for a new master planning document for Amman to bring order to the chaotic expansion of the city. The 2008 Metropolitan Growth Plan (Amman Plan) was led by Mayor Omar Ma'ani and implemented through the new Amman Institute.[34] Drafted with the assistance of several Canadian urban planners, the new plan stood out for two dimensions of its new spatial imaginary. First, Amman would get a "new downtown" in the sense of a luxury commercial and residential zone located in affluent West Amman.[35] Second, the "old" downtown in the actual city center would be refurbished and upgraded, renewing an earlier effort to create a space that invoked Jordan's Islamic and Bedouin heritage. This refurbished original city center would remain commercial but be redesigned as a site for leisure that would appeal to all classes as well as to tourists. To signal the start of Amman's new future, the city was given a new modern logo in 2009.[36]

Abdali Boulevard

Megaprojects are central to many urban renewal schemes—large, multiuse complexes involving a combination of public and private capital (typically at least $1 billion). They take years to complete and are often constructed in phases, but they are envisioned to have long-term and large-scale transformative effects socially, culturally, and economically. In practice, megaprojects loom over adjacent neighborhoods, at times appearing almost fortress-like with security stationed at "public" entrances. Megaprojects also work as techniques of exclusion, designed as bourgeois spaces realized by razing sometimes entire neighborhoods and erasing their history and place-making. Urban "renewal" of this sort—a euphemism that works to obscure the violent destruction of existing communities—works in the service of the needs of the elite; basic services for the working classes (let alone the impoverished) are secondary concerns, if considered at all. As privatized public spaces, everyone can ostensibly access them; in practice, many are made to feel unwelcome or are literally excluded. Such real and perceived limits to public access are a major component of the militarized management of a city,[37] and as such they are central to struggles over the right to the city.

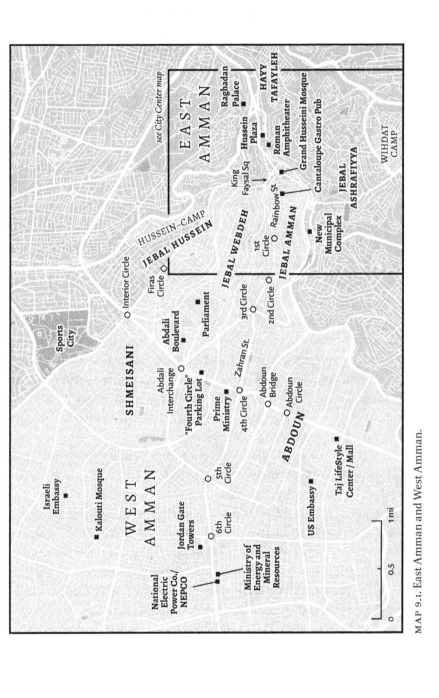

MAP 9.1. East Amman and West Amman.

262   CHAPTER 9

Amman's "new downtown" centers around the $1.5 billion Abdali Boulevard megaproject, located partly on state-owned land, including the former site of the General Intelligence Directorate constructed in 1970. Here was where activists were for decades detained and tortured (sometimes to death), so the site literally embodies a neoliberal vision built on the foundations of a violent security state. Other luxury projects have contributed to the sharpening of the West Amman spatial imaginary since the late 1990s, including the Jordan Gate Towers, five-star hotels at the Fifth Circle, the Taj Lifestyle Center (mall) in Abdoun, and numerous clubs, apartment buildings, and high-end restaurants. But the Abdali Boulevard project is the centerpiece of the king's vision for a new Jordan, delivering a space in the bustling capital that conforms visually to global expectations and whose place-making signified affluence, cosmopolitanism, and global connections. Its many glass-sided skyscrapers tower above the rest of the city, announcing that Jordan's exciting future has already arrived.

The project is overseen by the National Resources Investment and Development Corporation, known as Mawared. Created in 2001 to manage the sale of publicly owned military sites to private developers, Mawared has become a financially and administratively independent corporation owned by the Jordanian Armed Forces.[38] The king heads the Mawared board of directors, and the project has substantial outside financiers, including from the Gulf and Lebanon. Profits from Mawared-led sales are used to develop other military projects and to support the military pension plan.

In the mid-2000s, the Greater Amman Municipality (GAM) pressured landowners around the designated site to sell their properties to Mawared, which would then manage the sales to the Abdali Boulevard developers. One such building was owned by the Abu Ghazaleh investment group, which had received permission in 2005 to expand its building on land it owned. When the GAM suddenly halted that expansion ostensibly to study it further, the Abu Ghazaleh group mounted a protest at the property. Banners on the building declared, "These buildings under construction have had all the permits for construction required since 2005 . . . but the GAM has put a halt to this project to study it. When will the GAM finish this study, and to whose benefit?" The GAM removed the signs to avoid negative publicity, and, after four years in court, it appropriated the land, which Mawared promptly sold to Gulf investors

PROTESTING GLOBAL ASPIRATIONS   263

FIGURE 9.1. Artist rendering of the "glitzy" and "gleaming" Abdali Boulevard construction site in 2008.

for the Abdali project.[39] The government seized a considerable number of other privately owned residences and businesses in the area through eminent domain.[40]

Besides razing an entire neighborhood, Abdali Boulevard brought other class-related changes to the neighborhood. The Abdali bus and shared taxi (*sarvees*) transport terminal, for example, was moved 2.8 miles north to Tabarbour, severely limiting inexpensive public transportation in and out of the area. As ground was broken for the project in 2006, posters, advertising, and the promotional website described the multiuse megaproject in the language of glitz, glamor, lifestyle, luxury, and cosmopolitanism. In 2008, billboards around the gaping hole at the site of the old General Intelligence Directorate headquarters previewed the luxury lifestyle to come. Glamorous women are shown being photographed by paparazzi behind a velvet rope, indexing a secular and cosmopolitan lifestyle of the rich and famous. Such images aim to connect Amman to similar spaces globally, deploying recognizable tropes that work to produce neoliberal aspirations of access to that exclusivity.

Construction stalled for several years following the global financial crash of 2008, however, leaving residents to navigate the maze of barricades, gaping holes, and closed streets around the site—what Abu-Hamdi calls a "landscape of ruination" that remained for nearly a decade.[41] Time seemed to halt at the precise space where the king hoped to launch Amman into a high-speed global

FIGURE 9.2. Billboard at the Abdali Boulevard construction site in 2008. Source: Jillian Schwedler.

future. That vision, however, did not include protests and demonstrations. In 2013, Abu-Hamdi interviewed a Mawared director of marketing, Fahmi Saifi, who told her that the original 2005 plan for the project included a large plaza with seating around the perimeter. He even showed her on a three-dimensional model where the plaza—still present on the model—would have been located above the underground Abdali Mall. But they ultimately decided to remove it, he said, because they were afraid that it would be used for protests.[42]

The first phases of Abdali Boulevard finally opened in 2017, but multiple glass towers hovering over the pedestrian plaza and the underground Abdali Mall remain unoccupied. In January 2020—my most recent visit due to the pandemic—dozens of advertising signs along the plaza promoted not goods and services offered in the shops; instead the glowing yellow signs simply noted that those spaces were available for advertising from "Pikasso: Advertising Concessionaire of the Boulevard." The "future today" was shiny but hollow—with a literal sense of emptiness—for the new "downtown," many of its buildings, and the nation.

Oriental Urbanity and Plans for a New "Old" City Center

The state attempted to juxtapose this fast-paced and globally connected Jordan, as embodied in Abdali Boulevard and other neoliberal sites, with its slow historic past by refurbishing the capital's historic downtown area. Except for backpackers and tourists visiting the heritage sites, we have seen that the downtown area is primarily used by working-class Jordanians and Iraqi refugees for its low-end shops, used clothing stores, refurbished furniture and appliances, and inexpensive cafés. The Hashemite Plaza opposite the Roman amphitheater is often packed on weekends, evenings, and during Ramadan nights. The old city center is a vibrant and thriving place.

But not the right kind of place for the state's purposes. The plan for the area is to make it more friendly to tourists and Amman's elite by "cleaning it up" and more directly connecting the area (and thus Jordan) to an imagined past that meets local and foreign expectations of an oriental Middle Eastern city like Jerusalem, Cairo, or Damascus. As we have seen, the state has long hoped to market Jordan's Roman, Islamic, and Biblical sites for tourism, and it saw unutilized potential in old Amman.[43] Already with the 1968 city plan, the downtown area was reimagined as a magnet for foreign tourism. State planners and officials now again felt that, despite the area's archaeological sites, the city still lacked the atmosphere of an old city that could be marketed globally. One official working on the plan described the objective as creating a new "heritage" zone as "a reflection of timeless cultural identity."[44] Just as Nakib showed with the Gulf states, the Hashemite regime also sought to erase its modern period of state-building and even Amman's distinct historic architecture of the early twentieth century. The Philadelphia Hotel, for example, dated to the 1920s and was one of the famed examples of early Transjordanian architecture; it saw many famous guests, including T. E. Lawrence ("of Arabia"). But the hotel was demolished over the strident objections of local architects during the 1984 reconstruction of Hashemite Plaza. Another midcentury building and historic site for political debate, the University of Arab States café (across from the Grand Husseini Mosque), was destroyed in the early 2000s to put up a generic office building.

The GAM launched a new plan for creating a new "old" downtown in September 2001. With the aid of a Japanese loan of $58.8 million, the plan imagined a corridor between the historic Jebal Qalaa (with its Roman citadel ruins) and the Roman amphitheater. The deputy mayor of Amman described

266   CHAPTER 9

the objective of creating "orientalist fountains . . . , kiosks and a traditional marketplace" and redecorating "the entrances to some shops in a traditional Arabesque motif."[45] A new national museum would narrate Hashemite history and its centrality to Jordan's past and future, the same kind of narrative conveyed in the Royal Automobile Museum discussed above. In the King Hussein Gardens in West Amman, another elaborate relief wall art similarly conveys this journey from past into the future. Just as Abdali Boulevard embodied Jordan's glistening and fast-paced global future, the refurbished downtown would offer a counterpoint that represented Jordan's slow-paced past, meeting generic orientalist expectations with Arabesque designs, romantic cafés, and souvenir stores selling "culture" in the form of handmade pottery, ornate glass-and-brass water pipes, and Bedouin-style jewelry. To achieve that vision, however, many existing tenants and businesses would need to be relocated.

As of this writing, the downtown remains little changed save for the opening of an upscale art gallery and the refurbishment and expansion of a few shops.[46] Outside of Jebal Amman and Jebal Webdeh—the oldest neighborhoods in West Amman, which some now consider part of East Amman or even a central Amman spatial imaginary due to their heritage preservation (by private owners, not the state) of early twentieth-century homes—other parts of the city have not experienced rapid gentrification or widespread renovation of historic buildings. Unable to easily alter the atmosphere of the area, one plan sought to at least improve its appearance. In 2007, the entirety of the original downtown area was the focus of a GAM campaign, "Coloring the Present, Building the Future."

The project aimed not to upgrade infrastructure and services, however, but merely to put a fresh coat of paint on those buildings. The "upgrade" would do little more than improve the view for those gazing across the downtown valley at East Amman from the growing number of bars, cafés, restaurants, and art galleries in Jebal Amman and Jebal Webdeh.[47] Indeed, the radically different levels of state investments—facilitating a multibillion-dollar megaproject for West Amman and a coat of paint for East Amman—could not have been more obvious.

The spatial imaginaries of West Amman and East Amman were visually connected, however, with the fast-paced global future of the Abdali Boulevard towers visible from East Amman's hills and Jordan's slow and timeless past

FIGURE 9.3. Author selfie at the rooftop Cantaloupe Gastropub in Jebal Amman in West Amman, with East Amman's Jebal Ashrafiya reflected in the mirrors. Source: Jillian Schwedler.

providing a backdrop to West Amman's upscale clubs, cafés, and restaurants. History could be viewed across the valley from a (safe) distance—and with table service. Or the past could be directly accessed by descending the steep stairways leading to the old city center. The return trip required one to climb out of the past and into the gleaming future of cosmopolitan West Amman, with its services, luxuries, and global connections.

GLOBAL GEOGRAPHIES OF PROTEST AND REPRESSION

What are Jordan's connections? As we have seen from its founding until today, the Hashemite regime could not sustain its authority without fiscal and security assistance from foreign sources, and those alliances have been well studied.[48] Jordan is also connected to regional and international geographies of trade, labor flows, neoliberal investment, and—crucially—networks of securitization. Far from the spatial imaginary of a sovereign, territorial state

268   CHAPTER 9

that gained independence in 1946, the Hashemite regime moved in the 1950s from existential reliance on British largess to that from the United States.[49] Pete W. Moore even characterizes Jordan as a US protectorate effectively unable to make budgetary decisions without approval from Washington.[50] The United States asserts a kind of prerogative power in Jordan, at times seeming to forget that it is ostensibly a sovereign independent state. In July 2015, for example, US Secretary of Defense Ashton Carter landed at a Jordanian air base without a civilian Jordanian official waiting to greet him, having not notified the regime of his visit. The move was an embarrassing violation of protocol, as any sovereign state should approve all arrivals into its territory. More than a diplomatic faux pas, the incident underlines the extent to which the United States treats Jordan like a US territory.[51]

This section explores these and other global connections, including how protests in Jordan evoke connections to protests in the region and globally, how Jordan is located in regional and global security arrangements, and how both protests and state power are shaped by those connections. These preliminary discussions each invite additional research to flesh out the dynamics of these geographies of power and dissent.

Connecting Protests Regionally and Globally

Protesters often invoke connections with regional or global issues. Solidarity protests are widespread, and even protests about domestic issues can be inspired by protests elsewhere. The Occupy Wall Street protests in the United States in fall 2011, for example, were launched around the question posed to Americans, "Are you ready for your Tahrir moment?" The slogan, published in *Adbusters*, called on people to extend the geography of Egypt's revolution and the Arab uprisings into the United States by mounting their own encampments and remaining there until they achieved the change they sought. Global solidarities among protest movements have been widely studied, and that literature does not need to be rehearsed here.

In Jordan, we have already seen people take to the street for more than a century in solidarity with protests elsewhere in the Arab region. After World War I, people in the Transjordanian area expressed solidarities with those protesting in Greater Syria and later Iraq, Palestine, and Syria. The mid-twentieth century saw a wide range of Arab nationalist and leftist protests: in solidarity with people outside of Jordan, in support of Egypt's Gamal Abdul Nasser, against the Baghdad Pact and Suez War, and against Jordan's participation in the Yemen civil war, to give just a few examples. The late twentieth and early twenty-first centuries saw nationwide solidarity protests with the people of Iraq and Palestine. Protests in front of embassies always invoke regional or global connections, whether in solidarity with those people or in opposition to that state's policies or actions. In December 2018, for example, unemployment protesters in Amman donned yellow vests in solidarity with the eponymous protests in France.[52] Global and regional connections are thus central to a large number of solidarity and oppositional protests in Jordan.

Pedagogies of Repression

While protesters build affinities and solidarities with protesters in other states and regions, states shore up their power by forging security alliances with other regimes, both within the region and globally. Since the British-Jordanian security alliance expired in March 1957, Jordan's most important security ally has unquestionably been the United States. Washington has provided more than $20 billion in assistance to Jordan since 1951, and aid has nearly quadrupled since 2005. In 2001 the two countries signed a bilateral free trade agreement, and in 2018 they signed a nonbinding memorandum of understanding to provide $6,375 billion in bilateral foreign assistance over five years. In 2019 alone, Washington provided more than $1.5 billion, including $1.082 billion through USAID and $425 million in foreign military financing. An additional $1.5 billion was intended to assist with Syrian refugees, and $8.6 million aimed to help mitigate the spread of the coronavirus.[53]

Jordan and the United States have also held joint military exercises since the 1990s under the name Infinite Moonlight. US General David Petraeus told a Senate Armed Services Committee in April 2009 that Jordan was "at the forefront of police and military training for regional security forces."[54] During an October 2009 joint training mission in Jordan, US General Craig McKinley, chief of the US National Guard Bureau, described the Hashemite regime as the "lynchpin" to a "peaceful central command" in the region. Since 2010, Jordan has hosted Eager Lion, a two-week military exercise organized by the United States and including militaries from numerous other nations. Each year at the conclusion of that exercise, the United States leaves behind substantial military equipment and sometimes personnel. In 2013, for example, these included patriot missile batteries, F-16 fighters, and some seven hundred US military personnel.[55] On average, Jordan routinely hosts more than three thousand US troops.[56]

Military exercises suggest interactions between two sovereign states. Jordan's entanglements with the United States, however, are more spatially and economically complicated than that (as indeed they are in many countries). As they do in many places across the globe, US expertise, personnel, and military equipment flow across the Jordanian terrain, in arms sales and via military joint exercises but also in the techniques that structure Jordan's geography of repression. The US Central Intelligence Agency, for example, casts a long shadow over the kingdom, with agents on Jordanian soil working with the General Intelligence Directorate to help quash opposition since at least the 1970s.[57] More recently, Jordan has created a series of militarized spaces of exception that are saturated with US power and expertise and raise questions about where one state ends and the other begins. Take the King Abdullah II Special Operations Training Center (KASOTC, pronounced "ka-so-tic"), located fifteen miles north of Amman and possibly the world's largest training facility for special forces.[58] It was created in 2009 from designs by the US Army Corps of Engineers and built by a US construction firm with $99 million in Department of Defense funding. The 6,000-acre enclave—modeled on Blackwater's compound in North Carolina—is enclosed by razor wire and guarded by tall sentry towers. It is owned by Mawared (the army-owned developer behind Abdali Boulevard) but administratively run by private US contractors.[59] It has trained police and military units in countries where the United States was intervening heavily, thus participating in state-building in Afghanistan (training the US-allied Afghan Special Forces) and Iraq (training the new Iraqi police).[60] KASOTC is not officially a US training center, but in practice it functions as such because ViaGlobal, a private US company, operates, manages, and maintains the center, even if Jordanians conduct the actual training.[61]

While KASOTC represents the extension of US power onto Jordanian soil, it also has reach beyond Jordanian sovereign territory by way of the spread of techniques for repression. Its public website lists numerous course offerings, including "crowd control," a curriculum for riot police focused on techniques for preventing, containing, and dispersing protests. The built environment for instruction includes a mock city and a mock refugee camp—conveying that these are the kinds of spaces in which enemies will need to be apprehended and defeated. Although empty of actual inhabitants, these built environments are made "real" with a war-time soundscape and smellscape, including loud explosions and hundreds of specialized scents such as "dead body," manufactured by ScentAir in Charlotte, North Carolina.[62] Trainees learn to "conquer" enemies as well as the constraints of the built environment, inscribing meaning in those spaces as "missions" leave material evidence via destruction and bullet-riddled buildings.

Perhaps most bizarre, KASOTC is not only used for police and military training; it is connected to a geography of "extreme sport" competitions like the Ninja Games. Since 2009, it has hosted a competition called the Warrior Challenge, what the organizers describe as "the Olympics of counterterrorism." Shana Marshall more aptly describes it as "Disneyland for Mercenaries,"[63] where military teams from multiple governments compete alongside corporate-sponsored teams for trophies in events such as "hostage rescue." Josh Eells covered the 2013 competition for the *New York Times*, which included an American team sponsored by International Defense Systems, a private supplier of tactical equipment and ballistics gear.[64] The event blurs the lines between public and private security, which is a key technique for securing neoliberal investments. And it appallingly also treats policing as a game.

Another Mawared-owned space of exception is also funded by the United States: the Jordan International Police Training Center (JIPTC, pronounced "gypsy"). Located in the desert East of Amman, JIPTC trains police and gendarmerie from across the region. US Lieutenant General Keith Dayton served as the chief of the Office of the US Security Coordinator for Israel and the Palestinian Authority from 2005 to 2010, overseeing the training of Palestinian Authority forces at JIPTC by Dyncorp (a US private military contractor) along with Jordanian forces from various agencies. Jordan's own gendarmerie troops trained during that period are known as Dayton's Forces and are reputed among activists to be the most brutal in repressing protests. In a 2009 speech to the conservative pro-Israel think tank, the Washington Institute for Near East Policy, Dayton described JIPTC-trained Palestinian forces as engaging in violent raids that were "surprisingly well coordinated" with Israel. JIPTC, he went on to say, featured "a US-Jordanian police training cadre and a US-developed curriculum that is heavy on human rights, proper use of force, riot control, and how to handle civil disturbances."[65] But in practice, JIPTC was where Jordanian forces helped train Palestinian Authority forces to torture and repress Palestinians in the West Bank and Gaza, taking over work usually done by Israel.[66]

A final center is also outward reaching, sending not expertise but military equipment across the region and globe. In 1999, the king issued a royal decree that created the King Abdullah II Design and Development Bureau (KADDB, pronounced "kad-bee") as a military-industrial arm of the Jordanian Armed Forces. Mawared owns the land on which KADDB sits. Promotional materials tout the center's partnership with regional and global defense firms as well as a Malaysian commercial entity. Equipment and gear for domestic policing is in high demand, particularly among Arab states. As Marshall writes, KADDB markets many products designed for riot control, reconnaissance, and surveillance, including the Stallion armored vehicle with .50 caliber weapons stations. The Stallion is advertised for use in "peacekeeping, internal security and patrols." Its SkyWatch drone is advertised as ideal for "dignitary protection" and the oversight of prisons and "border entries."[67]

The KADDB Industrial Park operates as a space of exception, exempt from building and land taxes, import fees, customs duties, and corporate income taxes. It is the first free trade zone in the region to specialize in military production.[68] One of KADDB's affiliates is the Jordan International Security Company LLC (JoSecure), established in 2004 "to provide security services for government and national private and public entities."[69] Jordan also hosts the Special Operations Forces Exhibition and Conference (SOFEX) in Amman every other year, a defense fair that likewise focuses on Jordan's manufacturing sector for domestic policing and commando raids. These training and industrial zones, particularly those with US ties, extend Jordan's reach regionally and globally, working alongside other neoliberal zones of exception to produce nodes (spaces) of tightly networked connections that skip over territories in between. They connect Jordan to regional and global security spatial imaginaries, as discussed in the next section.

Jordan at the Regional and Global Scales

Jordan has been active in conflicts globally, providing small contingents to join conflicts led by allies (especially the United States) and well as participating in UN peacekeeping missions in places like Haiti, Bosnia, and Angola.[70] As we have seen, Jordan's refusal to join the US-led coalition to oust Iraqi troops from Kuwait in 1990–91 cost it dearly, and it does not want a repeat of that situation. Jordan is rumored to provide "black sites" where foreign forces (notably the United States and its proxies) can interrogate and torture prisoners without legal repercussions. It allowed some use of Jordanian soil and intelligence during the Iraq War in 2003, although it went to great pains to hide that cooperation from a citizenry widely outraged at the US-led invasion.

Key to these spaces of exception and cooperation within and across "foreign" conflicts are shared ideas about allies and enemies, and those ideas shape protest repression. The Hashemite regime's spatial imaginaries of "enemies" extends beyond localized spaces to reach across the region and even globally. One powerful example is King Abdullah II's 2004 invocation of a "Shi'i crescent," a geography of Shi'i dominance and violence purported to extend from Lebanon to Bahrain. In that spatial imaginary, concentrated Shi'i communities in multiple states are loyal to Iran and threaten Sunni communities in their midst as well as in neighboring states. The Shi'i Crescent spatial imaginary was welcomed by the United States, Israel, Saudi Arabia, and other Gulf states, and it has allowed those states to make moral claims against Iran and its allies. For the Hashemite regime, anchoring itself on the "Sunni" side of this discursive battlefront brought financial gains from Gulf states. Gulf investments in Jordan dramatically increased in the 2000s, allowing it to position itself as a buffer between Iranian influence (in Iraq, Syria, and Lebanon) and Israel and Saudi Arabia.[71] The spatial imaginary of a creeping Shi'i menace also worked to shore up the regime's status as a space of stability in a region of turmoil, but one in need of continual financial and military support to prevent the precarity and "crisis" times that loomed on the horizon.

With the 2011 uprisings, the Gulf monarchies joined the United States in escalating economic and materiel support to the Hashemite regime, and we have already seen that this aid enabled the regime to distribute largess as one means of deflating protests. Given the divergent political visions of Jordan's multisectoral protests at the time, a unified movement calling for the fall of the regime was highly unlikely. But Jordan's regional and global allies were concerned enough to deploy a combination of repression, co-optation, and patronage to prevent the protests from escalating.

274   CHAPTER 9

The idea that Jordan effectively functions as a US protectorate came into focus during this period. As the uprisings spread in 2011, the Obama administration talked up democracy promotion but maintained its support for its repressive regional allies, including Jordan. Moore summed up the US commitment to supporting Jordan during this period by describing the kingdom as "Washington's Bahrain in the Levant"—Bahrain being the home of the US Fifth Fleet, the logistics hub for the US Navy in the region.[72] As part of these security alliances, Jordan has been involved not only in training police and gendarmeries across the region but also in repressing protests outside its own territory. This role in aiding other states' domestic repression is not new. Beginning in the 1960s, Jordan sent units to Oman during the Dhofar rebellion to help crush challenges to the regime, as it did with Yemen in an effort to stop the Free Officers' overthrow of the monarchy. It sent troops to Afghanistan alongside US troops after September 2001.

During Bahrain's uprising in March 2011, Jordan sent several hundred gendarmerie officers, who were rumored to have received bonuses for the assignment. The Saudi army moved tanks—many manned by Pakistani nationals in Saudi uniforms—across a causeway into the capital city Manama to buttress Bahrain's brutal crushing of the peaceful protesters at the Pearl Roundabout. Gulf states falsely portrayed the Bahraini uprisings as led by Shi'i instigators, leveraging the Shi'i Crescent spatial imaginary to justify violent repression. Rumors circulated in Jordan at the time that its own gendarmerie officials had suggested to Bahrain that it should dismantle the Pearl Roundabout statue, the colossal (and somewhat failed) attempt to erase the symbol of the revolution from the built environment. Bahrain subsequently urged Saudi Arabia and the other Gulf states to step up their aid to Jordan. The Gulf Cooperation Council (GCC) even dangled the possibility that Jordan and Morocco—the two surviving Arab monarchies outside of the Gulf—might be invited to join. Many Jordanian activists laughed or scoffed at the prospect, however, given that Jordan is not located in the Gulf. To many of my interlocutors, the GCC was little more than a club for the survival of the region's remaining monarchies. Jordan was never extended GCC membership, but aid to Jordan increased over the next years, particularly as Syrian refugees flowed into Jordan and some Gulf states became increasingly involved in supporting rebel groups fighting in Syria. Some Jordanian officials, however, complained that portions of promised aid were never delivered.[73]

Jordan also joined the US-led intervention in the Syrian war, which led to the horrific December 2014 Islamic State murder of Jordanian pilot Mu'ath al-Kasasbeh. After his capture, members and supporters of the Kasasbeh family mounted protests in front of the Royal Court, calling for a withdrawal of Jordan's air force from the conflict. A video of Kasasbeh's caged immolation death sparked thousands of Jordanians to take to the streets nationwide, but especially in Karak, the historic base of the Kasasbeh. In Amman, protesters gathered at the Interior Circle and at the Sons of Karak Diwan in the West Amman neighborhood of Dabouq.[74] Various security forces were present at most of these protests, but police did not interfere even when protesters blocked roads with burning tires.

Despite the more than seventy years of the Jordanian-US alliance, the Donald Trump administration proved more interested in the Saudi-US-Israeli alliance than in Jordan, particularly in the face of the "Iranian threat" that the three states all touted. Washington's retreat from playing a leading role in the region had political effects in Jordan that involved the state's response to nationwide protests. Writer and activist Hisham Bustani argues, for example, that the regime responded quickly to the 2018 *Habbit Huzayran* protests because it found itself regionally and internationally exposed, with little influence in the emerging Saudi-US-Israeli axis. Jordan was no longer needed to play the role of mediator between Israel and Saudi Arabia because the two states were engaging directly under the Trump administration. Jordan's shifting importance in these regional and global security arrangements explains the regime's muted response to those protests, including the Fourth Circle statement by the crown prince to the gendarmerie that citizens had a right to protest and should be protected.[75]

Many Jordanians are, of course, aware of the state's economic, military, and security entanglements regionally and globally, and they talk of how those connections have shaped the forms and practices of repression against protests inside Jordan. Activists take note of the escalated violence by Dayton's Forces, and they condemn Jordan's close cooperation with Israeli security sectors. Some activists believe that the state has adopted more aggressive and humiliating techniques for repression as a direct result of security cooperation with Israel. Ma'ani protesters in 2002, for example, expressed outrage at what they described as "Israeli-style" tactics during the curfew: police aggressively

276   CHAPTER 9

searching house to house, treating everyone as already guilty, trashing drawers and cupboards, and dumping out containers of flour and rice ostensibly in search of weapons.

Finally, regional and global security ties shape how the state responds to certain protests, particularly those making claims against key allies. In November 2019, for example, families of dozens of Jordanians who were detained in Saudi Arabia protested outside of Parliament under the campaign, "Detainees without Charges in Saudi Arabia." They demanded information and assistance from the regime in securing the release of their family members, with whom they had no contact. Appeals to the Saudi embassy received no reply, however, so they turned to their own government for assistance. The regime did not intervene, which most of the protesters believed was due to Jordan's reliance on aid from Saudi Arabia.[76]

SPACES AND GEOGRAPHIES OF POWER AND DISSENT

To tie the threads of the argument together, let's zoom in to one more neoliberal space, the Aqaba Special Economic Zone, and then pivot to look north toward the capital. We have already seen that Aqaba has luxury resorts, secular elite enclaves, and a port operated by Al Maabar, an entity of the government of Abu Dhabi. Pristine beaches, world-class scuba diving, and all manner of services attract high-end tourists. Gulf investors also funded the $1 billion Saraya Aqaba megaproject,[77] and the city has Jordan's only pedestrian crossing into Israel, which tourists use for day trips to the Israeli port of Eilat.

Neoliberal Aqaba, however, belies the poverty of many who live in the area, including those who were forcibly relocated to outlying housing. We have seen how residents of the Shalaleh neighborhood protested their forced relocation, and thousands of dockworkers mounted demonstrations for years. In 2018, unemployed workers organized several sit-ins at Aqaba government buildings, including one at the king's office that was broken up by the police. Frustrated and desperate, some forty of the workers decided to take their grievances to the capital to make their claims directly to the regime's center of power. To emphasize their desperation, they decided to travel on foot.

As they departed Aqaba on February 14, 2019, they ascended north on the Desert Highway past Wadi Rum, which British officer T. E. Lawrence famously traversed with Bedouin troops during the Great Arab Revolt of 1916–18. The location is now a nature preserve, attracting world-class rock climbers and other nature lovers. Tourists can enjoy glamping—in luxuriously appointed (and air-conditioned) tents or pods that cost hundreds of dollars a night and often include room service. Queen Rania held her lavish fortieth birthday party in Wadi Rum in August 2010, reportedly including six hundred Jordanian and international guests. Photographs of the ill-timed event appeared in newspapers, on television, and in virtual spaces, just months after the Manifesto of the Retired Servicemen critiqued the regime's decadence and accused the queen of corruption. A decade later, people still invoke the extravagant party during protests about corruption, unemployment, and water shortages. The fast-paced jet-setting lifestyle that brought haute-couture-dressed guests from around the globe contrasted starkly with the slow march to the capital of barefoot unemployed workers.

Continuing north, the workers arrived in Ma'an, where they were joined by more unemployed. Here is where Abdullah I had camped for several months beginning in late 1920, staying carefully within the Hijaz spatial imaginary to which most Ma'ani tribes felt affective connection—which many still do. The march continued north past the highway interchanges that make blocking traffic with burning tires more difficult—but not impossible. They moved along the same north-south trade and pilgrimage corridor so prized by the Ottoman Empire, passing Ma'an prison, where the wives of Karaki rebels were detained and Habis Majali was born in 1910. At the town of Hussayniya they veered left to meet the King's Highway, another north-south road that follows the ancient Roman route connecting Damascus to Heliopolis in Egypt. Climbing steep roads into the mountains, the workers ascended some 3,200 feet by the time they reached Tafıleh during the wet winter months. Locals along their route provided shelter and food, and more unemployed joined at every stop as their march attracted national attention; unemployed workers in the north, who were not along the Aqaba march's path, were inspired to start their own marches. Government officials traveled from Amman to meet the main march at least twice, but their promises of jobs failed to persuade the workers to return home. The unemployed continued to march north through Karak, where Ottoman troops threw rebels to their deaths from the heights of the Crusader castle during the Karak Revolt of 1910. Much of the remaining route was downhill. The march passed Dhiban, where the day-wage labor activists

278   CHAPTER 9

decided in 2006 to travel to the capital to protest—the same activists who organized Jordan's first protests during the uprising period. As they continued north through Madaba, they traversed the historic lands of the Bani Sakhr, many of whom are still resentful that the state forced the Fayiz family to sell historic Bani Sakhr grazing land for the construction of the Queen Alia Airport in the 1970s.

Along the way, the march passed through multiple spatial imaginaries, starting from the Hijaz region and into the southern portions of historic Greater Syria. They traversed lands that were understood as the domains of various tribal confederations. They followed the centuries-old trade and pilgrimage corridor, areas that cohered in the twentieth century as the East Bank radical nativist spatial imaginary of the "true" sons of Jordan affectively connected to the lands east of the Jordan River. The marchers came from across Jordan, moving from the spatial imaginary of the economically neglected East Bank outer governorates and slowly converging on the cosmopolitan capital and Jordan's center of economic power and global connection. Amman was no longer the small town where, in 1923, Sultan led the Adwan through town on horses to make their demands on the fledgling Hashemite regime. The modern city that the unemployed workers encountered in February 2019 was a sprawling but deeply divided metropolis, characterized by the separate spatial imaginaries of impoverished East Amman and affluent West Amman, the latter of which was being reshaped by neoliberal urbanization as part of the king's vision for a new Jordan.

The march that started in Aqaba entered West Amman on February 21, with its skyscrapers, luxury hotels, gated complexes, and high-end boutiques and restaurants—the very neoliberal vision that excluded and eluded the workers. But the king's vision for a new Jordan also proved somewhat hollow. Construction had been halted for years on the still half-built skyscrapers of the Jordan Gate Towers on Zahran Street, an ill-conceived project that Abu-Hamdi aptly describes as "surrendering public space to build a neoliberal ruin."[78] The towers and their cranes have sat frozen for a decade, with the project suffering from collapsed floors that killed workers and narrow nearby streets unable to accommodate the traffic the finished towers would bring. Other projects, like the Royal Village residential complex and Limitless Towers, were also failures, revealing Abdullah II to be less than effective at stewarding Jordan

FIGURE 9.4. An anti-gas deal protest on Zahran Street with the unfinished Jordan Gate Towers in the background. Construction has been stalled for a decade, but the cranes offer a visible reminder that the project is unfinished. Source: Jillian Schwedler.

into a high-paced, limitless future. Even Abdali Boulevard—the showpiece megaproject realizing Amman's transformation into a fast-paced and globally connected city—was half occupied, its advertising spaces unused. Long-planned rapid transit lanes also sat unfinished, to be used only by Islamists looking for a place to protest while social distancing during the coronavirus pandemic in 2020.

As the unemployed workers walked slowly through a city that was supposed to be fast paced and globally connected, they were welcomed by Islamist leaders and joined by separate marches from Irbid, Mafraq, and Ajloun. The workers did not, however, stop at government offices such as the Prime Ministry on the Fourth Circle, or even Parliament—familiar protest locations in the capital. Instead, they descended from the city's hills into the old city center, not the one of the king's orientalist imagining but the dirty and bustling space for low-end commerce. They even walked past Amman's century-old, go-to place for protests, the Grand Husseini Mosque. Their destination was the Royal Court, a location symbolizing not government authority but the Hashemite regime itself. In the adjacent Hashemite Plaza, they established an encampment and refused to leave until they were given jobs. The regime of course knew they were coming, and the Chief of the Royal Court, Youssef Issawi, spoke with them almost daily. The workers refused the first jobs they were offered, however, insisting on permanent positions with benefits in the major industries (e.g., mining, potash, and the port). Although those industries had all been privatized, the state secured some 350 jobs for the workers within a few weeks, and then the Royal Court provided buses to transport them home in a few hours.[79]

As news of the march's success spread, more unemployed workers marched to the capital, first from Ma'an and the southern Badia (desert) area,[80] and then from across Jordan throughout the next year, all camping at the Royal Court. One mounted a hunger strike to increase pressure on the regime to speed up its response.[81] These marches of the unemployed became part of the protest repertoire, with their own spatial and temporal dynamics as well as symbolic destination. The encampments also worked as a kind of appropriation of public space. A banner mounted at the site by Dhiban workers in January 2020, for example, remained for days after the workers had left, labeling the area as "Dhiban District" and the protesters as "The Unemployed." With their occupation of public space and place-making, they and their banner marked the location as "Dhiban-unemployed-poverty" in contrast to "palace-king-wealth." These East Bank protests assert their moral and material claims directly at the king, holding Abdullah II responsible for his failure to provide Jordanians with even the most basic, dignified life.

The Periphery Converges on the Center

A careful examination of the multiple spatialities of protest is an illuminating entry point for bringing into view the incongruities of Jordan's state-making, state-maintaining, and geographies of economic and political power. These marches of the unemployed see the economic periphery converge on the capital to make claims directly on the regime. In this sense Jordan's peripheries are not merely spatially outlying areas or zones of economic exclusion—although

FIGURE 9.5. A banner at the Royal Court reading, "Dhiban District: The Unemployed," left behind after a sit-in of Dhiban residents who walked to the capital in January 2020. Source: Jillian Schwedler.

they can be both—but something closer to mobile frontiers that bring conflict to squeeze the center. This moving contention happens through the mobilization of actors outside of Amman and in the ways in which protesters ratchet up their claims through their spatial choices about where to protest and their insistence on establishing sustained encampments. These protesters increase the potency of their claims without growing the numbers beyond a few hundred through their slow movement marking determination and desperation. Their claims are made more contentious, too, through their choice of location, addressing their claims not to the government but to the Hashemite regime itself. This idea of a periphery/frontier in motion both reflects features of the built environment but also helps to shape it. And, finally, Jordan's economic peripheries may be peripheral to Amman and the Hashemite regime's neoliberal ambitions for the vision for a new Jordan, but they are not peripheral to the spatial imaginaries to which they are affectively connected.

Abdullah II's new Jordan remains a fiction, an unrealized vision marked by half-occupied skyscrapers, vacant stores, and stalled constructions visible across West Amman. In 2018, 71 percent of Jordanians saw the economy as the most important problem facing the country, and almost half of all Jordanians reported considering emigrating for economic opportunity.[82] The reality of growing inequality, stagnant wages, environmental destruction, water shortages, and outright poverty occupy the minds of many Jordanians, and they do not hesitate to express their grievances by protesting—the only means of expressing dissent that seems to bring results. The regime tries to appear responsive to some of the claim-making that Jordanians do during protests: it offers jobs, suspends subsidies, promises reform, and appoints a new prime minister while calling for national dialogue. Although enduring reforms remain elusive, protests continue to shape the ongoing state-maintaining project, which in turn shapes public discourse about political and economic reforms.

What do these protests portend for Abdullah II and the Hashemite regime? We have seen how open public criticism escalated from the veterans' manifesto in 2010 onward, and some Jordanians are even calling for the end to the monarchy. East Bank protesters, in particular, are no longer parsing language or leaving the referenced "you" in their claim-making open to interpretation (as they did in the "you, in Dabouq" chant that referenced the neighborhood where much of the royal family resides). They are openly asserting moral and material claims on the king and holding him personally accountable. One common protest chant explicitly registers this shift: "Why beat around the bush? Abdalluh, you are the one responsible!"[83]

Corruption remains one of the main grievances, and perceptions of corruption in government have increased from 66 percent in 2010 to 89 percent in 2018, with trust in government nosediving from 72 to 38 percent during the same period.[84] In 2019, the Bani Hassan tribal confederation posted to social media a statement about corruption, calling the king and queen demigods (ansaf al-aliha) who promoted policies that financially benefit themselves but not the Jordanian people. Issued by "the Hirak of the Bani Hassan Tribe," the statement directly called for the abolishment of the monarchy. Other powerful tribes endorsed the statement, including the Bani Abbadi and Bani Hamida, although prominent figures from each tribe also denounced it.[85] A group of retired military officials formed what they called the National Follow-up

Committee and also issued several statements in early 2019 calling for limits on the king's powers and the abolishment of the Royal Court offices for the queen and other royal family members.[86] But even with all this dissent, East Bank tribal communities remain central to the regime's support base, the source of the regime's most ardent loyalists. Central to the argument here, however, is that these acts of protest and dissent continue to shape state-maintaining in Jordan, and they index that a growing number are not only critical of the regime's policies but question its authority to rule.

CONCLUSION

Protesting Jordan argues for considering protests not (only) as events that social movements organize or as ruptures to "normal" or institutional politics. Public claim-making, in its many forms, can be a regular part of the political landscape, even in authoritarian contexts. In this way, protests can be surprisingly central to the "normal" functioning of the state, even playing a role in state-maintaining by adhering to established spatial and temporal routines. Repertoires for protest and repression—including the spatial routines of individual protest locations—are publicly known and tend to be relatively stable, but they are nevertheless available for innovation and adaptation as protesters and state actors encounter each other in the street. Even routine protests give transformative eventful moments a foundation on which to build. Therefore, narrating and analyzing a history of protest through spatial and geographic lenses, and at multiple scales, provides a rich entry point for theorizing not only about protests themselves but also about processes and techniques of state-making, state-maintaining, and the mutual constitution of state and society. And as I have shown for the period of the Arab uprisings, eventful moments do occur, albeit infrequently, and if we consider their political effects beyond questions of whether protests "succeed," we see that they, too, have long-term consequences for state-maintaining.

Protests also shape and are shaped by the built environment. The spatialities and symbolism of individual locations in the built environment affect the form and impact of protests mounted there, just as protests are themselves a form of place-making, a king of liminal "space-in-progress." I have also shown how some spaces (e.g., free-trade zones, neoliberal urbanism) are more tightly connected with regional and global spaces and practices than they are with large swaths of the national territorial state and even spaces adjacent to them. Carefully unpacking geographies of power and dissent, geographies of economic and political investments, and spaces of inclusion and exclusion help show us how the local and the global coproduce politics at the national level.

Protesting Jordan invites comparison with the geographic and spatial dynamics of protests elsewhere, and not only to "similar" cases of Arab or authoritarian states or even the global south. Indeed, we might fruitfully explore, for example, the spatial dynamics of repertoires for protest and repression across neoliberal urban spaces globally or with attention to the variations of the built environment and their spatial imaginaries within and across the city, nation, and region. States train each other in repressive techniques, just as protesters learn from movements and protests elsewhere. Bringing these connections into focus can further enrich our understanding of repertoires of protest and repression as well as how state power is challenged and maintained. One might also consider how economic, social, and political centers and peripheries are situated spatially, moving beyond conventional formulations of scale to explore localized and national spaces as constitutively multiscalar. The specifics of state-making and state-maintaining in a given case are shaped not just by those who gain a monopoly on the use of violence in a territory but by the techniques they deploy to do so.

And, finally, we have explored the multiple temporalities of protests as well as official state narratives and projects, assessing patterns and innovations across decades or even centuries, while also attending to the microdynamics of protests over the course of minutes or hours. A long view of protest dynamics illuminates patterns and turning points that are not readily apparent when focusing on movements or limited periods of heightened protest. A microanalysis helps us recognize localized spatial routines, thus enabling us to more readily recognize deviations from them. Understanding temporality also helps identify challenges to the state and explains the direction and form of political change. That is, attention to the temporalities of claim-making—the narratives of the past and present as well as visions for the future, in addition to how people affectively connect different periods or episodes of protest—can show us, for example, how a dozen people holding a sustained sit-in under a tent in a seemingly peripheral place can pose a greater challenge to the state than a crowd of several thousand conforming to the known spatial and temporal routine for protests in the capital's city center. Careful attention to the ideas invoked and advanced during protests also brings into view the spatial imaginaries that structure the moral and material claims of diverse peoples and communities.

Ending a book is difficult. The reader will decide if I have made my case, and I hope scholars will take me up on my invitation to think in ways that do not treat states as stand-alone cases or protests as events to be abstracted from complex historical contexts. As a key form of contentious public claim-making, protests are integral to multiple and complex sets of institutions, networks, and practices that interconnect within and across the built environment and national borders. The goal is not only to give voice and agency to people and their claims and to better understand why states deploy repression unevenly. My aim has also been to center diverse forms of protest discursively in the built environment, unpacking their role in state-making and the reproduction of power and its many configurations. Only then can we harness our potential to imagine and shape better futures.

Notes

All translations are my own unless otherwise indicated.

CHAPTER 1

1. *Khubz, huriyya, 'adala ijtima'yya!*

2. Martínez 2018a: 176. See also Simmons for a study of protests around basic foods (water and corn) in Latin America (2017).

3. Ali and Jarrar 2018; see also Ghitis 2018.

4. Sawalha 2018.

5. The Union of Professional Associations distanced itself from the protests that spread after the first strike. Some Jordanians believe that it had received guarantees that its demands would be met. Ali and Jarrar 2018.

6. These events will be referred to hereafter as the *Habbit Huzayran* protests.

7. Ababneh 2018; Doughan 2019.

8. *Italat lisanihi 'ala galalat al-malik.*

9. *Al-khatu al-hamra.*

10. *'Aqd ijtima'i.*

11. "Tribes" are not homogeneous entities, and degrees of affective connection among the "members" of these larger units vary over time and space; see chaps. 2 and 4 for more discussion.

12. Abu Sneineh 2018.

NOTES TO CHAPTER 1

13. Quoted in Abu Sneineh 2018.

14. As Tarrow notes, Tilly's definition of repertoires evolved from a list of tactics into "a set of cultural creations that both reflect structural developments and take on a life of their own. The latter occurs, for Tilly, as actors test the boundaries of the possible, elites respond to these innovations, new performances are refined and diffused, and new structures evolve out of these interactions. Performances are not only what people do when they act collectively; it is what they know how to do" (Tarrow 2021: 1893).

15. Wood (2000), for example, shows how insurgencies can be central to driving supposedly "top-down" reforms by incumbent elites.

16. Chenoweth and Stephan 2012; Chenoweth 2019.

17. Brownlee et al. 2015.

18. In coming chapters, I engage the rich scholarship on the uprisings that has moved away from this variation-finding and outcome-oriented approach.

19. McAdam et al. 2000.

20. To reflect pronunciation, *hayyih* and *habbih* are rendered *hayyit* or *habbit* when followed by a noun.

21. For example, see Assaf 2015 on the Balqa Revolt and the discussion about the Adwan Revolt in chap. 2 here.

22. Tilly 2008.

23. For example, Benedict Anderson 1983; Tilly 1985.

24. Chalcraft 2016.

25. Neep (2021) makes a similar case for examining state-making as beginning during the Ottoman period.

26. Lynch 2012; Abu-Rish 2012a.

27. Morton 2007; Cox and Nilsen 2014.

28. E.g., Scott 1999; Tilly 2000; Sewell 2001; Auyero 2003; Tilly 2003; Marston 2003; Martin and Miller 2003.

29. See the literature reviews in Leitner et al. 2008 and Oslender 2016.

30. D. Mitchell 1996; Mitchell and Staeheli 2005; Thrift 2006; Jessop et al. 2008; Nicholls et al. 2013; al-Nakib 2018; Hatuka 2018; Soudias and Sydiq 2020. These and others are discussed in coming chapters.

31. D. Mitchell 2018: 3.

32. Brenner 2019.

NOTES TO CHAPTERS 1 AND 2   289

33. Thompson 1971. The notion of a "moral economy" of political dissent was further developed by Scott 1976, 1985.

34. Trouillot 1995: 2.

35. Trouillot 1995: 9.

36. Gibreel 2018a.

37. *'Ashrin sanna jalis, ma dhal la akhdhar wa la yabis!*

38. *Battalna nahki ya'eesh, laysh namut wa inta ta'eesh?* A variation is: *Battalna nahki ya'eesh, ihna namut wa inta ta'eesh!* (We stopped saying "long live you," we die and you live!).

39. *Ya'eesh jalalat al-malik al-mu'azam!*

40. *Diritna 'urdunniyya qabl al-thawra al-'arabiyya!*

41. The view of the Hashemites as foreigners to the Transjordanian area dates to their arrival in 1920; see M. Wilson 1987 and Brand 1995.

42. Davenport and Moore emphasize the need to take seriously the ways in which foreign actors—particularly the United States—have a major impact on the dynamics and trajectories of regime responses to protests in the region and indeed globally (2012: 709).

43. Geographers debate the concept of scale and an alternative "flat" ontology. See Marston et al. 2005; Leitner et al. 2008; and Brenner 2019. I find considerable value in multiscalar analyses.

44. Jessop et al. 2008.

45. Soss 2021: 89.

46. McAdam and Sewell argue that in the study of contentious politics, "certain temporal rhythms have been emphasized at the expense of others" (2001: 89).

47. Jordan markets for tourism several Biblical sites, such as the location on the Jordan River where Jesus was baptized and Mount Nebo, where Moses was shown the Holy Land.

48. A growing number of scholars have begun advocating for an increase in the number of ethnographic studies of contentious politics, which are particularly rich ground for theory building. See Tarrow 2021; Fu and Simmons 2021.

CHAPTER 2

1. The literature on spatial imaginaries is considerable. Geographers variously treat them as performative discourses, semiotic orders, representational discourses, or simply worldviews. For a review of the debates, see Josh Watkins 2015.

NOTES TO CHAPTER 2

2. Nicholls et al. 2013: 6.

3. Schayegh 2017: 2 calls these "transpatializations."

4. Bourdieu 1970; T. Mitchell 1988.

5. Scott 1999; Harvey 1989, 2003.

6. Amawy 1994: 164–65.

7. Brand 1995; Shryock 1997; Alon 2016.

8. Shryock 1997; Alon 2007, 2016.

9. Musa and al-Mahdi 1959: 3–4.

10. Tell 2000: 37.

11. Schayegh 2017: 3, 7–8.

12. Allinsen 2016: 58–59.

13. Nicholls et al. 2013: 7.

14. Kazziha 1972: 14–19.

15. The stone is a stele with a Canaanite inscription.

16. Rogan 1994: 39–40; Alon 2016: 16.

17. Kazziha 1972: 21–23.

18. The historical site of the kingdom of Moab.

19. Gubser 1985: 15.

20. Johns 1994: 27–28.

21. In 1855, Karak was part of the Ottoman district of Ajloun. In 1967, it was moved into the new subdistrict of Balqa. In 1872, yet another new province sought to combine Salt, Karak, and Jawf.

22. Rogan 1994: 41–43.

23. Johns 1994: 29.

24. That light footprint did little to challenge "the succession of tribal elites, based in Karak, which operated in a manner resembling in certain ways the rulers of the little city-states of pre-Crusader Syria. These Arab Lords of Karak were not the savage Bedouins of the Ottoman sources and European travelers' tales." Rather, they were a sophisticated local authority who maintained their autonomy and control over the region's commercial and political life (Johns 1994: 27–28).

25. Rogan 1994: 44–45.

26. A small group of Algerians were settled in Karak in the mid-nineteenth century for a few years.

27. Rogan 1994: 46–48.

28. Anand et al. 2018: 3.

29. Scott 2009.

30. T. Mitchell 2002a.

31. Rogan 1994: 49.

32. Musa and al-Mahdi 1959: 3.

33. Rogan 1994: 50.

34. Rogan 1994: 50.

35. Alon 2016: 29.

36. Gubser 1985: 106.

37. *Arth al-Urdun* n.d.

38. Ochsenwald 1973: 300.

39. Tell 2000: 40.

40. Gubser gives the most detailed account of the revolt (1985: 106–10).

41. Ochsenwald 1973: 302.

42. Rogan 1994: 53–54.

43. Gubser 1985: 106–7.

44. Rogan 1994: 55.

45. Salt and Ajloun had by 1910 been administered by the Ottomans for forty-three years but Karak for only seventeen years (Gubser 1985: 110).

46. Gubser 1985: 110.

47. Gubser 1985: 107–8.

48. Ochsenwald 1973: 302.

49. Alon 2016: 31.

50. Krishan 2016.

51. Habis would join the Arab Legion in 1932 and become a major military leader in Jordan, later serving as a member of the Council of Notables for the last two decades of his life.

52. Agriculture and local modes of production are central to this story. Industries in Salt and Ajloun (farming, milling, and export of agricultural goods and flour) all required large initial investments and sustained activities. By comparison, trade was central to the Karaki economy, with local agriculture sold primarily for consumption in the surrounding region (rather than for export). I am grateful to José Ciro Martínez for stressing this distinction to me.

53. Tell 2013: 47.

54. Rogan 1994: 57.

55. Tell 2000: 39.

NOTES TO CHAPTER 2

56. Alon 2016.

57. Tell 2000: 35.

58. The Ibn Jazi, e.g., supported the Ottomans while the Abu Tayi backed the Hashemites.

59. Tell 2000: 45, citing Bidwell 1917: 101. "By agreement with Jamal Pasha, absolute ruler of Syria during the war, the tribes of Karak were exempted from conscription in return for supplying auxiliaries to the Ottoman forces operating in their vicinity."

60. Alon 2016: 34.

61. Tell 2000: 45–46; see also Alon 2016: 32–36.

62. An Ottoman counterattack, however, drove six thousand Saltis to Jerusalem. When they returned a year later, many found their homes and shops destroyed by the Ottomans (Madain 2020; see also Alon 2016: 36–37).

63. Clark 2018: 41.

64. Pursley 2015.

65. Brand 1995: 48.

66. Ma'anis today proudly describe their town as Jordan's first capital.

67. Alon 2016: 50–51.

68. Alon 2006; 2016: 50–51.

69. Alon 2007: 21.

70. Reimer 2005: 190.

71. Reimer 2005 shows how local authorities both resisted and encouraged the creation of municipal administration in these years. Also see Clark 2018.

72. Alon 2007: 21–25.

73. Alon 2006; 2016.

74. Viewing the defeat as a sign of the weakness of the new emir's authority, another local shaykh in Jabal Ajloun forced the closure of the new regime's local office (Alon 2007: 45).

75. The Kura townspeople returned the arms and horses they had seized and paid reparations for the soldiers who had been killed in the fighting. Sharayiri, Shurayda's rival, was removed from his cabinet post.

76. Betty Anderson 2005: 44.

77. Alon 2016; Clark 2018: 41–42.

78. The Bani Sakhr moved from the Hijaz into the central Transjordanian area in the late eighteenth century (Gubser 1985: 15).

79. Alon (2006) offers the most comprehensive examination of the revolt.

80. Alon 2006: 7.

81. Tell 2013: 68.

82. Salibi 2006: 101–8.

83. Tell reports that proregime counterprotests broke out in Amman amid fears that Istiqlalis—Arab nationalists perceived as coming largely from Damascus—might join the Adwanis and create an expanded anti-Hashemite movement (2013: 68).

84. Massad 2001: 20.

85. Alon 2006: 32, 31, 32.

86. The remaining prisoners were banished to the Hijaz in western Arabia, where they remained under the supervision of Abdullah's father in Jeddah. In March 1924, Abdullah issued a general amnesty, and the Adwani were allowed to return home.

87. Shryock 1997: 88.

88. Al Tal 2006: 28.

89. Alon 2006: 38.

90. Shryock and Howell 2001.

91. Alon 2006: 8.

92. Doughan 2019: 62; Assaf 2015.

93. Alon 2007: 60.

94. Clark 2018: 43.

95. Robins 2004: 47.

96. Amadouny 1994: 143–44, 146.

97. Scott 2009: 13.

98. Alon 2016: 51.

99. In 1927, demonstrations broke out in Irbid against the Rutenberg Concession Company that allowed the Palestine Electric Corporation to control Transjordanian access to the Yarmouk River (Dieterich 2003).

100. Betty Anderson 2005: 50.

101. Betty Anderson 2005: 51.

102. Robins 2004: 32.

103. Not to be confused with the Muslim Brotherhood (*Ikhwan al-Muslimeen*), founded in Egypt by Hassan Banna in 1928; see also T. Mitchell 2002b.

104. Pursley 2015.

105. Bocco and Tell 1994: 113.

106. Tell 2013: 79.

107. Bocco and Tell 1994: 114–16.

108. Clark 2018: 45.

109. Allinson 2016.

110. Bocca and Tell 1994: 122–23.

111. Bocco and Tell 1994: 124, 125.

112. In 1925, for example, the Nimr family of the Adwan tribal confederation complained to the British that the Ottomans had stolen a tract of their land in 1915. The British authorities found merit to their claim and returned the land to tribal control.

113. Fischbach 1994: 100; Betty Anderson 2005: 45.

114. Land settlement began in the north in 1933—where the towns and much land had long been centrally administered—and only reached the more rebellious southern towns of Karak in 1945 and Tafileh and Ma'an in 1949 (Fischbach 1994: 80–81).

115. In some cases, tribal leaders who had registered lands in their name under the Ottomans found themselves as new property owners of large swaths of land, which they could administer as landlords or exploit as they wished (N. Hourani 2016: 22).

116. Al Tal 2006: 42.

117. N. Hourani 2016: 29.

118. In 1927, the Arab Legion set up a passport office in Amman, even though the borders of the new state were not yet fixed either on paper or on the ground.

119. Betty Anderson 2005: 16, 210n11.

120. Fischbach 1994: 96–97; Amadouny 1994: 141.

121. Located opposite Salt's Grand Mosque, the square was the site of the First Salt Conference in the 1920s and has since been a key location for political demonstrations. In 1935, students from the Salt Preparatory School protested Zionist immigration to Palestine in Ayn Square. It was also the site of massive protests in 1955 against the Baghdad Pact, which resulted in the death of two locals, and it saw repeated protests against the treaty between the British and the Hashemites (Jarrar 2018).

122. In 1933, a German consul was attacked by crowds in Karak because he was mistaken for a Jew trying to buy Transjordanian land (Dieterich 2003).

123. Alon 2007: 120–21.

124. Tell 2005: 89; Alon 2007: 120–24.

125. *Al-Rai* 2007; Alon reports that he fled to Syria (2007: 120).

126. Dieterich 2003.

127. M. Wilson 1987: 125; Tell 2005: 89.

128. Bocco and Tell 1994: 126.

129. Kalisman 2015.

130. Activists Issa Madanat and Yaqoub Zayadin from Karak, along with Nabih Irshaydat from Irbid, were behind the establishment of the first Marxist cells in Jordan.

131. Al-Sijill 2009.

132. Gubser 1985: 22.

133. Al-Sijill 2009.

134. Harris 1958: 174.

CHAPTER 3

1. Sewell 2001: 53.

2. Hatuka 2018: 39.

3. "Nonhuman" things, as Deleuze observes, can be the "bearers of ideal events which do not exactly coincide with their properties, their actions and reactions: the edge of a knife" (1986: 118).

4. D. Mitchell 2018: 3.

5. Harvey 2003.

6. Sewell 2001: 61.

7. Hatuka 2018: 33–40.

8. Exceptions include efforts by political authorities to restrict protests to certain "approved" spaces; see Mitchell and Staeheli 2005.

9. Sewell 2003; 2018.

10. Keith and Pile 1997; Mitchell and Staeheli 2005; D. Mitchell 2018; Hatuka 2018.

11. Navickas 2016: 19; see also Thrift 2006.

12. Auyero 2003.

13. Exceptions discussed in later chapters include Schielke and Winegar 2012; Schwedler 2010, 2012, 2013a, 2013b; Gregory 2013; Tripp 2013; Khalaf 2013; Schwedler and King 2014; Al-Nakib 2014; Gunning and Baron 2014; Said 2015; Ziada 2015; AlSayyad and Guvenc 2015; Bayat 2016; Ghannam 2016; El-Chazli 2016; Sharp and Panetta 2016; Ketchley 2017; and Bishara 2021.

14. Lefebvre 1992: 14.

15. Schwedler 2012; 2018a; 2018b; 2020.

16. Debruyne and Parker 2015: 8, 21.

17. Cited in Rogan 1994: 52.

18. Potter et al. 2007: 7–8.

19. Potter et al. 2007: 7.

20. Al Tal 2006: 32.

NOTES TO CHAPTER 3

21. Abu-Dayyeh 2006: 84–85.

22. Amadouny 1994: 130.

23. Al Tal 2006: 35, 36, 44.

24. Alon 2016.

25. Shami 2007: 119.

26. Potter et al. 2007: 9.

27. Dieterich 2002: 16.

28. Al Tal 2006: 45.

29. Amadouny 1994: 141.

30. Tell 2005: 89.

31. Munif 1996: 274.

32. Abu-Dayyeh 2006: 83.

33. As Boulby 1999: 14.

34. N. Hourani 2016: 22–25.

35. Batatu 1978: 545–59.

36. Shami 2007: 221.

37. Kalisman 2015.

38. Shami 2007: 221.

39. It was Hussein's eighteenth birthday according to the Muslim calendar (AH); according to the CE calendar, he was seventeen and a half.

40. Aruri 1972: 69.

41. As Boulby argues, "The industrial development policy encouraged the emergence of an industrial East Bank elite that included landlords who acquired their wealth under the emirate and who had gradually transferred their wealth into industry. Financiers, wealthy merchants, and real estate owners concentrated in Amman. . . . A construction boom in urban centres, especially in the city of Amman, provided employment for thousands" (1999: 23).

42. Betty Anderson 2005: 9–11.

43. Satloff 1994: 92, 93.

44. The others were former prime minister Said al-Mufti and Salameh al-Tuwal. At the time, Nabulsi was former ambassador to London but was not currently in a government position.

45. *New York Times* 1954a.

46. When the election results were finally announced, two leftists were elected.

47. Satloff 1994: 97.

48. H. Hourani et al. 1999. The gathering, a major step in the Non-Aligned Movement of states seeking to remain unaligned with either side of the Cold War, also included Egypt, Iran, Iraq, Lebanon, Libya, Saudi Arabia, Syria, the Sudan, Turkey, and the Mutawakkilite Kingdom of Yemen.

49. *New York Times* 1955a.

50. The United Nations Relief and Works Agency for Palestinian Refugees in the Near East.

51. *New York Times* 1955b.

52. *New York Times* 1955c.

53. Pratt 2020: 44–47.

54. Gilroy writes that in Jerusalem, crowds attempted to push through the doorway of the US consulate, where they broke twenty-six windows with rocks and tore down the US flag. Arab Legion forces showered the crowds with tear gas and fired warning shots in the air (1956: 1).

55. Associated Press 1956: 2.

56. United Press 1956.

57. *New York Times* 1956b.

58. Associated Press 1956: 2.

59. Pratt 2020: 45–47.

60. Author's interview, Amman, February 21, 1997.

61. Pratt 2015.

62. Clark also reports that young officers were frustrated by the slow pace of Arabization of the army (2018: 48–49).

63. Brewer 1956.

64. Brewer 1956.

65. Yom 2016: 165.

66. *New York Times* 1957.

67. Caruthers 1957: 1–2.

68. Robins 2004: 100.

69. Clark notes that by the late 1950s, the army was Jordan's largest employer (2018: 51).

70. Robins 2004: 101.

71. Kaplan 1972; Yom 2016: 166–68.

72. Betty Anderson 2005: 186.

73. Robins 2004: 100.

74. Umm Ishaq recalled her father's participation in Wihdat protests for several weeks after the alleged coup attempt. Author's interview, Amman, February 23, 2008.

75. Yom 2016: 175.

76. In August 1962, Jordan signed a "treaty of alliance" with Saudi Arabia that was perceived by many as a form of union (Susser 1994: 54).

77. Abu Khalil 2019b.

78. Quoted in Susser 1994: 63, 65.

79. Susser 1994: 66.

80. Born in 1901 in Safed, in northern Palestine, he migrated with his family to Transjordan in the 1920s.

81. Susser 1994: 68.

82. Author's interview with student activist at the time, Amman, February 23, 2016.

83. Robins 2004: 115–16.

84. Yom 2016: 165.

85. Pappé 1994: 176–79.

86. Katz 2005.

87. Pappé 1994: 72.

88. Zakariah 2010: 56.

89. Yom 2016: 185.

90. Robins 2004: 131.

91. Robins 2004: 131.

92. Ahmad Tuqan replaced Muhammad Da'oud, both Jordanians of Palestinian descent.

93. Susser 1994: 138–41.

94. Robins 2004: 132.

95. On the General Intelligence Directorate and its expansion after Black September, see Moore 2019.

96. Brand 1995: 54.

97. Clark 2018.

98. Doughan writes, "Elderly Jordanians who are linguistically savvy would often boast that they can tell where someone is from just by noticing that person's *lahja* (dialect)" (2017: 78–79).

99. Soffner 1994: 36.

100. Pappé 1994: 72.

101. The projects for Amman were in 1955, 1968, 1978, and 1988. Abu-Dayyeh 2006: 83.

102. Potter et al. 2007: 23.

NOTES TO CHAPTERS 3 AND 4   299

103. Abu-Dayyeh 2004: 80.

104. Abu-Dayyeh 2004: 86.

105. King 1955: 30.

106. Housing would be built underneath bridges connecting the hills, with enough space for roads to run along the valleys as passageways out of the city center. Roads would be organized in a grid pattern as much as possible, with the exceptions of roads that followed natural contours, particularly along the wadi floors.

107. Abu-Dayyeh 2004: 88.

108. Al Tal 2006: 52. The map accompanying the plan marks the neighborhoods of Shmeisani and Umm Uthayna.

109. Abu-Dayyeh 2004: 90.

110. Al Tal 2006: 69.

111. Newcombe's successor, Czech Victor Lorenz, adopted a plan of minimalist intervention, seeking to work with existing patterns of urban growth and flows of people rather than trying to alter them. His vision of developing the downtown area led to the covering of the Sayl of Amman, the seasonal stream that flowed through town. See Abu-Dayyeh 2004: 90–91.

112. N.A. 1968: 54; italics added.

113. Al Tal 2006: 70n38.

114. Al Tal 2006: 79–80.

115. N. Hourani 2016: 32; see also Potter et al. 2009.

116. Bou Akar 2018; Menoret 2020.

117. Clark 2018: 96; see also Gubser 1985: 114.

118. Clark 2018 provides a comprehensive look at the shifts in administration across Jordan from the Ottoman period to the present. On the 1970s, see 95–99.

119. I am grateful to Stacey Philbrick Yadav for encouraging me to draw out this point.

120. Finlay 1987: 135, 139.

121. Camerapix 1994: 70.

122. Ham and Greenway 2003: 98.

CHAPTER 4

1. Brand 1995; Lynch 1999; Abu-Odeh 1999; Massad 2001; Naamneh 2017; Clark 2018.

2. Doughan 2017; Alon 2016: 23.

3. Ryan 2018: 105.

NOTES TO CHAPTER 4

4. Personal correspondence, June 8, 2021.

5. Brand 1995: 49.

6. Larzillière 2015.

7. Hasso 2005: 17–22; Larzillière 2015; LaCouture 2020.

8. Schwedler 2006: 44–46.

9. Moore 2019: 249.

10. *New York Times* 1974.

11. Fry 1974.

12. Martínez 2018b: 168.

13. Clark 2018: 55.

14. Baylouny 2008; Moore 2019.

15. Author's interview, Amman, January 14, 2016.

16. For more on these protests, see Brand 1988: 217–20; Hasso 2005: 21; and Amr 2014. Khorino 2000 provides a detailed look at student activism over several decades.

17. Amr 2014.

18. For a personal narrative of the events by Ramzi Khub, one of the student organizers, see Taleanews 2012.

19. Out of a student body of some 11,000 at that time.

20. Amr (2014) reports that the forces included regular police, riot police, the army, central security, and Badia (desert) forces. Ajlouni (2016) offers the most comprehensive account, including numerous documents; see also Khorino 2000. Otoum's 2014 novel, a fictionalized narrative of the protests at Yarmouk University in May 1986, sparked controversy for exaggerating the role of the Muslim Brotherhood in those events. Otoum was subsequently detained by the *mukhabarat* following a story about the novel's contents in al-Jazeera. See *Akeed* 2016 and Amr 2014.

21. Hasso 2005: 21.

22. Moore 2010.

23. Foreign Broadcast Information Service, July 17, 1983.

24. Foreign Broadcast Information Service, March 30, 1982.

25. Moore: 2004: 1–3; 145–73.

26. Moore 2010.

27. Ryan 1998.

28. Parker and Moore 2007.

29. Jarrar 2017.

30. International Crisis Group 2003: 4.

31. Brynen 1992: 88.

32. Author's interview with Khaled Ramadan, Amman, April 1, 2002.

33. Harvey 2007: 2, 25.

34. Wedeen 2019: 25.

35. Dean 2014: 151.

36. International Crisis Group 2003: 11.

37. Jarrar 2017.

38. For example, see Lust-Okar 2005: 169; Clark 2018: 56–57.

39. The Palestinian and Jordanian flags are identical save for the Hashemite star.

40. Personal conversation, June 1, 2021. Ryan was never able to confirm the students' story.

41. Center for Strategic Studies 2003 is the most comprehensive treatment of the Maʿan protests and violent repression.

42. International Crisis Group 2003: 4.

43. Author's multiple interviews, Amman, 2016–19. I learned of these pamphlets in 2016 but have not been able to locate any original documents.

44. International Crisis Group 2003: 7–8.

45. Mufti 1999; for a review of the debate about political openings as mechanisms of control, see chap. 2 in Schwedler 2006.

46. Free and fair procedurally, but the lower house would be constrained in that any legislation it passed would need to be approved by the king-appointed upper house, the Council of Notables.

47. Ryan 1998; Martínez 2017a.

48. See Schwedler 2006 and Clark 2006 for the evolution of leftist-Islamist animosity toward cooperation around limited issues.

49. That vision was articulated in the 1990 National Charter, although it held no force of law.

50. Baylouny 2008.

51. Andoni and Schwedler 1996; Ryan 1998: 60.

52. Author's interview with Isa Madanat, Amman, February 21, 1997.

53. Andoni and Schwedler 1996: 41.

54. Andoni and Schwedler 1996: 40.

55. Author's interviews, Karak, November 1996.

56. Thoraya El-Rayyes, personal correspondence, July 21, 2020.

57. Hanieh 2013: 129.

58. Dieterich provides the most comprehensive accounting of these events (1997: 165–67). From a prominent family from Tafileh, Shubaylat was elected to Parliament in the by-elections of 1984 (when the king recalled the Parliament suspended in 1967) and again in 1989. He was arrested in August 1992 at the end of that parliamentary session (when he lost immunity as a parliamentarian) and convicted of belonging to an illegal organization and possessing illegal explosives and automatic weapons. Residents of Tafileh protested his sentence at the court building; he was pardoned two days later.

59. Dieterich 1997: 163–73.

60. Schwedler 1998.

61. These protests are examined in greater detail in Schwedler 2002a.

62. International Crisis Group 2003: 5.

63. The circumstances surrounding the youth's death are detailed in International Crisis Group 2003: 5.

64. The regime had recently arrested Muhammad al-Shalabi, a cleric known as "Abu Sayyaf," who was associated with the militant Islamist group al-Takfir wa al-Hijra, which is illegal in Jordan. Shalabi was arrested at a checkpoint after having escaped from a hospital, although Shalabi reported that he had left the hospital freely and stopped to rest at his father's house in Ma'an. The regime suspected Ma'anis of aiding in his escape. For more details, see Schwedler 2002a.

65. Author's interview of Ma'ani activist, Amman, December 19.

66. United Nations World Population Prospects 2001.

67. Abu-Ghazaleh 2006: 155–56.

68. Abu-Hamdi 2016.

69. Munif 1996.

70. Abu-Ghazaleh 2006; Rawashdeh and Saleh 2006; Potter et al. 2009; Al-Husban and Al-Shorman 2013; N. Hourani 2014a; Abu-Hamdi 2016a, 2016b.

71. Noor 2003: 319. Queen Noor notes that the mood of the demonstrations turned from anger and outrage to "euphoria" when Iraq fired Scud missiles that reached Tel Aviv; days later the "mood on the streets was close to boiling over" (Noor 2003: 330–31).

72. Quoted in Schwedler 1998.

73. Author's interviews, Amman, January 1998.

74. Abu-Hamdi 2016a.

75. Noor 2003: 170.

76. Al Tal 2006: 199, 195–96.

77. Author's interview, Amman, November 23, 2001.

78. Schwedler 2003a.

79. Clark argues, "The blacklists proved to be a turning point for many centrists, liberals, and much of the public. Not only were many centrists and liberals on the lists, but the lists essentially criminalized all dealings with Israel when they were in fact accepted under law. The lists were also a direct attack on the legitimacy of the regime, not just the government—something that discomforted many people" (2018: 296n13); see also Kornbluth 2002:100.

80. Muasher 2011: 11.

CHAPTER 5

1. Ghannam 2016; Foucault 1984 [1967].

2. This section builds substantially on Schwedler 2018a, 2018b.

3. Zolberg 1972: 183; Tarrow 1993.

4. Sewell 2005: 100; Della Porta 2008.

5. Bishara 2015.

6. Graeber 2007: 24.

7. Tarrow 1993: 283–84.

8. Author's interview, Amman, January 25, 2020.

9. She has also been harassed and arrested, but her membership in a powerful tribal family brings a significant degree of protection.

10. Foreign Broadcast Information Service June 16, 1990.

11. Kornbluth 2002.

12. Dieterich 1997: 169.

13. Schwedler 2005.

14. Schwedler 2002a.

15. The song was written in 1934 by Palestinian poet Ibrahim Tuqan, and the music was written by Lebanese composer Muhammad Fuliefil. It was adopted as the Iraqi national anthem in 2004.

16. Adely 2012b: 67.

17. *Al-Dustour*, October 8, 2000.

18. Kornbluth 2002: 102.

19. *Albawaba* 2000; author's interview with activist and writer Hisham Bustani (who was among those attempting to reach Ma'an), Amman, April 15, 2002.

20. During that period, the Israeli Defense Forces swept through several towns and

cities under Palestinian control, destroying hundreds of buildings in Jenin, Nablus, and several smaller towns.

21. Tarawneh 2009a.

22. Schwedler 2003a.

23. Formed in 1990 as the Jordanian branch of the Popular Front for the Liberation of Palestine.

24. Author's interview with anonymous policeman, June 12, 2009.

25. N. Hourani 2014a: 652.

26. Author's interview with Ibrahim Alloush, Amman, June 2008.

27. Author's interview at Islamic Action Front offices, Amman, December 10, 2003.

28. Author's interview with activist Aida Dabbas, Amman, 1997.

29. Tilly 2008.

30. Author's interview at a Kalouti protest, June 2, 1010, name withheld by request.

31. Israelis suffered thirteen deaths, including four by friendly fire.

32. The throwing of a shoe is symbolic, invoking the December 14, 2008 incident in which an Iraqi journalist threw both of his shoes at President George W. Bush during a press conference in Baghdad.

33. Wikileaks 2009c.

34. *7iber* 2009.

35. Rivetti 2019.

CHAPTER 6

1. See, e.g., Pearlman 2013; Matthies-Boon 2017; Jumet 2017; Ketchley 2017; Allam 2018; Armbrust 2019; and Allam 2020.

2. Clark 2018: 91–92.

3. Phillips 2019: 16.

4. Abu Sneineh 2018.

5. For a the most detailed look at Snayd and Dhiban activism, see Lundberg 2018: 59–89.

6. Ababneh 2016: 92, 93.

7. Moss 2014: 273–74.

8. Ababneh 2016: 94.

9. Adely 2012a.

10. Ababneh 2016: 94.

11. As Ababsa notes, "The area's residents were given free housing in the district

of al-Karama, located 5 km from the town centre. Their plight is complicated by the fact that residents of North Shalaleh are originally from Gaza, with Egyptian travel documents and thus devoid of Jordanian nationality" (2011b: 54). See also Debruyne 2013: 214.

12. Sukarieh 2015: 391.

13. Debruyne 2013: 322. Tell notes that some dockworkers feared that the privatization of the port would lead to a loss of housing for the workers (2015: 6). Christophersen writes that those who were employed before the port had been privatized also objected to the lack of overtime, longer work hours, and the downgrading of their health insurance benefits (2013: 16–17).

14. Adely 2012a.

15. Wikileaks 2009a.

16. Tell 2015: 6.

17. Tell credits the nativist writer Nahed Hattar for encouraging the veterans' interest in public-sector labor struggles (2015: 7).

18. Moss 2014: 274.

19. Phenix Center 2011; see also LaCouture 2020 for the most comprehensive account of Jordan's multisectoral labor movement.

20. Adely 2012a.

21. Tell 2015: 7.

22. See also Yom 2014b: 235.

23. El-Rayyes 2017: 17–19.

24. Author's interviews in Amman and Salt, 2010.

25. Clark presents a detailed examination of the splintering of tribal units along clan lines (2018: 173–78).

26. Kreishan was giving shelter to a man who had allegedly cashed bad checks, and the police stormed his home in an effort to apprehend that man.

27. WikiLeaks 2009c.

28. Jessica Watkins 2014.

29. Munif 1996.

30. Ababsa 2011b: 47.

31. Ababsa 2011b: 48.

32. Clark 2018: 118, 173–78. Although amalgamation was a decade old, new districts had been proposed for the 2011 municipal election. Each municipality would receive only one electoral district, whereas previously each had several.

33. *Wasta*, literally "pull," is the ability to use one's connections, for example, to help one get a job, get one's child into a good college, or get an arrested activist released. Some Jordanians consider *wasta* to be a form of corruption, while others view it as a traditional means of securing the well-being of one's own family or clan.

34. Clark 2018: 177.

35. Personal correspondence, August 10, 2020.

36. The "alternative homeland" idea is that the Israeli-Palestinian conflict will be resolved by transferring Palestinians from Israel/Palestine to lands east of the Jordan River, namely, into Jordan; see also David 2011.

37. Baylouny 2008; Abu-Rish 2014: 300.

38. I am grateful to José Ciro Martínez for pointing out that my reading of the manifesto focuses on this particular point.

39. Debruyne and Parker 2015.

40. Tell 2013; interviews in Abu-Rish 2012b, 2012c. Lama Abu Odeh 2011 criticizes Tell for utilizing his position as a supposedly objective historian to advance a nativist position.

41. Tell 2015: 8.

42. Tell 2015: 8.

43. Tariq Tell quoted in Abu-Rish 2012c.

44. Jarrar and Melhem 2019.

45. Brown 2017: 104.

46. Phillips 2019: 18.

47. Lundberg 2018: 60.

48. Phillips 2019: 18.

49. Quoted in International Crisis Group 2012: 8.

50. Nashef 2013: 503.

51. Personal correspondence with Laryssa Chomiak, June 1, 2021; see also Chomiak 2011.

52. Bustani 2011a.

53. Brown 2017: 104.

54. Ryan 2018: 32.

55. Colla 2012.

56. Bustani 2011a.

57. Author's estimates based on multiple published sources and interviews.

58. Shadid and Bronner 2011.

59. Ammon 2011a.

60. Adely 2012a.

61. Christophersen 2013: 26.

62. Moss 2014: 275–76.

63. Ryan 2018: 48–49.

64. Greenberg 2011a.

65. Bustani 2011a.

66. Nashef 2013: 508.

67. Debruyne 2013: 335.

68. International Crisis Group 2012: 6n35.

69. Tell 2015: 9.

70. *Ammon* 2011b.

71. *Al-Ahram* 2011.

72. *Ammon* 2011h.

73. *Ammon* 2011i.

74. Bouziane and Lenner 2011: 149.

75. Yom 2014b: 234; Ababneh 2019.

76. Ababneh 2019: 54.

77. Yom 2014b: 234.

78. For example, Yom and al-Khatib 2012; Yom 2014a, 2014b; Ryan 2018.

79. See, e.g., the video of a June 2012 protest in Ajloun posted by Mihna News 2012.

80. Doughan 2019: 60.

81. Ababneh 2016: 89.

82. Yom and al-Khatib 2012.

83. Including Karak, Tafileh, Dhiban, Irbid, Mafraq, Ajloun, Jerash, Salt, Ma'an, and Shoubak.

84. Author's interviews, Ma'an and Amman, 2012 and 2016.

85. Lundberg 2018: 100–101.

86. Doughan 2020: 5.

87. Abu-Rish 2012c.

88. Christophersen 2013: 25, 31–32.

89. Bustani 2011a.

90. N. Hourani 2014a: 655.

91. Yom 2014b: 234.

92. Bouziane and Lenner 2011: 156.

308 NOTES TO CHAPTER 6

93. International Crisis Group 2012: 3.

94. Documented in the 2011 al-Jazeera documentary, "Bahrain: Shouting in the Dark."

95. This section expands substantially on the analysis presented in Schwedler 2013a; for the most comprehensive account of the encampment, see Lundberg 2018.

96. Nashef 2013: 503.

97. Jadaliyya 2011.

98. International Crisis Group 2012: 16.

99. Bouziane and Lenner 2011: 151.

100. Nashef 2013: 504.

101. Quoted in International Crisis Group 2012: 17. Kalaldeh's objection to criticizing the *mukhabarat* needs to be put in the context of his participation in the Social Left Movement with other radical nativists, including Nahed Hattar, who later admitted that some in the movement were at the time coordinating with the *mukhabarat*.

102. Lundberg 2018: 33n5; see also Debruyne and Parker 2015.

103. Jabir 2011.

104. Anon. 2011.

105. Lundberg 2018: 33.

106. Anon. 2011.

107. Cited in Nashef 2013: 505.

108. *Jadaliyya* 2011.

109. Bustani 2011b.

110. Brown 2017: 107.

111. Ryan 2018: 71.

112. Associated Press 2011.

113. Fioroni 2015: 42.

114. Clark (2018) argues that privatization was slowed because of concerns that wealthy Palestinians, who dominated the private sector, would gain control of many industries. The regime privatized seeking partners of East Bank descent.

115. Fioroni 2015: 31, 34.

116. International Crisis Group 2012: 23. The military veterans group expressed support for the demonstrators and criticized the harsh repression.

117. *Jordanzad* 2011.

118. Abu-Rish 2014: 295–96.

NOTES TO CHAPTER 6   309

119. Some opposition groups did not participate, saying that they no longer trusted the Muslim Brotherhood, which had taken the lead in organizing the event.

120. Helfont and Helfont 2011.

121. Fahim 2011.

122. Sharif 2011. The man is now teasingly known as Abu Manqal.

123. *7iber* 2011.

124. Kershner 2011.

125. Sherwood 2011.

126. Greenberg 2011b.

127. Agence France-Presse 2011a; author's interviews with activists, 2012–13, Amman.

128. Agence France-Presse 2011b.

129. Moss 2014: 276.

130. Snayd was convicted on July 27 under Article 164 of the Penal Code, which prohibits gatherings with the intention of committing a crime or disturbing public order.

131. Moss 2014: 276; Seeley 2012.

132. The police did not try to protect the office even though an Agence France-Presse journalist had reported a threatening call just hours earlier. The loyalists broke into the office and destroyed furniture and equipment while at least one journalist remained inside; Committee to Protect Journalists 2011.

133. Hussein 2011.

134. Moss 2014: 276.

135. International Crisis Group 2012: 24. Yom reports that the counterprotesters may have been other members of Bani Hassan families (2014b: 235).

136. Ammon 2011e.

137. The protest had been scheduled for a week earlier, but the interior ministry recommended delaying to avoid clashes with other Bani Hassan members who threatened a counterdemonstration. International Crisis Group 2012: 44.

138. International Crisis Group 2012: 24.

139. Cited in International Crisis Group 2012: 25.

140. Abu-Hamdi 2016b.

141. Moore 2019: 260. Dhahabi was also the *mukhabarat* official who had a relationship with activist Khaled Kalaldeh and nativist writer Nahed Hattar, and why Kalaldeh objected to the criticism of the *mukhabarat* at the March 24 Youth encampment.

142. The Islamic Action Front had announced in September that it would boycott the December elections.

143. Ammon 2011c.

144. A confusing system of "virtual districts" introduced in 2010 was abandoned, but the East Bank advantage remained: Amman has one seat for 114,000 voters; Tafileh has one for 25,000. International Crisis Group 2012: 6–7; Ryan 2018: 122–32.

145. Ammon 2011d.

146. Quoted in Christophersen 2013: 35.

147. Christophersen 2013: 36.

148. International Crisis Group 2012: 9n61.

149. N. Hourani 2014a: 655. Many rents had already been increased, particularly in the downtown area.

150. Ammon 2011f.

151. Ammon 2011g.

152. Luck 2011a.

153. Tarawneh 2012b.

154. Adely 2012a.

155. Fioroni 2015: 47.

156. Moss 2014: 276.

157. Quoted in Trend News Agency 2012.

158. Al Arabiya 2012.

159. The rape of a child under fifteen is punishable by death, but the rapist of a youth fifteen or older can be exonerated by Article 308 if he marries his victim for three years.

160. Tobin 2014: 65–66.

161. Debruyne and Parker 2015.

162. Ammon 2012c.

163. Ammon 2012a.

164. Seeley 2012a.

165. *7iber* 2012.

166. Wagemakers 2020.

167. Abu-Rish 2012a.

168. Kirkpatrick 2012a.

169. Ammon 2012b.

170. *Al-huriyya min Allah, mish min 'undik Abdullah!*

NOTES TO CHAPTERS 6 AND 7   311

171. Kirkpatrick 2012b.

172. *Arba'in harami ma' 'Ali Baba, arba'in harami;'Ali Baba al-thani ra'i al-fasad, 'Ali Baba al-thani; Ma nigaf 'a gasrak nish-had makarem, ma nigaf 'a gasrak; Walla walla 'asrak Abdallah al-thani, walla walla 'asrak; Rizigna beed allah la mahuu beedak, rizigna beed allah; Hinna abeed alla, mahna abeedak, hinna abeed allah.*

173. Kirkpatrick 2012c.

174. Wedeen 1999.

175. L. Anderson 1991; Herb 1999.

176. Lynch 2012; Schenker 2012; Hamid and Freer 2011.

177. Yom 2012; Lynch 2013; Yom and Gause 2012.

178. *Al-Jazeera* 2019.

179. Al-Jazeera documentary, "Jordan's Angry Tribes," 2019.

CHAPTER 7

1. Morton 2007; Cox and Nilsen 2014.

2. Author's interview with an activist, Amman, January 15, 2019.

3. Ryan found similar tensions among activists (2018: 181–83).

4. Brown 2017: 102.

5. Freij 2014.

6. Frost 2018; Human Rights Watch 2020.

7. Tarawneh 2012a.

8. Martínez 2018b: 179.

9. Baylouny and Klingseis 2018: 104; Baylouny 2020.

10. Petra News Agency 2014.

11. Baylouny and Klingseis 2018: 113.

12. For more details on Jordan's move toward nuclear power, see Seeley 2014.

13. Quoted in Schwedler 2014.

14. Fioroni 2015: 47.

15. Al-Khoshman 2019.

16. Ersan 2019c.

17. Sukarieh 2015: 392.

18. Al-Ajlouni and Hartnett 2019.

19. Gibreel 2018b. *La wala', wa la antima', illa li rabb al-samma'.*

20. Maan New Agency 2015.

21. *Gaz al-'adu'u ihtilal.*

312 NOTES TO CHAPTER 7

22. Ryan 2016 is the most comprehensive analysis of the first years of the movement.

23. Rothchild 2019.

24. Ersan 2019a.

25. Al-Maqar 2015.

26. Tarawneh 2009a.

27. Bustani 2018.

28. José Ciro Martínez, personal correspondence, August 25, 2019.

29. Tilly 2000; see also Tilly 2003 on the spatial concepts of *proximity* and *mobility*.

30. José Ciro Martínez, personal correspondence, August 25, 2019.

31. Ersan 2020a.

32. Ryan 2019: 33.

33. Nashef 2013: 501.

34. AlSayyad and Guvenc 2015: 11.

35. Gregory 2013: 240.

36. AlSayyad and Guvenc 2015: 10.

37. Tobin 2014: 66.

38. Tripp 2013: 256–308.

39. Schwedler 2003.

40. Author's interview with activist Aida Dabbas, June 5, 2003, Amman.

41. Ryan 2016.

42. On "radical dabke" in Syria during and after the uprising, see Silverstein 2012; 2015.

43. Schwedler 2005.

44. See the statement of the Jordan National Campaign to Drop the Gas Agreement with the Zionist Entity (2015). Portions of the tribunal can be seen at https://www.youtube.com/watch?v=TUKF3-gpGHw.

45. Tarawneh 2009b.

46. Tarawneh 2016.

47. Harel 2019. Walking on Israeli flags is common at protests and during times of heightened Israeli violence, as we saw in chap. 5 with the flag painted on the entrance floor of the Professional Associations Complex. Kyle Craig reported similarly in spring 2021 during anti-Israeli protests in Amman that children drew the Star of David on paper as a makeshift flag that they stepped on, and Israel flags were painted on many trash cans.

48. Author's interview with an anti-gas deal activist, Amman, January 20, 2020.

49. Butler 2011; see also Tripp 2013: 71–133; Gregory 2013.

50. Gregory 2013: 242n25.

51. Graeber 2007.

52. In Egypt, the state similarly responds with disproportionate violence to another piece of cloth: rainbow (queer pride) flags. In 2018, two concert goers in Egypt were arrested for waving a rainbow flag at a concert of Mashrou' Leila, a Lebanese alt-rock band known for its progressive politics, provocative lyrics, and openly gay lead singer. A few months later, police searched concertgoers attending a Red Hot Chili Peppers concert not for weapons but for rainbow flags; see Al-Araby 2019. One of those arrested at the Mashrou' Leila concert, Sarah Hegazi, was a lesbian LGBT activist. She was tortured in prison for three months and granted asylum in Canada after her release, where she died by suicide in June 2020. As we will see in chap. 8, her image was briefly the subject of a piece of public political art in Amman.

53. Ababneh 2016.

54. *Majhulu al-nasab*, orphans with no legal status because they could not prove citizenship. See *Khabirni* 2012.

55. Hiari 2012; Farahat and Cheney note that the government promised to address their concerns but those promises remained unfulfilled (2015: 146). A year later, a twenty-three-year-old of unknown parents set himself on fire in front of the Ministry of Social Development after the minister refused to meet with him to discuss living "a life without dignity." He died by suicide on June 13, 2013, less than a day after his self-immolation.

56. Baylouny 2020.

57. Jarrar and Melhem 2019.

58. Quoted in Abu Sneineh 2018.

59. Phillips 2019: 19.

60. Personal correspondence, July 18, 2020.

61. Jarrar 2018.

62. Moss 2014: 275.

63. Jarrar 2018.

64. One humorous exception came in July 2010. As Human Rights Watch 2011 reported, "police briefly arrested Amina Tariq under the Public Gatherings Law for conducting an unlicensed peaceful street protest to promote vegetarianism by covering herself in lettuce."

65. Faysal based her accusations on the recent doubling in the price of automobile insurance, given that Abu Ragheb owned several major auto insurance companies in the kingdom.

66. Ryan 2019: 34.

67. Al-Shaqiri 2019.

68. The laws replaced the Law of Information System Crimes adopted in August 2010.

69. MENA Rights 2019.

70. Ghazal 2018.

71. NapoleonCat 2019 estimates that as of December 2019, Jordan had 5,764,000 individual users, some 55.8 percent of its population (including noncitizens), of whom 58.1 percent were men and 62.8 percent of whom were aged 18–34.

72. Human Rights Watch 2019 notes that Masha'aleh was convicted on April 30, 2019, of insulting the king and sentenced to two years in prison, later reduced to one.

73. Phillips 2019: 16.

74. Human Rights Watch 2019.

75. For a firsthand account of a foreign researcher's repeat "interviews" with the *mukhabarat*, see Clark and Schwedler 2018.

76. The queen has also led other marches, including one in 2008 against traffic accidents.

77. Nanes 2003: 124.

78. Nanes 2003: 127.

79. Nanes 2003: 126.

80. For example, see this interview from 2012: http://www.cc.com/video-clips/ar2432/the-daily-show-with-jon-stewart-king-abdullah-ii-of-jordan-pt--1.

81. Bustani 2019.

82. *Jordan Times* 2018b.

CHAPTER 8

1. Bouziane and Lenner 2011: 152.

2. D. Mitchell 2018: 3.

3. Lambert 2015: 5.

4. Lambert 2015: 4.

5. Harvey 2003: 113.

6. Lambert 2015: 3.

7. Ababsa notes that those camps functioned for fifty years as "extra-territorial pockets within Jordanian towns" until the Housing and Urban Development Corporation launched the Community Infrastructure Programs in 1997 (2011b: 52).

8. Ababsa 2011b: 41.

9. Fawaz et al. 2015: 10.

10. Sewell 2001: 55–56.

11. The typology of erasures, enclosures, and exclusions is first introduced in Schwedler 2018b: 208–10 and further developed in Schwedler 2020.

12. I am grateful to Donna Murch for sharing this with me during a workshop at the University of Massachusetts, Amherst, in 2016.

13. Parker 2009: 112.

14. Achilli (2015) provides the most comprehensive study to date on Wihdat Camp and its development and history. The street was also the location where the opening scene to the film *The Hurt Locker* was filmed.

15. Achilli 2015: 55–7.

16. Khalaf 2013.

17. Fibiger 2017: 204.

18. Fibiger 2017.

19. Bayat 2016: 131–33.

20. Schielke and Winegar 2012: 14.

21. Schielke and Winegar 2012: 16.

22. Personal conversation, January 27, 2020.

23. Al-Nakib 2014: 733.

24. Gregory 2013: 239.

25. Hiari 2012.

26. Hamrani 2018.

27. *7iber* 2010.

28. Shokr 2011.

29. El-Ghobashy 2011; Schwedler and King 2014.

30. Said 2015; Ziada 2015.

31. *Jafra News* 2018.

32. Ababneh 2018; Sawalha 2018.

33. Gibreel 2018b.

34. Gibreel 2018b.

35. The university president was given the power to appoint the student body

NOTES TO CHAPTERS 8 AND 9

president and half of the members of the eighty-seat Student Council, allowing open elections for only the remaining forty members. Even supporters of the decision agreed that the move was aimed at curtailing the influence of Islamist students, who had dominated the council for several years and had organized multiple protests on the campus grounds.

36. K. Wilson 2008: 109.

37. Solidarity Center 2005; Fine 2013.

38. Lambert notes that curfews are part of a technique through which state authorities decide which bodies are "authorized" for which spaces (2015: 5).

39. Abu al-Hayja 2020.

40. Tarawneh 2005.

41. Tarawneh 2006.

42. Khalaf 2006.

43. D. Mitchell 2013: 50–52.

44. Massey 2005: 12

45. Lambert 2015: 5.

CHAPTER 9

1. Benedict Anderson 1983: 11–12.

2. Kanna 2001.

3. Al-Nakib 2020: 59.

4. Al-Nakib 2020: 58.

5. Al-Nakib 2020: 60.

6. Al-Nakib 2020: 68.

7. Bsheer 2020.

8. They are Shaykh Hussein (who led the Great Arab Revolt during World War I), Abdullah I, Talal, Hussein, Abdullah II, and his eldest son, Crown Prince Hussein.

9. Humeid 2015.

10. Assaf 2015.

11. Doughan 2019: 62.

12. Katz 2005.

13. Al Rabady and Abu-Khafajah 2015.

14. Parker 2009: 111.

15. Abu-Hamdi 2016: 75.

16. Clark 2018.

17. Abu-Hamdi 2018; Moore 2018.

18. The International Monetary Fund is often invoked simply as *al-sunduq*—the Fund.

19. Ababneh 2018.

20. Phillips 2019: 17.

21. Ababsa 2011b: 52.

22. Ong 2006.

23. Fine 2013: 64.

24. Moore 2003, 2005.

25. Fine 2013.

26. Ababsa 2011b: 54.

27. Schwedler 2010b.

28. Sukarieh 2015: 400–406.

29. Control of the site has changed hands over the years.

30. Lefebvre 1992; D. Mitchell 2003.

31. Lefebvre 1992: 386–87.

32. N. Hourani 2016: 32.

33. Ababsa 2011a; Abu-Hamdi 2018.

34. Beauregard and Marpillero-Colomina 2011.

35. Daher 2009, 2013.

36. Khirfan and Momani 2013; Debruyne and Parker 2015.

37. Lambert 2015: 5.

38. Parker 2009: 115; N. Hourani 2014b, 2016: 40–42.

39. Abu-Hamdi 2016: 83.

40. Abu-Hamdi 2017.

41. Abu-Hamdi 2018; see also Khawaja 2015.

42. Personal conversation, June 25, 2021, Brooklyn.

43. Rabady et al. 2014.

44. N. Hourani 2016: 36.

45. Quoted in Dieterich 2002: 16.

46. Abu Khalil 2019b.

47. Hazaimeh 2007.

48. For example, see Schlaim 1987; Brand 1994; Ryan 2002; Yom 2016.

49. Brynen 1992; Ryan 2002.

50. Moore 2012.

318 NOTES TO CHAPTER 9

51. Moore 2018.

52. Harel 2019.

53. US Department of State 2020.

54. Quoted in Elmer 2009.

55. N. Hourani 2014a: 657.

56. Sharp 2020: 1.

57. Moore 2018.

58. Schuetze 2017: 434.

59. Marshall 2013; Schuetze 2017.

60. Ryan 2020.

61. Schuetze 2017: 435.

62. Marshall 2013.

63. Personal correspondence, August 15, 2020.

64. Eells 2013.

65. Dayton 2009.

66. Perry 2011.

67. Marshall 2013.

68. As Marshall continues, "The bureau's website boasts of the park's 'reliable electricity and water' and 'attractive landscaping,' as well as its 'ongoing support for issuance of documentation, invoice certification, [and] transfer of ownership of goods and other paperwork required for international trade.' The park's amenities include a ballistic missile lab and a 'high-security environment,' all subsidized by the Jordanian government. This last feature is probably provided by KADDB subsidiary JoSecure, which also has contracts to provide security at the 'Aqaba Special Economic Zone, Jordanian Customs, the Public Security Directorate, the General Intelligence Directorate, the Greater Amman Municipality, and the Jordanian Petroleum Refinery Company. In 2009, JoSecure launched a joint venture with the Swiss firm Securitas to lease armored vehicles to private companies and provide armed protection for cash-in-transit vehicles" (2013).

69. JoSecure.com 2020.

70. Ryan 2020.

71. Bustani 2013.

72. Moore 2012.

73. Ryan 2020.

74. Al-Aloul 2015.

NOTES TO CHAPTER 9 319

75. Bustani 2018.

76. Ersan 2019b.

77. Peters and Moore 2009: 275.

78. Abu-Hamdi 2016b.

79. Harel 2019.

80. Abu Khalil (2019a) offers one of the best analyses of these marches.

81. Harel 2019.

82. Arab Barometer 2019.

83. *Laysh inleff aw laysh indour; Abdallah, inta al-mas'uul.*

84. Arab Barometer 2019.

85. Harel 2019.

86. On April 3, 2021, former crown prince Hamzah—the one whom protesters during the 2012 *Habbit Tishreen* protests called to replace Abdullah II on the throne—was put under house arrest at his palace in Dabouq for his alleged participation in a plot to overthrow the king. Eighteen others were arrested, although all but two were released without charge. One of those remaining, Bassam Awadullah, was a former minister who had overseen Jordan's privatization of state industries in the 2000s, and his name was often invoked at protests as a corrupt government official.

References

JORDANIAN NEWSPAPERS, PERIODICALS, AND WEBSITES

7iber (online, Arabic and English)

Akeed (online, Arabic)

Al-Dustour (Arabic)

Al-Ghad (Arabic)

Al-Maqar (Arabic)

Al-Rai (Arabic)

Al-Sabeel (Arabic)

Al-Shofa (online, Arabic)

Al-Sijill (online, Arabic)

Al-'Urduniyyah (online, Arabic)

Ammannet (online, Arabic)

Ammon (online, Arabic)

Jafra News (online, Arabic)

Jordan Times

Jordanzad (online, Arabic)

Khabirni (online, Arabic)

Maan News Agency (online, Arabic)

Roya News (online, Arabic)

Shihan (Arabic)

The Star

REFERENCES

NEWSPAPER ARTICLES, BLOG ENTRIES, AND SHORT ONLINE PIECES

7iber. 2009. "Protests Near Israeli Embassy Turn Ugly." July 10. https://www.7iber. com/2009/01/jordanian-protests-by-the-israeli-embassy-turn-ugly/.

———. 2010. "Photos: Sit-in protest in Amman Against the Egyptian Wall" (Arabic). January 4. http://www.7iber.com/2010/01/protest-against-egyptian-wall/.

———. 2011. "Photos: Protest in Front of Ministry of Interior" (Arabic). July 21. https:// www.7iber.com/2011/07/photos-protest-in-front-of-ministry-of-interior/.

———. 2012. "Photos and Sound: Protests in Jabal Hussein and in Front of Raghadan Palace" (Arabic). November 16. https://www.7iber.com/2012/11/photos-sound-pro-tests-in-amman-thursday-nov15/.

Ababneh, Sara. 2018. "Do You Know Who Governs Us? The Damned Monetary Fund": Jordan's June 2018 Rising." *Middle East Report Online*, June 30. https://merip. org/2018/06/do-you-know-who-governs-us-the-damned-monetary-fund/.

Abu al-Hayja, Muhammad. 2020. "A Human Chain in Rejection of the Annexation Decision." *Ammannet*, June 27. https://ammannet.net/أخبار/سلسلة-بشرية-رفضاً-للقرار-الضم-شاهد.

Abu Khalil, Ahmad. 2019a. "Before the Unemployed Arrived in Amman" (Arabic). *7iber,* March 18. https://www.7iber.com/society/before-unemployed-protesters-ar-rived-in-amman/.

———. 2019b. "Marginalization Shifts in Downtown Amman: Twenty Years of the Fantasy of Modernization." *7iber,* June 24. https://www.7iber.com/environment-ur-ban/marginalization-shifts-in-the-heart-of-amman/?fbclid=IwAR0OIsuNyD-58Vt2UzQ1dOHQL8PJIqxpsczoEwnEkt81qfqO1v2YJ4PGKfto.

Abu Odeh, Lama. 2012. "Materialist Analysis in the Service of a Nationalist Thesis: Response to Interview with Tariq Tell on the Hirak Siyasi in Jordan." *Jadaliyya,* September 17. http://www.jadaliyya.cxom/Details/27026/Materialist-Analysis-in-the-Service-of-a-Nationalist-Thesis-Response-to-Interview-with-Tariq-Tell-on-the-Hirak-Siyasi-in-Jordan.

Abu-Rish, Ziad. 2012a. "Getting Past the Brink: Protests and the Possibilities of Change in Jordan." *Jadaliyya,* November 15. http://www.jadaliyya.com/pages/index/8375/getting-past-the-brink-protests-and-the-possibilit.

———. 2012b. "On the Nature of the Hashemite Regime and Jordanian Politics: An Interview with Tariq Tell (Part 1)." *Jadaliyya,* August 22. http://www.jadaliyya. com/Details/26928/On-the-Nature-of-the-Hashemite-Regime-and-Jordanian-Politics-An-Interview-with-Tariq-Tell-Part-1.

————. 2012c. "Jordan's Current Political Opposition Movements and the Need for Further Research: An Interview with Tariq Tell (Part 2)." *Jadaliyya*, August 22. http://www.jadaliyya.com/Details/26928/On-the-Nature-of-the-Hashemite-Regime-and-Jordanian-Politics-An-Interview-with-Tariq-Tell-Part-1.

Abu Sneineh, Mustafa. 2018. "In Struggling Jordan, Grassroots Movements Are Demanding Political Change." *Middle East Eye*, July 10. https://www.middleeasteye.net/news/struggling-jordan-grassroots-movements-are-demanding-political-change.

Agence France-Presse. 2011. "Jordan Demo Demands Israeli Embassy Closure." *Your Middle East*, September 16. http://www.yourmiddleeast.com/news/jordanian-demo-demands-israeli-embassy-closure_1557.

Ahram, al-. 2011. "Jordan Tribesmen Block Airport Road in Land Protest." February 16. http://english.ahram.org.eg/News/5742.aspx.

Ajlouni, Laith Fakhri al-, and Allison Spencer Hartnett. 2019. "Making the Economy Political in Jordan's Tax Revolts," Middle East Report Online, Feburary 24. https://merip.org/2019/02/making-the-economy-political-in-jordans-tax-revolts/ (accessed January 9, 2020).

Akeed. 2016. "'The Story of the Soldiers': Truth Versus Falsehood." December 7. https://akeed.jo/en/post/1248/_The_Story_of_the_Soldiers_Truth_Versus_Falsehood.

Albawaba. 2000. "Jordan Police Stop Six Activists from Joining Anti-Israeli Protest." December 17. http://www.albawaba.com/news/jordan-police-stop-six-activists-joining-anti-israeli-protest.

Ali, Doa, and Shaker Jarrar. 2018. "Jordan's Strike and Uprising: No Alternative to Alliances from Below," *7iber*, June 3. https://www.7iber.com/politics-economics/jordans-strike-and-uprising/.

Aloul, Hasan al-. 2015. "Demonstrations in Amman and a Riot in al-Karak after the Martyrdom of al-Kasasbeh" (Arabic). *Khaberni*, February 3. http://www.khaberni.com/news/141752.

Ammon. 2011a. "Protests in Karak, Dhiban. Silent Sit-in in Aqaba Calling for Govt to Resign" (Arabic). January 28. http://en.ammonnews.net/article.aspx?articleNO=11444#.XPl-gS2ZPOR.

————. 2011b. "Probe Launched into Zarqa Incident, Srour to Meet Protesting Tribes" (Arabic). February 14. http://en.ammonnews.net/article.aspx?articleno=11543#.XPmOoi2ZPOR.

————. 2011c. "Protesters Continue to Demand Separate Municipalities" (Arabic).

October 5. http://en.ammonnews.net/article.aspx?articleno=18921#.XPmHzS2Z-POR.

———. 2011d. "Protest Against 'Neoliberalism' in Front of the US Embassy in Amman" (Arabic). October 15. http://en.ammonnews.net/article.aspx?articleno=14115#.XPmQUS2ZPOR.

———. 2011e. "Jordanian Tribal Coalition Mobilizes for Reform" (Arabic). November 16. http://en.ammonnews.net/article.aspx?articleno=14533#.XPmOxy2ZPOR.

———. 2011f. "Work Stoppage in Aqaba Port Disrupts Operations" (Arabic). December 7. http://en.ammonnews.net/article.aspx?articleno=15045#.XPmLdi2ZPOR.

———. 2011g. "757 ASEZA Day-laborers Granted Employment, Corruptions Cases Referred to ACC" (Arabic). December 22. http://en.ammonnews.net/article.aspx-?articleno=15045#.XPmLdi2ZPOR.

———. 2011h. "Yarmouk Students Protest 'Security Grip,' High Tuition" (Arabic). April 17. http://en.ammonnews.net/print.aspx?Articleno=11907.

———. 2011i. "Tribal Brawls in Universities, Mu'tah Suspends Classes" (Arabic). April 14. http://en.ammonnews.net/print.aspx?Articleno=11888.

———. 2012a. "Govt Plans to Amend Retirement Law after Military Retirees Protest" (Arabic). November 10. http://en.ammonnews.net/article.aspx?articleno=18921#.XPmHzS2ZPOR.

———. 2012b. "Violent Riots, Protests, Looting Erupt in Protest of Price Hikes" (Arabic). Ammon, November 14. http://en.ammonnews.net/article.aspx?articleNO=19016#.WyoYIS2ZNE4.

———. 2012c. "Karak Hirak Towards Tarawneh's Visit to the Governorate." Ammon, June 22. https://www.ammonnews.net/article/123846.

———. 2013a. "Protesters in Amman Slam Jordanian Regime" (Arabic). March 15. http://en.ammonnews.net/article.aspx?articleno=20466#.XPmQKi2ZPOR.

———. 2013b. "Intense Chants in Front of Husseini Mosque" (Arabic). March 15. http://www.ammonnews.net/article/147537.

Amr, Muhammad. 2014. "Hadith al-Junud: Towthiq al-Tarikh wa Rahan al-Rowayah 'al-Islamiyya'" (Arabic). 7iber, June 17. https://www.7iber.com/2014/06/review-ayman-otoom-novel/.

Anon. 2011. "My Experience on March 25." 7iber, March 30. https://www.7iber.com/2011/03/my-experience-on-march-25/.

Arab Barometer. 2019. *Arab Barometer V: Jordan Country Report.* Princeton, NJ: Arab Barometer.

Arabiya, Al. 2012. "Jordan's King Orders Release of Jailed Activists" (Arabic). April 15. https://www.alarabiya.net/articles/2012/04/15/207973.html.

Araby, al-. 2019. "Egypt Police Checking for Rainbow Flags at Red Hot Chili Peppers." March 17. https://www.alaraby.co.uk/english/news/2019/3/17/egypt-police-checking-for-rainbow-flags-at-pyramids-concert.

Arth al-Urdun. n.d. "The al-Shobak Revolution: 1900 and 1905" (Arabic). http://jordanheritage.jo/shobak-revolution-1905/.

Associated Press. 2011. "Israel 'Evaculates Jordan Embassy' amid Protests in Amman." *Guardian*, September 15. http://www.theguardian.com/world/2011/sep/15/israel-evacuates-jordan-embassy-amman.

Associated Press. 2011. "Islamists Clash with Supporters of Jordan's King." *New York Times*, April 15. http://www.nytimes.com/2011/04/16/world/middleeast/16jordan.html?_r=1&hpw.

———. 1956. "Gunfire Kills a Rioter." *New York Times,* January 8, p. 2.

Brand, Laurie, and Fayez Hammad. 2012. "Just What Does Jordan's Abdullah Understand?" Middle East Channel, *Foreign Policy*, January 17. https://foreignpolicy.com/2012/01/17/just-what-does-jordans-abdullah-understand/.

Brewer, Sam Pope. 1956. "Jordan Nationalism Rises: Palestinian Refugees Lead Demonstrations Celebrating General Glubb's Ouster." *New York Times*, March 10.

Bustani, Hisham. 2011a. "The Alternative Opposition in Jordan and the Failure to Understand Lessons of Tunisian and Egyptian Revolutions." *Jadaliyya*, March 22. http://www.jadaliyya.com/Details/23816/The-Alternative-Opposition-in-Jordan-and-the-Failure-to-Understand-Lessons-of-Tunisian-and-Egyptian-Revolutions.

———. 2011b. "Jordan's New Opposition and the Traps of Identity and Ambiguity." *Jadaliyya*, April 24. http://www.jadaliyya.com/Details/23912/Jordan%6os-New-Opposition-and-the-Traps-of-Identity-and-Ambiguity.

———. 2013. "Up to Now, the Regime Has Been Successful in Absorbing the Movement and Fragmenting It." *Your Middle East*, January 8. https://yourmiddleeast.com/2013/01/08/aeoeup-to-now-the-regime-has-been-successful-in-absorbing-the-movement-and-fragmenting-itae%C2%9D/.

———. 2018. "The Decisive Moment of Change: How to Turn the 'Jordan Strike' Protests into Popular Gains" (Arabic). *7iber*, June 4. https://www.7iber.com/politics-economics/how-to-turn-jordan-protests-into-popular-gains/.

———. 2019. "The IMF Still Rules: How the Authority Uses Protests to Deepen

326 REFERENCES

Liberalization and Absolutism" (Arabic). *7iber*, August 24. https://www.7iber.com/ politics-economics/قودندنصلا-مكح-طقسي-مل/.

Butler, Judith. 2011. "Bodies in Alliance and the Politics of the Street," *transversal texts*, September, https://transversal.at/transversal/1011/butler/en.

Caruthers, Osgood. 1955. "Revolt in Jordan Has Many Facets: British Pressure on Country to Join Baghdad Pact Seen as Ill-Timed Maneuver." *New York Times*, December 23.

———. 1957. "Jordan Extremists Threatening Strike." *New York Times*, April 24, 1–2.

Committee to Protect Journalists. 2011. "In Jordan, Attacks on the Press Go Unpunished." June 21. https://cpj.org/2011/06/in-jordan-attacks-on-the-press-go-unpunished.php.

David, Assaf. 2010. "The Revolt of Jordan's Military Veterans." *Foreign Policy* online, June 16. http://foreignpolicy.com/2010/06/16/the-revolt-of-jordans-military-veterans/.

Eells, Josh. 2013. "Sleep-Away Camp for Postmodern Cowboys." *New York Times*, July 19. https://www.nytimes.com/2013/07/21/magazine/sleep-away-camp-for-postmodern-cowboys.html?pagewanted=2&_r=0&hp.

El Chazli, Youssef. 2016. "A Geography of Revolt in Alexandria, Egypt's Second Capital." *MetroPolitics.eu*, February 23. http://www.metropolitiques.eu/A-Geography-of-Revolt-in.html.

Elmer, Jon. 2009. "The 'Green Zone' Called Jordan." *Electronic Intifada*, November 17. https://electronicintifada.net/content/green-zone-called-jordan/8540.

Ersan, Mohammad. 2019a. "Jordanians and Palestinians Rally in Amman against Trump's 'Deal of the Century.'" *Middle East Eye*, June 22. https://www.middleeasteye.net/news/jordanians-and-palestinians-mobilize-amman-against-trumps-deal-century.

———. 2019b. "Dozens of Jordanians Jailed in Saudi Arabia without Charge or Justice." *Middle East Eye*, November 27. https://www.middleeasteye.net/news/saudi-arabia-jails-jordanian-citizens-without-charge-or-justice.

———. 2019c. "Jordan Fears Striking Teachers Will Inspire New Wave of Widespread Protest." *Middle East Eye*, September 10. https://www.middleeasteye.net/news/jordans-government-fears-nationwide-teachers-strike-may-engulf-other-sectors.

———. 2020. "'Black Day': Hundreds Rally in Jordan Over 'Treasonous' Gas Deal with Israel." *Middle East Eye*, January 3. https://www.middleeasteye.net/news/black-day-hundreds-rally-jordan-over-treasonous-gas-deal-israel.

Fahim, Kareem. 2011. "Jordanian Police Break Up a Peaceful March with Beatings." *New York Times*, July 15. https://www.nytimes.com/2011/07/16/world/middleeast/16jordan.html.

Freij, Muath. 2014. "Protesters Attempt to Storm Israeli Embassy in Amman." *Jordan Times*, July 9. http://www.jordantimes.com/news/local/protesters-attempt-storm-israeli-embassy-amman.

Frost, Lilly. 2018. "Patriots without Passports." *American Center for Oriental Research Blog*, January 18. https://www.acorjordan.org/2018/01/18/patriots-without-passports/?fbclid=IwARotjcv5tbX7ssOl6IoLoWCFmghcz7du4uNInJud5GkrOm-V97z6DEFl9-U4.

Ghannam, Farha. 2016. "The Rise and Decline of a Heterotopic Space: Views from Maidan al-Tahrir." *Jadaliyya*, January 25. https://www.jadaliyya.com/Details/32895/The-Rise-and-Decline-of-a-Heterotopic-Space-Views-from-Midan-al-Tahrir.

Ghazal, Mohammad. 2018. "New Cybercrime Law Will Restrict Media Freedom, Public Opinion." *Jordan Times*, November 21. http://jordantimes.com/news/local/'new-cybercrime-law-will-restrict-media-freedom-public-opinion'.

Ghitis, Frida. 2018. "Anti-Austerity Protests Rattle Jordan, Reverberating across the Middle East." *World Politics Review*, June 7.

Gibreel, Dana. 2018a. "Roundup of Day Four of Protests in Jordan." *7iber,* June 4. https://www.7iber.com/politics-economics/roundup-of-day-four-of-protests-in-jordan/.

———. 2018b. "The People's Thursday: How Did the Third Sit-in Pass?" (Arabic). *7iber*, December 15. https://www.7iber.com/politics-economics/jordanians-protest-thursday-third-consecutive-week/.

Gilroy, Harry. 1956. "Rioters in Jordan Stone U.S. Center, Burn AID Building." *New York Times*, January 7, 1–2.

Graeber, David. 2007. "On the Phenomenology of Giant Puppets: Broken Windows, Imaginary Jars of Urine, and the Cosmological Role of the Police in American Culture." *Libcom.org*, https://libcom.org/files/puppets.pdf.

Greenberg, Joel. 2011a. "Jordan Protesters Attacked by Government Supporters in Amman." *Washington Post*, February 18. http://www.washingtonpost.com/wp-dyn/content/article/2011/02/18/AR2011021804081.html.

———. 2011b. "In Jordan, Low Turnout for Anti-Israeli March." September 15. https://www.washingtonpost.com/world/middle-east/israel-clears-embassy-staff-ahead-of-jordan-protest/2011/09/15/gIQA75LwTK_story.html.

REFERENCES

@HalaAlkbar. 2018. "Breaking: The Crown Prince Visits the Fourth Circle, Thanks Security and Requests the Protection of Citizens" (Arabic). Twitter, June 3, 8:47 p.m. https://twitter.com/HalaAkhbar/status/1003437933335105536.

Hamrani, Nabil. 2018. "Sit-ins Turn Parliament Sidewalk into 'Hyde Park'" (Arabic). *al-Sabeel*, February 1. http://assabeel.net/news/2018/1/31/اعتصامات-تحول-رصيف-البرلمان-الى-هايد-بارك.

Harel, Z. 2019. "Ongoing Protests in Jordan Threaten to Destabilize the Regime." *MEMRI*, March 11. https://www.memri.org/reports/ongoing-protests-jordan-threaten-destabilize-regime.

Hazaimeh, Hani. 2007. "Coloring the Present, Building the Future." *Jordan Times*, August 31.

Helfont, Samuel, and Tally Helfont. 2011. "Jordan's Protests: Arab Spring Lite?" *Foreign Policy Research Institute*, July 3. (The publication date of July 3 cannot be correct because the protest discussed in the piece happened July 15; the correct date is likely July 30.) https://www.fpri.org/article/2011/07/jordans-protests-arab-spring-lite/.

Hiari, Sandra. 2012. "Why Amman's Public Space Stops at the 4th Circle." *7iber*, July 24. http://www.7iber.com/2012/07/why-ammans-public-space-stops-at-4th-circle/.

Human Rights Watch. 2011. "World Report 2011: Jordan, Events of 2010." https://www.hrw.org/world-report/2011/country-chapters/jordan.

———. 2019. "Jordan: Crackdown on Political Activists: Charges Restrict Free Expression." June 4. https://www.hrw.org/news/2019/06/04/jordan-crackdown-political-activists.

———. 2020. "Jordan: Stepped Up Arrests of Activists, Protesters; Little Progress on Women's Rights," January 14. https://www.hrw.org/news/2020/01/14/jordan-stepped-arrests-activists-protesters.

Humeid, Ahmad. 2015. "The 80s Refusing to Leave: Shmeisani and the Death of Ammani Human-scale Urban Modernity." *BeAmman*, December 3. http://beamman.com/index.php/on-the-street/places/item/307-the-80?fbclid=IwAR0YkjCj5PGiRApqT2VYktz8pKh3Na9mF-nHoamI2MoPq5M9mD7OAyV7BcY (accessed January 8, 2020; originally posted on *360east*).

Hussein, Mohammad Ben. 2011. "Political Parties Condemn Attack on Karak Protesters." *Jordan Times*, August 11.

International Crisis Group. 2003. "Red Alert in Jordan: Recurrent Unrest in Maan." *Middle East Briefing*, February 19.

———. 2012. "Dallying with Reform in a Divided Jordan." *Middle East/North Africa Report* no. 118, March 12.

Jabir, Jabir. 2011. "What Happened at the Interior Circle Yesterday?" (Arabic). *7iber*, March 25. https://www.7iber.com/2011/03/march24-protests/.

Jadaliyya. 2011. "Jordan's March 24 Youth Sit-in Violenty Dispersed (Videos)." *Jadaliyya*, March 26. http://www.jadaliyya.com/pages/index/1012/jordans-march-24-youth-sit-in-violently-dispersed-.

Jafra News. 2018. "The Governor of the Capital Prevents a Fourth Sit-in" (Arabic). *Jafra News*, February 1. http://www.jfranews.com.jo/post.php?id=194358&fbclid=I-wAR04EVU5AxvWLjmM-hNkYnUE1soJ-rioRCJv1ZPgc1L8l22yIRBzN-92gK0.

Jarrar, Shaker. 2017. "How the Uprising Happened: Background and Diaries of the [1989] *Habbit Nisan*" (Arabic). *7iber*, April 30. https://www.7iber.com/politics-economics/how-did-1989-uprising-happen/?fbclid=IwAR3gj9GZRk84gCoqumUMpoFidjBaFt9xZ4QMjlz0bhjp4OoT2sK0gwc--2k.

———. 2018. "Al-Ayn Square Sit-in in Salt: Restoring History and Eroding Political Channels" (Arabic). *7iber,* March 14. https://www.7iber.com/politics-economics/demonstrations-in-salt-city/.

Jarrar, Shaker, and Yazan Melhem. 2019. "Lifting the Lid on Society: The Dhiban Brigade's Path to Poverty and Unemployment" (Arabic). *7iber*, March 10. https://www.7iber.com/society/theeban-road-to-poverty-and-unemployment/.

Jazeera, al-. 2019. "Jordan's Angry Tribes" (documentary). July 4. https://www.aljazeera.com/programmes/peopleandpower/2019/07/jordan-angry-tribes-190704085944812.html.

Jordan Times. 2018. "King: Jordan Will Terminate Baqoura, Ghumar Annexes in Peace Treaty." October 21. https://www.jordantimes.com/news/local/king-jordan-will-terminate-baqoura-ghumar-annexes-peace-treaty.

Jordanzad. 2011. "The Youth Hirak: 'The People Want to Reform the Regime' Written on Bank Notes" (Arabic). *Jordanzad*, July 18. http://www.jordanzad.com/index.php?page=article&id=49902.

Kershner, Israel. 2011. "Anti-Israeli Rally in Jordan Also Exposes Arab Rifts." *New York Times*, September 15. http://www.nytimes.com/2011/09/16/world/middleeast/israeli-diplomats-leave-jordan-ahead-of-protest.html?_r=0.

Khabirni. 2012. "People of Unknown Parents Take Over the Fourth Circle" (Arabic). *Khabirni*, July 6. https://www.khaberni.com/news/مجهولو-النسب-يفترشون-أرض-الرابعة-78858.

REFERENCES

Khalaf. 2006. "Are We Ready for Freedom of Speech?" *What's Up in Jordan?* blog, January 25. http://ajloun.blogspot.com/2006/01/are-we-ready-for-freedom-of-speech.html.

Khoshman, Afaf, al-. 2019. "Jordanian Female Teacher Activism in the Most Recent Teachers Strike." *7iber,* December 2. https://www.7iber.com/society/jordanian-female-teacher-activism-in-the-most-recent-teachers-strike/.

Kirkpatrick, David D. 2012a. "Protests in Jordan Continue, with Calls for Ending the King's Rule." *New York Times,* November 15. https://www.nytimes.com/2012/11/16/world/middleeast/protesters-in-jordan-call-for-ending-king-abdullah-iis-rule.html.

———. 2012b. "Protesters Come Up Empty in Jordan." *New York Times,* November 16. https://www.nytimes.com/2012/11/17/world/middleeast/protesters-in-jordan-seek-ouster-of-the-king.html.

———. 2012c. "Jordan Protesters Dream of Shift to King's Brother." *New York Times,* November 21. https://www.nytimes.com/2012/11/22/world/middleeast/jordan-protesters-dream-of-shift-to-prince-hamzah.html.

Krishan, Mahmoud. 2016. "When the Turks Imprisoned the Wife of Shaykh Rafifan al-Majali, She Gave Birth to Habis in Ma'an Prison" (Arabic). *Al-Dustour,* July 29. https://www.addustour.com/articles/23536.

Lynch, Marc, ed. 2012. *Jordan, Forever on the Brink.* POMEPS Briefings 11, May 9. https://pomeps.org/wp-content/uploads/2012/05/POMEPS_BriefBooklet11_Jordan_Web.pdf.

———. 2013. "Does Arab Monarchy Matter?" *Foreign Policy,* August 31. https://foreignpolicy.com/2012/08/31/does-arab-monarchy-matter/.

Maan News Agency. 2015. "Ministry: Death Toll from Gaza Offensive Topped 2,310." January 3, 2015. http://www.maannews.com/Content.aspx?id=751290.

Madain, Mathew. 2020. "Remembered One Hundred Years Later: Al-Salt, Transjordan, and the First World War." *Oxford Middle East Review,* July 3. https://omerjournal.com/2020/07/03/remembered-one-hundred-years-later-al-salt-transjordan-and-the-first-world-war/?fbclid=IwAR09tQPW85h-4dleo84TZPW-WkvoQkjBamosT7v-OnStBERuoH_cwKVCA9nw.

Maqar, al-. 2015. "Security Prevents Protesters from Reaching the French Embassy" (Arabic). January 16. https://maqar.com/2015/01/16/الأمن-يمنع-محتجين-من-التوجه-للسفارة-ال/.

MENA Rights Group. 2019. "Latest Cybercrime Law Amendments Once Again Risk

Curbing Free Speech in Jordan," April 11. https://www.menarights.org/en/articles/latest-cybercrime-law-amendments-once-again-risk-curbing-free-speech-jordan.

Mihna News. 2012. "Ajloun Underground Corruption" (Arabic). January 14. https://www.youtube.com/watch?v=fYYP-KHK86s.

Moore, Pete. 2003. "The Newest Jordan: Free Trade, Peace and an Ace in the Hole." Middle East Report Online, June 26. https://merip.org/2003/06/the-newest-jordan-free-trade-peace-and-an-ace-in-the-hole/.

———. 2012. "Washington's Bahrain in the Levant." *Middle East Report Online*, May 23. https://merip.org/2012/05/washingtons-bahrain-in-the-levant/.

———. 2018. "The Fiscal Politics of Rebellious Jordan." *Middle East Report Online*, June 21. https://merip.org/2018/06/the-fiscal-politics-of-rebellious-jordan/.

NapoleonCat. 2019. "Facebook Users in Jordan, December 2019." December. https://napoleoncat.com/stats/facebook-users-in-jordan/2019/12.

New York Times. 1954a. "Rioters in Jordan Burn U.S. Building: Damaged Information Services, Library in Amman Election Disorders—3 Are Slain," October 17.

———. 1954b. "Further Disorders Reported in Jordan," October 19.

———. 1955a. "Jordan Riots Reported: 40 Dead or Hurt in Outbreaks against Joining Baghdad Pact," December 17.

———. 1955b. "Jordanians Riot on Baghdad Pact: One Civilian Killed in Amman, Jericho Project Damaged—King Urges Unity," December 20.

———. 1955c. "Jordan Premier Out amid Rioting on Baghdad Pact," December 20, 1955.

———. 1956a. "Jordan Curfew Relaxed," January 13.

———. 1956b. "Jordan Is Calm as Curfew Ends: Riot Toll of 50 Dead or Hurt and Damage of $420,000 Revealed after Blackout," January 15.

———. 1957. "Jordanians Go Wild as British Tie Ends," March 15.

———. 1974. "Mutiny Reported at a Jordan Camp," February 7.

Nusairat, Tuqa. 2021. "Jordan Was Never Boring. A Vibrant Protest Movement Has Been Ignored for Too Long." MENA Source blog of the Atlantic Council, April 9. https://www.atlanticcouncil.org/blogs/menasource/jordan-was-never-boring-a-vibrant-protest-movement-has-been-ignored-for-too-long/.

Perry, Mark. 2011. "Dayton's Mission: A Reader's Guide." *Al-Jazeera English*, January 25. https://www.aljazeera.com/palestinepapers/2011/01/2011125145732219555.html.

Petra News Agency. 2014. "Man Killed during Demonstrations over Water in Beit Ras." *Jordan Times*, July 13. http://www.jordantimes.com/news/local/man-killed-during-demonstrations-over-water-beit-ras.

Pratt, Nicola. 2015. "A History of Women's Activism in Jordan: 1946–1989." *7iber*, May 26. http://www.7iber.com/society/a-history-of-womens-activism-in-jordan-1946-1989/.

Pursley, Sara. 2015. "'Lines Drawn on an Empty Map': Iraq's Borders and the Legend of the Artificial State" (Part 1). *Jadaliyya*, June 2. http://www.jadaliyya.com/Details/32140/%60Lines-Drawn-on-an-Empty-Map%60-Iraq's-Borders-and-the-Legend-of-the-Artificial-State-Part-1.

Queenrania.jo. 2008. "Queen Rania Joins Thousands of Citizens in a March to Reduce Traffic Accidents" (Arabic). May 10. https://www.queenrania.jo/ar/media/articles/may-9-2008-queen-rania-joins-jordanians-kafa-awareness-march.

Rai, al-. 2009. "Rashid Khuzaʻi Fraihat: One of the Nation's Men and Fighters" (Arabic). July 27. http://alrai.com/article/344704/الرأي/أرشيف-الرأي-الخبازي-عي-من-رجال-الوطن-ومواطنيها-الألمة.

Rothchild, Alice. 2019. "A Pipeline Protest in Amman." *Mondoweiss*, May 2. https://mondoweiss.net/2019/05/pipeline-protest-amman/?utm_source=rss&utm_medium=rss&utm_campaign=pipeline-protest-amman&utm_source=Mondoweiss+List&utm_campaign=025c3409e2-RSS_EMAIL_CAMPAIGN&utm_medium=email&utm_term=0_b86bace129-025c3409e2-398518161&mc_cid=025c3409e2&mc_eid=d23cc52c61.

Salameh, Dalal, and Dana Gibreel. 2018. "Day Five Roundup: Al-Mulki's Government Resigns and Protests Continue." *7iber*, June 5. https://www.7iber.com/politics-economics/day-five-roundup-al-mulkis-government-resigns-and-protests-continue/.

Sawalha, Rand. 2018. "Why I Joined the Protests in Jordan." *Al-Jazeera*, June 6. https://www.aljazeera.com/indepth/opinion/joined-protests-jordan-180606084649506.html.

Seeley, Nicholas. 2014. "The Battle over Nuclear Jordan." *Middle East Report*, no. 271 (Summer).

———. 2012. "If Change Comes to Jordan, It Won't Start in Amman." *Christian Science Monitor*, December 18. https://www.csmonitor.com/World/Middle-East/2012/1218/If-change-comes-to-Jordan-it-won-t-start-in-Amman.

Shadid, Anthony, and Ethan Bronner. 2011. "Protests Unsettle Jordan While Most Other Neighbors Stay Calm." *New York Times*, January 28. http://www.nytimes.com/2011/01/29/world/middleeast/29region.html?_r=0.

Shaqiri, Omar, al-. 2019. "To Muddle Relations with a Foreign Country: Three Arrested after a Demonstration against the 'Deal of the Century'" (Arabic). *7iber*, July 15. https://www.7iber.com/politics-economics/موقوف-نوف-بعد-مسيرة-م-ضهانه-ةلصفق-قةللدرقن/.

Sharif, Mouin. 2011. "With a Baton, not a Grill, Oh Pasha" (Arabic). *7iber*, July 27. https://www.7iber.com/2011/07/baton-not-grill/.

Sherwood, Harriet. 2011. "Egypt Declares State of Alert after Israeli Embassy Broken into." *Guardian*, September 9. http://www.theguardian.com/world/2011/sep/10/egypt-israeli-embassy-broken-into.

Sijill, al-. 2009. "Al-Karak in the Fifties: A Political Cauldron" (Arabic). April 16. https://www.al-sijill.com/sijill_items/sitem6686.htm?fbclid=IwARogbd8aUqIU-vjzz-VWuCn5ugf6iFgVAkfizx225eAVFTBckXzZr1cPIgLo.

Taleanews. 2012. "The Goals of Yarmouk University 1986" (Arabic). May 15. https://al-taleanews.com/مفلف-ع-نج-إحادث-جامعة-اليرمومك-1986/?fbclid=IwAR11RZ2gFLd-6oWTr4vZpbrsFQAHUCs4peLCcEa_Wvr5vdb93HXCl8Emee98.

Tarawneh, Naseem. 2005. "Amman: City of Circles Gets a Square?" *Black Iris*, December 15. http://black-iris.com/2005/12/15/jordan-building-a-freedom-square/.

———. 2006. "Hashemite Yard to Become Freedom Square." *Black Iris*, March 21. http://black-iris.com/2006/03/21/hashemite-yard-to-become-freedom-square/.

———. 2009a. "Anti-Normalization Protesters Beaten in Jordan: Permission To Speak Freely Sir?" *Black Iris*, July 6. http://black-iris.com/2009/07/06/anti-normaliza-tion-protesters-beaten-in-jordan-permission-to-speak-freely-sir/.

———. 2009b. "The Art of Protesting." *Black Iris*, January 20. http://black-iris.com/2009/01/20/the-art-of-protesting/.

———. 2012a. "Protesting Internet Censorship outside of Parliament Today." *Black Iris*, September 11. http://black-iris.com/2012/09/11/protesting-internet-censor-ship-outside-parliament-today/.

———. 2012b. "Poll: Majority of Jordanians Don't Support Protests, Except If You're Overthrowing the Government." *Black Iris*, January 19. http://black-iris.com/2012/01/19/poll-majority-of-jordanians-dont-support-protests-ex-cept-if-youre-overthrowing-the-government/.

———. 2016. "The Jordan-Israeli Gas Deal and Our Perpetual Déjà Vu." *Black Iris*, October 6. http://black-iris.com/2016/10/06/the-jordan-israeli-gas-deal-and-our-perpetual-deja-vu/.

Trend News Agency. 2012. "Jordan's First All-Women Protest Calls for Prisoner Release." March 18. https://en.trend.az/world/arab/2004931.html.

United Press. 1956. "City Fined for Attack." *New York Times,* January 14.

Yom, Sean L. 2012. "The Survival of the Arab Monarchies." *Foreign Policy: The Middle East Channel,* November 12. https://foreignpolicy.com/2012/11/12/the-survival-of-the-arab-monarchies/.

Yom, Sean L., and Wael al-Khatib. 2012. "Jordan's New Politics of Tribal Dissent." *Foreign Policy: The Middle East Channel,* August 7. https://foreignpolicy.com/2012/08/07/jordans-new-politics-of-tribal-dissent/.

———. 2018. "Youth Revolts and Political Opposition in Jordan." *Monkey Cage* blog of *the Washington Post,* December 20. https://www.washingtonpost.com/news/monkey-cage/wp/2018/12/20/youth-revolts-and-political-opposition-in-jordan/?utm_term=.e50d7f75a54b.

Ziada, Hazem. 2015. "What Brings Them There? Reflections on the Persistent Symbolism of Tahrir Square." *Jadaliyya,* April 2. https://www.jadaliyya.com/Details/31939/What-Brings-them-There-Reflections-on-the-Persisting-Symbolism-of-Tahrir-Square.

DOCUMENTS

Dayton, Lt. Gen. Keith. 2009. Comments Given at the Washington Institute for Near East Policy, Program of the Soref Symposium, Michael Stein Address on U.S. Middle East Policy, May 7. https://www.washingtoninstitute.org/html/pdf/DaytonKeynote.pdf.

Fry, Mr. 1974. State RCI Operations Center to Mr. McCants, White House Situation Room, "Mutiny of Armored Brigade in Jordan," February 3, doc. no CIA-RDP78S01932A000100020008–8.

Jordan National Campaign to Drop the Gas Agreement with the Zionist Entity. 2015. *Statement on the Gas Tribunal.* https://gastribunaljo.wordpress.com.

King, George W. 1955. *Final Report of the United Nations Field Town Planner,* ed. and approved by Max Lock (Amman, Jordan).

A Masterplan for Improving Visitor Services and Activities in Amman. December 1968. Amman.

National Committee of Retired Servicemen. 2010. Manifesto, April 1. http://allofjo.net/web/?c=153&a=20972.

Newcombe, Vernon. 1964. "Town and Country Planning in Jordan." *Town Planning Review* 35, no. 3 (October): 238–52.

———. 1967. "Planned Development in Jordan." *Town and Country Planning* 38 (August): 413–15.

Preliminary Study on the City Center Development for Municipality of Amman, The Hashemite Kingdom of Jordan. 1978.

US Department of State Bureau of Near Eastern Affairs. 2020. "U.S. Relations with Jordan: Bilateral Relations Fact Sheet." June 30. https://www.state.gov/u-s-relations-with-jordan/.

WikiLeaks. 2009a. "Aqaba Port Strike Leads to Security Crackdown." August 4. https://www.wikileaks.org/plusd/cables/09AMMAN1749_a.html.

———. 2009b. "Riots in East Amman Highlight Larger Concerns about Government." November 9. https://wikileaks.org/plusd/cables/09AMMAN2451_a.html.

———. 2009c. "Tribal Clashes with Police Erupt in Ma'an." November 16. https://wikileaks.org/plusd/cables/09AMMAN2490_a.html.

MEMOIRS, JOURNALS, BIOGRAPHIES

Alon, Yoav. 2016. *The Shaykh of Shaykhs: Mithqal al-Fayiz and the Tribal Leadership of Modern Jordan.* Stanford, CA: Stanford University Press.

Ashton, Nigel. 2008. *King Hussein of Jordan: A Political Life.* New Haven, CT: Yale University Press.

Assad, Nassir al-Din El-. 2008. *Muhammad Ahmad El-Assad: Biography and Memoir* (Arabic). Amman: Dar al-Fatah.

Noor, Queen. 2003. *Leap of Faith: Memoirs of an Unexpected Life.* New York: Miramax.

Susser, Asher. 1994. *On Both Banks of the Jordan: A Political Biography of Wasfi al-Tall.* Portland, OR: Frank Cass.

NOVELS

Otoum, Ayman al-. 2014. *The Story of the Soldiers* (Arabic). Amman: Dar al-Marefa.

Munif, Abd Al-Rahman. 1996. *Story of a City: A Childhood in Amman.* Translated by Samira Kawar. London: Quartet Books.

UNPUBLISHED MASTER'S THESES AND DOCTORAL DISSERTATIONS

Al Tal, Raed. 2006. "Structures of Authority: A Sociopolitical Account of Architectural and Urban Programs in Amman, Jordan (1953–1999)." PhD diss., Binghamton University.

Debruyne, Pascal. 2013. "Spatial Rearticulations of Statehood: Jordan's Geographies of Power under Globalization." PhD diss., Ghent University.

Khawaja, Hadeel. 2015. "Public Spaces under Threat: Scenes from Amman." Master's thesis, École Polytechnique de l'Université François Rabelais de Tours.

Lundberg, Arvid. 2018. "Openness as Political Culture: The Arab Spring and the Jordanian Protest Movements." PhD diss., Stockholm University.

Musa, Majd Abdallah Nemer. 2013. "Constructing Global Amman: Petrodollars, Identity, and the Built Environment in the Twenty-First Century." PhD diss., University of Illinois at Urbana–Champaign.

Rayyes, Thoraya El-. 2017. "Micro-dynamics of Distributional Politics in Jordan: Insights from al-Karak." Master's thesis, St. Antony's College, Oxford University.

SCHOLARLY BOOKS AND ARTICLES

Ababneh, Sara. 2016. "Troubling the Political: Women in the Jordanian Day-Waged Labor Movement." *International Journal of Middle East Studies* 48, no. 1 (February): 87–112.

———. 2019. "The Struggle to Re-Politicize the Political: The Discourse on Economic Rights in the Jordanian Popular Movement, 2011–2012." *POMEPS Studies 36: Youth Politics in the Middle East and North Africa*, 54–59. Washington, DC: Project on Middle East Political Science.

Ababsa, Myriam. 2011a. "Social Disparities and Public Policies in Amman." In *Cities, Urban Practices, and Nation Building in Jordan, ed.* Myriam Ababsa and Rami Daher, 205–31. Beirut: Press d'Ifpo.

———. 2011b. "Citizenship and Urban Issues in Jordan." In *Cities, Urban Practices, and Nation Building in Jordan, ed.* Myriam Ababsa and Rami Daher, 39–64. Beirut: Press d'Ifpo.

Abu-Dayyeh, Nabil I. 2004. "Persisting Vision: Plans for a Modern Arab Capital, Amman, 1955–2002." *Planning Perspectives* 19 (January): 79–110.

Abu El-Haj, Nadia. 2001. *Facts on the Ground: Archaeological Practice and the Territorial Self-Fashioning in Israeli Society.* Chicago: University of Chicago Press.

Abu-Ghazalah, Samer. 2006. "Le Royal in Amman: A New Architectural Symbol for the 21st Century." *Cities* 23, no. 2: 149–59.

Abu-Hamdi, Eliana. 2016a. "Bureaucratizing the City: Moderated Tribalism, Regime Security, and Urban Transformation in Amman, Jordan." *Traditional Dwellings and Settlements Review* 27, no. 11: 23–37.

———. 2016b. "The Jordan Gate Towers of Amman: Surrendering Public Space to Build a Neoliberal Ruin." *International Journal of Islamic Architecture* 5, no. 1: 73–101.

———. 2017. "Neoliberalism as a Site-specific Process: The Aesthetics and Politics of Architecture in Amman, Jordan." *Cities* 60: 1–11.

———. 2018. "Amman: Ruination in the City of Lost Nations." *Middle East Report*, no. 287 (Summer): 18–21.

Abu-Odeh, Adnan. 1999. *Jordanians, Palestinians, and the Hashemite Kingdom of Jordan.* Washington, DC: United States Institute of Peace.

Abu-Rish, Ziad. 2014. "Protests, Regime Stability, and State Formation in Jordan." In *Beyond the Arab Spring: The Evolving Ruling Bargain in the Middle East,* ed. Mehran Kamrava. London: Hurst.

Achcar, Gilbert. 2013. *The People Want: A Radical Exploration of the Arab Uprising.* Berkeley: University of California Press.

———. 2016. *Morbid Symptoms: Relapse in the Arab Uprisings.* Stanford, CA: Stanford University Press.

Achilli, Luigi. 2015. *Palestinian Refugees and Identity: Nationalism, Politics and the Everyday.* New York: I. B. Tauris.

———. 2021. "The Deep Play: Ethnicity, the Hashemite Monarchy, and the Arab Spring in Jordan." In *Minorities and Statebuilding in the Middle East: The Case of Jordan,* ed. Paolo Maggiolini and Idir Ouahes, 151–73. Cham, Switzerland: Palgrave Macmillan.

Adely, Fida. 2012a. "The Emergence of a New Labor Movement in Jordan." *Middle East Report*, no. 264 (Fall): 34–37.

———. 2012b. *Gendered Paradoxes: Educating Jordanian Women in Nation, Faith, and Progress.* Chicago: University of Chicago Press.

Ajlouni, Kamil Muhammad Salih al-. 2016. *The History of Yarmouk University and Its Events, 1976–1986* (Arabic). Amman: Ward Books.

Allam, Nermin. 2018. "Activism amid Disappointment: Women's Groups and the Politics of Hope in Egypt." *Middle East Law and Governance* 10, no. 3: 291–316.

———. 2020. "Affective Encounters: Women, Hope, and Activism in Egypt." In *Arab Spring: Modernity, Identity and Change*, ed. Eid Mohamed and Dalia Fahmy, 135–55. New York: Palgrave.

Allinsen, Jamie. 2016. *The Struggle for the State in Jordan: The Social Origins of Alliances in the Middle East.* New York: I. B. Tauris.

Alon, Yoav. 2006. The Balqa' Revolt: Tribes and Early State-Building in Transjordan." *Die Velt des Islams* 46, no. 1: 7–42.

REFERENCES

———. 2007. *The Making of Modern Jordan: Tribes, Colonialism, and the Modern State.* New York: I. B. Tauris.

Al Rabady, Rama, and Shatha Abu-Khafajah. 2015. "'Send in the Clowns': Re-inventing Jordan's Downtowns in Space and Time: Case of Amman." *Urban Design International* 20, no. 1: 1–11.

AlSayyad, Nezar, and Muna Guvenc. 2015. "Virtual Uprisings: On the Interaction of New Social Media, Traditional Media Coverage and Urban Space during the 'Arab Spring.'" *Urban Studies* 51, no. 11: 2018–34.

Amadouny, Vartan M. 1994. "Infrastructural Development under the British Mandate." In *Village, Steppe and State: The Social Origins of Modern Jordan*, ed. Eugene L. Rogan and Tariq Tell, 128–61. London: British Academic Press.

Amawy, Abla M. 1994. "The Consolidation of the Merchant Class in Transjordan during the Second World War." In *Village, Steppe and State: The Social Origins of Modern Jordan*, ed. Eugene L. Rogan and Tariq Tell, 162–86. London: British Academic Press.

Anand, Nikhil, Akhil Gupta, and Hannah Appel. 2018. *The Promise of Infrastructure.* Durham, NC: Duke University Press.

Anderson, Benedict. 1983. *Imagined Communities: Reflections on the Origin and Spread of Nationalism.* London: Verso.

Anderson, Betty. 2005. *Nationalist Voices in Jordan: The Street and the State.* Austin: University of Texas Press.

Anderson, Lisa. 1991. "Absolutism and the Resilience of Monarchy in the Middle East." *Political Science Quarterly* 106 (Spring): 1–15.

Andoni, Lamis, and Jillian Schwedler. 1996. "Bread Riots in Jordan." *Middle East Report*, no. 201 (Fall): 40–42.

Armbrust, Walter. 2019. *Martyrs and Tricksters: An Ethnography of the Egyptian Revolution.* Princeton, NJ: Princeton University Press.

Aruri, Naseer. 1972. *Jordan: A Study in Political Development 1921–1965.* The Hague: Martinus Nijhoff.

Assaf, Abdullah Mutlaq al-. 2015. *The Balqa Revolt and the Majid-ian State Project.* Amman.

Auyero, Javier. 2003. "The Geography of Popular Contention: An Urban Protest in Argentina." *Canadian Journal of Latin American and Caribbean Studies* 28, nos. 55/56: 37–70.

Batatu, Hanna. 1978. *The Old Social Classes and the Revolutionary Movements of Iraq:*

A Study of Iraq's Old Landed Classes and of Its Communists, Ba'thists, and Free Officers. Princeton, NJ: Princeton University Press.

Bayat, Asef. 2017. *Revolution without Revolutionaries: Making Sense of the Arab Spring.* Stanford, CA: Stanford University Press.

Baylouny, Anne Marie. 2008. "Militarizing Welfare: Neo-liberalism and Jordanian Policy." *Middle East Journal* 62, no. 2 (Spring): 277–303.

———. 2020. *When Blame Backfires: Syrian Refugees and Citizen Grievances in Jordan and Lebanon.* Ithaca, NY: Cornell University Press.

Baylouny, Anne Marie, and Stephen J. Klingseis. 2018. "Water Thieves or Political Catalysts? Syrian Refugees in Jordan and Lebanon." *Middle East Policy* 25, no. 1 (Spring): 104–23.

Beauregard, Robert A., and Andrea Marpillero-Colomina. 2011. "More Than a Master Plan: Amman 2025." *Cities* 28, no. 1 (February): 62–69.

Bidwell, Robin. 1917 (1986). *Arab Personalities of the Early Twentieth Century.* New York: Oleander Press.

Bishara, Dina. 2015. "The Politics of Ignoring: Protest Dynamics in Late Mubarak Egypt." *Perspectives on Politics* 13, no. 4 (December): 958–75.

Bocco, Riccardo, and Tariq M. Tell. 1994. *"Pax Britannica* in the Steppe: British Policy and the Transjordan Bedouin." In *Village, Steppe and State: The Social Origins of Modern Jordan,* ed. Eugene L. Rogan and Tariq Tell, 108–27. (London and New York: British Academic Press.

Bou Akar, Hiba. 2018. *For the War Yet to Come: Planning Beirut's Frontiers.* Stanford, CA: Stanford University Press.

Boulby, Marion. 1999. *The Muslim Brotherhood and the Kings of Jordan, 1945–1993.* Atlanta: Scholars Press.

Bourdieu, Pierre. 1970. "The Berber House and the World Reversed." *Social Science Information* 9, no. 2 (April): 151–70.

Bouziane, Malika, and Katharina Lenner. 2011. "Protests in Jordan: Rumblings in the Kingdom of Dialogue." In *Protests, Revolutions, and Transformations: The Arab World in a Period of Upheaval,* ed. Center for Middle Eastern and North African Politics, Working Paper no. 1 (July): 148–65.

Brand, Laurie. 1988. *Palestinians in the Arab World: Institution Building and the Search for a State.* New York: Columbia University Press.

———. 1994. *Jordan's Inter-Arab Relations: The Political Economy of Alliance Making.* New York: Columbia University Press.

———. 1995. "Palestinians and Jordanians: A Crisis of Identity." *Journal of Palestine Studies* 24, no. 4 (Summer): 46–61.

Brenner, Neil. 2019. *New Urban Spaces: Urban Theory and the Scale Question.* New York: Oxford University Press.

Brooke, Steven, and Neil Ketchley. 2018. "Social and Institutional Origins of Political Islam." *American Political Science Review* 112, no. 2: 376–94.

Brown, Daniel P. 2017. "How Far 'Above the Fray'? Jordan and the Mechanisms of Monarchical Advantage in the Arab Uprisings." *Journal of the Middle East and Africa* 8, no. 1 (April): 97–112.

Brownlee, Jason, Tarek Masoud, and Andrew Reynolds. 2015. *The Arab Spring: Pathways of Repression and Reform.* New York: Oxford University Press.

Brynen, Rex. 1992. "Economic Crisis and Post-Rentier Democratization in the Arab World: The Case of Jordan." *Canadian Journal of Political Science* 25, no. 1 (March): 69–97.

Bsheer, Rosie. 2020. *Archive Wars: The Politics of History in Saudi Arabia.* Stanford, CA: Stanford University Press.

Buehler, Matt. 2018. *Why Alliances Fail: Islamist and Leftist Coalitions in North Africa.* Syracuse, NY: Syracuse University Press.

Camerapix. 1994. *Spectrum Guide to Jordan.* Ashbourne, UK: Moorland Publishing.

Center for Strategic Studies. 2003. *Ma'an: Ongoing Crisis* (Arabic). Amman: Center for Strategic Studies at the University of Jordan.

Chalcraft, John. 2016. *Popular Politics in the Making of the Modern Middle East.* New York: Cambridge University Press.

Chenoweth, Erica. 2019. *Women's Participation and the Fate of Nonviolent Campaigns: A Report on the Women in Resistance (WiRe) Data Set.* Broomfield, CO: One Earth Future Foundation.

Chenoweth, Erica, and Maria J. Stephan. 2012. *Why Civil Resistance Works: The Strategic Logic of Nonviolent Conflict.* New York: Columbia University Press.

Colla, Elliot. 2012. "The People Want." *Middle East Report,* no. 263 (Summer).

Chomiak, Laryssa. 2011. "The Making of a Revolution in Tunisia." *Middle East Law and Governance* 3, no. 2: 68–83.

Christophersen, Mona. 2013. *Protest and Reform in Jordan: Popular Demand and Government Response 2011 to 2012.* Oslo: Fafo Institute.

Clark, Janine Astrid. 2006. "The Conditions of Islamist Moderation." *International Journal of Middle East Studies* 38: 539–60.

———. 2018. *Local Politics in Jordan and Morocco: Strategies of Centralization and Decentralization.* New York: Columbia University Press.

Clark, Janine Astrid, and Jillian Schwedler. 2018. "Encountering the Mukhabarat State." In *Political Science Research in the Middle East and North Africa: Methodological and Ethical Challenges,* ed. Janine Clark and Francesco Cavatorta, 23–34. New York: Oxford University Press.

Cox, Laurence, and Alf Gunvald Nilsen. 2014. *We Make Our Own History: Marxism and Social Movements in the Twilight of Neoliberalism.* London: Pluto Press.

Daher, Rami Farouk, ed. 2009. *Amman: Neoliberal Urban Management.* Amman: Diwan.

———. 2013. "Neoliberal Urban Transformations in the Arab City: Meta-narratives, Urban Disparities and the Emergence of Consumerist Utopias and Geographies of Inequalities in Amman." *Environnement Urbain/Urban Environment* 7: 99–115.

Davenport, Christian, and Will Moore. 2012. "The Arab Spring, Winter, and Back Again? (Re)Introducing the Dissent-Repression Nexus with a Twist." *International Interactions* 38, no 5: 704–13.

Dean, Mitchell. 2014. "Rethinking Neoliberalism." *Journal of Sociology* 50, no. 2: 150–63.

Debruyne, Pascal, and Christopher Parker. 2015. "Reassembling the Political: Placing Contentious Politics in Jordan." In *Contentious Politics in the Middle East,* ed. Fawaz Gerges, 437–67. New York: Palgrave Macmillan.

Deleuze, Gilles. 1986. *Cinema 1: The Movement-Image.* Translated by Hugh Tomlinson and Barbara Habberjam. Minneapolis: University of Minnesota Press.

Della Porta, Donatella. 2008. "Eventful Protest, Global Conflicts." *Distinktion: Journal of Social Theory* 9, no. 2: 27–56.

Dieterich, Renate. 1997. "'To Raise One's Tongue against His Majesty'—Islamist Critique and Its Response in Jordan: The Case of Laith Shubeilat." In *Encounters of Words and Texts,* ed. Lutz Edzard and Christian Szyska, 159–76. Zurich: Georg Olms Verlag.

———. 2002. "Orientalizing the Orient: Renovating Downtown Amman." *ISIM Newsletter* (October): 16.

———. 2003. "Electrical Current and Nationalist Trends in the Transjordan: Pinhas Rutenberg and the Electrification of Amman." *Die Welt des Islams* 43, no. 1: 88–101.

Doughan, Yazan. 2017. "Imaginaries of Space and Language: A Historical View of the Scalar Enregisterments of Jordanian Arabic." *International Journal of Arabic Linguistics* 3, no. 2: 11–109.

. 2019. "The Reckoning of History: Youth Activists, Tribal Elders, and the Uses of the Past in Jordan." *POMEPS Studies 36: Youth Politics in the Middle East and North Africa,* 61–63. Washington, DC: Project on Middle East Political Science.

. 2020. "The New Jordanian Patriotism after the Arab Spring." *Middle East Brief,* no. 134 (March). Crown Center for Middle East Studies, Brandeis University.

El-Ghobashy, Mona. 2011. "The Praxis of the Egyptian Revolution." *Middle East Report,* no. 258 (Spring).

Farahat, Hind, and Kristen E. Cheney. 2015. "A Façade of Democracy: Negotiating the Rights of Orphans in Jordan." *Global Studies of Childhood* 5, no. 2: 146–57.

Fawaz, Mona, Mona Harb, and Ahmad Gharbieh. 2015. "Beirut: Mapping Security." *Funambulist: Politics of Space and Bodies,* no. 1 (September): 8–13.

Fibiger, Thomas. 2017. "Potential Heritage: The Making and Unmaking of the Pearl Monument in Bahrain." *Journal of Arabian Studies* 7, no. 2 (December): 195–210.

Fine, Janice. 2013. *Emergent Solidarities: Labor Movement Responses to Migrant Wokers in the Dominican Republic and Jordan.* Washington, DC: Solidarity Center.

Finlay, Hugh. 1987. *Jordan and Syria: A Travel Survival Kit.* Victoria, Australia: Lonely Planet.

Fioroni, Claudie. 2015. "From the Everyday to Contentious Collective Action: The Protests of Jordan Phosphate Mines Company Employees between 2011 and 2014." *Workers of the World (International Journal on Strikes and Social Conflicts)* 1, no. 7 (November): 30–49.

Fischbach, Michael R. 1994. "British Land Policy in Transjordan." In *Village, Steppe and State: The Social Origins of Modern Jordan,* ed. Eugene L. Rogan and Tariq Tell, 80–107. London: British Academic Press.

Foucault, Michel. 1984 [1967]. "Of Other Spaces: Utopias and Heterotopias." *Architecture/Movement/Continuité* (October): 1–9.

Fu, Diane, and Erica S. Simmons. 2021. "Ethnographic Approaches to Contentious Politics: The What, How, and Why." *Comparative Political Studies* 54, no. 10: 1698–1721.

Gregory, Derek. 2013. "Tahrir: Politics, Publics, and Performances of Space." *Middle East Critique* 22, no. 3: 235–46.

Gubser, Peter. 1985. *Politics and Change in Al-Karak, Jordan: A Study of a Small Arab Town and Its District.* Boulder, CO: Westview Press.

Gunning, Jeroen, and Ilan Baron. 2014. *Why Occupy a Square? People, Protests, and Movements in the Egyptian Revolution.* Oxford: Oxford University Press.

Ham, A., and P. Greenway. 2003. *Jordan.* 5th ed. Victoria, Australia: Lonely Planet.

REFERENCES 343

Hamid, Shadi, and Courtney Freer. 2011. *How Stable Is Jordan? King Abdullah's Half-Hearted Reforms and the Challenge of the Arab Spring*. Policy Briefing. Doha: Brookings Doha Center.

Hanieh, Adam. 2013. *Lineages of Revolt: Issues of Contemporary Capitalism in the Middle East*. Chicago: Haymarket Books.

Harris, George I. 1958. *Jordan: Its People, Its Society, Its Culture*. New Haven, CT: Hraf Press.

Harvey, David. 1989. *The Condition of Postmodernity*. London: Wiley-Blackwell.

———. 2003. *Paris, Capital of Modernity*. New York: Routledge.

———. 2007. *A Brief History of Neoliberalism*. New York: Oxford University Press.

Hasso, Frances S. 2005. *Resistance, Repression, and Gender Politics in Occupied Palestine and Jordan*. Syracuse, NY: Syracuse University Press.

Hatuka, Tali. 2018. *The Design of Protest: Choreographing Political Demonstrations in Public Space*. Austin: University of Texas Press.

Herb, Michael. 1999. *All in the Family: Absolutism, Revolution, and Democracy in Middle Eastern Monarchies*. Albany: State University of New York Press.

Hourani, Hani. 1978. *The Economic and Social Structure of Transjordan (1921–1950)* (Arabic). Beirut: Palestine Liberation Organization Research Center.

Hourani, Hani, Mahmoud Rimawi, and Hussein Abu Rumman. 1999. *Hukumat Suleiman al-Nabulsi, 1956–1957*. Amman: Markaz al-Urdun al-Jadid li al-Dirasat.

Hourani, Najib. 2014a. "Neoliberal Urbanism and the Arab Uprisings: A View from Amman." *Journal of Urban Affairs* 36, no. S2: 650–62.

———. 2014b. "Urbanism and Neoliberal Order: The Development and Redevelopment of Amman." *Journal of Urban Affairs* 36, no. S2: 634–49.

———. 2016. "Assembling Structure: Neoliberal Amman in Historical Perspective." *Urban Anthropology* 45, nos. 1, 2: 1–62.

Husban, Abdel Hakim K. al-, and Abdulla Al-Shorman. 2013. "The Socioanthropological Dynamics of the Urban Evolution of the Contemporary Amman City." *Anthropos* 108, no. 1: 219–25.

Husban, Abdel Hakim K. al-, and Mahmood Na'amneh. 2010. "Primordial Ties Vis-à-vis Citizenship: The Particularlity of the Jordanian City." *Orient* 1 (January): 57–64.

Jessop, Bob, Neil Brenner, and Martin Jones. 2008. "Theorizing Sociospatial Relations." *Environment and Planning D: Society and Space* 26: 389–401.

Johns, Jeremy, 1994. "The *Longue Durée*: State and Settlement Strategies in Southern Transjordan across the Islamic Centuries." In *Village, Steppe and State: The Social*

Origins of Modern Jordan, ed. Eugene L. Rogan and Tariq Tell, 1–31. London: British Academic Press.

Jumet, Kira D. 2017. *Contesting the Repressive State: Why Ordinary Egyptians Protested during the Arab Spring*. New York: Oxford University Press.

Kalisman, Hilary Falb. 2015. "Bursary Scholars at the American University of Beirut: Living and Practising Arab Unity." *British Journal of Middle Eastern Studies* 42, no 4: 500–617.

Kanna, Ahmad. 2011. *Dubai: The City as Corporation*. Minneapolis: University of Minnesota Press.

Kaplan, Stephen S. 1972. "United States Aid and Regime Maintenance in Jordan, 1957–1973." *Public Policy* (Spring): 189–217.

Katz, Kimberly. 2005. *Holy Places and National Spaces: Jerusalem under Jordanian Rule*. Gainesville: University Press of Florida.

Kazziha, Walid. 1972. *The Social History of Southern Syria (Trans-Jordan) in the 19th and Early 20th Century [sic]*. Beirut: Beirut Arab University.

Keith, Michael, and Steven Pile. 1997. *Geographies of Resistance*. London: Routledge.

Ketchley, Neil. 2017. *Egypt in a Time of Revolution: Contentious Politics and the Arab Spring*. New York: Cambridge University Press.

Khalaf, Amal. 2013. "Squaring the Circle: Bahrain's Pearl Roundabout." *Middle East Critique* 22, no. 3: 265–80.

Khatib, Lina, and Ellen Lust. 2014. *Taking to the Streets: The Transformation of Arab Activism*. Baltimore: Johns Hopkins University Press.

Khirfan, Luna, and Bessma Momani. 2013. "(Re)branding Amman: A 'Lived' City's Values, Image and Identity." *Place Branding and Public Diplomacy* 9, no. 1: 49–65.

Khirfan, Luna, Bessma Momani, and Sahra Jaffer. 2013. "Whose Authority? Exporting Canadian Urban Planning Expertise to Jordan and Abu Dhabi." *Geoforum* 50, no. 8: 1–19.

Khorino, Samir. 2000. *The Jordanian Student Movement: 1948–1998* (Arabic). Amman: Al-Urdunn al-Jadid.

Kornbluth, Danishai. 2002. "Jordan and the Anti-Normalization Campaign, 1994–2001." *Terrorism and Political Violence* 14, no. 3: 80–108.

Lambert, Léopold. 2015. "Introduction: Militarized Cities." *Funambulist: Politics of Space and Bodies*, no. 1 (September): 2–7.

Larzillière, Pénélope. 2015. *Activism in Jordan*. Zed Books.

Lefebvre, Henri. 1992 [1974]. *The Production of Space.* London: Blackwell.

Leitner, Helga, Eric Sheppard, and Kristin M. Sziarto. 2008. "The Spatialities of Contentious Politics." *Transactions of the Institute of British Geographers* 33, no. 1 (January): 157–72.

Luck, Taylor. 2011. "Islamists Return to the Streets in 'Friday of Affirmation.'" *Jordan Times,* January 27.

Lust-Okar, Ellen. 2004. *Structuring Conflict in the Arab World.* New York: Cambridge University Press.

Lynch, Marc. 1999. *State Interests and Public Spheres: The International Politics of Jordan's Identity.* New York: Columbia University Press.

Marshall, Shana. 2013. "Jordan's Military-Industrial Complex and the Middle East's New Model Army." *Middle East Report,* no. 267 (Summer).

Marston, Sallie A. 2003. "Mobilizing Geography: Locating Space in Social Movement Theory." *Mobilization* 8, no. 2: 227–33.

Marston, Sallie A., John Paul Jones III, and Keith Woodward. 2005. "Human Geography without Scale." *Transactions of the Institute of British Geographers* 30, no. 4: 416–32.

Martin, Deborah. G., and Byron Miller. 2003. "Space and Contentious Politics." *Mobilization* 8, no. 2: 143–56.

Martínez, José Ciro. 2017. "Leavening Neoliberalism's Uneven Pathways: Bread, Governance and Political Rationalities in the Hashemite Kingdom of Jordan." *Mediterranean Politics* 22, no. 4: 464–83.

———. 2018a. "Leavened Apprehensions: Bread Subsidies and Moral Economies in Hashemite Jordan." *International Journal of Middle East Studies* 50: 173–93.

———. 2018b. "Site of Resistance of Apparatus of Acquience? Tactics at the Bakery." *Middle East Law and Governance* 10: 160–84.

Massad, Joseph. 2001. *Colonial Effects: The Making of National Identity in Jordan.* New York: Columbia University Press.

Massey, Doreen. 2005. *For Space.* New York: SAGE Publishers.

Matthies-Boon, Vivienne. 2017. "Shattered Worlds: Political Trauma amongst Young Activists in Post-Revolutionary Egypt." *Journal of North African Studies* 22, no. 4: 620–44.

McAdam, Doug, and William H. Sewell Jr. 2001. "It's About Time: Temporality in the Study of Social Movements and Revolutions." In *Silence and Voice in the Study of Contentious Politics,* ed. Ronald R. Aminzade et al., 89–125. New York: Cambridge University Press.

McAdam, Doug, Sidney Tarrow, and Charles Tilly. 2001. *Dynamics of Contention*. New York: Cambridge University Press.

Menoret, Pascal. 2020. *Graveyard of Clerics: Everyday Activism in Saudi Arabia*. Stanford, CA: Stanford University Press.

Mitchell, Don. 1996. "Political Violence, Order, and the Legal Construction of Public Space: Power and the Public Forum Doctrine." *Urban Geography* 17: 152–78.

———. 2003. *The Right to the City: Social Justice and the Fight for Public Space*. New York: Guilford Press.

———. 2013. "The Liberalization of Free Speech: Or, How Protest in Public Space Is Silenced." In *Spaces of Contention: Spatialities and Social Movements*, ed. Walter Nicholls, Byron Miller, and Justin Beaumont, 47–68. New York: Routledge.

———. 2018. "The Lightning Flash of Revolt." In *Revolting New York: How 400 Years of Riot, Rebellion, Uprising, and Revolution Shaped a City*, ed. Neil Smith and Don Mitchell, 47–67. Athens: University of Georgia Press.

Mitchell, Don, and Lynn A. Staeheli. 2005. "Permitting Protest: Parsing the Fine Geography of Dissent in America." *International Journal of Urban and Regional Research* 29, no. 4 (December): 796–813.

Mitchell, Timothy. 1988. *Colonizing Egypt*. Cambridge: Cambridge University Press.

———. 2002a. *Rule of Experts: Egypt, Techno-politics, Modernity*. Berkeley: University of California Press.

———. 2002b. "McJihad: Islam in the U.S. Global Order." *Social Text* 73, vol. 20, no. 4 (Winter): 1–18.

Moore, Pete. 2004. *Doing Business with the State: Political Reform and Economic Crisis in Jordan and Kuwait*. New York: Cambridge University Press.

———. 2005. "QIZs, FTAs, USAID, and the MEFTA: A Political Economy of Acronyms." *Middle East Report*, no. 234 (Spring).

———. 2010. "Guilty Bystanders." *Middle East Report*, no. 257 (Winter).

———. 2019. "A Political-Economic History of Jordan's General Intelligence Directorate: Authoritarian State-Building and Fiscal Crisis." *Middle East Journal* 73, no. 2 (Summer): 242–62.

Morton, Adam David. 2007. *Unravelling Gramsci: Hegemony and Passive Revolution in the Global Economy*. London: Pluto Press.

Moss, Dana M. 2014. "Repression, Response, and Contained Escalation under 'Liberalized' Authoritarianism in Jordan." *Mobilization* 19, no. 3: 261–86.

Muasher, Marwan. 2011. "A Decade of Struggling Reform Efforts in Jordan." *Carnegie Papers* (May). Washington, DC: Carnegie Endowment for International Peace.

Mufti, Malik. 1999. "Elite Bargains and the Onset of Political Liberalization in Jordan." *Comparative Political Studies* 32, no. 1 (February): 100–129.

Musa, Sulayman, and Munib al-Mahdi. 1959. *The History of Jordan in the Twentieth Century* (Arabic). Amman.

Naamneh, Mahmoud M. 2017. "Memories of Clashes, Clashes of Memories: The 1970s Events and the Making of National Identity in Jordan," *International Journal of Education and Social Science* 4, no. 2 (February): 56–66.

Nakib, al-, Farah. 2014. "Public Space and Public Protest in Kuwait, 1938–2012." *City* 18, no. 6: 723–34.

———. 2018. "Legitimizing the Illegitimate." *Traditional Dwellings and Settlements Review* 29, no. 2 (Spring): 7–22.

———. 2020. "Modernity and the Arab Gulf States: The Politics of Heritage, Memory, and Forgetting." In *Routledge Handbook of Persian Gulf Politics*, ed. Mehran Kamrava. New York: Routledge.

Nanes, Stefanie Eileen. 2003. "Fighting Honor Crimes: Evidence of Civil Society in Jordan." *Middle East Journal* 57, no. 1 (Winter): 112–29.

Nashef, Hania A. M. 2013. "Jordan Unrest: Did Royal Tweets Absorb Some of the Anger?" In *Social Media Go to War: Rage, Rebellion, and Revolution in the Age of Twitter*, ed. Ralph D. Berenger, 87–105. Spokane, WA: Marquette Books LLC.

Navickas, Katrina. 2016. *Protest and the Politics of Space and Place, 1789–1848.* Manchester: Manchester University Press.

Neep, Daniel. 2021. "'What *Have* the Ottomans Ever Done for Us?' Why History Matters for Politics in the Arab Middle East." *International Affairs* (online first look): 1–17.

Nicholls, Walter, Byron Miller, and Justin Beaumont, eds. 2013. *Spaces of Contention: Spatialities and Social Movements.* New York: Routledge.

Nugent, Elizabeth R. 2020. *After Repression: How Polarization Derails Democratic Transition.* Princeton, NJ: Princeton University Press.

Ochsenwald, William L. 1973. "Opposition to Political Centralization in South Jordan and the Hijaz, 1900–1914." *Muslim World* 63, no. 4: 297–306.

Ong, Aihwa. 2006. *Neoliberalism as Exception: Mutations in Citizenship and Sovereignty.* Durham, NC: Duke University Press.

Oslender, Ulrich. 2016. *The Geographies of Social Movements: Afro-Colombian Mobilization and the Aquatic Space.* Durham, NC: Duke University Press.

Pappé, Ilan. 1994. "Jordan between Hashemite and Palestinian Identity." In *Jordan in the Middle East 1948–1988: The Making of a Pivotal State*, ed. Joseph Nevo and Ilan Pappé, 61–91. London: Frank Cass.

Parker, Christopher. 2009. "Tunnel-bypass and Minarets of Capitalism: Amman as Neoliberal Assemblage." *Political Geography* 28: 110–20.

Parker, Christopher, and Pete W. Moore. 2007. "The War Economy of Iraq." *Middle East Report*, no. 243 (Summer).

Pearlman, Wendy. 2013. "Emotions and the Microfoundations of the Arab Uprisings." *Perspectives on Politics* 11, no. 2: 387–409.

Peters, Anne Mariel, and Pete W. Moore. 2009. "Beyond Boom and Bust: External Rents, Durable Authoritarianism, and Institutional Adaptation in the Hashemite Kingdom of Jordan." *Studies in Comparative International Development* 44: 256–85.

Phillips, Colfax. 2019. "Dhiban as Barometer of Jordan's Rural Discontent." *Middle East Report, nos. 293–94 (Fall/Winter): 15–19.

Potter, Robert B., Khadija Darmame, Nasim Barham, and Stephen Nortcliff. 2009. "Ever-growing Amman." Special issue: *Jordan: Urban Expansion, Social Polarisation and Contemporary Urban Planning Issues. Habitat International* 33: 81–92.

———. 2007. "An Introduction to the Urban Geography of Amman, Jordan." *Geographical Paper* no. 182 (June). Reading, UK: University of Reading.

Pratt, Nicola. 2020. *Embodying Geopolitics: Generations of Women's Activism in Egypt, Jordan, and Lebanon.* Oakland: University of California Press.

Rabady, Rama Al, Shaher Rababeh, and Shatha Abu-Khafajah. 2014. "Urban Heritage Governance within the Context of Emerging Decentralization Discourses in Jordan." *Habitat International* 42: 253–63.

Rawashdeh, Samih Al, and Bassam Saleh. 2006. "Satellite Monitoring of Urban Spatial Growth in the Amman Area, Jordan." *Journal of Urban Planning and Development* 132, no. 4 (December): 211–16.

Reimer, Michael J. 2005. "Becoming Urban: Town Administrations in Transjordan." *International Journal of Middle East Studies* 37: 189–211.

Rivetti, Paola. 2019. *Political Participation and the Unintended Consequences of Reformism in Iran: From Khatami to the Green Movement.* London: Palgrave).

Robins, Philip. 2004. *A History of Jordan.* New York: Cambridge University Press.

Rogan, Eugene L., 1994, "Bringing the State Back: The Limits of Ottoman Rule in Jordan, 1840–1920." In *Village, Steppe and State: The Social Origins of Modern Jordan*, ed. Eugene L. Rogan and Tariq Tell, 32–57. London: British Academic Press.

Ryan, Curtis R. 1998. "Peace, Bread and Riots: Jordan and the International Monetary Fund." *Middle East Policy* 6, no. 2 (October): 54–66.

———. 2002. *Jordan in Transition: From Hussein to Abdullah.* Boulder, CO: Lynne Rienner Publishers.

———. 2016. "Reviving Activism in Jordan: The Movement against Israeli Gas." *Middle East Report*, no. 281 (Winter): 6–9.

———. 2018. *Jordan and the Arab Uprisings: Regime Security and Politics beyond the State.* New York: Columbia University Press.

———. 2019. "Resurgent Protests Confront New and Old Red Lines in Jordan." *Middle East Report*, nos. 292–293 (Fall/Winter): 30–34.

———. 2020. "Jordan: The Military and Politics in the Hashemite Kingdom." In *Oxford Research Encyclopedia of Politics, October 27, 2020.* https://oxfordre.com/politics/view/10.1093/acrefore/9780190228637.001.0001/acrefore-9780190228637-e-1945.

Said, Atef. 2015. "We Ought To Be Here: Historicizing Space and Mobilization in Tahrir Square." *International Sociology* 3, no. 4 (July): 348–66.

Salibi, Kamal. 2006. *The Modern History of Jordan.* London: I. B. Tauris.

Schayegh, Cyrus. 2017. *The Middle East and the Making of the Modern World.* Cambridge, MA: Harvard University Press.

Schenker, David. 2012. *As Jordan Stumbles, the U.S. Response Is Crucial.* Policy Watch 1984. Washington, DC: Washington Institute for Near Eastern Affairs.

Schielke, Samuli, and Jessica Winegar. 2012. "The Writing on the Walls of Egypt." *Middle East Report*, no. 265 (Winter): 13–17.

Schlaim, Avi. 1987. *Collusion across the Jordan: King Abdullah, the Zionist Movement, and the Partition of Palestine.* Oxford: Clarendon Press.

Schuetze, Benjamin. 2017. "Simulating, Marketing, and Playing War: US-Jordanian Collaboration and the Politics of Commercial Security." *Security Dialogue* 48, no. 5: 431–50.

Schwedler, Jillian. 1998. "Protesting Sanctions against Iraq." Interview with Aida Dabbas, *Middle East Report*, no. 208 (Fall).

———. 2002a. "Don't Blink: Jordan's Democratic Opening and Closing." *Middle East Report Online*, July 3, 2002. https://www.merip.org/mero/mero070302.

———. 2002b. "Occupied Maan: Jordan's Closed Military Zone." *Middle East Report Online*, December 3. https://merip.org/2002/12/occupied-maan/.

———. 2003. "More Than a Mob: The Dynamics of Political Demonstrations in Jordan." *Middle East Report*, no. 226 (Spring): 18–23.

———. 2005. "Cop Rock: Protest, Identity, and Dancing Riot Police in Jordan." *Social Movement Studies* 4, no. 2 (September): 255–75.

———. 2006. *Faith in Moderation: Islamist Parties in Jordan and Yemen.* New York: Cambridge University Press.

———. 2010a. "Jordan's Risky Business as Usual." *Middle East Report Online,* July 30, 2010. https://merip.org/2010/06/jordans-risky-business-as-usual/.

———. 2010b. "Amman Cosmopolitan: Spaces and Practices of Aspiration and Consumption." *Comparative Studies in South Asia, Africa, and the Middle East* 30, no. 3 (November), 547–62.

———. 2012. "The Political Geography of Protest in Neoliberal Jordan." *Middle East Critique* 21, no. 3 (December): 259–70.

———. 2013a. "Jordan." In *Dispatches from the Arab Spring,* ed. Paul Amar and Vijay Prashad, 243–65. Minneapolis: University of Minnesota Press.

———. 2013b. "Spatial Dynamics of the Arab Uprisings." *PS: Political Science and Politics* 46, no. 3 (April): 230–34.

———. 2014. "The Nuclear Project Is Bound to Fail." Interview with Bassel Burgan, *Middle East Report,* no. 271 (Summer): 24–25.

———. 2015. "Comparative Politics and the Arab Uprisings." *Middle East Law and Governance* 7, no. 1 (April): 141–52.

———. 2018a. "Routines and Ruptures in Anti–Israeli Protests in Jordan." In *Microfoundations of the Arab Uprisings: Mapping Interactions between Regimes and Protesters,* ed. Frédéric Volpi and James M. Jasper, 67–88. Amsterdam: Amsterdam University Press.

———. 2018b. "Political Dissent in Amman, Jordan: Neoliberal Geographies of Protest and Policing." In *Rethinking Neoliberalism: Resisting the Disciplinary Regime,* ed. Sanford Schramm and Marina Pavlovskaya, 197–212. New York: Routledge.

———. 2020. "Material Obstacles to Protest in the Built Environment: Insights from Jordan." *Contention: A Multidisciplinary Journal of Social Protest* 8, no. 1 (Summer): 70–92.

———. 2021. "Against Methodological Nationalism: Seeing Comparisons as Encompassing through the Arab Uprisings." In *Rethinking Comparison: Innovative Strategies for Qualitative Political Inquiry,* ed. Erica Simmons and Nicholas Rush Smith, 172–89. New York: Cambridge University Press.

Schwedler, Jillian, and Ryan King. 2014. "Political Geography." In *The Arab Uprisings Explained: New Contentious Politics in the Middle East,* ed. Marc Lynch, 160–79. New York: Columbia University Press.

Scott, James C. 1976. *The Moral Economy of the Peasant: Rebellion and Subsistence in Southeast Asia*. New Haven, CT: Yale University Press.

———. 1985. *Weapons of the Weak: Everyday Forms of Resistance*. New Haven, CT: Yale University Press.

———. 1999. *Seeing Like a State: How Certain Schemes to Improve the Human Condition Have Failed*. New Haven, CT: Yale University Press.

———. 2009. *The Art of Not Being Governed: An Anarchist History of Upland Southeast Asia*. New Haven, CT: Yale University Press.

Sewell, William H., Jr. 2001. "Space in Contentious Politics." In *Silence and Voice in the Study of Contentious Politics*, ed. Ronald R. Aminzade et al., 51–88. New York: Cambridge University Press.

———. 2005. *Logics of History: Social Theory and Social Transformation*. Chicago: University of Chicago Press.

Shami, Seteney. 2007. "'Amman Is Not a City': Middle Eastern Cities in Question." In *Urban Imaginaries: Locating the Modern City*, ed. Alev Çinar and Thomas Bender, 208–35. Minneapolis: University of Minnesota Press.

Sharp, Deen, and Claire Panetta, eds. 2016. *Beyond the Square: Urbanism and the Arab Uprisings*. New York: UR/Urban Research.

Sharp, Jeremy M. 2020. "Jordan: Background and U.S. Relations." Washington, DC: Congressional Research Service. https://fas.org/sgp/crs/mideast/RL33546.pdf.

Shokr, Ahmad. 2011. "The 18 Days of Tahrir." *Middle East Report*, no. 258. http://www.merip.org/mer/mer258/18-days-tahrir.

Shryock, Andrew. 1997. *Nationalism and the Genealogical Imagination: Oral History and Textual Authority in Tribal Jordan*. Berkeley: University of California Press.

Shryock, Andrew, and Sally Howell. 2001. "'Ever a Guest in Our House': The Amir Abdullah, Shaykh Majid al-Adwan and the Practice of Jordanian House Politics, Remembered by Umm Sultan, the Widow of Majid." *International Journal of Middle East Studies* 33: 247–69.

Silverstein, Shayna. 2015. "Syria's Radical Dabka." *Middle East Report*, no. 263 (Summer).

Simmons, Erica. 2017. *Meaningful Resistance: Market Reforms and the Roots of Social Protest in Latin America*. Cambridge: Cambridge University Press.

Soffner, Arnon. 1994. "Jordan Facing the 1990s: Location, Metropolis, Water." In *Jordan in the Middle East 1948–1988: The Making of a Pivotal State*, ed. Joseph Nevo and Ilan Pappé, 26–44. London: Frank Cass.

Solidarity Center. 2005. *Justice for All: The Struggle for Worker Rights in Jordan*. Washington, DC: Solidarity Center.

Soss, Joe. 2021. "On Casing a Study versus Studying a Case." In *Rethinking Comparison: Innovative Strategies for Qualitative Political Inquiry*, ed. Erica S. Simmons and Nicholas Rush Smith, 84–106. New York: Cambridge University Press.

Soudias, Dimitris, and Tareq Sydiq. 2020. "Introduction: Theorizing the Spatiality of Protest." *Contention* 8, no. 1 (Summer): 1–3.

Sukarieh, Mayssoun. 2015. "The Notion of Arab Culture and the 'Colonial Present.'" In *A Companion to the Anthropology of the Middle East*, ed. Soraya Altorki, 391–410. London: Blackwell.

Susser, Asher. 2011. "Jordan 2011: Uneasy Lies the Head." *Middle East Brief* no. 52, Crown Center for Middle East Studies (June). Waltham, MA: Brandeis University.

Tarrow, Sidney. 1993. "Cycles of Collective Action: Between Moments of Madness and the Repertoire of Contention." *Social Science History* 17, no. 2 (Summer): 281–307.

———. 2021. "Progress outside of Paradise: Old and New Comparative Approaches to Contentious Politics." *Comparative Political Studies* 54, no. 10: 1885–1901.

Tell, Tariq M. 2000. "Guns, Gold, and Grain: War and Food Supply in the Making of TransJordan." In *War, Institutions and Social Change in the Middle East*, ed. Steven Heydemann, 33–58. Berkeley: University of California Press.

———. 2013. *The Social and Economic Origins of Monarchy in Jordan*. New York: Palgrave.

———. 2015. "Early Spring in Jordan: The Revolt of the Military Veterans." Carnegie Middle East Center, November 4, 2015. https://carnegieendowment.org/files/ACMR_Tell_Jordan_Eng_final.pdf.

Thompson, E. P. 1971. "The Moral Economy of the English Crowd in the Eighteenth Century." *Past and Present* 50: 76–132.

Thrift, Nigel J. 2006. "Space, Place, and Time." In *The Oxford Handbook of Contextual Political Analysis*, ed. Robert E. Goodin and Charles Tilly, 341–61. New York: Oxford University Press.

Tilly, Charles. 1985. "War-making and State-making as Organized Crime." In *Bringing the State Back In*, ed. Peter B. Evans et al., 169–91. London: Cambridge University Press.

———. 2000. "Spaces of Contention." *Mobilization* 5, no. 2 (June): 135–59.

———. 2003. "Contention over Place and Space." *Mobilization* 8, no. 2 (June): 221–25.

———. 2008. *Contentious Performances*. Cambridge: Cambridge University Press.

Tobin, Sarah A. 2012. "Jordan's Arab Spring: The Middle Class and the Anti-Revolution." *Middle East Policy* 19, no. 1 (Spring): 96–109.

———. 2014. "'God Save the King?' The Evolution of Protest in Jordan in Light of the Arab Spring." In *Middle East: Conflicts and Reforms*, ed. Mohammed M. Aman and Mary Jo Aman, 57–70. Washington, DC: Westphalia Press.

Tripp, Charles. 2013. *The Power and the People: Paths of Resistance in the Middle East.* New York: Cambridge University Press.

Trouillot, Michel-Rolph. 1995. *Silencing the Past: Power and the Production of History.* Boston: Beacon Press.

Wagemakers, Joas. 2020. *The Muslim Brotherhood in Jordan.* New York: Cambridge University Press.

Watkins, Jessica. 2014. "Seeking Justice: Tribal Dispute Resolution and Societal Transformation in Jordan." *International Journal of Middle East Studies* 46, no. 1 (February): 31–49.

Watkins, Josh. 2015. "Spatial Imaginaries Research in Geography: Synergies, Tensions, and New Directions." *Geography Compass* 9, no. 9 (September): 508–22.

Wedeen, Lisa. 1999. *Ambiguities of Domination: Politics, Rhetoric, and Symbols in Contemporary Syria.* Chicago: University of Chicago Press.

———. 2019. *Authoritarian Apprehensions: Ideology, Judgment, and Mourning in Syria.* Chicago: University of Chicago Press.

Wilson, Kate. 2008. "Cultural Collateral Damage: The Cancellation of Jordan's Jerash Festival 2006." Special issue: Post 9/11 Arabic Theatre and Performance, *Journal of Dramatic Theory and Criticism* 23, no. 1 (Fall): 93–113.

Wilson, Mary. 1987. *King Abdullah, Britain, and the Making of Jordan.* Cambridge: Cambridge University Press.

Wood, Elisabeth. Jean. 2000. *Forging Democracy from Below: Insurgent Transitions in South Africa and El Salvador.* New York: Cambridge University Press.

Yom, Sean. 2014a. "Tribal Politics in Contemporary Jordan: The Case of the Hirak Movement." *Middle East Journal* 68, no. 2 (Spring): 229–47.

———. 2014b. "The New Landscape of Jordanian Politics: Social Opposition, Fiscal Crisis, and the Arab Spring." *British Journal of Middle Eastern Studies* 42, no. 3: 284–300.

———. 2016. *From Resilience to Revolution: How Foreign Interventions Destabilize the Middle East.* New York: Columbia University Press.

Yom, Sean, and F. Gregory Gause III. 2012. "Resilient Royals: How Arab Monarchies Hang On." *Journal of Democracy* 23, no. 4 (October): 74–88.

Zakariah, Muhamad Hasrul. 2010. "The Uprising of the Fedayeen against the Government of Jordan, 1970–1971: Declassified Documents from the British Archive." *International Journal of West Asian Studies* 2, no. 2: 47–64.

Zolberg, Aristide R. 1972. "Moments of Madness." *Politics and Society* 2, no. 2 (March): 183–207.

Index

Ababsa, Myriam, 157, 257

Abbadi, Ahmad Uwaydi, 191–92

Abbadi tribe, 166, 168; protests, 171, 282

Abdali: development in 1960s, 91–92; interchange, 243–44, *245*, *261*, 247; transportation terminal, 263. *See also* Abdali Boulevard

Abdali Boulevard, 270, 279, *280*; main discussion, 260–66, *261*, *263*; planned plaza above Abdali Mall, 264

Abdoun, 91, 118, 120, 217, 233, 261–62, *261*; Bridge, 233, *261*; Circle, 120, *261*; protests at the US embassy, 233. *See also* Taj Lifestyle Center

Abdullah I bin Hussein, Emir and King: arrival in Transjordanian area, 15, 29, 43–60, 69–75; aspirations for a larger domain, 32–33, 43, 61, 75; assassination, 76

Abdullah II bin Hussein, King, 119, 124,

148, 164, 181, 221, 223–24, 273, 282; anger toward, 12, 18–19, 169, 199, 278, 280; assent to throne, 97, 118, 152; economic policies, 13, 255–56, 260; efforts to silence dissent, 124, 126, 169, 186–88, 190–92; and the social contact, 2; support for, 183, 222; unpopularity, 152–53, 159, 182; vision for a new Jordan, 25, 250–55, 282

Abu-Hamdi, Eliana, 121, 259, 263–64, 278

Abu-Rish, Ziad, 174

Adwan Revolt, 47–50, 52; remembrance of, 49–50, 254, 278, 293n83

Adwan tribal confederation, 33–34, 44, 52; battle with Ottoman forces, 33–34; Great Arab Revolt, 42; supporting the king against protesters, 82. *See also* Adwan Revolt

affect and: analysis, 151; Arab nationalism, 59, 75; Arab uprisings, 162, 165,

356 INDEX

affect and (*continued*)
185; attachments to place, 2, 10, 14,
27–9, 31, 33, 50, 57, 93, 99–101, 117, 151,
251, 277, 287n11; militarized space,
228–29; protests, 5, 21–22, 59, 76, 80,
110, 127–29, 136, 148–49, 151–52, 186
Afghanistan protests, 118
Ahmad Suleiman al-Najdawi Street, 135
Ajarma protests, 178
Ajloun, *30*; Black September, 87; British
administrative district, 42; Caucasians settled in, 31–32; criticism of
the king, 182, 191; industry, 291n52;
merchants, 28, 35; Ottoman conscription, 39–40; Ottoman district,
290n21, 291n45; Prince of, 52, 58–59;
protests, 46, 52, 58–59, 79, 156, 165,
169, 185, 191, 279, 292n74, 307n79,
307n83. *See also* Ajloun Revolt; Kura
Revolt
Ajloun Revolt, 52, 58–59
Ajlouni, Muhammad, 219
Algerian independence demonstrations,
83
Alon, Yoav, 47, 49, 58
Al Ma'abar, 13, 276
Al Tal, Raed, 123
Amman, *30*, 105, *121*, 122, *261*, *267*; cosmopolitan, 259–66; early Hashemite
period, 69–67; early protests, 72–74;
early settlements, 62–66, 68–69,
69; *Fedayeen*, 93; growth, 68, 74–77,
86–88, 119, 128, 231; militarization,
227–49; Oriental urbanity, 265–67;
protest repertoires, 79–80, 120–23,

124–26, 129; tourist guides, 95–96;
urban planning, 89–93, 123. *See
also* East Amman; Greater Amman
Comprehensive Development Plan;
Greater Amman Municipality;
Metropolitan Growth Plan; West
Amman
Amman, Jebal. *See* Jebal Amman
Amman Plan. *See* Metropolitan Growth
Plan
Anderson, Benedict, 251
Anderson, Betty, 52, 77
anti-austerity protests, 2, 8, 25, 98–99,
114–15, 121, 126, 185, 215, 223. *See also*
Habbit Huzayran protests; Habbit
Nisan protests; Habbit Tishreen
protests
anti-gas deal (with Israel) protests,
200, 206–7, 209–12, 214–15, 240, 279,
313
antinormalization (with Israel) Committee, 124–25, 135–36, 140, 145, 147, 160,
174, 176, 193–94, 200, 209, 220
antinormalization (with Israel) protests,
24, 124–25, 131–34, 135–36, 211. *See
also* Kalouti protests
Aqaba, *30*; anti-gas deal (with Israel)
protest, 207; development, 14, 76–77,
199, 257–59, 276–78; dockworker
protests, 154–55, 164, 199; Great Arab
Revolt, 42; *Habbit Nisan* protests,
111; neoliberal zone, 153–54, 199, 251,
255, 257–59, 276, 318n68; trucking
industry, 106–7; unemployed march,
206, 276–78. *See also* Aqaba Special

Economic Zone Authority; Shalaleh protests

Aqaba Special Economic Zone Authority (ASEZA), 154, 180, 257, 276–78

Arabiyyat, Abd al-Latif, 124

Arab Kingdom of Syria, 43

Arab Legion, 48, 54, 59, 69, 77–82, 103, 291n51, 294n118, 297n54

Arab nationalism, 32, 58, 60, 75–77, 80, 82–83, 122, 138, 253

Arab Solidarity Agreement, 80

Arab Spring. *See* Arab uprisings

Arab uprisings, 8, 101, 163, 165, 170, 174, 179, 182, 185, 193; analyses of, 7, 21–22, 67, 129–30, 150–53, 189; commemoration of, 16; Jordan, 150–92; connections to other protests, 268, 273–74; slogans 1, 165, 187, 190, 236–37, 240

Arar (poet), 52

ASEZA. *See* Aqaba Special Economic Zone Authority

Ashrafiya, Jebal. *See* Jebal Ashrafiya

Awadullah, Bassam, 210, 319n86

Awamleh, Mahmoud al-, 118

Ayn Square protests, 57, 110, 123, 310n121

Baghdad: learning protests in, 60, 76, 269; shoe thrown at George W. Bush in, 304n32; solidarity with protests in, 60

Baghdad Pact, 78; protests, 78–80, 269, 294n121

Bahrain, 169–70, 189, 236–37, 239, 273–74, 308

bakery protests, 196

Bakhit, Marouf al-, 164, 168, 170, 173, 179, 248

Balqa, 46–49, 167–68; Caucasians settled in, 32; Great Arab Revolt, 42, 44; resistance to Ottomans, 33, 39, 290n21. *See also* Adwan Revolt; Adwan tribal confederation; Bani Sakhr tribal confederation

Balqa Applied University, 167

baltajiyya, 140, 145–46, *146*, 148, 166, 168, 172–73, 202

Bandung Conference, 78

Bani Hamida tribal confederation, 3, 55; Ottoman revolts, 33; protests, 178–79; statement about corruption, 282

Bani Kinana protests, 197

Bani Sakhr tribal confederation, 55–56, 62, 166, 278, 292n78; Great Arab Revolt, 42; Ikhwan raids, 54; Ottoman revolts, 34, 39–40; protests, 3, 20, 35, 47, 56, 166–67, 178, 197; relations with Abdullah I, 44–45, 48–49, 51, 54, 70, 82. *See also* Adwan Revolt; Bani Sakhr Tribal Sons for Reform; Coalition of 36 Manifesto; Gaylani Revolt

Bani Sakhr Tribal Sons for Reform, 167

Bani Tamim revolts, 33

Baqa'a Camp, 86, 217, 234; protests, 131–32, 166, 174, 184, 199, 245

Baqoura and Ghumar protests, 224

batons at protests, 124, 173, 175, 178, 202

Battle of Karama. *See* Karama, Battle of

Bayat, Asef, 236

Baylouny, Anne Marie, 214

INDEX

Bedouin, 29, 35, 40, 43–45, 50, 58, 106, 266; defined, 31, 55, 99–100, 110; hardships, 54–55; military recruitment, 55–56, 81, 106–7; national identity, 98, 102, 175, 209, 253, 260; raids and revolts, 33, 37–39, 37, 40, 53–55, 66, 276; seasonal migration, 32; settlement, 32, 70; support for the king, 82. *See also* Adwan Revolt; Arab Legion; Gaylani Revolt

Beirut, 47, 76, 79, 93; learning protests in, 60, 76; militarization 228

Beit Ras protests, 197

blacklists, 125, 133–34, 303, 319n79

Black September, 24, 63, 112, 119, 122, 131, 227, 231, 234, 253; main discussion, 84–103. *See also* Fedayeen; Palestinian Liberation Organization

blockades at protests. *See* roadblocks at protests

Bouziane, Malika, 169

boycotts, 53, 60, 125, 132–34, 160, 310n142

Brand, Laurie, 44, 88, 102

Brenner, Neil, 13

Brizat, Ali, 3, 153, 161

Brown, Michael, 234

Bsheer, Rosie, 252

Burgan, Basel, 130, 197, 218, 220

Bustani, Hisham, 162, 201, 223, 275, 303n19

Cairo, 265; learning protests in, 76; Tahrir protests, 163, 171, 176, 236–37, 239, 242

Campaign Against So-Called Crimes of Honor protests, 222–23

Cantaloupe Gastro Pub, *261*, *267*

Caucasian refugees, 31, 35

censorship protests, 196

Chalcraft, John, 9

Charlie Hebdo protests, 242

Chenoweth, Erica, 6

Circassian refugees, 31, 35

citizenship protests, 196

Clark, Janine Astrid, 42, 88, 94, 157–58

Coalition of 36 manifesto, 166

Committee for the Revival of the Teachers' Professional Association, 156. *See also* teachers' protests

Communist Party. *See* Jordanian Communist Party

containment of protests, 234, 264, 247; defined, 244–47

coronavirus pandemic, 194; effect on protests, 247–48, 279

Corruption Dabke, 187–88, 209

countermanifesto, 159–60

counterprotests, 7, 12, 82, 145–46, 152, 165, 172–78, *175*, 181–83, 190. See also *baltajiyya*

Craig, Kyle, 238, 269

curfews, 78–79, 111, 115, 118–19, 208, 245–47, 275, 316

Cybercrimes Law, 208, 214, 218–19

Da'ajna protests, 178

Dabke. *See* Corruption Dabke

Dabouq, 18, 275, 282, 319n86

Dahabtuna protests, 167. *See also* students

Damascus, *30*, 46–47, 194, 265; affective ties to, 28–29, 32, 70; Hashemite interest in, 32, 43; learning protest in, 52, 60, 76; Ottoman administration, 35–36, 38–39; Syrian uprising, 165; trade with, 31, 35–36, 277

Dara'a, 52, 165

Darak Forces. *See* gendarmerie

Day Wage Labor Movement: emergence of 153–54; protests, 153–54, 160–61, 177, 199, 202, 205, 213–14, 258, 277. *See also* Brizat, Ali; Snayd, Muhammad

Deal of the Century protests, 200, 217

Dean, Mitchell, 108

Debruyne, Pascal, 67

Deir Abu Sa'eed protests, 109

Department of Lands and Surveys, 56–57

Desert Patrol, 55

Dhahabi, Muhammad al-, 179, 309n141

Dhiban, 256–57, 277; Happy Farm almond tree farm, 256; protests, 1, 110–11, 153–54, 161–62, 177, 185, 199, 206, 208, 213–14, 219, 280–81, *281*, 304n5, 307n83; unemployment, 153. *See also* Day Wage Labor Movement

dockworkers protests, 154–55, 164, 166, 180, 276, 305n13

dogs at protests, 124, 132

Doughan, Yazan, 50, 88, 168, 254

Druze Revolt, 39, 50–51

Earth Day protests, 196

East Amman, 92, 95–96, 120, 128, 134, 157, 169, 235 *261*. *See also* Amman

East Bank identity, 99–102. *See also* nativist nationalism

Economic Consultative Council, 255

Economic Dialogue Committee, 170

Egypt, *30*, 43, 297n48, 313n52; counter-coup massacre, 194, 223; migrant workers from, 88, 155; Muslim Brotherhood, 293n103; protests, 104, 237; relations with, 80–85; ties with, 28, 70; uprising, 8, 163–64. *See also* Cairo

Egyptian embassy protests, 164, 242

elections, 53, 77, 79, 83, 110, 112–14, 134; laws, 124–25, 160, 170, 172, 179; protests, 160, 172, 179; student, 167, 179, 310, 316

Elkhairy, Nidal, 202–23, *203*, cover art

encampments. *See* tents and encampments

enclosures of protest spaces, 234, *241*, 315n11; defined, 239–42

Ensour, Abdullah, 183–84, 197

erasure of protests, *238*, 315n11; defined, 235–39

ethnography of place, 127–48; defined, 127–29

eventful moments, 21, 130, 165, 193, 283; defined, 149–51

exclusions from protest spaces, 234, 240, 242–44; defined 242–43, 315n11

exposures of protest spaces, 315n11; defined, 234–35

360 INDEX

Facebook, 158, 208; harassment for posts, 218; use by loyalists, 173; use for protests, 162, 170–71, 176, 196, 199, 207–8, 214, 219, 242–43

Falahat, Abd al-Hadi, 124

Farouk, King, 76

Fayiz, Fares al-, 3

Fayiz, Faysal al-, 161

Fayiz, Hind al-, 19, 130

Fayiz, Mithqal al-, 45, 47, 54, 60, 70

Faysal, Toujan, 217, 314n65

Faysal I (king of Iraq), 32, 43, 76

Faysal II (king of Iraq), 60

Fawaz, Mona, 228

Fedayeen, 85–87, 93–94, 97, 101–3, 228

Ferguson, Missouri, 234

Fifth Circle, 262; protests, 197, 221

Firas Circle, *71*, *261*; protests, 187

fires set at protests, 77–79, 109–11, 119, 156, 177, 184, 185

Foucault, Michel, 127

Fourth Circle, 126, *229*, *261*; art about *Habbit Huzayran* protests at, 202, *203*, 204, cover; "Fourth Circle" parking lot protests, 211–12, 243–44, 246–47, *247*, *261*; protests, 147, 154, 163–65, 173, 181–82, 184, 197, 199–200, 202, *203*, 204–5, 210–11, 213, 217, 219, 242, 275, 279; restricting access to, 229, *229*, 235, 240, 242–44, 246–47, *247*; *The Fourth Circle* news show, 219; underpasses, 232–33, *233*. *See also* Prime Ministry

Freedom Flotilla demonstration, 125, 210

Freedom Square, 248

Freedom4EmadHajjaj hashtag. *See* Hajjaj, Emad

French embassy protests, 202, 242

Free Tafileh Movement, 168, 180

Fridays for the Future marches, 196

Furayhat family, 52

GAM. *See* Greater Amman Municipality

Gardens Street protest, 243

Gaylani Revolt, 60

GCC. *See* Gulf Cooperation Council

gendarmerie, 15, 197–98, 211, 217, 219, 225, 240, 242–43; art critical of, 2024, *203*, cover; during the uprising, 155–56, 165, 167, 170–78, 180–81, 184; 195; formation of, 137; Kalouti protest behavior, 137, 139–46, *141*, *142*, *146*, 148, 200, 204; Ottoman period, 38; sent to Bahrain, 274–75; tearing down tents, 213–5; training, 271

General Intelligence Directorate (*mukhabarat*), 92, 103, 132, 159, 172, 179, 218, 262–63, 270, 298n95; creation of, 87; interrogation by, 220

Ghannam, Farha, 127

Gharaybeh, Mothanna, 220

Ghor. See Jordan River Valley

Ghor Safi protests, 132

Glubb, John Bagot, 55, 80; demonstrations against, 80

Graeber, David, 212, 224

graffiti, 208, 237–39, *238*

Grand Husseini Mosque, 70, *71*, 72, 90, *261*, 265; atmosphere of protests at 127–28, 153, 207; during the uprising,

162–65, 174–75, *175*, 181, 183–86;
Islamist preference for protesting at,
204–5, *205*, 232; protests, 70, 74–75,
78–79, 81, 83, 85, 92, 106, 109–10,
115–16, *116*, 120–21, 123, 132, 135, 137,
147–48, 152, 199–200, 202, 210, 221,
231, 280; spatial constraints,
249
Great Arab Revolt, 8, 133, 188, 191, 254–55,
276; commemoration, 18–19, 72, *73*;
main discussion, 41–43, 49
Greater Amman Comprehensive Development Plan, 122
Greater Amman Municipality (GAM),
179, 257, 262
Greater Syria, 10, 32, 35–36, 39, 43, 68,
159, 187, 268, 278; affective ties to, 28,
64, 165; division of, 42
Gregory, Derek, 208, 212
Gubser, Peter, 61
Gulf Cooperation Council (GCC), 274
Gulf War protests, 117–18

Habashneh, Nima, 196
Habbit Huzayran protests, 67, 194, 199,
202, 205, 211, 223, 243, 253–54, 256,
275; art about, 202–4, *203*, cover;
main discussion, 2–3, *3*, 6, 18
Habbit Nisan protests, 2, 18, 101, 163, 183,
185, 199, 223, 253; impact and legacy,
112–13, 117, 123, 126, 131; main discussion, 106–11; thirtieth anniversary,
170
Habbit Ramadan protests. *See* Habbit
Huzayran protests

Habbit Tishreen protests, 2, 191, 193, 212,
240, 319n86; main discussion, 183–87
Hadid tribesmen battle, 54
Hajaya protests, 178
Hajjaj, Emad, 218
Hamzah bin Hussein, Prince, 159, 182,
188, 190–91, 319n86
Harvey, David: militarization of Paris,
227; neoliberalism defined, 107–8
Hashemite Plaza, 123, 241, *242*, *261*; Free-
dom Square in, 248
Hashemite University protests, 196
Hashimi Camp, 85
Hattar, Nahed, 158, 160, 207, 305n17,
308n101, 309n141
Haussmann, George-Eugène, 66, 227, 234
Hatuka, Tali, 65–66
Hayy Tafayleh, 111, *261*, 204, 254;
baltajiyya from, 168; Corruption
Dabke, 187; mock trial, 169; protests,
111, 115, 157, 168–69, 184, 187, 261
Hegazi, Sarah, 239, 313n52
Helfont, Tally and Samuel, 175
Hiber (7iber), 144, 169
Hijaz, 64
Hijaz Railway, *30*, 39–40, 45, 55, 63, 66,
68–69; raids, 36–37, *37*; station in
Amman, 69; suspension of service,
107
Hirak groups: emergence, 167–69;
post-uprising period, 195, 200–201,
205–6, 208, 219, 243–44, 256, 282;
protests during uprising period,
164, 174, 177–80, 183, 188, 193; youth
characteristics, 167–68

362 INDEX

Hmouz, Rana, 219
Homeland's Call loyalist demonstration, 172
honor killing protests, 2, 10, 78, 94, 197, 208, 222–23
hotel bombings demonstrations, 228
Humman, 31
Hussein, Jebal. *See* Jebal Hussein
Hussein bin Abdullah II, Crown Prince, 159, 316n8
Hussein bin Ali, Sharif, 41–43
Hussein bin Talal, King, 316n8; ascent to the throne, 76; aspirations for larger domain, 15, 32, 43; death, 118, 159, 182; *Fedayeen* and Black September, 83–93; first decade of rule, 77–83; Gulf War, 117–18; Jordanization, 97–98, 105; neoliberalism, 108, 152, 185, 255; peace with Israel, 117; response to protests, 111–14
Hussein Camp, *71*, 75, 85, *261*
Hourani, Najib, 92
Hussayniya protests, 109, 111, 277
Huwaytat tribal confederation, 42, 106

Ibn Saud, 54
identity: East Bank, 99–102; Palestinian, 102. *See also* nativist nationalism
Ikhwan raids, 53–54
IMF. *See* International Monetary Fund
infrastructure, 5, 36–37, 64–66, 70, 76, 89, 170, 226, 315n7; Amman, 94–95, 107, 111, 120, 153, 228, 232–33, 249, 256, 259, 266; communication, 32, 36, 39; negative effects on Bedouin,

39; pipeline, 56, 58, 66; port, 76, 106, 154–55, 166, 180, 256–57, 276, 280, 305n13; sabotage of, 7, 13, 24, 36, 53, 58, 73, 81, 201; 315; as a technique of power, 36, 50–51, 66, 70. *See also* Hijaz Railway
Interior Circle, 170, *261*; protests, 170, 172, 181–84, 212, 275; restricting access to, 240. *See also* Habbit Tishreen protests; March 24 Youth
International Monetary Fund (IMF), 18, 98, 106–8, 113–14, 126, 153, 163, 183–84, 204, 224, 255–56, 317n18. *See also* anti-austerity protests; Habbit Huzayran protests; Habbit Nisan protests; Habbit Tishreen protests
International Women's Day protests, 196
internet, 196, 207–8, 218. See *also* Cybercrimes Law; Facebook; Twitter; YouTube
Intifada, 8, 98; solidarity protests, 98, 105, 110, 118, 122, 129, 131–35, 152, 206, 213, 234
Iran: Baghdad Pact, 78; impact of Iran-Iraq war, 105; Shi'i Crescent spatial imaginary, 15, 273, 275
Iraq, 15, *30*, 117, 159, 179, 273; affective ties to, 28, 76; Al-Qaeda in, 228; challenges to monarchy 60, 76; economic impact of war, 105–6, 111; Hashemite confederation, 83–84; mandate period, 32, 35, 42–43; overthrow of monarchy, 83–84; Petroleum Company, 56; protests in, 60, 75–76, 165; protests in solidarity with, 111, 115,

117–19, 121–22, 125, 152, 159, 195, 209; refugees, 265, 268–70; World War II, 59–60. *See also* Baghdad; Baghdad Pact; Gaylani Revolt

Irban protests, 178

Irbid, *30*, 69, 74; *Fedayeen* control, 87; protests, 46–47, 77, 84–85, 104–5, 109, 111–12, 118, 132, 166–70, 180, 184, 197, 199–200, 206–7, 218–19, 293n99, 295n130, 307n83; strikes, 51, 58; unemployed march, 279. See *also* Irbid Popular Movement; Kura Revolt; Yarmouk University

Irbid Popular Movement, 168

Irshaydat, Nabih, 295n130

Islamic Action Front party: attacks against, 178, 181; boycott of first uprising protests, 162; election boycott, 160, 310n142; protests, 124; 136–37, 140,159, 162–64, 169, 183, 202, 204, 216, 232, 246; refusal to join cabinet, 170. *See also* Muslim Brotherhood

Israel, 124, 271–73, 275–76, 306n36; 1948 war, 74; 1967 war, 85; embassy, 129, 135–36, 143, 176, 200, 221, *261*; *Fedayeen* attacks, 86; peace treaty, 114, 117, 124–25, 134, 160; protests against, 24, 85, 86, *86*, 104, 109, 117, 119, 121, 124–25, 171, 174, 195, 198, 200, 211, 221, 224, 312n47; trade fair protests, 207, 209. *See also* anti-gas deal (with Israel) protests; antinormalization protests; blacklists; Kalouti protests; Operation Cast Lead protests; Operation

Defensive Shield protests; Operation Protective Edge protests

Issawi, Youssef, 280

Jafr protests, 109

Jayeen protests, 161–63, 169, 171–73, 220

Jebal Amman, *71*, 79, 92, 120, 244, *261*, 266, *267*; political graffiti, 238, *238*. *See also* Prime Ministry; Rainbow Street; Zahran Street

Jebal Ashrafiya, *71*, *261*, 267

Jebal Druze, *30*, 49

Jebal Hussein, *71*, 75, *261*; protests, 184, 187. *See also* Firas Circle

Jebal Jofa, *71*

Jebal Qala, *71*, 265

Jebal Taj, *71*

Jebal Webdeh, *71*, 92, 120, 244, *261*, 266; political art, 239

Jerash, 90; protests, 85, 111, 167, 169, 178, 185, 199, 206, 307n83

Jerusalem, *30*, 36, 48, 55, 85, 240, 254, 265; King Abdullah I assassination in, 76; protests, 78–79, 83–85, 131, 292n62, 297n54

JIPTC. *See* Jordan International Police Training Center

Jordan Cement Industrial Workers strike, 85

Jordan Friends of the Environment protests, 197

Jordan Gate Towers, *261*, 262, 278, *279*

Jordanian Armed Forces, 103, 111, 171, 262, 272. *See also* Mawared

364 INDEX

Jordanian Communist Party, 60, 79, 101, 136, 138

Jordanian Democratic Popular Unity Party, 136, 138, 145, 160, 162, 218, 237

Jordan International Police Training Center (JIPTC), 271–72

Jordanization, 24, 102–9, 111–13, 115, 117, 119, 121, 123, 125–26, 253; main discussion, 97–103

Jordan River Valley, *30*, 32, 35, 109, 132, 255; *Fedayeen* control of, 87

Jordan University. *See* University of Jordan

Jordan University of Science and Technology (JUST), 105; protests 105, 109

JUST. *See* Jordan University of Science and Technology

Kabariti, Abd al-Karim, 114–15

KADDB. *See* King Abdullah II Design and Development Bureau

Kalouti Group, 176

Kalouti Mosque, 128, *261*

Kalouti protests, 24, 126, 152, 176, 194, 199–200, 204, 209, 212–13, 240, 242; main discussion, 128–48, *139*, *141*, *142*, *146*; restricting access with fence, 240. *See also* Kalouti Group

Kanna, Ahmad, 252

Karak, *30*, 34, 60, 100–101, 168, 170, 277, 290n1, 290n24, 290n26, 291n45, 292n59, 294n114, 294n122, 295n130; affective ties, 28; mandate-period revolts, 46–47; opposition to the Organic Law, 52; Ottoman revolts,

34–37, 39–42; protests, 1, 57, 60–61, 70, 110–12, 114–15, 122, 132, 160–61, 164, 168–69, 178, 180, 185, 195, 199, 206–7, 247, 275, 277, 307n83; shoe protests, 183; teachers strike, 156, 160. *See also* Karak Revolt

Karak Revolt, 24; main discussion, 39–42

Karama, Battle of, 86, 171

Karama protests, 174

Kasasbeh, Mu'ath, 275

KASOTC. *See* King Abdullah II Special Operations Training Center

Khalaf, Amal, 236

Khalaldeh, Khaled, 220, 308n101, 309n141

Khalayla protests, 167

Khalayla Youth Movement protests, 167

Khasawneh, Awn al-, 179–80, 182

Khuzai, Rashid al-, 52

Kidman, Nicole, 166

King Abdulla I bin Hussein. *See* Abdullah I bin Hussein, Emir and King

King Abdulla II bin Hussein. *See* Abdullah II bin Hussein, King

King Abdullah II Design and Development Bureau (KADDB), 272

King Abdullah II Special Operations Training Center (KASOTC), 270–71

King Faysal Street, *71*, 72–74, *73*, 77–78, 81, 92, 123, *261*

King Faysal Plaza. *See* King Faysal Street

King Hussein. *See* Hussein bin Talal, King

King Hussein Gardens, 172, 196, 254, 266

Kura, 170. *See also* Kura Revolt

Kura Revolt, 46–7, 292n75

Kurdi, Walid, 174, 210

Kuwait: protests, 165, 239, 273; Gulf War, 117, 121, 273; Safat Plaza closure, 239

Lajjun, 31

Lambert, Léopold, 227, 316n38

land reform, 56–7, 179

landlords; 214, 294n115, 296n41; protests against, 180; protests by, 169, 180–81

Lebanon, *30*, 101, 199, 262, 273, 297n48; mandate period, 42, 54, 101; protests, 165

Lefebvre, Henri, 64, 67, 259

Lenner, Katharina, 169

Lèse-majesté, 2, 118

Limitless Towers, *261*, 278

Ma'an, 29, *30*, 39–40, 58, 81, 157, 161, 168, 170, 178, 180, 185, 195, 219, 247, 260, 277, 280; Abdullah's arrival, 15, 42–44; curfews, 111, 118–19; locust invasion of, 54; Osama Bin Laden demonstrations, 119; protests, 107, 109, 111–12, 115, 118–19, 124, 132–33, 152, 206; *Shamiyya* and *Hijaziyya* neighborhoods, 43; transit hub, 51, 70; transport industry, 105–7

Ma'anash protests, 199, 205, 211, 243–44

Ma'ani, Omar, 179, 260

Madaba, *30*, 35, 55, 153; affective ties, 28; protests, 4, 39, 111, 206, 214, 278

Madaba Street police station, 234. *See also* Wihdat Camp

Madain, Mathew, 42

Madanat, Isa, 79, 295n130

Mafraq, *30*; protests, 167, 178, 180, 197, 279, 307

Majali, Bandar, 40

Majali, Habis, 40, 81, 100, 277, 291n51

Majali, Hazza, 76, 79

Majali, Muhammad, 34

Majali, Qadr, 39

Majali, Rafifan, 40

Majali, Salih, 39

Majali family, 34, 41, 44, 79, 115, 277; Palestinian heritage, 34, 100101

manifestos, 158–60, 166, 277, 282. *See also* Coalition of 36 manifesto; veterans' manifesto

manqal protest, 176

Mansour, Hamzeh, 140, 181

March 24 Youth protest, 177, 181, 183, 194, 208, 212–13, 226, 235, 240; main discussion, 170–73

Marj al-Hamam, 132

Marshall, Shana, 271–72

Martínez, José Ciro, 196

Masha'aleh, Sabri, 214, 219

Masri, Taher, 132, 170

Massey, Doreen, 248

material obstacles to protest: main discussion, 230–48. *See also* containment of protests; enclosures of protest spaces; erasures of protests; exclusions from protest spaces; exposures of protests

Mawared, 262, 264, 270, 272

Mawtini, 133, 142–43, 171, 209

Mazar protests, 185

McAdam, Doug, 8, 289n46

366 INDEX

Mecca, 31, 85
Medina, 36, 85
Menoret, Pascal, 93
Metropolitan Growth Plan, 260.
militarization: defined, 226–30
Ministry of Education protests, 115
Ministry of Energy and Mineral Resources protests, 200, *261*. *See also* anti-gas deal (with Israel) protests
Ministry of Supply, 103, 108
Ministry of the Interior, 78, 137, 216, 309n137; protests, 76, 170, 176. *See also* Interior Circle
Ministry of Transportation protests, 183
Mish Sakitin protests,199, 206, 211
Mitchel, Andrew Park, 70, 72
Mitchell, Don, 13, 66, 227
Mleih protests, 214
Moabite Stone destruction, 33
Mobile Force, 53
mock trials at protests, 169, 209–10; anti-gas deal (with Israel), 210; Hayy Tafayleh, 169
Moore, Pete W., 268, 274
Moss, Dana M., 116, 178, 205
Muasher, Marwan, 207
Muhammad Ali invasion, 34
mukhabarat. See General Intelligence Directorate
Mulki, Hani, 199, 214
Municipal Complex, 123–25, 128, *261*; protests, 175–76, 200, 202, 207, 249
Municipal Council of Amman, 68
Munif, Abd al-Rahman, 70, 74, 92
Mufti, Sa'id al-, 296

Muslim Brotherhood, 103, 162; Black September, 103; calls for the fall of the regime, 184; Egyptian, 237; fear of, 193; involvement in Hirak groups, 169, 174, 183; parade guards, 204–5, *205*; protests, 78, 81, 135–38, 140, 159, 163–64, 172, 175, 178, 181, 183–84, 202, 216, 232, 293, 300, 309; split of, 193–94. *See also* Islamic Action Front party
Mustada protests, 111

Nabulsi, Suleiman, 60, 61, 77, 80–82, 296n44
Nakba protests, 174
Nakib, Farah al-, 239, 252–53, 265
Naksa protests, 174
Naqab protests, 109
Nasser, Gamal Abdul, 77, 80, 82–85, 87, 231, 269
Nasser, Kamel, 220
National Committee of Retired Servicemen, 158–60. *See also* veterans' manifesto
national dialogue, 131, 215, 282; Committee, 170, 173
National Electric Power Company (NEPCO), *261*; protests, 200. *See also* anti-gas deal (with Israel) protests
nationalism. *See* Arab nationalism; nativist nationalism
National Resources Investment and Development Corporation. *See* Mawared
nativist nationalism, 12, 20, 25, 99, 155,

159–60, 168, 189, 191, 207, 209, 278, 305n17, 306n141, 308n101; defined, 101; early articulation of, 48. *See also* Hattar, Nahed

Navickas, Katrina, 67

neoliberalism, 3, 26, 67, 98, 114, 126, 159, 199, 256; defined, 107–8. *See also* anti-austerity protests

New Camp. *See* Wihdat Camp

nontransgressive protests: defined, 143

nuclear energy protests, 130, 197, 218

Obaydat, Ahmad, 132, 159–60

Occupy Wall Street, 268; solidarity protests, 179

officers' revolt, 103–4

Omar bin Abd al-Aziz Street, 135

Ong, Ayhwa, 257

Operation Cast Lead protests, 144

Operation Defensive Shield protests, 133

Operation Protective Edge protests, 199

Organic Law protests, 51–53, 63, 70

Ottoman Empire, 31–41. *See also* Karak Revolt; Kura Revolt; Shoubak Revolt

Palestine, 15, 28, *30*, 32, 35, 42–45, 47–48, 52, 54, 58–59, 61, 70, 99; identity in Jordan, 100, 102, 159; partition of, 74–75, 85; protests in, 77; solidarity protests, 104, 109, 121, 133, 174, 176, 195, 198–99, 240–41, 243. *See also* antinormalization (with Israel) protests; anti-gas deal (with Israel) protests; Black September; Kalouti protests; Palestinian Liberation

Organization; Palestinian Revolts; Palestine solidarity protests; Right of Return march; Shaykh Jarra protests

Palestinian Liberation Organization, 85, 87–88, 103, 105, 171

Palestinian refugees, 10, 61–62, 74–75, 85–86; protests, 75, 83. *See also* Baqa'a Camp; Hashimi Camp; Hussein Camp; Widhat Camp; Zarqa Camp

Palestinian Revolts, 58; solidarity protests, 58, 73

Palestinians from Gaza protests, 196

Palestinian solidarity protests, 58, 61, 77, 105–6, 221–22; contemporary overview, 131–34. *See also* anti-normalization (with Israel) protests; anti-gas deal (with Israel) protests; Kalouti protests; Operation Cast Lead protests; Operation Defensive Shield protests; Operation Protective Edge protests; Palestinian Revolts; Right of Return march; Shaykh Jarra protests

pandemic. *See* coronavirus pandemic

Parker, Christopher, 67, 254–55

Parliament, 47, 70, 77, 79–80, 83–84, 92, 124, 126, 130, 160, *261*; closing space for protest at, 241; opposition dominated, 112–14; protests at, 2, 125, 132, 147, 154, 161, 163–64, 180–81, 183, 200, 206, 217, 221–22, 276, 279

Pearl Roundabout protests, 235–37; 274

Penal Code, 124; Article 164, 217, 309n130; Article 195, 2; Article 308, 182

368 INDEX

people's court. *See* mock trials at protests

petitions, 36, 39–40, 45, 47, 52, 222

phosphate workers' protests, 174, 181, 197

Popular Arab Jordanian Committee for Resisting Submission and Normalization, 132. *See also* antinormalization (with Israel) protests; Kalouti protests

Popular Front for the Liberation of Palestine, 87, 304n23

Portsmouth Treaty protests, 75

Pratt, Nicola, 78

Prime Ministry, *161*; protests at, 60, 70, 126, 147, 154, 163, 197, 210, 232–33, 244. *See also* Fourth Circle

Professional Associations Complex, 103–4; protests, 110–11, 123–25, 131–33, 154, 210–11. *See also* Union of Professional Associations

Progressive Democratic Jordanian Tendency, 160–61

property owner protests, 57, 262–63

protests: defined, 6–9; effects of the built environment on, 66–68, 231–34; effects of urban sprawl on, 231–32; outcome-oriented analyses of, 6–7; terms in Arabic, 2, 8; traveling for, 205–7; uprising analyses, 150–52; that work for the regime, 222–24. *See also* eventful moments; material obstacles to protest; routine protests

Public Gatherings Law, 114, 125, 170, 216–17

Public Security Directorate, 83, 137, 156,

Qasimi, Jamal al-Din al-, 68

QIZs. *See* Qualified Industrial Zones

Qualified Industrial Zones (QIZs), 15, 245; protests, 246. *See also* Aqaba Special Economic Zone Authority; King Abdullah II Design and Development Bureau

Queen Alia Airport, 166

Queen Noor Street protests, 243. *See also* Fourth Circle protests

Queen Rania. *See* Rania, Queen

Rabia, 134

Raghadan Palace 70, 82, *261*; protests, 184

Ragheb, Ali Abu, 217, 314n65

Rahaba protests, 46

Rainbow Street, 239, *261*, 313; protests, 182

Ramtha, 165

Rania, Queen, 159, 232; birthday party, 277; criticism of, 4, 166, 187, 191, 277; Palestinian solidarity march, 221–22

Ras al-Ayn, 63, 68, 200, 244

Razzaz, Omar, 199

refugees, 10–11, 45, 74, 122, 214; Caucasian, 31, 35; Circassian, 31, 35; Druze, 50; in early Amman, 10, 35, 62, 88, 92; Iraqi, 265; Lebanese, 88; Syrian, 224, 269, 274; Turkomen, 31, 35. *See also* Baqa'a Camp; Hashimi Camp; Hussein Camp; Palestinian refugees; Widhat Camp; Zarqa Camp

repertoires, 7–9, 67, 150; for protests, 4–5, 23–25, 32, 36, 39, 47, 61, 71, 73, 79, 84, 109, 111, 154, 158, 201–15, 280; for

INDEX 369

repression, 13, 113, 195, 215–22; rules of, 130; spatial, 153

Rifa'i, Samir, 84, 101, 163

Rifa'i, Zayd, 101, 103, 109, 112, 161, 163–64, 183

Rifa'i family: branches in Lebanon and Syria, 101; Palestinian heritage

Right of Return march, 131–32, 174

Right of Return protest quilt, 209

roadblocks at protests: Egypt's uprising, 243; by police, *139*, 156, 175, *175*, 184, 197–98, 201–2, 207, 242–43, 244, *245*; by protesters, 4, 48, 51, 109, 111, 114, 132, 143, 166–67, 171, 184–85, 197, 215, 228, 247, 275

Robins, Philip, 87

Rogan, Eugene, 34, 40

routine protests, 4, *116*; defined, 129–31; main analysis, 146–49. *See also* Kalouti protests

Royal Court, 25, 83, 118, 128; protests, 154, 168, 184, 206, 213, 219, 222, 241, 251, 275, 280, *281*, 283

Royal Village, 278

Ryan, Curtis, 101, 110, 301n40, 311n3, 312n22

Sa'ad, Kahiri, 173

Sahab protests, 178

Salhoub protests, 178

Saifi, Fahmi, 264

salafi protests, 101, 119, 173

Salman, Muhammad bin, 217

Salt, *30*, 36, 47, 62, 69–70; affective ties, 28, 35; Great Arab Revolt, 42, 44;

Ottoman control, 39, 41, 290n21, 291n45; Ottoman revolt, 33; protests, 1, 51–52, 57, 85–86, 110–11, 115, 156, 160–61, 167, 169, 180, 184, 215; resistance to Abdullah I, 62. *See also* Ayn Square

Salt Preparatory School protests, 294

Sami Pasha, 39–40

Samuel, Herbert, 45

Saudi Arabia, 23, *30*, 76, 252–53; 273; Bedouin migration, 35; detained Jordanians, 276; intervention in Bahrain, 170, 274; pilgrimage, 106; regional security network, 15, 273–75; Yemen war, 83. *See also* Arab Solidarity Agreement; Ikhwan militias; Mecca; Medina

Save the Homeland demonstration, 183

Schielke, Samuli, 237

Sewell, William, 231, 289n46

Shakir, Zayd bin, 103

Shalaleh protests, 155, 257, 276

Shami, Seteney, 76

Sharayiri, Ali Khulqi, 46, 292n75

Shaykh Jarra protests, 240–41

Shmeisani, 91–92, 95, 120, 123, 131, 244, *261*, 299n108

shoe protest. *See* Karak

Shoubak, *30*; affective ties, 28; protests, 109, 168–69, 307n83. *See also* Shoubak Revolt

Shoubak Revolt, 37–39

Shryock, Andrew, 49

Shubaylat, Layth al-, 118, 136, 302

Shunaykat, Mustafa, 220

370 INDEX

Shurayda, Khulayb al-, 46–47
Shi'i Crescent spatial imaginary, 15, 273, 275
Sisi, Abd al-Fattah al-, 236
Snayd, Muhammad, 153–54, 161, 177, 214, 219, 304, 309. *See also* Day Wage Labor Movement
social contract, 2, 10, 15, 61–62, 93–94, 152, 159, 182, 186, 188
SOFEX. *See* Special Operations Forces Exhibition and Conference
Soss, Joe, 20
spatial imaginary, 32–33, 35; colonial, 42, 51, 57, 89–93; competing, 41–42, 57–58; defined, 28–29; East Bank, 64, 88; national, 59, 74–75, 88
Special Operations Forces Exhibition and Conference (SOFEX), 272
Sports City Complex, 222, *261*
students, 133, 300n19, 315n35; activism, 300n16; *Dahabtuna* protests, 167; protests, 52, 60–61, 74, 76, 78, 83–84, 87, 98, 104–5, 109–10, 135, 164, 245–46; support for teachers strike, 156; violence on campuses, 15658, 167, 174. *See also* Hashemite University protests; Salt Preparatory School protests; University of Jordan; Yarmouk University protests
Sultan Pasha Atrash. *See* Atrash, Sultan Pasha
Sumayya Street, 234. *See also* Wihdat Camp
Syria, *30*, 43, 81, 84–85, 268, 273–74; activist divisions over, 194; Bedouin

migration into, 35; uprising, 165, 169, 188, 193. *See also* Arab Solidarity Agreement; Daraa; Druze Revolt; Greater Syria; United Arab Republic

Tabanja, Ahmed, 219
Tabarbour bus terminal, 263
Tafileh, *30*, 70, 118, 294n114, 302n58; 307n83; affective ties, 28; curfews, 247; early Hashemite revolts, 46; electoral district, 310n144; Great Arab Revolt, 42; king's motorcade incident, 177; Ottoman revolt, 40; protests, 58, 110–11, 115, 132, 168–69, 180–83, 185, 195, 206, 247, 277; women's protest, 181. *See also* Free Tafileh Movement
Taj Lifestyle Center, *261*, 262; protests, 233
Talal bin Abdullah I, King, 76
Tall, Wasfi al-, 84, 87
Tarawneh, Fayez, 182–83, 242–43
Tarawneh, Husayn al-, 52
Tarawneh, Naseem, 210, 248
Tarrow, Sidney, 8, 130
taxes, 1, 32, 45–46, 51, 54, 194, 199, 256; protests, 1, 5, 31, 33–35, 3739, 45–47, 49, 54, 162, 194–95, 199, 272. *See also* Habbit Huzayran protests
Taybeh protests, 109, 184
teachers' protests, 6, 76, 117, 135, 156, 160–61, 164, 169, 185, 197–98
tear gas at protests, 115, 124, 144, 157, 178, 180, 183, 184, 197, 230, 297n54
Tell, Tariq, 41–42, 155, 158–60, 166

Tell, Wahbi al-, 52

Tell, Wasfi al-. *See* Tall, Wasfi al-

temporality: defined, 21–22; life-cycle analyses, 21, 152; pacing, 22; of uprising protests, 182, 185–92

tents and encampments at protests, 133, 144–45, 154, 167, 171–73, 177, 179–80, 183–85, 194–95, 199, 201, 208, 224–26, 235, 240, 243, 277, 280; main discussion, 212–15

Terrorism Law, Prevention of, 217–18

Thompson, E.P., 16

Tilly, Charles, 8, 206

transgressive protests: defined, 143

Tribal Control Board, 55

tribes, 54–55; anger over loss of land, 166–67; basic affiliation, 29, 31; identity, 99–102; violence among, 156–58; weakening authority, 41, 259

Tripp, Charles, 208–9

Trouillot, Michel-Rolph, 16–17

Trump, Donald, 275

Trump, Ivanka, 166

Tuqan, Ahmad, 87, 298n92

Turkomen refugees, 31, 30, 35

Tuwal, Salameh al-, 296

Twitter, 158, 199, 207

unemployed protests, 18–19, 168, 180; marches to Amman, 206, 219, 276–81

Union of Professional Associations: general strike, 1, 185; protests, 110, 123–24, 131–32, 136, 162, 164, 179, 185, 195, 201, 210, 216, 287n5. *See*

also Professional Associations Complex

United Arab Republic, 83

United States, 98, 117; embassy, 120, 221, 261; foreign aid, 81; military assistance, 269–70; protests against, 87, 118, 120, 221, 131, 176, 179, 217–18

Unity party. *See* Jordanian Democratic Popular Unity Party

University of Jordan, 83, 181; protests, 84, 104, 109, 246

Urban Planning Ordinance, 72

veterans' manifesto, 158–60, 277, 282, 306n38

virtual spaces for protest, 207–8

Wadi Musa, 30, 42; protests, 109; revolts, 50–51

Wahhabi raids. *See* Ikhwan raids

water cannons at protests, 124, 132, 144

water scarcity protests, 196–97, 213–15

Webdeh, Jebal, *see* Jebal Webdeh

Wedeen, Lisa: legitimacy defined, 188; neoliberalism defined, 108

West Amman, 92, 95–96, 120, 121, 128–29, 134, 157, 179, 235, 253, 261; spatial imaginary, 230. *See also* Amman

WhatsApp, 219

Wihdat Camp, 75, 261; *Fedayeen*, 85; protests, 83, 85, 90, 199, 228, 234, 245, 261, 298, 315n14. *See also* Madaba Street police station; Sumayya Street

INDEX

Wikileaks, 176
Winegar, Jessica, 237

Yarmouk, 109–10; protests, 104, 110, 167, 214. *See also* Yarmouk University protests
Yarmouk University protests, 104–5, 109–10, 167, 214, 300n18
Yellow Vest solidarity protests, 269
Yemen, 274; protests over Jordanian intervention in, 83, 269
YouTube, 170, 173, 312n44
Young Turk Revolution, 39

Zabn protests, 56
Zahran Street, 120, 126, 197, 201, 221, 232, 240, 244, *261*, 278–79; renovations, 232–33. *See also* Fifth Circle; Fourth Circle; Prime Ministry
Zarqa, 53, 74, 82, 103, 112, 166–67, 173, 200, 207. *See also* officers' protest
Zarqa Camp, 74
Zayadin, Yaqoub, 60, 295n130
Zayed, Muhammad bin, 218
Zaytouna University, 167
Zawahra protests, 167

Stanford Studies in Middle Eastern
and Islamic Societies and Cultures

Joel Beinin and Laleh Khalili, editors

EDITORIAL BOARD
*Asef Bayat, Marilyn Booth, Laurie Brand, Timothy Mitchell, Jillian Schwedler,
Rebecca L. Stein, Max Weiss*

Media of the Masses: Cassette Culture in Modern Egypt   2022
ANDREW SIMON

States of Subsistence: The Politics of Bread in Contemporary Jordan   2022
JOSÉ CIRO MARTÍNEZ

Between Dreams and Ghosts: Indian Migration and Middle Eastern Oil   2021
ANDREA WRIGHT

Bread and Freedom: Egypt's Revolutionary Situation   2021
MONA EL-GHOBASHY

Paradoxes of Care: Children and Global Medical Aid in Egypt   2021
RANIA KASSAB SWEIS

*The Politics of Art: Dissent and Cultural Diplomacy in Lebanon, Palestine,
and Jordan*   2021
HANAN TOUKAN

The Paranoid Style in American Diplomacy: Oil and Arab Nationalism in Iraq   2021
BRANDON WOLFE-HUNNICUTT

Dear Palestine: A Social History of the 1948 War   2021
SHAY HAZKANI

A Critical Political Economy of the Middle East and North Africa   2021
JOEL BEININ, BASSAM HADDAD, and SHERENE SEIKALY, editors

Between Muslims: Religious Difference in Iraqi Kurdistan   2020
J. ANDREW BUSH

Showpiece City: How Architecture Made Dubai   2020
TODD REISZ

Archive Wars: The Politics of History in Saudi Arabia   2020
ROSIE BSHEER

The Optimist: A Social Biography of Tawfiq Zayyad   2020
TAMIR SOREK

Graveyard of Clerics: Everyday Activism in Saudi Arabia   2020
PASCAL MENORET

Cleft Capitalism: The Social Origins of Failed Market Making in Egypt   2020
AMR ADLY

The Universal Enemy: Jihad, Empire, and the Challenge of Solidarity   2019
DARRYL LI

Waste Siege: The Life of Infrastructure in Palestine   2019
SOPHIA STAMATOPOULOU-ROBBINS

Heritage and the Cultural Struggle for Palestine   2019
CHIARA DE CESARI

Banking on the State: The Financial Foundations of Lebanon   2019
HICHAM SAFIEDDINE

Familiar Futures: Time, Selfhood, and Sovereignty in Iraq   2019
SARA PURSLEY

Hamas Contained: The Rise and Pacification of Palestinian Resistance   2018
TAREQ BACONI

Hotels and Highways: The Construction of Modernization Theory in Cold War Turkey   2018
BEGÜM ADALET

Bureaucratic Intimacies: Human Rights in Turkey   2017
ELIF M. BABÜL

Impossible Exodus: Iraqi Jews in Israel   2017
ORIT BASHKIN

Brothers Apart: Palestinian Citizens of Israel and the Arab World   2017
MAHA NASSAR

Printed in the USA
CPSIA information can be obtained
at www.ICGtesting.com
JSHW021748231223
54086JS00002B/2